Ian Keown's
European Hideaways

Other Books by the Author:
(*Available from Harmony Books)

KLM's Holland
Arthur Frommer's Guide to Athens
Very Special Places: A Lovers' Guide to America
*Ian Keown's Caribbean Hideaways

Ian Keown's
European
Hideaways

With additional material by
Jane Abrams, Eleanor Berman, Susan Hannah,
Cynthia Proulx, Doris Saatchi, Bob Scanlon,
and Ila Stanger

Illustrations by Abby Merrill

Harmony Books/New York

Harmony Books
a division of Crown Publishers, Inc.
One Park Avenue, New York, New York 10016
Illustrations by Abby Merrill

Published simultaneously in Canada by General Publishing Co., Ltd.
Printed in the United States of America.

Library of Congress Cataloging in Publication Data

    Keown, Ian.
    Ian Keown's European hideaways.

    1. Europe—Description and travel—1971–
—Guide-books. I. Title. II. Title: European
hideaways.
D909.K39 1980   914′.04′55   79-26017
ISBN 0-517-538237 cloth
ISBN 0-517-538245 pbk.
10 9 8 7 6 5 4 3 2 1
First Edition

CONTENTS

Acknowledgments/xi
Introduction/1
Scotland, England and Ireland/13

Isle of Eriska Hotel (*Ledaig*)/14
Inverlochy Castle (*Fort William*)/17
Taychreggan Hotel (*Lochaweside*)/19
Creggan's Inn (*Strachur*)/21
Culloden House (*Inverness*)/23
Newton Hotel (*Nairn*)/24
Meldrum House (*Old Meldrum*)/26
Tullich Lodge (*Ballater*)/27
Dunkeld House Hotel (*Dunkeld*)/29
Ballathie House Hotel (*near Perth*)/30
Greywalls (*Gullane*)/32
Turnberry Hotel (*near Ayr*)/33
Miller Howe (*Windermere*)/36
Sharrow Bay Country House Hotel (*Lake Ullswater*)/38
White Moss House (*near Grasmere*)/41
The Grosvenor Hotel (*Chester*)/42
The Lygon Arms (*Broadway*)/44
Hunstrete House (*near Bath*)/45
The Close at Tetbury (*Tetbury*)/47
Whatley Manor (*Easton Grey*)/49
The Bear (*Woodstock*)/50
Chewton Glen Hotel (*New Milton*)/52
Ye Olde Bell Hotel (*Hurley-on-Thames*)/54
Maison Talbooth (*Dedham*)/56
Number 16 (*London*)/58
Blakes Hotel (*London*)/60
Brown's Hotel (*London*)/62
Newport House (*Newport*)/64
Ashford Castle (*Cong*)/65
Dromoland Castle (*Newmarket-on-Fergus*)/67
Fitzpatrick Castle (*Dublin*)/68

Denmark/71

Store Kro (*Fredensborg*)/72
71 Nyhavn Hotel (*Copenhagen*)/73
Hotel Hesselet (*Nyborg*)/75
Falsled Kro (*Millinge*)/76
Steensgaard Herregardspension (*Millinge*)/78

Holland and Belgium/81

Hotel-Restaurant Lauswolt (*Beetsterzwaag*)/82
De Wiemsel (*Ootmarsum*)/83
Pulitzer Hotel (*Amsterdam*)/85
Hotel de l'Europe (*Amsterdam*)/88
Kasteel Neubourg (*Gulpen*)/90
Kasteel Wittem (*Wittem*)/91
Waterland (*Velsen-Zuid*)/94
Auberge De Kieviet (*Wassenaar*)/96
Auberge du Moulin Hideux (*Noirefontaine*)/98
Hôtellerie du Prieuré de Conques (*Herbeumont sur Semois*)/100
Hôtellerie Trôs Marets (*Malmédy*)/102

Germany/105

Parkhotel Fürstenhof (*Celle*)/106
Kommende Lage (*Rieste*)/107
Schlosshotel Lembeck (*Dorsten*)/109
Parkhotel Wasserburg Anholt (*Isselburg*)/111
Alte Thorschenke (*Cochem*)/112
Schloss Zell (*Zell*)/114
Waldhotel Jagdschloss Niederwald (*Assmannshausen*)/115
Hotel Schwan (*Östrich/Winkel on the Rhine*)/117
Burghotel auf Schönburg (*Oberwesel on the Rhine*)/118
Zum Ritter (*Heidelberg*)/120
Schloss Heinsheim (*Bad Rappenau*)/122
Schlosshotel Friedrichsruhe (*Friedrichsruhe*)/123
Hotel Markusturm (*Rothenburg*)/125
Hotel Eisenhut (*Rothenburg*)/127
Parkhotel Adler (*Hinterzarten*)/129
Clausing's Posthotel (*Garmisch*)/132
Hotel Alte Post and Hotelvilla (*Wangen*)/134

France/137

Hôtel Ritz (*Paris*)/138
Hôtel de l'Université (*Paris*)/141
L'Hotel (*Paris*)/143
Hôtel Lutece (*Paris*)/145
La Résidence du Bois (*Paris*)/147
Château d'Audrieu (*Audrieu*)/149
Auberge du Vieux Puits (*Pont-Audemer*)/151
Manoir du Vaumadeuc (*Pléven-Plancoët*)/153
Château d'Artigny (*Montbazon*)/155

Domaine des Hauts de Loire (*Onzain*)/158
La Tortinière (*Montbazon*)/159
Hôtellerie du Bas-Bréau (Barbizon)/161
Auberge des Templiers (*Les Bézards*)/163
L'Hôtellerie de la Poste (*Avallon*)/166
Hôtellerie du Moulin des Ruats (*Avallon*)/169
Chez La Mère Blanc (*Vonnas*)/171
Hôtel de la Verniaz (*Evian-les-Bains*)/172
Hôtel Les Prés Fleuris (*Evian*)/174
L'Auberge du Père Bise (*Talloires*)/175
Moulin du Roc (*Champagnac de Belair*)/178
Le Vieux Logis (*Trémolat*)/181
Le Métairie (*Mauzac*)/182
Château de Mercuès (*near Cahors*)/184
Hôtellerie le Prieuré (*Villeneuve-lez-Avignon*)/186
Château de Rochegude (*Rochegude*)/188
L'Auberge de Noves (*Noves*)/189
Le Mas d'Entremont (*Aix-en-Provence*)/191
Le Mas des Herbes Blanches (*Joucas*)/192
L'Oustau de Baumanière (*Les Baux-de-Provence*)/194
Hôtel Byblos (*St.-Tropez*)/198
Hôtel du Cap (*Cap d'Antibes*)/201
Château du Domaine St.-Martin (*Vence*)/203
Le Mas d'Artigny (*St.-Paul-de-Vence*)/207
Auberge Le Hameau (*St.-Paul-de-Vence*)/208
Le Cagnard (*Haut-de-Cagnes*)/209
Hôtel La Voile d'Or *(Cap Ferrat)*/211
L'Hôtellerie du Château de la Chèvre d'or (*Eze Village*)/213
Hôtel Le Cap Estel (*Eze-Bord-de-Mer*)/215
Hôtel Le Vistaero (*Roquebrune-Cap-Martin*)/218

Austria and Switzerland/221

Hotel Schloss Mönchstein (*Salzburg*)/222
Hotel Goldener Hirsch (*Salzburg*)/224
Hotel Schloss Fuschl (*Salzburg-Hof*)/226
Hotel Goldener Adler (*Innsbruck*)/228
Schlosshotel Igls (*Igls*)/230
Hotel Grünwalderhof (*Patsch bei Igls*)/232
Hotel Hirschen (*Langnau*)/234
Hotels Drachenburg, Waaghaus and Garni (*Gottlieben*)/235
Le Vieux Manoir (*Murten-Meyriez*)/237
Hotel Château Gütsch (*Lucerne*)/239
The Grand Hotel (*Bürgenstock*)/241

Hotel Monte Rosa (*Zermatt*)/244
Hotel Alex (*Zermatt*)/246
Hôtellerie Tenne (*Zermatt*)/247

Italy/249

Hotel Villa d'Este (*Cernobbio*)/250
Hotel Castello di Pomerio (*Pomerio d'Erba*)/251
Albergo Splendido (*Portofino*)/253
Grand Hotel Miramare (*Santa Margherita Ligure*)/255
Hotel Cenobio dei Dogi (*Camogli*)/256
Hotel Due Torri (*Verona*)/258
Hotel Victoria (*Verona*)/260
Hotel Gritti Palace (*Venice*)/261
Hotel Cipriani (*Venice*)/263.
Hotel Gabrielli Sandwirth (*Venice*)/266
Villa Cipriani (*Asolo*)/268
Hotel d'Inghilterra (*Rome*)/270
Hotel Lord Byron (*Rome*)/272
Hotel San Pietro (*Positano*)/273
Hotel Punta Tragara (*Capri*)/275
La Scalinatella (*Capri*)/277
Grand Hotel Quisisana (*Capri*)/279
Hotel Cervo (*Sardinia*)/281
Hotel Cala di Volpe (*Sardinia*)/283
Hotel Pitrizza (*Sardinia*)/285
Villa Igiea Grand Hotel (*Sicily*)/287
San Domenico Palace Hotel (*Sicily*)/289

Greece/291

Akti Myrina Hotel (*Lemnos*)/292
Amalia Hotel (*Delphi*)/295
Xenia Palace Bungalows (*Nafplion*)/296

Portugal and Spain/299

Pousada do Castelo (*Obidos*)/300
Estalagem Albatroz (*Cascais*)/302
Lennox Country Club Hotel (*Estoril*)/303
Hotel do Guincho (*Cascais*)/304
Hotel Palacio dos Seteais (*Sintra*)/307
York House (*Lisbon*)/308
Hotel Principe Real (*Lisbon*)/310
Pousada de Palmela (*Palmela*)/312

Hotel do Mar (*Sesimbra*)/314
Quinta das Torres (*Azeitão*)/316
Pousada de São Filipe (*Setúbal*)/317
Pousada dos Lioios (*Evora*)/319
Pousada do Infante (*Sagres*)/320
Casa de São Gonçalo da Lagos (*Lagos*)/322
Estalagem do Cerro (*Albufeira*)/324
Pousada de São Bras (*São Bras de Alportel*)/325
Hostal de la Gavina (*S'Agaró*)/327
Parador Marqués de Villena (*Alarcón*)/329
Hotel Doña Maria (*Seville*)/330
Parador Nacional Condestable Davalos (*Ubeda*)/332
Parador Nacional San Francisco (*Granada*)/334
Parador Nacional Gibralfaro (*Málaga*)/335

Contents

Added Attractions/339

The Rates—and how to figure them out/373

The Reps and Tourist Information/385

In the course of researching and writing this guidebook I was given a lot of help by a lot of people. Since I invariably omit some names from the list of acknowledgees, I will begin by thanking all those people who are *not* listed here simply because I don't have their business cards or letterheads at hand. My apologies, but thank you nevertheless.

For the others, my great gratitude. Among them, in approximately alphabetical order, Marchesini Adelino, Marguerite Aumann Allen, Myriam Bin, Walter Bruderer, Constant Cachin, Ed Conradsen, Peter Esterhazy, Hank Fisher, Peter ffrench-Hodges, Winston Fitzgerald, Nils Flo, Andrew Glaze, George and Pat Gosden, Evelyn Heyward, Lucille Hoshabjian, Jerry Jansse, Joyce Kowalk, Peter Kuhn, Herb Livesey, Tony Madeira, Gerhard Markus, Elizabeth Moulin, Ann Neville, Charles Nicholas, Kurt Nielsen, Charles Ocheltree, Peter Steward, Odette Taminiau, Barbara Taylor, Giorgio Valentini, Hedy Wuerz. A special thanks to Beth Crouch, Julie Wilson, Victoria Adams, my Phi Beta Kappa typist, Bob Mckinnon for speedy deliveries, and Harriet Bell, my editor, for being exceptionally cooperative and flexible with schedules.

Above all, a special thanks to my colleagues who devoted so much of their time for piddling reward, if any. They are identified throughout the guide by their initials, but I thought you might also like to know something about them.

J.A. Jane Abrams is a contributing editor to "Know Your America"; her byline has appeared in several magazines, including *House & Garden, Woman's Day* and *Apartment Life.* She is currently a travel writer on the staff of the *New York Daily News.*

E.B. Eleanor Berman is the author of three books, the most recent of which is *Re-entering,* also published by Crown. Her background includes agency copywriting, publishing and public relations, and she has written articles for *Newsday, Harper's Bazaar* and *Travel & Leisure.*

C.P. Cynthia Proulx was my coauthor on *Guide to France for Loving Couples,* an earlier incarnation of the present guide. She has also written for *Saturday Review, Viva, Travel & Leisure* and other publications.

S.H. Susan Hannah flies for Pan Am on weekends, spends the rest of her time ensconced in Columbia University, where she is well on her way to a Ph.D. in anthropology.

D.S. Doris Saatchi has a copywriting background, and now lives in London. Whereas your author gets to travel from hotel to hotel in a rented Simca, Doris and her husband are more likely to drive up in a Rolls-Royce, or, as in the case of the Costa Smeralda, to cruise in aboard a 100-foot yacht.

R.E.S. Bob Scanlon is a New Yorker by birth and inclination but currently lives in Houston, Texas, where he writes advertising copy for Shell, Houston Opera and other clients.

I.S. Ila Stanger, a New York writer, was features and travel editor of

ACKNOWLEDGMENTS

Harper's Bazaar, contributor to *Saturday Review* and *Family Circle,* and is currently executive editor of *Travel & Leisure.*

Five of us have, at one time or another, worked for the advertising agency Ogilvy & Mather, and since we learned a lot there, this might be a convenient opportunity to say a collective thank you to two of our mentors—David Ogilvy and Cliff Field.

This is another book of special places.

For special people.

It's all about stately country-house hotels with chandeliers and crystal, old country inns where the great lovers of bygone days trysted, castle hotels in parks with pergolas and pheasants, the elusive "great little restaurants" with wonderful food and a few cozy rooms beside a millstream.

It's a dreambook for people who want to snuggle up in four-poster beds and have breakfast served on a silver tray with a sculptured silver coffeepot. Or sit beneath ancient linden trees on a lakeside terrace and dine on *l'omble-chevalier meunière* and a bottle of Cheval Blanc. These are special places for travelers who can appreciate the finer—and simpler—things in life: a crackling log fire and a very slow cognac. A glass of wine in a vine-covered arbor. Watching salmon leap in a Highland stream. Drowsing in a mimosa-scented garden on the Riviera. Picnicking in a pine-scented meadow in the Alps. *European Hideaways* will, I hope, help you *experience* Europe rather than merely sample the highlights. This is the Europe promised by the brochures which so often eludes today's travelers in this whirlwind world of cheap fares, jumbo coaches and crowds.

Ground Rules

European Hideaways is a guidebook primarily for lovers. Lovers and romantics and escapists. Maybe even idealists. It's for travelers who refuse to settle for the humdrum and the run-of-the-mill.

What it sure as hell is NOT is a guidebook for irrepressible swingers and crapshooters, night owls and barflies, the kind of travelers who *must* have a television in every room and beauty parlors in every lobby.

This guidebook describes more than 200 handpicked inns, château-hotels, resorts, *auberges, paradores, pousadas, alberghi.* It describes them, moreover, in more detail than you normally find in guidebooks. In some cases, too much detail, you may think. But what all this information does is let you size up your options *before* you make your reservations and helps you choose the hotel that best suits your taste—and, in the end, that kind of information more than pays for the cost of the guide.

These are places where you can, on the whole, escape noise, piped music, jukeboxes, plastic, tour groups, conventions, children, formula smiles and formula decor. The kind of places you usually hear about only by word of mouth or by diligent research through scores of guidebooks, directories, magazine articles and brochures, places you *think* you'd like to stay in, but you're not really sure what they're like. Think of this book as your talent scout.

Every hotel in this guidebook has been visited *personally,* if not by me, then by one of my colleagues. In most cases, each visit has involved inspecting three or four rooms in each hotel, but in many cases we've been collared by proud owners or enthusiastic assistants who have traipsed us through almost *every* room. (The record, I believe, is 20 rooms in a single 40-room hotel.)

No one pays to be in this guidebook. It is completely independent. This means, alas, that all the cost of research comes out of the author's pocket.

Pet Peeves

Piped music. This is becoming a universal torment. It's not just the noise—it's the incongruity. Presumably, the intention of background music is to create a mood or atmosphere, but invariably it oozes safe pop tunes with treacly orchestrations, mindless marshmallow music that has nothing to do with the character of the country or the establishment. What on earth does "Bless Your Indian Hide" have to do with a well-heeled inn in the middle of Belgium's Ardennes?

In some cases, to be sure, the music may be live and authentic, in which case the problem is likely to be one of excessive amplification. It seems that no musician anywhere in the world can perform without microphones and amplifiers, and few of them seem to understand that in a good restaurant dining and good conversation, not the performer, are the priorities.

Throughout this guide we've noted the presence of music, piped or live; if it's intrusive, we say so, and you can make your decision accordingly. If you arrive at a hotel or restaurant or lounge and the music is going full blast, ask the innkeeper/maître d'hôtel/bartender to turn it off, or, with live performers who are less manageable than tapes, to lower the volume.

Television. Many hotels in this guide put a total embargo on television. Some tolerate TV but banish the set to a special lounge where the sound won't interfere with guests who'd rather not hear "Gunsmoke" in German. *Very* few of these hotels have sets in lobbies or bars or public lounges, and they're usually the kind of hotels where the staff will understand and respect your wishes if you ask to have the volume turned down. TV in guest rooms is something quite different since you don't have to switch it on if you don't want to; if your neighbors' set disturbs you, call the front desk (but make sure you get the offending room number correct). When TV is included in the list of facilities in these pages, this should not be taken as a recommendation but merely as a reference.

Children. Some hotels practically hoist up the drawbridge at the very sight of them. Others allow them in subject to certain age limitations. Some accept them reluctantly but give them special dining hours, and so on. There must be some reason why innkeepers feel that way, and this coincides more or less with the way many readers (many of whom are parents) feel about children in hotels. Most of the hotels in this guidebook are not really suitable for children, who will consequently be bored out of their skulls and turn cantankerous.

It may seem callous, but there's no point in searching out some romantic spot, spending perhaps a lot of money to get there, then having your peace and quiet shattered by loutish children. Or, perhaps, by loutish *families,* since the parents are often more to blame than the children. (For example, this little tidbit from the travel section of a leading newspaper: "The waitresses smiled indulgently as Jim's father, in a burst of Middle Western chauvinism, taught his two grandchildren the football fight songs of the universities of Chicago and Wisconsin. 'On Wisconsin' echoed through the sedate inn as a group of Japanese tourists looked on incredulously." As well they might.) We should point out that many parents share this point of view, since many of them, trying to escape their own families for a few days, are unlikely to be thrilled by the prospect of other people turning a hideaway into a rumpus room. If you are concerned about an overdose of children, check the P.S. at the end of each listing in this guide; if a hotel has special regulations, you'll read about them there; if there are none, you may have to consider avoiding school vacations (which vary from country to country, so maybe you'd better check out the subject with the hotel in advance).

Conventions. The object of a convention is to whip up enthusiasm. The object of a hideaway is escape. They don't mix. Most of the hotels, inns and resorts in this guidebook, therefore, do not accept conventions. However, most of them must rely to some extent on commercial business, especially in the off-season. Some of these hotels would go under without occasional seminars, workshops, board meetings and so on. But such meetings are a different kettle of fish altogether. So, although most of the places listed in these pages shun placard-waving, funny-hat-wearing, beer-swilling conventioneers, they will accept small groups of high-level executives, administrators, professors and others who can usually (not always, but usually) be relied upon to conduct themselves in an unobtrusive manner. In the case of the smaller hotels, they may insist on a group taking over the entire hotel, in which case you will have no problem because you won't be staying there anyway. Otherwise, check with the hotel in advance; most of these hotels will understand your concern and will advise you accordingly; indeed, some of them may take it upon themselves to alert you to the presence of a group. The P.S. at the end of each listing also gives you, where appropriate, a clue to the hotel's policy regarding groups.

Checking In

Nobody cares. My colleagues and I have made a point of asking innkeepers specifically if there will be any problems for guests sharing rooms but not passports, and without exception the attitude seems to be it's none of the innkeeper's business—unless one of the parties seems to be too young or operating professionally. In some countries (and only in some hotels in those countries) the receptionist will ask for one or both passports, which he or she will retain overnight. Don't lose any sleep (or pleasure). This is merely a formality. It does not mean that your credentials are being checked out with Interpol. In Spain it's still against the law for unmarried couples to cohabit, and the procedure there is simply for the male only to hand over his passport and complete the form. If the lady is liberated and insists on using her own name, she can—in a separate room. In Italy, guests checking in together must be over 18 years of age.

In most cases you can get by with signing a noncommittal M/M; in some cases both parties may be required to complete a registration card. Either way, it's no embarrassment to anyone other than, perhaps, yourselves.

Caution: Many hotels add the names registered to their mailing lists and you will later receive all sorts of interesting newsletters or updated rate sheets. In case you're somewhere you're not supposed to be with someone you're not supposed to be with and you don't want someone else to find out a few months later, ask the receptionist (better still, the manager) to keep your name *off all mailing lists.*

Signing Checks

If you find you must sign in under an assumed name, a *nom de plaisir* so to speak, there's no point in then trying to pay your bill with a credit card or check that uses your regular name. In such cases, pay an early visit to the manager or cashier to explain the situation. Also, if you have registered as husband and wife make sure that both of you remember which name to sign on the room-service bill when breakfast arrives; and be sure that both of you know how to spell it. It's not fair to the waiter to have someone ask, "Is it K-E-O-W-N or K-E-W-O-N?"

Language

We always check out how many members of the staff speak or at least understand English. In virtually every hotel in this guidebook front-desk personnel are fluent enough to eliminate the possibility of misunderstandings due to language. In most of the hotels, you will encounter no problems communicating with dining-room staff. In about half of them you'll have no problem communicating intelligently with maids and porters. Where there *is* likely to be a language problem, we will alert you in the P.S. section at the end of each listing.

Reservations

The ideal way to see Europe is simply to travel around by car or train in a footloose way and stop for the night where and when you feel like it.

Unfortunately, these days there are too many Japanese, Arabs, Germans, Britons, Dutch, Danes, Swedes and Antipodeans with similar ideas, and finding the inn you want is not always possible at the last minute. And there's nothing more frustrating, is there, than being all set to tumble into bed only to find you don't have a bed to tumble into? So don't take chances: *always make a reservation in advance.*

That's good advice for any hotel but doubly so in the case of most of those in this guide; because they *are* special they may be the first to be booked, and in any case, many of them have so few rooms that they are full most of the time. That's another point: don't count on the seasons anymore—even if it's a time of year when the hotel *should* be empty, it may still be full, simply because so many people seem to be on the move these days.

Above all, if you want a special room or a particular type of bed, it's essential that you reserve as far in advance as possible. Here and there throughout this guide we recommend rooms which we feel have particular attractions; innkeepers hate us for this, because it makes their lives complicated since everyone then wants the same rooms. All the more reason why you should reserve far in advance. Remember also that you have a better chance of getting the best rooms if you plan to stay several nights.

For adventurous lovers who're willing to risk last minute go-as-you-please reservations, I've listed telephone numbers: call ahead early enough in the day so that you can still make alternative arrangements if your first choice is not available. For lovers who think ahead, here are the other ways of going about reservations:

1. Travel agents. The agent who books your flight, rental car and train tickets can also arrange your hotel reservations, probably for no extra fee. Agents will also attend to the business of deposits and confirmations— which, be warned, can be pesky and time-consuming if you have to do it yourselves for six or eight or a dozen hotels. However, travel agents may not be familiar with some of the smaller inns and hotels listed in these pages, and since they may be reluctant to send their clients to places they don't know, they may try to steer you to inns and hotels they *do* know. Stand firm. If necessary, show them this guidebook.

2. Hotel representatives. These are organizations which handle reservations either from travel agents or individual travelers. They can usually tell you *on the spot* whether or not rooms are available on the dates you have in mind, and they will make and confirm the reservation. The individual representative(s) is listed, where available, under each hotel, the telephone numbers and addresses of the major reps at the back of the book.

3. Cables/telex. You can contact the hotel directly, using either a cable or telex address, which is listed under each hotel. Of the two, telex is faster because the message goes direct to the reservations office of the hotel and you can get a reply within minutes. It's also cheaper. Moreover, telex is more reliable than the telephone because both parties have the reservation and confirmation in writing. (You can send cables or telexes via Western Union, ITT or RCA offices.)

Whichever method you choose, be sure your reservation is specific and clear. It should list the number of people in the party, date of arrival, time of arrival (especially if you are arriving late), flight number if you know it, number of nights you plan to stay, date of departure, whether you want twin beds or a double bed, bathtub or shower or both, upper floor or front or courtyard and so forth, whether you want your rate to be EP, CP, MAP or FAP. Finally, after all that, don't forget your name, return address or telephone number or telex number.

The Ratings

All the inns, hotels and resorts in this guide are, in one way or another, exceptional; but some obviously are more exceptional than others, and to try to make life easier for you, we've rated the individual establishments. This is helpful, I think, because character and personality and charm bear little or no connection with rates, and even less with the official government ratings of each country, which depend heavily on the mechanics of the business—elevators, room phones, TV, that sort of thing. However, you can assume that every inn, hotel and resort included in these pages meets high basic standards in terms of housekeeping, plumbing, bedding and so on—that goes without saying. Crowns represent *romantic* rather than functional qualities. Warmth rather than elevators, charm rather than color television, ambience and surroundings rather than direct-dial telephones and coin-operated laundromats. Therefore (and this is most important) crowns are *not* the equivalent of stars in other guides or tourist-office booklets. *Champagne bottles* evaluate the overall wining and dining experience. This takes into account the ambience of the dining room or terrace, the attitude and appearance of the dining-room staff rather than whether or not or how the bechamel sauce has been passed through a white tammy. This is not, in other words, an evaluation of the cuisine alone, for which we have neither the qualifications, subsidies, time nor indeed stomach to evaluate with the same efficiency as Michelin inspectors; but we *are* qualified, from long and harassed experience, to evaluate how guests are received by maîtres d'hôtel, how dishes are removed by busboys, how waiters present and serve the food and how they add or remove the appropriate cutlery. In other words, a hotel that rates only two champagne bottles might well deserve three for the food alone but loses out because the maître d' is a martinet or the waiter slops wine on the tablecloth; conversely, a waiter who clears away crumbs promptly and unobtrusively, or a maître d' who waits until you've *finished* munching or sipping before asking if

6

everything is all right, may compensate, in these ratings, for any shortcomings there may be in the pinch of cayenne in the *sauce Colbert*.

Here are the ratings:

For a one-night stand or stopover

For a weekend

For a week

Happily ever after

A good meal

Worth getting out of bed for

Something to look forward to

An experience

Less than $40 a night double

$40–$80

$80–$120

$120 and heavenward

Double or Single Beds?

Hotels nowadays, even the smaller romantic ones, seem to have more twin beds than double beds. However, most of the inns, hotels and resorts in this guide offer you a choice, provided you give them adequate warning (that is, when you make your reservation). If all the double beds have gone and you really must have one, most hotels will instruct their maids to push twins together to make a double, although this may not always be the case in smaller inns with limited maidpower or if you arrive late in the evening. If they *are* doubled-up twins, check the method of joining them together, because if they suddenly part at a crucial moment, it can be painful for one of you. (NOTE: If a hotel specifies "French beds," it probably means twin beds pushed together, made up as twins but covered with a communal bedspread.)

7

The Rates

Some guidebooks simply skip rates altogether; having put together more than a dozen guidebooks myself, I sympathize with those authors who steer clear of this complex subject. Rates are the single most frustrating part of writing a guidebook, for the type of rate varies from hotel to hotel, from season to season, from room to room, from location to location within the hotel. In these days of inflation, oil price hikes, added-value taxes and whatnot, the subject of rates is more unpredictable than ever. Hotels rarely know for sure what their rates will be twelve months from now.

However, we feel we owe it to readers to provide them with as much information as possible—and that certainly includes information on how much they are likely to pay. Here's how we've handled this irksome matter.

1. We quote official rates for all the hotels listed. Since the guidebook is researched almost a year before it appears in the bookstores, however, there was no way we could include detailed rates for 1980/81; therefore, the rates quoted are those which were in effect during the spring and summer of 1979. This way you have an accurate yardstick for *comparison*, one hotel versus another, one country versus another. *Use these rates as a guide only.* Add on, say, 10 percent for 1980, perhaps another 10 or 15 percent for 1981. Even if we were able to keep track of figures and rush them into print two or three times a year, you'd still have to confirm detailed rates with the hotels when you made your reservations. So, as we say, use these rates as a guide only.

2. We have separated the detailed rates from the individual hotel listings and placed them at the rear of the guide, so that they can be brought up to date occasionally without resetting the type for the entire guide. But to compensate for this, we have inserted a $ symbol beside each hotel to give you an idea, as you glance through the guide, of roughly how much you'll have to pay. For an explanation of the $, turn to page 7.

3. The rates quoted at any point in this guidebook are for *double rooms*—"for two people sharing," as the brochures say. They are mostly for room only (EP, or European Plan), but in several cases they are for room with breakfast (CP, or Continental Plan). In a few cases, hotels will quote only MAP or demipension rates, which are listed and identified. (See the chapter on rates for more details of the terms EP, CP, MAP, etc.)

4. When comparing prices, bear in mind that in some cases the rates may include incidentals (such as morning coffee and afternoon tea) and recreational facilities. If you want to play tennis, for example, it makes dollar-and-cents sense to stay at a hotel where tennis facilities are free.

A word about prices. At first glance, these rates may seem extravagant, but remember that what we are investigating here are special places. *Anything* out of the ordinary (be it hotel or car or dress) is likely to cost more. Peace and quiet and wide open spaces are among the most precious of commodities these days, and our very special places are more costly to operate than formula hotels with standard dimensions and furnishings. In any case, they're not *all* expensive. The listings, especially those in the category Added Attractions, include many hotels and inns and resorts where your double room, usually with breakfast included, costs less then $40 a night.

What you have to consider is the alternative. There are many outstanding hotels in these pages costing $40 to $80 a night for two people, but if you go to a city like Paris or London, you'll be hard pressed to find an *average* hotel at this price.

When you evaluate a hotel, don't look only at the price. Consider all the other attractions. A city hotel is likely to cost more than a country hotel because of the costs of lands, operation, salaries and so on; hotels in Venice are usually more expensive then equivalent hotels in, say, Rome because of the peculiar characteristics of this water-logged location. A hotel like the Ritz, which offers you a quiet courtyard in the heart of a city like Paris, presumably has to build the cost of that real estate into its rates.

How to Lick High Costs

1. Avoid peak seasons. Many hotels reduce their rates for a few months of the year, depending on location and the type of clientele. For example: the Château du Domaine St.-Martin and Le Mas d'Artigny in Vence, in the hills behind the French Riviera, reduce their rates by 25 percent in winter; if you visit Venice between mid-November and mid-March, you can save $25 on your room at the Gritti Palace.

2. Choose your hotel carefully. Check through the listing of facilities and details of meals. If you're going somewhere strictly for sightseeing, rather than resort life, you may be paying more than you have to by staying at a hotel with acres of sporting facilities (which are, somehow, built into the rate); likewise, if you don't have to eat a 5-course gourmet meal every day, don't stay at a hotel that *insists* on serving you banquets.

3. Demipension. On the other hand, although we always recommend staying at hotels that do *not* insist on guests taking meals there, you can often save money by taking a *demipension*, or Modified American Plan, rate—that is, a rate which includes lunch or dinner with room and breakfast. The menu may be more limited, but it may save a few dollars.

4. Packages. That's sometimes considered a dirty word among travelers, because it usually conjures up images of groups being herded into and out of buses. Nowadays, however, there are all kinds of promotional packages that allow travelers to get about on their own, *completely independently*, taking advantage of special promotional air fares which do not necessarily involve group travel. Because of all these fares, many tour operators and wholesalers are able to offer exceptional rates for all-inclusive tours incorporating inns and hotels that would normally crumble into dust at the very mention of "group tours." The types of package vary considerably—some offer guaranteed advance reservations, others allow you to make your reservations as you go along at designated hotels at prepaid rates—but since most of them include special rates for air fares *and car rentals*, they are worth looking into. Two World Tours in New York offers a choice of eleven drive-yourself tours with overnight or two-night stops at Relais-Châteaux hotels in France and Italy. (See under "Reps" at end of this guide for TWT's address.)

5. Car leasing. If you plan to spend a month or longer in Europe, consider the economies of *leasing* a car on a Purchase-Repurchase Plan. All you do is buy a car tax-free, with the contractual understanding that the manufacturer/dealer will buy it back at an agreed price, assuming that it is still in good condition. It may sound complicated, but in fact all you do is pay out the *difference* between the buying price and the selling price, in advance, and simply drive off in a brand-new car. We took advantage of this plan when researching parts of this guidebook, and by "owning" a car for 3 months we saved two-thirds of the rental charges. Two snags: servicing the new car is your responsibility, so you may have to plan your trip around the location of an authorized dealer who will honor the manufacturer's warranty; nonwarranteed maintenance and repairs are also your responsibility. Two companies which offer this plan are both French—Simca and Renault. You can get details in New York from Simca/Chrysler, 420 Lexington Avenue (for delivery in France); from ShipSide, 609 Fifth Avenue, for delivery at Schiphol Airport in Holland.

6. Tax-free cars. If you're toying with the idea of buying a European car in North America, consider combining the purchase of your car with a vacation in Europe. If you buy a Mercedes, Porsche or Jaguar, what you save on the tax-free price in Europe can pay for your air fares (probably more), even taking into consideration the cost of shipping the car back home. With a smaller, less expensive car, where the tax advantage is less, buying a car tax-free may more than offset the cost of renting.

As far as we can determine, the largest and most reliable organization selling tax-free cars in Europe is ShipSide, right next to the arrivals hall at Amsterdam's Schiphol Airport. ShipSide has been selling tax-free cars for more than twenty years, and they have something like three hundred models in their catalog. (For details, write to ShipSide, 609 Fifth Avenue, New York, N.Y. 10017; or telephone (212) 755-2080.)

7. Gasoline. It's expensive any way you look at it, and the only solution is to rent or buy a *small* car. However, Italy offers tourists a reduction (about one-third) by selling *benzina* coupons at frontiers. These special coupons are available only to motorists driving cars not registered in

Italy—so there's no point in renting a car in Italy and expecting to get a break on gasoline.

8. Eurailpass. If you plan to cover a lot of territory, the least expensive way to get around may be by train, using a Eurailpass. In case you're not familiar with it, the Eurailpass gives you unlimited travel, first class, for periods of 15 days to 3 months. In 1980, the 15-day ticket costs only $210. Quite apart from economy, a Eurailpass is convenient, because you just show it to the ticket collectors, and you never have to stand in line for tickets. European trains are first rate: they run on time, they're comfortable and clean, and the classiest of them have first-class dining cars and/or sleeping cars, and, in some cases, boutiques, bookstalls and beauty parlors.

Many of the inns, resorts and hotels described in this guide are within a short taxi ride of railroad stations, and you could easily chart a tour to romantic hideaways by train. A travel agent can give you details of Eurailpass and European train schedules; alternatively, contact the tourist offices of Germany, France or Switzerland, who represent European railroads in North America.

A Word about the Selection

On a continent as crowded as Europe, with its plenitude of heritage and history and sights and attractions, there are obviously more locations and hotels than can possibly be squeezed into *any* guide. Even when focusing only on romantic hotels, the selection is still overwhelming.

Some places, therefore, had to be ruled out in advance. One way to do this was size. For the purposes of this guide the cut-off point is 150 rooms, but this is by no means a hard-and-fast figure. Some larger hotels have been included because they have qualities that overcome their size. However, as things have turned out, our research has turned up mostly hotels which have fewer than a hundred rooms, and a few have only half a dozen. We concede that the arbitrary figure of 150 rules out many potential candidates, but a line had to be drawn somewhere.

The preference also lies with hotels away from the large metropolises, except in the case of those cities like Amsterdam, London, Paris and Rome that are romantic in their own right. Sorry, Düsseldorf, Rotterdam and Birmingham. However, many of the other hotels and inns are located close to major cities and can be used as bases for forays into the traffic and clutter when you feel like it.

The guide is arranged by country, northern climes first. We have kicked off with an offshore island called Britain, specifically with Scotland. I make no apology for this since my slightly soggy but lovely native land is among the most romantic of Europe.

Within each country (or pair of countries) hotels are organized more or less geographically, north-to-south, not in any form of preference.

SCOTLAND, ENGLAND and IRELAND

1. Isle of Eriska Hotel
2. Inverlochy Castle
3. Taychreggan Hotel
4. Creggan's Inn
5. Culloden House
6. Newton Hotel
7. Meldrum House
8. Tullich Lodge
9. Dunkeld House Hotel
10. Ballathie House Hotel
11. Greywalls
12. Turnberry Hotel
13. Miller Howe
14. Sharrow Bay Country House Hotel
15. White Moss House
16. The Grosvenor Hotel
17. The Lygon Arms
18. Hunstrete House
19. The Close at Tetbury
20. Whatley Manor
21. The Bear
22. Chewton Glen Hotel
23. Ye Olde Bell Hotel
24. Maison Talbooth
25. Number 16
    Blakes Hotel
    Brown's Hotel
26. Newport House
27. Ashford Castle
28. Dromoland Castle
29. Fitzpatrick Castle

Scotland

Isle of Eriska Hotel
Ledaig

WWWW XXX $$$

There is magic, a whisper of Brigadoon, in the very name. Eriska is separated from Earth by a channel only fifty yards wide, but once you've crossed the old iron bridge and squeezed through the rhododendron-lined driveway, you're in a world apart, a place of ineffable peace. Spacious lawns. Stands of beech and sycamore and fir. Accents of azalea and dahlias. Shaggy red Highland cattle graze in the pasture that runs down to the water's edge. Out in Loch Linnhe the island of Lismore lies becalmed, and beyond it the peaks of Mull pattern the horizon. At the heart of all this never-neverness stands a stalwart mansion of granite with sandstone trim, topped off by a tower with decorative battlements. Within, log fires beckon you into a hallway lined with bog oak, drawing rooms with overstuffed settees—a general air of gracious living.

The guest rooms are everything you would expect in an elegant country mansion: each is individually decorated, each is attractive, but if we were being perfectionists we'd try to snare Lismore or Kenera for the view, Iona for its tiny balcony up in the tower, or Shuna for its big double bed. Every room comes with hospitable little touches like heated towel rails, bath salts, sewing kits, fresh fruit, fresh flowers and hot-water bottles. Since some guests might want to have a cup of tea or coffee at odd hours, each room has an electric kettle and the makings of tea or coffee. But throughout Eriska the attention to the *refinements* of hospitality is exemplary. If you order tea for breakfast, the waiter will ask, "India or China?" If you order wine ahead of time and ask to have it decanted, it will be waiting for you at the table in a crystal decanter. And when the bartender is vacuuming his domain in the morning, he carefully closes the door so that the noise won't disturb guests having morning coffee in the hall.

A gong summons guests to dinner. Tables are set with silver napkin rings and silver candlesticks, soup is served from silver tureens. Carafes of water are garnished with thin slices of lime. Meals are served country-house style, a fixed menu with no choices (although you know at lunchtime what

14

you will be having for dinner and have an opportunity to ask for a simple substitute). The cuisine favors simple country fare—roast Aberdeen Angus beef, roast leg of lamb, haunch of venison, perhaps, served from the carving trolley. The herb bread is baked fresh in the Eriska ovens, the vegetables come fresh from the Eriska garden, the cream from the Eriska Jerseys, eggs from the free-ranging hens, salmon and lobster courtesy of Loch Linnhe.

What the Isle of Eriska offers, then, is an opportunity to sample gracious country-house living, the "upstairs" of Upstairs/Downstairs. Your host, the Honorable Robin Buchanan-Smith, has invested close to half-a-million dollars in restoring the 300-acre property and the Victorian mansion, originally the home of a Scottish shipowner. His background can only be considered unusual as preparation for a career as a successful innkeeper—former chaplain of the University of St. Andrews—but in case you expect to find some kind of doddering dominie, let me hasten to add that your host is the able-bodied gentleman in kilt and tweeds lugging baggage or checking the boiler or chopping logs for the fire. Sheena Buchanan-Smith is in charge of the kitchen, and her previous experience of

Isle of Eriska

catering was high teas at the manse, but you'd never suspect it once you've enjoyed her impeccable meals, the sort of self-indulgent desserts you'd never find in a Scottish manse—banana *brûlée*, peach mousse and ginger/orange roulade.

Of course, not everyone is enchanted with country-house life, and I've watched couples here who were bored and bewildered. But I've also seen stylish young couples having the time of their lives, because one of the attractions of Eriska is that you can get away to your own private nooks and crannies when you want to. By day, play tennis or croquet. Go for a ride on one of the Icelandic ponies. Wander off along the shore to scout for seals and otters. Go rowing on the loch or bay. There's plenty to see in the neighboring countryside, of course, but nothing I can think of that would lure me back across that iron bridge until the last possible moment. After dinner, find a quiet corner for backgammon or Scrabble. Or, if the evening is mild, take your drinks and slip off for a stroll in the garden. Listen to the stillness. Watch the moonbeams on Loch Linnhe. Pure magic.

Name: Isle of Eriska Hotel

Owners/Managers: Robin and Sheena Buchanan-Smith

Address: Ledaig, Connel, Argyll PA37 1SD

Location: From Glasgow, about 2½ hours by car via Oban; by Loganair to Oban; by train to Connel (where the Hotel Daimler will collect you for a small fee, if alerted in advance)

Telephone: (0631-72) 205 in Ledaig

Cables/Telex: (None)

Reps: (None)

Credit Cards: American Express

Rooms: 28

Meals: Breakfast 8:30–9:30, morning coffee in lounge for residents only, lunch 1–1:30, afternoon tea 4–4:30 (residents only), dinner 7:30–8:30; approx. cost of dinner for two $36; tie and jacket for dinner; room service during dining room hours

Entertainment: No piped music, no television, just conversation, backgammon or Scrabble, or the local malt whiskies—Tarisker and Glencoe

Sports: Tennis court (all-weather, "not lighted—but you can play to almost 11 in the evening in summer"), rowing boat, croquet, walks, pony

16

trekking on the island; golf and watersports in Oban

Sightseeing: Castles at Dunstaffnage and Barcaldine, Highland games at Oban, the lochs and glens and forests and ghosts of the Ancient Kingdom of Dalriada

P.S. Closed November to Easter

Scotland

Inverlochy Castle
Fort William

♕♕♕♕ ✗✗✗ $$$$

It's a mansion rather than a castle, its Scottish Baronial granite turrets protected, not by lookouts and moat, but by Oscar the Peacock and rhododendron bushes the size of guardhouses. It was built by Lord Abinger in 1863, and shortly thereafter he played host to his monarch, Queen Victoria; and if her great-great-granddaughter were to stay here today, she wouldn't look at all out of place. The two-story Great Hall is lined with antiques and topped by a delicately frescoed ceiling; portraits by Sir Benjamin West hang above carved mantels and brass andirons; and a hand-carved antique oak chest that would be front stage center in most other hotels is here tucked away behind a settee, repository for assorted tennis rackets and balls. The drawing rooms are palatial, the dining room is decked out with masterfully carved mahogany sideboards from the palace of a Norwegian king, and glistening with silverware from the heirloom collection of the present owners. A carved oak staircase leads up to a wood-paneled billiard room with a rare Burroughs and Watts marble-based table and lined with stags' heads from the Scottish Highlands and moose heads from America. Step into the satin-and-brocade refinement of the dozen bedchambers, and you may feel you've been born again—this time with a silver spoon in your mouth. (Most of them are booked months in advance, so take whatever you can get; but if you have a choice, my favorites are 6 and 20 among the rooms, 3 among the suites.)

Inverlochy is now owned by a Canadian family by the name of Hobbs, but when you see the pride, the painstaking protectiveness of manager Michael Leonard, you might get the impression that the castle is the personal property of that consummate professional. In the kitchen, Miss Mary Shaw, MBE, a diffident lady from the Outer Hebrides, conjures up orange soufflés that would put many Parisian-trained chefs to shame; a few   17 years ago she was created a Member of the British Empire by Queen Victoria's great-great, etc., the first woman in Britain to be honored in this way for services to gastronomy. Waiters and waitresses are recruited from a nearby hotel school—young but eager to please and proficient.

The staff may be young, the chef may be a lady from Lewis rather than Lyons, but everyone from Mrs. Hobbs down is a devotee of perfection. Even in France or Italy you'll be hard-pressed to find its equal. And although Inverlochy Castle ranks among the most expensive hostelries in Britain (the rates are enough to make a Scotsman choke on his whisky), let me offer you a word of advice: most people make a reservation for only one night, then regret having to leave next morning, so promise yourselves a couple of nights at least.

At the very least, get there early in the day to enjoy everything Inverlochy has to offer—the terraced gardens, the trout pond, 5,000 acres of forest and pasture, the roses and rhododendrons, the views of Ben Nevis on one side and the Western Highlands on the other. Tea on the terrace. Sherry in the lounge. A glass of Dew of Ben Nevis, the Inverlochy malt whisky, as a nightcap in one of the elegant drawing rooms. To say nothing of the pleasures of your sumptuous bedchamber. As Queen Victoria confided to her diary: "I never saw a lovelier or more romantic spot." True then, probably true today.

Name: Inverlochy Castle

Owners: The Hobbs Family

Manager: Michael Leonard

Address: Fort William, Inverness PH336SN

Location: Three miles *north* of Fort William. (That's important if you're driving from the south, because you have to go through town, then pass a sign saying "Inverlochy," another saying "Inverlochy Castle"—the ruined one—and yet another with the words "Inverlochy Castle Farm"; about half-a-mile beyond the latter you'll find a concealed entrance on the left side of the road.) If you give them plenty of advance notice, the hotel can arrange to meet you at any major railway station or airport (including Prestwick).

Telephone: Fort William 2127 (area code 0397)

Cables/Telex: (None)

Reps: Relais-Châteaux in U.S., Canada and Europe

Credit Cards: American Express, Visa

18   **Rooms:** 12, including 2 suites

Meals: Breakfast 7:30–10, morning coffee, lunch on request, afternoon tea, dinner at 8; 5-course dinner for two approx. $45–$50 (there is no formal menu, but "individual preferences are always recognized and pandered to whenever possible"); tie and jacket de rigueur; room service during dining room hours

Entertainment: "Absolutely no formal entertainment"

Sports: Tennis (all-weather court, but cramped), walking trails, trout fishing on the property; pony trekking and golf nearby (including an 18-hole course on *peat*)

Sightseeing: Drives up Glen Nevis, walks up Ben Nevis; the scene of Bonny Prince Charlie's Uprising at Glenfinnan, the Road to the Isles, Loch Ness, castles everywhere; Highland games at Fort William in August; West Highland Museum; trips by hydrofoil to Oban and points south

P.S. Closed October through March

Taychreggan Hotel
Lochaweside

W X $$

"Peat, we always burn peat... so much better for warming up the claret, you know," says John Taylor, and indeed there's a peat fire burning in the lobby to welcome you after your trek through Glen Nant to the shores of Loch Awe.

You get there along a narrow road that winds through eight miles of protected forests—spruce and oak and lodgepole pine—the route followed by cattle drovers of old, a sort of Highland Butterfield Trail. The old inn at Kilchrenan was where they rested for the night before swimming their cattle across the loch; Samuel Johnson, too, may have stayed here, and changed horses, on his peregrinations through the Highlands. The original inn, a whitewashed cottage by the edge of the loch, has probably not changed all that much in the years since, nor has the view of quiet loch (25 miles of it) and heathered hillside. But in recent years the interior has been revamped, and a new wing added at the rear, grouped around a cobbled courtyard with a well and flowers, and a glass-enclosed, plant-draped walkway to link the 17th and 20th centuries. It's an award-winning effort, done with flair and feeling, a happy blend of mellowed barn timbers with plate glass, hundred-

19

year-old Admiralty charts with Rya rugs, Yorkshire sandstone flooring with contemporary sofas and armchairs in mocha cut velvet upholstery. The dining room acquires an airy conservatory feeling with arched floor-to-ceiling windows, the white walls of the cozy bar are hung with ship models and stuffed capercaillies and salmon.

The guest rooms didn't fare quite so well, but the 22 rooms, small but comfortable, are adequate for a couple of nights. Come here, not for luxury, but for simple Scottish pleasures. A tranquil setting. A bench in the garden. A rowboat on the loch. Come for the coziness of the place, for this is the local pub and you may find yourselves sharing the bar with the local gillie in deerstalker hat or a christening party from the wee kirk in the village. The Taychreggan menu ranges from local trout and salmon to Danish *koldt bord* lunches (Tove Taylor is Danish), the 52-bin wine list is unusually eloquent: "strong in alcohol but with an equilibrium which makes it the most perfect match for salmon," or "a note of honey and meadow flowers, which matures to more substantial tones." A pleasant browse while you wait for the claret to warm up.

Name: Taychreggan Hotel

Owners/Managers: John and Tove Taylor

Address: Lochaweside, Taynuilt, Argyll

Location: Near Kilchrenan, or the shores of Loch Awe, about 20 miles from Oban via A85 and Glen Nant (B845)

Telephone: Kilchrenan 211 (area code 08663)

Cables/Telex: (None)

Reps: (None)

Credit Cards: American Express, Diners Club, Access, Barclaycard

---

Rooms: 22 (10 with private bathrooms, some with central heating, some with electric heaters)

Meals: Breakfast 8:15–9:30, lunch 1–2:15, afternoon tea 3:45, dinner 7:30–8:45; dinner for two approx. $20; informal dress but "long dresses are not out of place"; room service for breakfast only

---

Entertainment: (None)

Sports: Rowboats and motorboats at the inn; forest walks and horseback riding nearby, golf and tennis in Oban

---

Sightseeing: Highland games at Oban, Taynuilt and Inveraray; castles—
Stalker, Inveraray, Kilchern, Innis, Carnasserie

Creggan's Inn
Strachur

A long finger of loch shimmers in the seemingly endless twilight; whitewashed cottages accent low hills with patches of heather; a centuries-old chestnut tree stands guard beside a rocky headland, or *creagan* in the Gaelic. It is possible that this same tree sheltered Mary Queen of Scots when she stepped ashore here all those many twilights ago; the inn itself wasn't there in those days, being a relative youngster dating from the last century. Strachur itself is a true backwater, a hushed hamlet straggling along the shores of the loch—a general store, a post office, a shinty field in the grounds of the big white house just along the road from the inn. If the local shinty team has had a good game, you may find yourselves joining in the celebration at the inn; or the owners of the inn themselves, Sir Fitzroy and Lady Maclean, may stop by from the Big House to mingle with their guests. Sir Fitzroy is the very model of a British baronet: Eton, Cambridge, diplomatic service in Moscow and Paris, raconteur, parachuted behind German lines in Yugoslavia to be Churchill's liaison with Tito. He has written several books on journeys to Samarkand, Tashkent and other exotic points in Central Asia; Lady Maclean, in turn, is the author of several cookbooks.

Their inn claims to be no more than a traditional West Highland hostelry, a small whitewashed "farmhouse" building with black trim, and a recent addition that adds nothing to its external charm but does provide space for another dozen rooms and a lounge with large windows framing that tranquil view down the loch. Creggan's makes no pretence to luxury (only half its rooms have private bath or shower), but it attracts a loyal clientele, and Happy Rockefeller, who presumably could afford plusher spots, spent a week here when she was Mrs. Vice-President.

Certainly it's a quiet, pleasant stopover on a Highland tour, or a base for side trips into the surrounding lochs, or to nearby gardens, museums and castles (the Duke of Argyll's Inveraray Castle is just across the loch). And even if you cannot spend a night here, stop off for one of the Creggan's substantial afternoon cream teas—fresh-baked scones and pancakes, cream from the farm up the brae, homemade strawberry jams and cakes. Sample   21 tea and you may be tempted to stay for dinner. Sheila Ford, the Creggan's cook, serves up some unusual dishes like mackerel with gooseberry sauce, Loch Fyne herring rolled in oatmeal and venison pot roast; the sweet trolley is piled high with chocolate roulade, Grand Marnier gateau, strawberry cheesecake and other pleasures; the wine list is stocked with 64 vintages handpicked by Sir Fitzroy, among them, needless to say, several Yugoslavian labels. After dinner, have a malt whisky in the cozy bar (the local brand is Glencoe). Or go for a stroll along the loch, and sit on one of the park benches by the shore until the sun finally disappears behind the islands of Islay and Jura.

Name: Creggan's Inn

Owners: Sir Fitzroy and Lady Maclean

Manager: Laura Huggins

Address: Strachur, Argyll

Location: On the shores of Loch Fyne, 1½ hours by car from Glasgow via Loch Lomond and Rest-and-Be-Thankful, or via the Gourock-Dunoon car ferry and route A815

Telephone: Strachur 279 and 270

Cables/Telex: (None)

Reps: (None)

Credit Cards: American Express

Rooms: 25, half of them with private bathrooms

Meals: Breakfast 8–9:30, lunch 12:30–2, dinner 8–9:30; 3-course dinner for two approx. $20; tie and jacket preferred; room service for morning tea and continental breakfast only (served by Peggy the head housekeeper, on her "own" bone china)

Entertainment: Color TV in Loch Fyne lounge, occasional *ceilidhs*, or singsongs, in the bar, occasional pipers

Sports: Walking trails, golf, boat trips and pony trekking nearby

Sightseeing: The inn publishes its own list of attractions in the neighborhood, including Highland games at Dunoon, Inveraray, Oban; castles, gardens, museums at Inveraray, Glencoe, Crarae and elsewhere; and lovely scenery among the lochs, the Mull of Kintyre and the Kyles of Bute.

P.S. Occasional coach parties, a few groups of gardeners or nature lovers

Culloden House
Inverness

The name Culloden has a dolorous ring for the Scots, for it was here on the battlefield of Culloden that the Highland clans under Prince Charles Edward Stuart were finally vanquished by the Duke of Cumberland, known hereabouts as the Butcher of Culloden. The Prince, it is said, spent the night before the battle in a Renaissance castle which used to stand on the site of this hotel, but of the royal lodging no tangible sign remains. In its place you have this grand mansion, behind an ornate stone gateway and a lush lawn the size of a soccer field, its elegant 4-story facade and attendant wings mirrored in a duck pond. This 18th-century masterpiece, now designated a "building of special architectural and historical interest," was designed and build by the Adams, Scotland's preeminent creators of stately homes. They might quibble about some of the 20th-century trappings (like white plastic doors on room closets) but few guests would quibble about the conveniences and comforts—telephones beside bed *and* bath, trouser pressers, color television, fresh fruit, fresh flowers, and more towels than a Hilton. Your room is made up while you're downstairs dining off River Spey salmon or filet of Aberdeen Angus beef with chef's paté and red wine sauce, and service generally is attentive, but you get the feeling, judging from the way the same personnel keep popping up in varied roles, that management stretched its resources to the hilt when fixing the place up. Still, Kenneth McLennan—veteran hotelier, antiques dealer, rally driver, world authority on pheasant breeding—has created a desirable overnight stop, and as an ardent Scottish Nationalist he must have a special feel for the location. But one suspects that if that other nationalist, Bonnie Prince Charlie, turned up again today, he couldn't afford to spend the night here.

Name: Culloden House

Owner: Kenneth McLennan

Manager: James Whyte

Address: Inverness

Location: Three miles east of Inverness, one exit past the sign for Culloden on the main highway

Telephone: Culloden Moor 461 (area code 046372)

Telex: 75402

Reps: Scott Calder in U.S. and Canada, Prestige Hotels in Europe

Credit Cards: "All of them"

Rooms: 25, including one suite

Meals: Breakfast from 7 on, lunch 12:30–2, afternoon tea, dinner 7–11; dinner for two approx. $32 to $40, informal; room service around the clock

Entertainment: TV in guest rooms

Sports: Sauna/solarium, walking on 41 acres of grounds; golf, fishing, shooting, horseback riding nearby

Sightseeing: Culloden Moor Battlefield and Museum; Inverness Castle, Cawdor Castle; tour of whisky distilleries

P.S.   When last seen, Kenneth McLennan was dressed in paint-speckled overalls renovating his latest acquisition, Dalhousie Castle, 8 miles south of Edinburgh in a village called Bonnyrigg; it's a massive pile of a palace, which had been owned by the Earls of Dalhousie since the 13th century. It promises to be grander, more deluxe than Culloden House. For details, write: Dalhousie Castle, Bonnyrigg, Midlothian.

Newton Hotel
Nairn

It looks like a mini-Balmoral Castle, a gray mansion with crow-stepped gables and corbeling, ensign blowing stiffly from the topmost tower; spacious lawns and pastures open up panoramic views of the Moray Firth on one side, shut out town and traffic on the other. Inside, it's all paneling of Canadian pine, high ceilings with chandeliers, pastel walls with decorative stucco, and Isobel Ian, the resident manager, waiting in a stylish long dress to welcome guests to the candlelit dining room. After dinner you retire to the gold-draped drawing room, sink into a plump sofa, while a waitress pulls up a cart laden with coffee, liqueurs and malt whiskies. All very civilized. Charlie Chaplin used to love vacationing here "because no one paid any attention to him."

   In recent years, the emphasis seems to have moved to the dining room (the hotel is owned by an Inverness catering firm), where the menu feels like

24

an encyclopedia and the local fare takes on a continental flavor—and Aberdeen Angus beef is marinated in red wine, herbs and peppercorns to become *filet mignon avignonaise*. The young, attentive staff manages to create a suggestion of sophistication to match the menu. But they reserve one half of the dining room for guests staying two or three nights (whether those guests appear in the dining room or not) while one-night stands are herded into an alcove with the tour groups (classy tour groups, visiting castles and gardens and so on, but groups nevertheless). Consolation takes the form of a dessert trolley laden with 15 temptations, each one creamier than the next.

Tour groups are put up in a new courtyard wing in what was once the carriage house, where the decor is uninspired but the rooms are spacious and perfectly adequate; the most expensive rooms are in the main house, and, if you can, bag Room 106 overlooking the golf course and the sea; 226 and 112, both corner rooms, have garden views and enough space for practicing your golf swing.

If you're golfers, of course, you'll like Newton House because you just have to walk across the garden and across the street to get to the nearest links; if you're touring the Highlands, you'll find it a comfortable and convenient base; if you're passing your time simply as lovers, you'll find, like Chaplin, that no one pays any attention.

Name: Newton Hotel

Manager: Donald Curry, resident manager Isobel Ian

Address: Nairn

Location: In town, just off A96, about 7 miles east of Inverness Airport

Telephone: Nairn 53144 (area code 0667)

Cables/Telex: Robroy G/75470

Reps: (None)

Credit Cards: American Express

Rooms: 30, including 14 newer rooms in Newton Court, the former carriage house in the garden

Meals: Breakfast 8–10, lunch 12:30–2, afternoon tea anytime, dinner 7–9:30; 4-course dinner for two approx. $20 to $25; tie and jacket "expected"; room service at small extra charge

Entertainment: TV room

Sports: Tennis (1 court), sauna, putting; golf (9 holes and 18 holes) next door; fishing and game shooting by arrangement; beach nearby

Sightseeing: Cawdor Castle, Culloden Battlefield and Museum, Loch Ness, the Spey Valley whisky distilleries

P.S. Closed mid-October to early April; some tour groups for lunch or overnight stops

Meldrum House
Old Meldrum

The Laird of Meldrum himself may cook breakfast for you, but then again he may not, since the Honorable Robin Duff is a man of far-flung interests—chairman of Scottish ballet and broadcaster, formerly tutor to Yugoslavian princesses and adviser to the chief of state of Bundi in India. He comes from a long line of patriots and empire builders, and his family has lived here for some 700 years. His cocktail lounge, a grottolike snuggery, was his ancestors' kitchen in the 13th century, but most of this gray-stone mansion with pepperpot turrets and curly gables dates from later centuries. Prints and engravings of ancestors hang side by side on corridor walls with engravings of Indian scenes and political caricatures (one frame features a well-thumbed certificate of remission granted to an ancestor by a King of France). There are more family heirlooms and bibelots in the guest rooms, most of which have been recently refurbished. My preferences would be Rooms 2 or 8, but since there are only nine guest rooms in all, reservations are at a premium. Since it attracts a loyal and discerning clientele, you may find yourself elbow-to-elbow in the snuggery with ambassadors, ballet dancers, ex-Prime Ministers or oil tycoons who've discovered that business trips to Aberdeen are not such a bad idea after all when you can stay with the Laird of Meldrum.

Name:	Meldrum House
Owner:	Robin Duff
Manager:	Mrs. Kay Chatfield
Address:	Old Meldrum, Aberdeenshire

26

Location: In farming country northwest of Aberdeen, about 25 minutes from the city by car via route A947

Telephone: Old Meldrum 294 (area code 06512)

Cables/Telex: (None)

Reps: (None)

Credit Cards: Diners Club

Rooms: 9 (2 with semiprivate bathrooms)

Meals: Breakfast 8–9:30, continental breakfast 9:30–10, lunch 12:30–2, no afternoon tea, dinner 7–10; 4-course dinner for two approx. $25–$30; informal dress but tie and jacket "appropriate"; room service for breakfast only

Entertainment: TV in lounge

Sports: Walking on 300 acres of private grounds; golf in Old Meldrum; tennis, fishing, hunting nearby; watersports and beach in Aberdeen

Sightseeing: Castles—Crathes, Craigievar, Drum, Fraser—and stately homes—Haddo House and Leith Hall; Highland games in Old Meldrum in June; Pittmeden Gardens; the Whisky Trail (tour of distilleries); Aberdeen

P.S. Closed December through March

Tullich Lodge
Ballater

WWW XX $$

Mr. Jeeves shuffles over to greet you with as much dignity as a world-weary English sheep dog can muster, but soon loses interest, leaving you to take stock of his domain. Tullich Lodge is a sturdy turreted granite mansion, in a notch in the hillside above the River Dee, surrounded by birch and beech. From the lounge or lawn (where you can sip afternoon tea when the sun shines) there are classic views across Strathdee to Craig Coileach and to the Coyles of Muick and Lochnagar.

The interior is immaculate: an elegant L-shaped drawing room dominated by a grand piano and antique andirons; a library/lounge that's exactly the comfy sort of spot where you sit out a shower, browsing through

27

piles of magazines and volumes of Scott. In the dining room, windows are draped with French brocade, the walls are paneled with dark walnut from a mansion in India, the tables decorated with sprigs of heather or sprays of fresh flowers in wine goblets.

Dinner, as you might suspect, relies heavily on local produce— Aberdeen Angus beef, Highland lamb, grouse and pheasant, vegetables fresh from the Tullich garden. There's a good, moderately priced wine list to enhance the fastidious home cooking. The lodge has only ten rooms, all with private bathrooms, all with views, all furnished in country-house style; my favorite is the tower room, with panoramic view and spacious bathroom, but you may have to settle for whatever is available (no chore) since the lodge has its steady clientele of anglers, shooters and stalkers. If there is one reservation about Tullich Lodge it is that, while the regulars are tended with efficiency and deference, other guests *may* have to settle for service that's about as enthusiastic as Mr. Jeeves's welcome. Nevertheless, sun or shower, Tullich Lodge is a lovely spot to spend a few days relaxing and reading or exploring Royal Deeside. Forest tracks and old drove roads go winding off into the hills practically from the gate, and if you decide to venture forth, Neil Bannister and Hector Macdonald will rustle up a tasty picnic box for you—Stilton cheese, potted shrimp, rolls, crackers, fresh fruit, tea or coffee. Mr. Jeeves may tag along—until you come to the steep parts.

Name: Tullich Lodge

Owners/Managers: Neil Bannister and Hector Macdonald, proprietors

---

Address: Ballater, Aberdeenshire AB35SB

Location: On Royal Deeside, a mile or so east of Ballater proper, less than 30 miles west of Aberdeen on route A93

Telephone: Ballater 406 (area code 03382)

Cables/Telex: (None)

Reps: (None)

Credit Cards: American Express, Diners Club

Rooms: 10

Meals: Breakfast 8:30–9, lunch 1, afternoon tea, dinner 7:30–9; 3-course dinner for two approx. $20–$25; tie and jacket expected; limited room service during dining room hours

---

Entertainment: No TV, no radio, no piped music—just a bar with 34 different malt whiskies

Sports: Golf, tennis, horseback riding, woodland walks nearby

Sightseeing: Nine castles—Knock, Dunnotar, Midmar, Crahtes, Craigievar, Kildrummy, Corgarff, Braemar (all open to the public) and Balmoral (the gardens of which are open when the Royal Family is not in residence); highland games at Braemar, Ballater, Aboyne, Lonach and Aberdeen during August and September; excursions and picnics to the Linn of Dee, Glen Muick, Burn o' Vat and Forest of Birse; the Whisky Trail (a tour of local distilleries)

P.S. Closed January through March; no children under nine

Dunkeld House Hotel
Dunkeld

Afternoon tea is served on the terrace beside the River Tay. Salmon flip in the stream, birds chirrup in the larch and laurel, and a hundred acres of garden and woodland create a sense of solitude. But if you walk along the driveway to the gatehouse, then go right along the main street of Dunkeld you come to a village square with cobbled streets, and the cloistered hush of Dunkeld Cathedral. This was once the capital of ancient Scotland and over the centuries these cobbles have rung with the footsteps of kings and queens (James V, Mary Queen of Scots, Queen Victoria) and poets Burns and Wordsworth. The house itself, with its almost Teutonic lines and timber trim, was built as a shooting lodge for the 7th Duke of Atholl, at the turn of the century, then turned into a hotel ten years ago by the gracious Mrs. Miller. She has meticulously preserved the basic character of the lodge, with its pine paneled halls and wall tapestries, its formal dining room with cream-and-Wedgwood decor and tall windows looking out on the lawns and river. Catch a salmon and you can have the chef prepare it for dinner, but even if you don't, there's a fair chance you can still sit down to *darne de saumon au beurre* or *salmon Radziwill,* cooked in white wine with prawns.

Most of the Dunkeld's rooms have a view, or garden and/or river, but a few at the rear do not (specify that you don't want one of these "inner courtyard rooms," unless you want to save a few dollars). Of the others, Rooms 8, 8a and 11 are your best bets.

Name: Dunkeld House Hotel

Owner: Mrs. G. B. Miller

Manager: Mrs. B. B. Chadwick

Address: Dunkeld, Perthshire PH80HY

Location: On the banks of the River Tay, 15 miles north of Perth, 45 miles north of Edinburgh

Telephone: Dunkeld 243

Cables/Telex: (None)

Reps: (None)

Credit Cards: (None)

Rooms: 27 (21 have private bathrooms)

Meals: Breakfast 8–9:30, lunch 12:30–2, afternoon tea 4–5, dinner 7–9; 3-course dinner for two approx. $20–$25; tie and jacket preferred; room service during dining-room hours at a small additional charge

Entertainment: Dine and dance (old time and Scottish) on weekends, TV in guest rooms

Sports: Tennis (1 court), fishing (1½-mile beat), croquet, pitch-and-putt; golf nearby

Sightseeing: Dunkeld Cathedral and the restored village; Blair Castle, Glamis Castle and Scone Palace; Pitlochry Festival Theater in summer.

P.S. Closed November through mid-January

Ballathie House Hotel
near Perth

The conical towers may put you in mind of a chateau in France but that's the River Tay rather than the Loire that flows past the lawns. When it was built in 1850, Ballathie House had its own railroad station, and royalty came here for the hunting and fishing. Fishermen still have their separate

entrance, which tells you something about the clientele; but there's room enough in Ballathie's gardens and lounges for everyone—assuming you can get a room in the first place. All 22 guest chambers come equipped with dashing little Hitachi color television sets, wake-up alarms, radios, coffee/tea makers and heated towel racks; but only two of them face the river, so you'll almost certainly have to settle for views of lawns and oaks and sycamores (views that would be considered the major attraction in most hotels). The loveliest room in the house is the dining salon, with period furnishings, olive crushed-velvet upholstery, pastel green walls, an ornately carved white marble fireplace with wine racks where the crackling logs should be. Cuisine is predominantly continental but with its own Ballathie touches—hence, *entrecôte minute* with whisky sauce; and the menu also gives you an opportunity to sample some traditional Scottish fare, like cock-a-leekie soup and haggis.

Name: Ballathie House Hotel

Manager: Mrs. P. E. Brassey

Address: Kinclaven by Stanley, Perthshire PH14QN

Location: About 12 miles north of Perth, just off A93

Telephone: Meikleour 268 (area code 025083)

Telex: Ballathie 727396

Reps: (None)

Credit Cards: American Express, Access

Rooms: 22 (plus 16 rooms in a chalet tucked away in the garden and used mostly by fishermen)

Meals: Breakfast 7:30–9:30, lunch 12:45–2, afternoon tea 3:30–5, dinner 6:45 to 8:30; 5-course dinner for two approx. $28–$30; tie and jacket; room service for continental breakfast only

Entertainment: TV in guest rooms

Sports: Tennis (1 court), pool table, backgammon, hiking trails on 2,500 acres of woodland; golf nearby (a different *championship* course for every day of the week)

Sightseeing: (See Dunkeld House Hotel)

P.S. Closed December 1 to January 15, slack months February and June

Greywalls
Gullane

♛♛ ✗✗ $$

The clubhouse of the Honourable Company of Edinburgh Golfers is right next door, the 10th fairway runs past the rose garden, and beyond the Muirfield fairways, the Firth of Forth flows into the North Sea.

This unique country house is a diffident sort of place, its convex facade screened from the humdrum world by curvaceous walls (not gray but honey-colored) and four walled gardens. It was built as a holiday house by an Edwardian golf nut, and one of its frequent guests was King Edward VII himself, whose interests seem to have lain in directions other than golf; Lord Derby rented it one summer, but found it inadequate because the dining room wasn't large enough for his guests *and* his footmen—one for each diner.

Greywalls' two-dozen guest rooms are still immaculate (you get the impression the chambermaids must be as diligent in spotting specks of dust as golfers are in removing minuscule obstructions before putting); public rooms fairly glow with antiques and refined furnishings; log fires burn in the grates; the pine-paneled library is stacked with leatherbound encyclopedias, histories and the collected novels of various scribes. The dining room, now that His Lordship's footmen are no longer in attendance, is an *intime* enclave specializing in fish fresh from the Firth, prepared by a chef who practiced his trade at London's Dorchester and Chewton Glen Hotel.

Greywalls is very much a private country house (the Horlicks family of malted-milk fame), and those curving walls, be warned, welcome you into a world that's soft-spoken, almost genteel, certainly low-key—the sort of place where Jack Nicklaus can relax between rounds of the British Open and Yehudi Menuhin between recitals at the Edinburgh Festival. But if you plan to spend a few days exploring the countryside around Edinburgh (half-an-hour's drive to the west) or Sir Walter Scott's territory (an hour's drive to the south), Greywalls is the loveliest of nests to return to each evening.

Name: Greywalls

Owners: The Horlick Family

Manager: Alastair Keeling

Address: Gullane, East Lothian

Location: About 30 minutes east of Edinburgh (you can arrange to have the hotel pick you up at the airport)

Telephone: Gullane 842144 (area code 0620)

Cables/Telex: (None)

Reps: (None)

Credit Cards: American Express, Diners Club

Rooms: 25

Meals: Breakfast 8–9:30, lunch 12:45–2, dinner 7:30–8:45; 3-course dinner for two approx. $26; tie and jacket; room service during meal hours

Entertainment: TV lounge

Sports: Tennis (1 court); 9 golf courses within 5 miles; beach and riding nearby

Sightseeing: Edinburgh; Dirleton and Hailes Castles; the Scott Country, including Abbotsford (Sir Walter Scott's home), Mellerstain House and Dryburgh Abbey

P.S.   Closed mid-October to mid-April

Turnberry Hotel
near Ayr

WW X $$$

All the greats of recent golfing history have stayed here—Burt Lancaster, James Garner, Bing Crosby and Dwight D. Eisenhower. Every major British tournament has been played here. Golfers have been known to step off their jets at Prestwick, drive here, go straight to the course and tee off. And I've heard members of the staff muttering that sometimes you'd think more money was spent on the golf course than on the hotel. Which is not to say that oceans of money have not been spent on the hotel or that only golfers come here—Paul Newman played *tennis* here, and hosts of visitors come just to enjoy the serene setting, the panoramic view and the lovely, unspoiled countryside all around.

Turnberry was built by one of the British railway companies back in 1902, and neither the setting nor the hotel has changed much since then. It sits on a hillock well back from the roadway, its long cream-colored facade topped by a red roof dotted with dotted windows and dozens of chimneys

33

dating from the coal-burning, steam-train era. The hotel is still owned by British Railways, its British Transport Hotels division, which keeps the place in tiptop condition. The overall decor clings to the hotel's Edwardian heritage, and the elegant proportions of the place cover up the dullness of much of the furnishing; in the guest rooms, decor has sort of evolved, keeping pace with changing demands in comforts (TV, radio and phones in every room) if not in style, and in many of the rooms the most impressive feature is the grand old-style bathtub, the size of a bunker. You can save a few dollars by settling for a room at the rear without a view, but you'll be envious of people facing the firth, especially the tenants of Suite 170/2 which has a grand piano and a window alcove with dining table.

The Turnberry dining room itself is a large salon with tall windows overlooking the golf courses and river; smartly attired waiters do their best to create the atmosphere of an ocean liner, and although the cuisine hardly lives up to the setting, dinner can be a pleasant experience. The Turnberry chefs give you a chance to sample traditional Scottish dishes (Highland venison and crispy oatcakes) as well as more continental fare (*goujons de sole marat* and *escalope de veau à l'Anversoise*). The lengthy *carte des vins* lists a few oddities, like an Adgestone 1976 from England, a Corbières Château de Pech Redon 1975 from Languedoc and Penedes Torres Coronas 1974 from the hills behind Barcelona. The Turnberry bar stocks a bountiful range of those singularly Scottish *vins du pays*—Highland malt whiskies. Order yourselves a couple of Glenfiddichs. Take them out onto the terrace. Sip them slowly and admire the view. Palm trees grow in the garden, dogged evidence that the Gulf Stream flows nearby. From the terrace, steps and paths lead down the manicured hillside past the putting green, pitch-and-putt course and tennis courts; then across the roadway (one car every five minutes would constitute a traffic jam here) to the fairways that made Turnberry famous, great swatches of green interspersed with yellow whin and sandy bunkers. Off to the right, Turnberry Lighthouse; to the left, the rocky cupcake islet known as Ailsa Craig, and beyond the Firth of Clyde, the low hazy hills of Kintyre. This is one of the most tranquil corners of Scotland, and a couple of days of this kind of calm is like a week's vacation elsewhere. Especially on a long, leisurely twilight in summer, when as you drain your glasses not much short of midnight, the last golfers of the day approach the 18th green.

Name: Turnberry Hotel

Manager: C. J. Rouse

Address: Turnberry, Strathclyde

Location: Just south of Ayr and Prestwick International Airport, about half an hour by car

Telephone: Turnberry 202 (area code 06553)

Telex: 777779

Reps: BTH Hotels in U.S., Canada and U.K., Etap Hotels in Europe

Credit Cards: American Express, Diners Club, Barclaycard, Access, Carte Blanche

Rooms: 124, including a few suites

Meals: Breakfast 8–10, lunch 1–2:30, afternoon tea 4–5, dinner 8–9:30; 3-course dinner for two approx. $35–$40; tie and jacket for dinner; full room service around the clock

Entertainment: Dancing 3 times a week during summer, pianist in dining room, films shown twice weekly in summer, TV in every room

Sports: Two all-weather tennis courts, putting green, pitch-and-putt course, billiard room, indoor swimming pool, croquet, private beach, two championship golf courses (guaranteed starting times for hotel guests); fishing and horseback riding nearby

Sightseeing: Culzean Castle (with its special Eisenhower memorial suite); Dunure Castle, Kennedy Castle; Burns Country, including the poet's birthplace; walking on moor and glen and along the shore

For brief reports on other hotels in Scotland turn to the chapter on Added Attractions at the end of this guide.

England

Miller Howe
Windermere

♔♔♔ ✗✗✗ $$$

Dinner, says the prospectus, is "a 5-course event," and that promise is the key to the Miller Howe experience. The event, scheduled at "8 for 8:30," commences with dressy guests gathering in the three elegant, clublike lounges for sherry or whatever, well before the appointed half-hour when the first course appears on the tables. On a recent visit, the first course was grapefruit and orange with elderflower sorbet, followed by cauliflower and cheese soup with croutons and chopped chives, then duck liver paté with sherry aspic; all this in preparation for the *pièce de résistance*—poached local salmon with hollandaise sauce, and a gardenful of fresh vegetables—leeks in white wine, glazed carrots with lemon, purée of parsnips with toasted pine kernels, zucchini with toasted almonds, french bean sprouts, baked cabbage with nutmeg, minted new potatoes. All prepared to perfection. Only when you reach the dessert event do you have a choice—chocolate brandy roulade, Bacardi and lime jelly with shortbread, honey and malt whisky cream ice, poached peach with hot butterscotch sauce, to name just a few. There is, of course, an elaborate (and reasonably priced) wine list to complement such a feast, ranging from a Pineau de la Loire 1977 for under $5 a half bottle to a La Tache Domaine de la Romanée Conti 1971 for a cool $130 a bottle. Since it also lists several champagnes by the half bottle (including Taittinger and Roederer) you have no excuse for not celebrating. And I suspect that's the kind of mood you ought to be in when you visit Miller Howe.

"Theatrical" is the word you most often hear applied to Miller Howe, and there is indeed a touch of stagecraft in having guests assemble at 8 for 8:30, and (so I'm told, because I was spared the spectacle) having the chef appear with a giant platter of saddle of beef, followed around the dining room by spotlights.

Certainly the setting is expertly staged, by Noel Coward out of Terence Rattigan. The house itself is a Victorian manor distinguished mainly by two large chimneys like funnels and a glass-enclosed veranda. The interior has been fitted out in the most elegant manner with studded leather wing chairs, vitrines filled with Ilmenau porcelain, and Bristol glass, mocha-and-cream walls decorated with framed tapestries and steel engravings, coffee tables with piles of magazines and large books. At the rear, French doors open onto a flagstone terrace with white wrought-iron patio furniture, flower-decked fountains, splashes of rock pink and primulas, saxifrage and candytuft, and a couple of cherubs in a heavy necking session. Beyond the terrace, lawns and fields stretch away down to the lake.

Most of the guest chambers take advantage of the vista, and the few that do not (facing the garden or parking lot) cost several dollars less. Facing the lake, suites Troutbeck, Windermere and Ullswater have tape decks to go with all the other felicitous accouterments common to all the rooms (trouser presser, hair dryer, French of London Shampoo, Yardley Bath Oil, Riley Health Soap, intercom, radio, magazines and *binoculars*). I settled into Rydal, a smaller room at one end of the 2nd floor, facing the lake, but costing less because to see the lake you must peer through the branches of an oak tree that was tall and sturdy when Wordsworth was wandering around these parts looking at daffodils.

This singular hideaway is the creation of a man called John Tovey, who in his forty-odd years has managed to run theaters, hotels and a small corner of the British Empire when he served in the Colonial Office in Africa. I have never met him, but everyone seems to have the highest regard for his all-around abilities. He is responsible for the cooking, the decor, the details like binoculars and Clichy paperweights in every room, and, perhaps most of all, for instilling in his staff the same obsession with perfection and service. When you decide to enjoy the Miller Howe experience, arrive, if you can, in time for afternoon tea on the terrace. Tea appears on a large tray, a bulbous silver teapot, silver strainer, jug of hot water, Bavarian china piled high with cones and creamy cakes. While waiting for the tea to infuse, admire the view. The terrace with its stone walls dripping rock pinks and primulas, the bird bath surrounded by aubretia and candytuft. A wisp of smoke rising from a white farmhouse far up on the hillside. A sailboat tacking across the lake. Fields ribboned with stone walls. Clouds casting shadows on the peaks beyond the lake—Scafell, Hanging Knotts, Pike o' Stickle. With a view like this you *have* to be theatrical just to compete.

Name: Miller Howe

Owner/Manager: John Tovey

Address: Rayrigg Road, Windermere (Cumbria)

Location: In the Lake District, via route M6 Motorway (Exit 36), 1½ hours north of Manchester

Telephone: Windermere 2536 (area code 09662)

Cables/Telex: (None)

Reps: (None)

Credit Cards: American Express, Diners Club

Rooms: 13

Meals: Breakfast 9–10:30, no lunch but a plated salad dish can be prepared to take away, afternoon tea, dinner 8 for 8:30 (set menu of 5 courses); dinner for two approx. $42; room service for continental breakfast and drinks only

Entertainment: Taped classical music in the evening, various special events (e.g., cooking classes)

Sports: Nothing on premises though special advice is given on walking and car tours; nearby, tennis, golf, riding, squash, rowing, sailing and skiing

Sightseeing: Wordsworth House, Boat Museum, Railway Museum (steam railroads) and National Park House; historic homes (Levens Hall, Holker Hall); the Lake District National Park Centre has 32 acres of gardens and grounds on the shore of Windermere; local events include Sheep Dog Trials and sporting meets in the ancient tradition. Every morning at ten, Leonard Fitzjames, a retired army gentleman and expert on the Lakes, arrives at Miller Howe to help guests plan their days' sightseeing, walking, picnicking or pony trekking. His services are gratis.

P.S. Closed January 2 to last Thursday in March

Sharrow Bay Country House Hotel
Lake Ullswater

♔♔♔ ✗✗✗ $$$

Here is the luncheon I sat down to, at the table known as Window One, with uninterrupted view of lake and peaks competing with impeccable table settings and service: cream of pear and watercress soup; fresh Aberdeen sole and local salmon terrine with lobster sauce; lemon sorbet; roast leg of young English spring lamb, cooked on a bed of vegetables with a farci of lemon and parsley, *plus* a selection of fresh vegetables—cauliflower, zucchini, young carrots, sautéed potatoes—arranged on their platters like a

Japanese still life, each a work of art. For dessert, I passed up the sticky toffee sponge with cream since I was on some kind of diet and chose instead fresh rhubarb crumble with creamy egg custard, but I managed to sample the toffee sponge and can well believe that "people drive all the way from London for our sticky toffee sponge." This was one of the most enjoyable meals I've had *anywhere,* and it's easy to understand why Sharrow Bay enjoys such an exalted, insiders' reputation. The cuisine is the achievement of Francis Coulson, gentleman chef, antique buff, collector, decorator and one-time actor who came north from London thirty years ago to do what he had always wanted to do—run a small hotel with a first-rate restaurant. He chose his spot well.

Ullswater is, if anything, more serene, more virgin than Windermere. Only small boats and one old ferryboat ripple its waters, and the narrow winding road along its eastern shore ends in nowhere. A few miles down the lake's quietest shore from a village called Pooley Bridge (and well past the camp sites) you come upon a gray gatehouse and a driveway leading to the edge of the lake, and there, at the every edge of the lake, you find Sharrow Bay, a Victorian idea of a chalet in stone. It looks, actually, rather ungainly on the outside, but inside all is fair and graceful, a festival of Victoriana— porcelain and pots of flowers, gilt mirrors and bronze candelabra, Dresden figurines and chubby cherubs fill the hall and drawing room in happy higgledy-piggledydom.

In the guest rooms, lights are switched on *before* guests arrive ("having the lights on always seems to make it more like home"), sherry awaits you on the dressing table; all the rooms come with trouser pressers, hair dryers, radio, television, telephone, bedside copies of *Diary of a Country Lady,* and Scrabble. Such is the attention to the fine points of hostmanship here that Brian Sack and Francis Coulson supply not only the Scrabble but the dictionaries, too.

A dozen of the rooms are located in the main house, a few in a cottage in the garden (Beatrix is particularly attractive here), a few more in the gatehouse—all within strolling distance of lake and lounge. Grab whichever one you can get. If I had a choice, though, I'd opt for a room in the Bank House, a converted 18th-century farmhouse farther down the lake, sitting in its own garden above the lake. I'd take my glass of sherry out to the bench in the garden and admire a view that has to be one of the most tranquil in England, serenaded by finches and curlews. Francis Coulson has managed to retain all the low-linteled, whitewashed charm of his Cumbrian farmhouse while furnishing it in a manner that does credit to the word "Victorian"—antiques and bibelots everywhere, frilly little touches that tell you someone really *cares;* some of the bathrooms are so spacious they have upholstered armchairs. Bank House has its own breakfast room (you can, of course, have your breakfast served in your room), a country-house drawing room where you can have afternoon tea, but it's worth the short drive to the dining room for lunch or dinner.

At Sharrow Bay, your welcome is warm, the rooms are cozy. You'll want to stay here for *at least* a couple of nights—even without the sticky toffee sponge with cream.

Name: Sharrow Bay Country House Hotel

Owners/Managers: Francis Coulson and Brian Sack

Address: Ullswater (Cumbria) CA 10 2L2

Location: On the eastern shore of Ullswater, 6 miles from the M6 Motorway, 25 miles south of Carlisle and 100 miles north of Manchester

Telephone: Pooley Bridge 301 or 483 (area code 08536)

Cables/Telex: (None)

Reps: Relais-Châteaux in U.S., Canada and Europe

Credit Cards: (None)

Rooms: 27 rooms, 2 suites in 4 buildings (a few share bathrooms)

Meals: Breakfast 9–9:45, lunch 1–2:15, afternoon tea, dinner 7–8:45; cost of a 6-course dinner for two approx. $42; tie and jacket required; room service for breakfast and drinks (minibar in some rooms)

Entertainment: TV rooms, nothing scheduled publicly (although it has been known for the hosts to sit down at the piano and sing Noel Coward)

Sports: Swimming in Lake Ullswater; tennis, golf, riding, boating and walking trails nearby

Sightseeing: Hills and dales and hosts of golden daffodils, Gowbarrow National Park, historic Dalemain (jousting contests held here), horse trials at Lowther Castle in August (see also Miller Howe, Windermere)

P.S. The hotel is closed Dec. 3 to early March

White Moss House
near Grasmere

W XXX $$

Think of the perfect bed-and-breakfast stop—a 200-year-old stone house, between mountain and lake, surrounded by a garden, comfortably furnished, managed by a genial, dedicated husband-and-wife team and radiating cheeriness. Now add one of the finest country restaurants in all of England and you have White Moss House at Rydal Water.

White Moss once belonged to wordsmith Wordsworth, although he never lived there (something about buying it to give him voting rights in the town in order to block the introduction of one of those noisy, belching newfangled things called trains—in other words, the poet as antirailroad activist), but the setting is something he would surely have enjoyed. The Butterworths bought the place ten years ago, when they were bored with careers in corporate finance and school teaching, and decided to live in the country and open a small restaurant; their traditional English country fare soon acquired a reputation far and wide, but they wisely kept the restaurant small and added a small hotel. Dinner is served in a plain farmhouse-style dining room with low ceilings and brick walls, the candles, flowers and shiny silverware the only adornments to distract from the meal. Only eighteen guests dine here, never more since only one table is set aside for nonresidents (who must call in advance—usually days in advance). An air of expectation fills the room as the dishes appear. What will it be? Fresh salmon braid (prepared in a pastry shell with béchamel sauce), cucumber "de-seeded but never peeled," chopped parsley and other herbs fresh from the White Moss garden? Or ballotine of guinea fowl with crabapple jelly? Or hunters' pot served with herb scones, pickled damsons and spiced cabbage? Potted Stilton laced with port, or gingered pears with double cream and advocaat, or hot brandied blackberry and apple meringue nests, or Sussex pond pudding—and so on, a whole repertory of the kind of country-style home cooking that has earned plaudits from food guides ("one of the three best restaurants in the country") and TV appearances ("one of the seven best cooks in the country").

When you return to your room, you'll find that the maid has been in to tidy up and turn down the beds, and in the morning you'll be wakened by the maid delivering your early tea on fine china. When you blink your way downstairs, you'll sit down to another Butterworth specialty—a hearty country breakfast of Cumberland sausages, sweet-cured bacon, eggs, tomatoes, mushrooms, fried breads and black pudding (I won't explain it— just try it).

41

As if all that cooking were not enough to fill one lifetime, Mrs. Butterworth spends her spare time sewing padding to the coat hangers in your closet to match the drapes and bedspreads. You'll also find a hair dryer, trouser presser and his-and-her hot-water bottles. "We try to create an away-from-it-all atmosphere where phones and television and similar 'facilities' would intrude." They try, they succeed.

Name: White Moss House

Owners/Managers: Mr. and Mrs. J. A. Butterworth

Address: Rydal Water, Grasmere LA229SE

Location: Between Ambleside and Grasmere, a few miles from Exits 36 or 40 on the M6 Motorway

---

Telephone: Grasmere 295 (area code 09665)

Cables/Telex: (None)

Reps: (None)

Credit Cards: (None)

Rooms: 9, including 5 in the main house and 4 in a cottage nearby

---

Entertainment: Classical music, very much in the background, during dinner

---

Sports: Golf, tennis, boating, hiking, etc., nearby

Sightseeing: (See Miller Howe and Sharrow Bay hotels)

P.S. Closed November through March; no children under 15

The Grosvenor Hotel
Chester

This hideaway is smack dab in the center of a bustling city, but Chester has its tourist attractions, and the Grosvenor, despite its location, is quiet and very attractive. After a day's sightseeing, its bars are welcome havens—the long, cozy Wine Cellar Bar and the Arkle Bar, dominated by a large portrait of Arkle, a racehorse once owned by the Duchess of Westminster.

The Grosvenor was built as recently as 1865, but its architecture—all columns and half-timbering—was designed to blend in with its neighbors in a balustraded medieval street known as The Rows. Everything sparkles— windows and brass trim, the 200-year-old chandelier above the curving oak staircase in the lobby (its 28,000 chunks of crystal are cleaned by *hand*). The guest rooms are luxurious, all with color TV and stocked minibars, and two of the six suites have double bathrooms. Since it is a city hotel, and therefore popular with business people, you may want to come here on a weekend—to enjoy a good old-fashioned English dinner-dance, with salmon from the River Dee that runs past the city walls and trout from Earl Grosvenor's farm.

Name: The Grosvenor Hotel

Manager: Richard Edwards

Address: Eastgate Street, Chester CH11LT

Location: In the center of town, 35 miles west of Manchester

Telephone: Chester 24024

Cables/Telex: Grosvotel Chester/61240

Reps: HRI in U.S., Canada and Europe, Scott Calder in U.S. and Canada, Prestige Hotels in Europe

Credit Cards: American Express, Barclaycard, Access, Diners Club

Rooms: 100

Meals: Breakfast 7:30–10, lunch 12:30–2:30, afternoon tea on request, dinner 7–10; dinner for two approx. $50; tie and jacket in evening; room service around the clock

Entertainment: Dinner-dance Saturday evenings in winter

Sports: Golf nearby by arrangement

Sightseeing: Ancient Chester—2 miles of 2000-year-old Roman city walls, medieval alleys, cathedral, museums; nearby—Chirk Castle, Beeston Castle, Llangollen in Wales

P.S. Some conferences

The Lygon Arms
Broadway

♛♛ ✕✕ $$$

Broadway, with its mile-long broad way lined with traditional stone cottages, is one of the most famous villages in England, the Lygon Arms one of the most famous inns. Naturally then, you're likely to find crowds in the trio of lounges; nevertheless, the Lygon Arms is still a classic, well-run, friendly inn, and you can usually escape the day-trippers by slipping away to the garden courtyard at the rear.

Its gabled facade, with mullion windows peeping out from among the creepers, dates from the 16th century, and both Oliver Cromwell and Charles I sought refuge behind the entrance with its regal trappings. It has been expanded over the years, most recently with a wing of bedrooms in the garden and the modern additions, fabrics and conveniences have been tastefully fitted in with the old. The Inglenook Lounge, to the right of the entrance, is almost all fireplace and a few cabinets filled with antiques; the Russell Room (named for the owners) has acres of windows looking onto a flagstone terrace; the great hall dining room has a cathedral ceiling and stags' heads decor; the cuisine is predominantly English, with the emphasis on beef, fish and game.

Assuming you have a choice of rooms, both the old and new (or Orchard wings) are furnished with antiques, and basically only the plumbing is different, although the old wing has more charm, despite its sometimes undependable plumbing. Room 20, the Great Chamber, has a vaulted timber-and-plaster ceiling, chandelier and a huge four-poster bed; if you want lots of space, 51 in the new wing has a separate sitting room.

Name: The Lygon Arms

Manager: Peter Wilson

Address: Broadway, Worcestershire WR127DU

Location: On the main road in the village, at A424 (A44) and A46 in the Cotswold Hills, about 90 miles from London

---

Telephone: Broadway 2255 (area code 038681)

Telex: 338260

Reps: HRI, Scott Calder in U.S. and Canada, HRI, Prestige Hotels and Relais-Châteaux in Europe

---

44   **Credit Cards:**   All major cards (except Carte Blanche)

Rooms:	72

Meals: Breakfast 8–10, lunch 12:30–2, afternoon tea 4–5, dinner 7:30–9:15, candlelight supper by arrangement; dinner for two approx. $22, supper $24; tie and jacket; 24-hour room service, extra charge

Entertainment: The people in the bar, TV in rooms

Sports: Nearby—golf, riding, tennis, lawn bowling

Sightseeing: Tewkesbury Abbey, Wye Valley; cattle market in Banbury every Wednesday morning; fox hunting in winter; Stratford-upon-Avon

P.S. Some small groups for lunch (in separate wing)

Hunstrete House
near Bath

₩₩ ✗✗✗ $$

John and Thea Dupays, who created The Priory in Bath and elevated it to culinary eminence, decided a few years ago that they really wanted to be out in the country—with garden, flowers, fields and stables. So they acquired this Georgian mansion about eight miles from Bath, gave it the magical Dupays touch and welcomed their first guests in January, 1979. Hunstrete is a square gray block of manor, its severe lines softened by the clematis montana that frames the garden doorway; inside, though, all is sunny and cheerful. The tall walls of the public rooms are brightened with contemporary paintings (Thea Dupays is herself an artist of some note) and family antiques and bibelots. Each of the 13 guest rooms is named for a local bird, the tiniest as pretty as the largest, rates varying according to size and location. Dove, a corner room facing south and west, is large enough to feature both an enormous Venetian four-poster and a love seat that once belonged to Laurence Olivier and Vivien Leigh; Linnet, on the other hand, is a nest at the back of the house, less expensive but bright and sunny with buttercup-yellow wallpaper, wicker headboard and windows overlooking the croquet lawn.

The mansion sits on 90 acres of placid English countryside that once belonged to the abbots of Shastonbury, and beyond the croquet lawn, a door in the garden wall leads to a swimming pool and a brand-new enclosed all-weather tennis court. For guests who simply want to dawdle or cuddle, there are secluded benches dotted among the roses and hawthorn trees; an

45

Hunstrete House

alley of laurel trees leads to a lily pond, and behind the vegetable garden there's a "secret" garden with trees huddling protectively over a patch of lawn, for lovers rather than abbots. Hunstrete is a place of peace and quiet, screened from the winding country lanes by hedgerows and pasture and forests—yet close enough to town for performers or listeners attending the annual Bath Festival.

Name: Hunstrete House

Owners/Managers: John and Thea Dupays

Address: Hunstrete, Chelwood B5184NS (Avon)

Location: 8 miles southwest of Bath, about the same southeast of Bristol, on route A368, near Chelwood and Marksbury (ask in advance, and the hotel can arrange to collect you at Bristol Airport, Bristol or Bath railway stations)

Telephone: Compton Dando 578 and 579 (area code 07618)

Cables/Telex: (None)

Reps: (None)

Credit Cards: American Express

Rooms: 13 rooms

Meals: Breakfast 7:30–9:30 (anytime in room), lunch 1–2, dinner 7:30–9:15; dinner for two approx. $38; dress informal, "advisable for house guests to reserve a table when booking a room"; room service for breakfast, tea and drinks

Entertainment: TV in rooms

Sports: Tennis court, heated swimming pool, walking trails, croquet; nearby—golf, riding and trout fishing

Sightseeing: The 18th century city of Bath with its fine Roman remains (the Roman Baths with their hot springs are particularly impressive) and Georgian architecture (handsome streets, squares and crescents); the Bath Summer Festival with emphasis on 18th century music and drama; antiques fair (early May); to the south—Wells Cathedral, Stourhead Gardens and Longleat House; for drama, the Theatre Royal in Bath and the Old Vic in Bristol; Chewton Mending, a local farm producing handmade Cheddar cheese

P.S. Closed for two weeks at Christmas time; no children under 9; some groups, numbering no more than 30

The Close at Tetbury
Tetbury

WW XX $$$

Four hundred years ago a wealthy wool merchant built this handsome home on the main street of a small town in the Cotswolds, and even with major recent remodeling The Close is as English as can be; but you might get the impression you're in La Belle France when you pick up the menu—*les trois pâtés de poisson au beurre blanc,* shrimps with garlic and almond butter, *et tout ça.* Jean-Marie Lauzier and his French chief de cuisine aim to offer their English clientele the finest haute cuisine, and their dining room is highly regarded. The dining room is a big Adam-style salon overlooking a   47 walled garden with lily pads and dovecotes; and dinner here is something of an occasion (although we have had reports of disinterested service by waiters whose English is as inadequate as their manners). To ensure that guests take it seriously, cigars and pipes are banned from the dining room; but cigars and brandy are set out *after* dinner in the main lounge with domed ceiling and red-velvet upholstery.

Bedrooms in The Close are all different, but decor in the bathrooms always harmonizes with the bedrooms—even the bath salts and shampoo are color-coordinated; each room has trouser presser, room phone and color TV, fresh flowers in summer and dried flower arrangements in winter. The Elizabethan Suite is a charming winter nest up in the eaves; the Bank Suite overlooks the main street, noisy by day but quiet by night when you're tucked up in your four-poster with the green velvet curtains. Best of all perhaps, is the room called Doves, with a two-poster bed, lavender bath, lots of space and a dovecote right outside your window. It may not be the top choice in the Cotswolds, but it surely comes Close.

Name: The Close at Tetbury

Owners: The Greenhalgh & Lauzier Families

Manager: Robert Crompton

Address: 8 Long Street, Tetbury, Gloucestershire GL88AQ

Location: About 26 miles northeast of Bristol, on A433

Telephone: Tetbury 52272 and 52777 (area code 0666)

Cables: CloseTetbury

Reps: (None)

Credit Cards: American Express, Barclaycard, Diners Club

Rooms: 11

Meals: Breakfast 7:30–10 in rooms, 8–9:30 in dining room, lunch 12:30–1:45, dinner 7:30–9; dinner for two approx. $45; tie and jacket; room service by arrangement

Entertainment: Color TV in rooms

Sports: Nearby—riding, golf, tennis

Sightseeing: Cheltenham, Bath, Westonbirt Arboretum, antiquing in Tetbury

P.S.   "Not the kind of place people bring children to"

48

Whatley Manor
Easton Grey

WW X $$

You enter the estate along a driveway lined with yew trees, through a stone archway flanked by cherry trees; on the left, a courtyard encircled with stables, on the right the honey-colored manor draped in wisteria. Although the earliest parts of the house date from the 18th century, most of the farmhouse manor you see today dates only from the twenties, but constructed with native Cotswold stone, weathered slates and mullioned windows with leaded lights in the traditional manner. It was the dream manor of a Canadian millionaire, who was, among other enthusiasms, a polo buff—hence the abundance of stables.

The interior, too, is impressive—delicately carved pine fireplaces and a Cromwellian refectory table in the hallway, oak and pine paneling everywhere, tapestries and paintings on the walls. Guest rooms are, on the whole, unusually spacious and comfortable (even the bathrooms are carpeted) and what differentiates them is location. Three of the most interesting rooms are in the Tudor Wing opposite the main entrance, where Room 10 is a particularly handsome suite with Tudor stonework and arches, beamed ceiling and big double bed in light blue damask. In the manor itself, Room 1, in Wedgwood blue with gold trim, gets the sun in the morning *and* the afternoon, and each of its four windows has a padded seat to match the floral damask drapes and bedspreads. It's above the porte cochère, so you may have some noise from car doors and departing dinner guests; because it's above the kitchen, Room 9 costs a few dollars less, but like most of the rooms at Whatley, it has lovely views of gardens, wild lilac and almond trees, and pastures rolling off into the distance.

Lovely manor, lovely setting, pleasant staff—so I wish I could be more enthusiastic about Whatley, but the impression is strong that it's being run by a shoestring staff, and afternoon tea trays still in the drawing room when you retire for after-dinner coffee don't help. Maybe we expect too much just because the setting is so grand.

Name:	Whatley Manor
Owner:	Diana Parry
Manager:	Stephen Parry
Address:	Easton Grey, Malmesbury (Wiltshire)

Location: In the West Country, a few miles north of Bristol and Bath, between routes A46 and A429

Telephone: Malmesbury 2888 (area code 06662)

Cables/Telex: (None)

Reps: (None)

Credit Cards: American Express, Master Charge/Eurocard, Access

Rooms: 12 rooms

Meals: Breakfast 9–9:45, lunch 12:45–1:45, dinner 7:30–9; dinner for two approx. $15–$16; dress informal; room service for breakfast and drinks

Entertainment: Color television in all rooms; taped music in lounge

Sports: Heated swimming pool behind the Rose Garden, riding (experienced riders only), walking trails (20 acres), croquet, and trout fishing at the bottom of the garden; nearby, tennis, golf, and riding for beginners

Sightseeing: Malmesbury is the oldest borough in England (celebrates its 1100th anniversary in 1980, special events May–October); Mummers at Marshfield with morris dancing (September); the Duke of Beaufort's hounds (regularly, September through February)

P.S. Closed the two weeks after Christmas; no children under 7; small seminars in winter

The Bear
Woodstock

WW XX SS

This Woodstock is a pretty English country town, worth a visit in its own right, but more famous as the focal point for travelers visiting Blenheim Palace, where Winston Spencer Churchill was born in a broom closet, and Bladon Churchyard, where the great statesman is buried. Woodstock's Bear, of course, was hosting travelers for several hundred years before Blenheim was built, since it dates from the 13th century. This 600-year-old half-timbered inn stands in the center of town by the cobbled market square, flagged by a huge bear on the pub sign outside the door. It's all very cozy and casual, the epitome of a veteran coaching house; decorated with fireplaces and horse brasses, oil paintings of fox hunts and the framed "Rules of Cocking with Hoods and Spurs." Most of the Bear's staff have been here for decades (the Porters have owned it for 40 years), and the delightful head porter, Leslie James Longley, is a mine of information about everything relating to the town and surrounding countryside.

With all its nooks and crannies, you *need* a porter to show you to your room, all of which have room phones and color TV. If you want to pay the top rate, the splendid Blenheim Suite, in the courtyard, has stone walls and a fireplace (electric fire), a bay window facing the courtyard, twin beds and a small refrigerator. Nest 16, up under the eaves, facing the courtyard *and* the street, has low beamed ceiling, stone walls and autumn colors, and a balcony overlooking a church roof—and is said to be haunted by a crying baby.

Name: The Bear

Owners/Managers: The Porter Family

Address: Woodstock, Oxfordshire

Location: In the heart of town, about 8 miles west of Oxford on A34

Telephone: Woodstock 811511

Cables/Telex: (None)

Reps: (None)

Credit Cards: All major cards

Rooms: 33 (of which 28 are doubles with bath)

Meals: Breakfast 8–10, lunch 12:30–1:45, afternoon tea on request, dinner 7–9; dinner for two approx. $36, casual dress; around-the-clock room service slight extra charge

Entertainment: TV in rooms

Sports: Walking in the village and countryside

Sightseeing: Blenheim Palace, Bladon Churchyard, Oxford; Cheltenham Race Week (in March)

P.S. Some groups for lunch in summer

Chewton Glen Hotel
New Milton

♛♛♛ ✗✗✗ $$$

In a land of fine country-house hotels and country inns, here is a country Ritz. This red-brick mansion with green shutters and white trim is the sort of deceptively unpretentious country place that might belong to a bowlered-and-brollied gent from the City of London. A merchant banker, maybe, or a bullion trader. It basks in six acres of clipped and cosseted garden, surrounded in turn by 40 acres of pasture and forest, seemingly isolated but in fact only half a mile from seaside villages. The earliest parts of the house were built in the 1700s, and a century later it came into the possession of George Marryat, brother of Captain Frederick Marryat, adventurer and author; while staying here, the captain wrote his most famous novel, *Children of the New Forest,* inspired by the nearby nature preserve, a vast tract set aside by William the Conqueror as his private hunting ground. The mansion had declined into near dilapidation by the time it was taken over in 1967 by Martin Skan, who quit a lucrative family candy business to try his hand at innkeeping. Rather, at creating the perfect country-house hotel. Most budding innkeepers might call in a local decorator to help out with the interior, but Skan assigned a peer of the realm, a lord no less, to design the lobby, bar and suites; most innkeepers are lucky if they have an emergency generator of any kind, but here it's powered by a Rolls-Royce engine. At Chewton Glen the china is Wedgwood and Darlington, *Punch* and *Tatler and Bystander* are bound in leather, the bathtubs have armrests, and in some rooms they also have fingertip controls so that you can, with one languorous flick of your finger, adjust the temperature without changing position.

Expensive accouterments alone don't make a successful hotel, of course, and Skan had the foresight to hire managers (plural!) and a maître d'hôtel with grand hotel backgrounds, putting together a team for whom nothing less than perfection is the day-to-day norm. Likewise in the kitchen.

Skan and his French chef are, as you might have suspected by now, sticklers for the best ingredients, using whenever possible fresh local produce (lamb from Dorset, salmon from Christchurch), but the menu is predominantly French, *à la mode de la nouvelle cuisine.* A recent table d'hôte lunch, for around $20 per person, listed *pâté pantin* Ferdinand Wernert (a coarse pâtè of veal, pork and chicken, baked in pastry); roast ribs of selected Scotch beef served from the silver trolley or *filet de barbue* Albert (fresh brill cooked with bread crumbs and Noilly Prat and served with a sauce Albert); for dessert, a selection of sweets from what can only be described as the Trolley of a Dozen Dreams. Recommendations from the à la carte menu would be *escalope de saumon à l'oseille* or *filet de loup de mer mouginoise* (fresh sea bass cooked with a mousse of salmon, foie gras and chicken). The house wines are a 1976 Muscadet Cuvée du Destrier and a 1975 Bordeaux Superieur, Château LaFont d'Hubert—each for under $8 a bottle; the wine list itself is *formidable.* When you look around Chewton Glen, it's not surprising to learn that within a year of opening, the hotel had been awarded three stars by Britain's Automobile Association, and since then it has gone on to win almost every other plaudit. Now Skan is adding an indoor pool and a few deluxe suites in an extension of the former carriage house (of which the Colonel Beverly Suite would be my choice, with the original pine trusses as wall decor, arched french doors leading to a private patio, a stairway to a sleeping gallery, and a Jacuzzi in the bathroom). In the main house, eight boxrooms have been adroitly fashioned into up-in-the-eaves nests with country-elegant decor; if you want a terrace, ask for rooms 6, 7, 8, 10 or 11. In the end, which room you have is relatively unimportant. They're all impeccable, all individually decorated, and they all have room phones, color TV, sewing kits, thermos carafes for water. The important thing is to be there.

Soaking in a bathtub with armrests and fingertip controls, I have this fantasy: my guidebooks are outselling Harold Robbins' novels, I've spent a week at Chewton Glen, and just as I wind up a last game of croquet, the uniformed chauffeur walks across the lawn to tell me the limousine is waiting to take me to Southampton, where a first-class suite awaits me aboard the *Queen Elizabeth II.* Anything else would be an anticlimax.

Name: Chewton Glen Hotel

Owners: The Skan Family

Managers: David Brockett and Jo Simonini

Address: New Milton, BH256Q5 (Hampshire)

Location: On the south coast 20 miles from Southampton, 10 miles from Bournemouth

Telephone: Highcliffe 5341 (area code 04252)

Telex: 41456

Reps: Relais-Châteaux, HRI, Scott Calder in U.S.A. and Canada; Relais-Châteaux and HRI in Europe

Credit Cards: All major cards

Rooms: 55 rooms, 3 deluxe suites in the Coach House

Meals: Breakfast 7–9:45, lunch 12:30–2, dinner 7:30–9:30; dinner for two   53

approx. $40–$45; tie and jacket "definitely"; room service during dining room hours

Entertainment: Color television in the rooms

Sports: All-weather tennis court and heated swimming pool (indoor pool under construction), walking trails, putting green and snooker room; nearby—beach, watersports, riding, fishing, shooting, golf (12 courses within 20 miles)

Sightseeing: Stonehenge and Salisbury Cathedral are the prime attractions, but lovely old villages abound—Burley (typical forest village), Lymington (fine Georgian houses), Buckler's Hard (river town with Maritime Museum, boat trips available from here), Beaulieu (remains of 1204 monastery and Montagu Veteran Car Museum), Cranborne (medieval wall paintings) and Rockbourne (quaint cottages along a chalk stream)

P.S.   No children under 7; small business groups accommodated in the winter only

Ye Olde Bell Hotel
Hurley-on-Thames

♛♛ ✗✗ $$

The Old Bell first rang with the wassails of Benedictine monks, back in the 12th century. They lived in a monastery nearby, and to cover up their carousing a secret passage was built to join monk to mead without the locals knowing what was going on. Ye Olde Bell sits on a narrow street, in a village of high-walled narrow streets, a whitewashed, half-timbered inn with tiny windows and clumps of flowers around the base. A Norman door leads to a snuggery of beams and rafters, old maps and stuffed floral-print chairs; and at the rear, a flagstone terrace surrounded by shade trees and a brick wall, landscaped with rock gardens, fountains and a pergola draped with climbing roses. The horses mooning around in the pasture beyond the wall belong to a noted equestrienne, Mrs. Alder, who also happens to be the daughter of octogenerian Giulio Trapani, host at Ye Olde Bell for decades.

All the guest rooms have been spruced up in recent years, with modern plumbing and TV but traditional decor; if you have a choice, opt for Room 1 (overlooking the garden, with a balcony for breakfast or cocktails) or 2 (also with a garden balcony, but smaller).

54

The paneled dining room, beside the terrace, features lobster and turbot, grouse and pheasant in season, as well as some more unusual dishes. The staff outnumbers overnight guests 5 to 1, with no fewer than four gardeners to look after the grounds.

Ye Olde Bell is popular with diners yet it's less touristy than some of its more famous neighbors, which may be why Mickey Rooney and Broderick Crawford stay here, to enjoy the same qualities of privacy and quiet that appealed to the Benedictines in the beginning.

Name: Ye Olde Bell Hotel

Owners/Managers: The Trapani Family

Address: Hurley-on-Thames, Berks SL65LX

Location: Off A423, about 4½ miles northwest of Maidenhead, 20 to 30 minutes from London's Heathrow Airport

Telephone: Littlewick Green 4244 and 4282

Cables/Telex: (None)

Reps: (None)

Credit Cards: American Express, Barclaycard

Rooms: 9

Meals: Breakfast 7:30–9:30, lunch 12:30–2:30, afternoon tea on request, dinner 7:30–9:30; dinner for two approx. $35; jackets in the dining room (ties not necessary); room service 24 hours at no extra charge

Entertainment: Sitting in the garden, picnics by the river

Sports: Nothing at the inn; golf, riding, squash, tennis, swimming, boating nearby

Sightseeing: The Thames, Henley Regatta, Ascot Racetrack

P.S. No groups except for small parties during the sporting events at Henley and Ascot

Maison Talbooth
Dedham

♕♕♕ ✗✗✗ $$$

Picture a painting by John Constable. A winding river with willow trees dipping into its ripples. An old stone bridge and a half-timbered barn. By the edge of the river a terrace lined with marigolds or tulips, and behind it a split-level lawn with finely clipped grass. It's rural England in all its timelessness, except that this is the setting for a restaurant. Diners sit on the flagstone terrace sipping their sherries as they browse through the menu, wondering if the Talbooth gardener may not be so far off the mark when he claims that people come here for the garden as much as the food. Go for both.

Le Talbooth, the restaurant, now rates one star in the U.K. edition of the *Michelin Guide* and various symbols of honor in other guides, and it's the main reason why lovers drive to this Eden in Essex. It dates from the 16th century, a lopsided wattle-and-daub building with clematis climbing up the walls to the red-tiled roof, Tudor chimneys and tiny gable windows.

Maison Talbooth

The interior is snug with dark beams and mullioned windows, antique copper and Adams china. Once a tollbooth on the River Stour, it began its most recent incarnation in the early fifties as a tearoom—scones, cream, homemade jams and all that—and over the years Gerald Milsom has seen his tearoom evolve into one of the finest country restaurants in England. The browsers on the terrace have, luckily for them, plenty to linger over: to begin, sole creams with a shrimp sauce of a pâté of Stilton, port and celery; for the main course, fillet of pork with sage and peaches or *casserolette de sole Maître Queux* or steak and kidney pie. For dessert, regular visitors to Le Talbooth have no choice, skipping over the orange and madeira syllabub and iced Drambuie soufflé in deference to the Talbooth brandy snaps (so popular they require the fulltime attention of a pastry cook). For additional browsing, local oenologist Richard Wheeler has compiled an impressive wine list that ranges urbanely through vineyards famous and unsung—including the English Cavendish Manor—and features a selection of 50 wines for under $10 a bottle.

The most recent stage of the Talbooth's evolution is the Maison Talbooth, a big, buff-colored Victorian manor a mile or so up the road, transformed into a hotel to satisfy the cravings of guests who didn't want to drive all the way back to Mayfair and Kensington after their brandy snaps. Even more peaceful than the restaurant, with a view across the Vale of Dedham, are 10 comfortable, spacious suites—two with "moon baths" (circular sunken tubs, 6 feet in diameter), some with baldachins above the beds, all with Victorian Boudoir decor, television, bars and nice touches like clothes brushes and back scrubbers. The moon baths are in suites at the rear, and Room 2 has in addition a small patio with honeysuckle climbing the wall. Also on the ground floor, Room 10 has a floor-to-ceiling view across the front lawn, but it may be for lovers with strong nerves because people on the lawn also have a floor-to-ceiling view of Room 10. Upstairs, Room 5 facing the garden on one side; there's a small balcony at the back and an array of liquor is set out on a table made from an antique sewing machine. Rooms 6, 7 and 8 all have pretty decor and undisturbed views across the lawns to the Vale of Dedham.

The Vale has not changed all that much since Constable painted these landscapes, and Gerald Milsom can show you reproductions of Constable originals depicting this very Vale—complete with winding river, willows, bridge and the old tollhouse.

Name:	Maison Talbooth
Owner:	Gerald Milsom
Manager:	John Benstead

57

Address: Dedham, Colchester C07GHP (Essex)

Location: About 60 miles northeast of London (leave route A12 at the Stratford St. Mary sign, just beyond the Colchester sign)

Telephone: Colchester 322367 (323150 for Le Talbooth Restaurant) (area code 0206)

Cables/Telex: (None)

Reps: Relais-Châteaux in U.S.A., Canada and Europe

Credit Cards: American Express, Diners Club, Barclaycard, Access

Rooms: 10 suites

Meals: Breakfast 7:30 on, lunch 12:30–2, dinner 7:30–9; dinner for two approx. $28–$30; tie and jacket preferred; room service during dining room hours (minibars in rooms)

Entertainment: Television in rooms

Sports: No facilities on premises; tennis, golf, riding, walking and fishing nearby

Sightseeing: "Constable Country" (it was here John Constable painted his radiant landscapes); Colchester—the oldest recorded Roman town in England (the walls are still standing and there is a Castle Museum); the opening of the oyster season in Colchester; a bit further afield, Bury St. Edmunds (its name comes from the burial of the murdered Saint Edmund, King of East Anglia, whose body resides in the now ruined abbey)

P.S. Closed over Christmas; no children under 7; seminars are accepted, but they must reserve the entire hotel

Number 16
London

WW $$

Sumner Place in South Kensington is a trim parade of Edwardian houses, each five stories high, each with portico and steps, all painted the same shade of cream. It has a special nostalgic meaning for me because Sumner Place was my first address in London, when Number 16 was a boarding house, heating was by gas fire, water boiling by gas ring, and we all shared the bathroom on the second floor. That was many moons ago. More recently, in 1970, a couple of these townhouses were transformed by Michael Watson, "picture nut" and retired executive of a chain of hotels and restaurants. "It's fun to do all the things you can't do in a chain," he says, and London is the better for it, for what he has created is a gem of a small hotel. The reception-cum-lounge is in chic browns and beige, stairways are boldly emblazoned with splashes of royal blue and grenadier red, or thereabouts. Walls are decorated with Michael Watson's collection of original paintings, framed prints, engravings and reproductions of Holbein and Toulouse-Lautrec, lithos by Braque and Picasso. The guest chambers are as comfy as you could hope to come home to after a foot-wearing day of plodding through Harrods or Marks & Sparks, and each one has a minibar (soft drinks only, no liquor license as yet). Five of the rooms have full-size bathrooms, 2 share bathrooms, the remainder have showers. The Garden Room, looking out on a small patio at the rear, has a big double bed and full-scale bathroom.

Take your soft drinks (or hard drinks, for that matter, if you bring your own) into the garden at the rear, and you'd never know you were in London; there's no restaurant (no need for one, "dozens of good eating places in the neighborhood"), and breakfast is served in bed. Number 16 is not inexpensive, but by current London standards it's good value; and a cultured clientele—opera singers from Covent Garden, cellists and concert pianists, actresses and choreographers—is lured back time and again by its townhouse comfort, personal service and privacy.

Name: Number 16

Owner/Manager: Michael Watson

Address: 16 Sumner Place, London SW 7

Location: A few yards from South Kensington tube station, within walking distance of the Victoria and Albert Museum, Hyde Park and Harrods

Telephone: (01) 589-5232

Cables/Telex: Number 16 21879

Reps: (None)

Credit Cards: American Express, Diners Club

Rooms: 25 rooms (all but two with private bathrooms)

Meals: Breakfast early morning to midday; no other meals are served;   59

rooms have small refrigerators with mixers; liquor is available in the lounge on the honor system

Entertainment: Television in lounge, and on request in rooms

Sports: (None)

Sightseeing: London

P.S. No children under 10; by one of those quirks of history you find in Britain, all the houses on Sumner Place are owned by a 19th-century charity and all the rentals go toward cancer research

Blakes Hotel
London

WW X $$$$

First impressions suggest a trendy decorator has been let loose in the place, with no expense spared. In fact, the decorator was the owner, actress/model Anoushka Hempel. She spared no expense. A jaunty rattan-and-bamboo lobby is piled with cushions and potted plants; in the center, an iron stairway spirals down to a palm-studded restaurant with thirties' decor (quite attractive, quite new, but already being refashioned—chef and all). Guest rooms are spread over three townhouses and a mews at the rear; every room is individually designed, some to the point where you almost feel guilty about ruining the effect just by being there. The Bridal Suite in the mews (Room 58), decked out in shell-pink chintz with rust highlights, has a very large brass bed and a rolltop desk; in Room 48, also in the Mews, the headboard is a black shantung screen of wood and silk, and everything else is black to match, including the terry towel bathrobes; Room 41 has a lace counterpane, heavy pile carpeting, antique mirrors, white captain's chairs and white café table (it's also small and therefore one of the less expensive chambers). And so on.

Blakes is not cheap but it attracts a classy clientele of grand prix drivers, actors and pop stars. Executives plump for the suites—each of which has a "music center" (tapes, color TV, radio) and pullman kitchen. For upward of $200 you can have a suite with mirrored bathroom, washer and dryer, big brass bed, a huge antique wardrobe and a wooden floor hand-painted by students from the Royal Academy of Art (it's Room 73); or one with a large four-poster bed, a haremful of pillows, bouncy sofas, cane chairs, mirrored bathroom with flower-filled wicker baskets—the whole kit and caboodle (walls, carpets, towels, bathrobes, bathtub, stool) in a modish blue gray. Obviously, a place to check into when you're in town with an expense account—or a *very* special date.

Name: Blakes Hotel

Owner: Mrs. Anoushka Hempel

Manager: Leonard Burrows

Address: 33/35 Roland Gardens, London SW 7

Location: In South Kensington, about 15 minutes by the underground or bus to Piccadilly, near Victoria and Albert Museum and Harrods

Telephone: (01) 370-6701

Cables/Telex: Blakes 21879

Reps: (None)

Credit Cards: American Express, Diners Club, Visa, Barclaycard, Access

Rooms: 40 rooms, 10 suites

Meals: Breakfast 7:30–10:30, lunch 10:30 on, dinner 7–11; dinner for two approx. $40; dress casual; complete room service 24 hours (suites have cooking facilities and refrigerators)

Entertainment: Taped music in the lounge and dining room, color television in rooms

Sports: Sauna on premises

Sightseeing: London

P.S. No tours, no conventions, probably not many children

Brown's Hotel
London

W X $$$$

Mayfair. Townhouses where dukes and dowagers, bishops and baronets once lived. Oak-paneled lounges. Afternoon tea in silver teapots. Cucumber sandwiches. Velvet-padded chairs and an escritoire when you sign in. A concierge who gets your name and number right the first time. Brown's Hotel is actually eleven townhouses on two famous London streets—Albemarle and Dover—and over the years it has ministered to a most distinguished roster of guests: Teddy Roosevelt stayed here the night before he got married, Franklin D. and Eleanor honeymooned here; J. P. Morgan and Alexander Graham Bell, Rudyard Kipling, the Count of Paris, kings, queens and princesses. "But do famous people stay here today?" I asked Manager Bruce Banister, and before he could say Gilbert O'Sullivan, through the revolving doors came Sir Cecil Beaton.

Of the hotel's 127 rooms, a hefty proportion are singles, mostly on the upper floors; of the remainder, each one is different although they all have period furnishings (much of it dating from the original Victorian inn), a few have minibars and, on the lower floors, double-glazed windows. There's also an attractive oak-paneled restaurant, L'Aperitif, serving mostly French and continental dishes.

Brown's may not be the grandest hotel in London. Nor the most comfortable. For some, it may not even be all that romantic. But it does have a special quality that other hotels cannot match even with all their drugstores and boutiques and beauty salons. It has character. The kind of character that's built on a long tradition of service. Soft-spoken, well-mannered—very *Mayfair*.

Name: Brown's Hotel

Owners: Trust Houses Forte

Manager: Bruce Banister

Address: Albemarle Street, London W1A4 SW

Location: A few steps from Piccadilly and close to the Green Park tube station which is now on the direct underground route from Heathrow airport

Telephone: (01) 493-6020

62 **Cables/Telex:** 28686

Reps: Trust Houses Forte and Golden Tulip Worldwide in U.S.A., Canada and Europe

Credit Cards: All major cards

Rooms: 127 rooms, 3 suites

Meals: Breakfast 7:30–10, lunch 12:15–2:30, dinner 6–10; dinner for two approx. $50–55; jacket required; room service around the clock with full meals from 7:30 to 10:15; minibars in 80 of the rooms

Entertainment: Television in rooms

Sports: (None)

Sightseeing: London

P.S. No group tours or conventions

For brief reports on other hotels in England and Wales turn to the chapter on Added Attractions at the end of this guide.

Ireland

Newport House
Newport

The eggs come from Grandma's hens, the meat from Grandma's butcher, and the hotel's home-smoked salmon is worth the trip on its own. Meals (English with continental overtones) are served by young Austrians in formal waiter attire, all in hushed voices. Like everything else at Newport House. This is very much a family-owned, family-run, genteel country house, and if you're not here for the fishing, you'd better have a bagful of good novels or be prepared to look into each other's eyes all day. There are, to be sure, plenty of excursions in the surrounding countryside, picnics by the river, walks in wood and garden.

The house dates from the 1600s, when it was the home of The O'Donels, and has been owned by the present family since World War II. It's a formal Irish-Georgian country home with a small cobbled courtyard at the rear (the best rooms are here); the small lobby is dominated by a stuffed brown trout, the center hall has a high glass-domed ceiling and ornate red carpeting usually covered with green plastic to protect it from the dripping leggings of the fishermen. The lounge and bar have seen better days. Ditto the tweed-and-brogue guests. But the food *is* good, and if you really want to get away from it all, this is as far as you probably want to go.

Name:	Newport House
Owner:	Francis Mumford-Smith
Manager:	Owen Mullins
Address:	Newport, County Mayo
Location:	On Clew Bay, 60 miles north of Galway
Telephone:	Newport (Mayo) 12 or 61
Cables:	Irish Tourist Board Office, Westport (County Mayo)

Reps: None—but arrangements can be made through the Irish Tourist Board in New York

Credit Cards: American Express, Diners Club, Barclaycard

Rooms: 24, some without private bath

Meals: Breakfast 8–10, lunch 12:30–2:30, afternoon tea on request, dinner 7:30–9; 3-course dinner for two approx. $22–$25; dress optional—from hearty tweeds to banker blue; room service by arrangement—but reluctantly

Entertainment: People watching

Sports: Billiard room, croquet, fishing (the hotel owns the river); riding, fishing and shooting nearby

Sightseeing: Westport House and Zoo, Connemara, Yeats Country

P.S. Closed October through March; few children, and those usually shunted off to the games room; no day trippers, a few small unobtrusive fishing parties

Ashford Castle
Cong

♦♦♦ ✗✗ $$$

Windsor West! Towers and turrets, stone walls and white trim, battlements and portcullis, it stands in formal gardens with fountains on a 500-acre estate beside the shores of Lough Corrib. Your room will have a view of lake or river, forest or golf course. Gold-draped lounges are hung with suits of armor. You dine in a 200-seat hall with carved ceilings and chandeliers, served by attentive, uniformed waiters who bring you platters of Rossmore oysters or fresh salmon pie. After dinner, you can sip and snuggle in the dimly lighted Dungeon Bar, or, on summer evenings, wander, goblets in hand, through half-a-mile of rose gardens.

The oldest parts of Ashford were built in 1228 by William de Burgo, who sailed over with Prince John. It's been a hotel since 1939, but completely modernized and enlarged at a cost of $8 million or thereabouts (very cleverly, it's hard to tell the difference between old and new) when it

65

was bought in 1972 by the present owner, an American with Irish ancestry. Americans love it, but they seem to be the kind of Americans who respect the castle's Irish heritage—and, no doubt, their own. For the most part the rooms are all luxurious, with huge tubs, heated towel racks and immense towels, although plumbing in the older part of the building sometimes allows you to keep track of neighbors' bathing habits. Each room is individually decorated, furnished mostly with antiques and period pieces. Room 326, in the old section, is particularly spacious, with heavily draped windows looking out on the garden and lake, and a double bed large enough for Prince John and half his courtiers.

Ashford is well run, formal but friendly, the epitome of gracious living. And the setting is magnificent. As one colleague advises: make your reservations in the next half hour.

Name: Ashford Castle

Owner: John A. Mulcahy

Manager: Rory J. C. Murphy

Address: Cong, County Mayo

Location: Between Lough Corrib and Lough Mask, 27 miles from Galway

Telephone: Castlebar 22644

Telex: 4749

Reps: Aer Lingus, Lismore Travel

Credit Cards: All major cards

Rooms: 72 rooms and 6 suites

Meals: Breakfast 8–10, lunch 1–2:30, dinner 7:30–9:30; 3-course dinner for two approx. $36 to $40; tie and jacket required; 24-hour room service, slight extra charge

Entertainment: Chopin on the grand piano between 7 and 9, Irish music in the Dungeon 10 to midnight

Sports: Tennis (2 courts), golf (clubs supplied), boating and fishing on the lake; horseback riding nearby

Sightseeing: The Mayo countryside, Connemara Pony Show in August

P.S. Closed January 15 through March 31; children "not encouraged"; no daytrippers, but perhaps some small groups or overnight visits

Dromoland Castle
Newmarket-on-Fergus

WWW XX $$$

Dreamland Castle. Mix a dash of American know-how, a splash of Irish charm and a soupçon of *snobbisme*, and you have the makings of this splendid caravanserai. It was once the home of The O'Briens, who built their first castle here in the 11th century, but what you see today—towers, crenellations, corbels and all—dates from the 18th century. In 1963 the castle was bought by an American industrialist, West Virginian but with an Irish background, who happened to like visiting the Oulde Sod, wanted a pleasant place to stay when he was there, so went out and bought himself a 50-room pleasant place with 400 acres of lawns and ponds, fairways and a vast kitchen garden. He called in a famous American designer, Carleton Varney, who restyled the interior with expensive but refined flair. All is bright, all is light. Carpets are emerald green for Ireland, chairs are in shades of yellow for sunshine, drapes are as colorful as the flowers in the kitchen garden. Guest rooms are luxurious; those in the castle itself are often huge, some in the Queen Anne Wing open onto a courtyard. Room 205 has a big bay window overlooking the lake, a sunny, warm room where you'll probably want to have your meals sent up. Room 206 is immense, with acres of scarlet carpeting for waltzing harmonizing with flowered wallpaper; the 1st Earl of Clarendon peers down from one wall, and two ladies (wives? good friends? no one knows for sure) hang on the wall above the bed. Palatial rather than cozy. But pricey—so give yourselves time to enjoy the pleasures of the place. Wander through halls full of O'Brien ancestors. Take a boat out on a lake. Play tennis on a deserted court. Stroll through gardens dotted with palm trees. Dine like courtiers in a red-and-gold salon overlooking the lake.

Name:	Dromoland Castle
Owner:	Bernard P. McDonough
Manager:	Patricia Barry
Address:	Newmarket-on-Fergus, County Clare
Location:	Near Shannon Airport, 2 miles north of Newmarket-on-Fergus
Telephone:	Shannon 71144
Telex:	6854

Reps: None; toll-free number in U.S. and Canada 800-624-1921

Credit Cards: All major cards accepted

Rooms: 67

Meals: Breakfast 7:30–10, lunch 1–2, afternoon tea 1–6, dinner 7–9; 3-course dinner for two approx. $35–$40; tie and jacket at dinner; 24-hour room service, small extra charge

Entertainment: Piano or guitar in bar after dinner, very relaxed

Sports: Tennis court, 9-hole golf course, 2 boats for lake or river fishing

Sightseeing: Medieval banquets at Bunratty Castle and Knappogue Castle, the Irish countryside

P.S. Closed November through March; a few small groups in summer

Fitzpatrick Castle
Dublin

₩ X̌ $$

Here's an alternative to staying in Dublin, although you won't completely escape the crowds because of the castle's nightly cabaret. It really was a full-blooded castle at one time, although it now looks more like a Walt Disney concept of what Sleeping Beauty's castle should be. About ten years ago it was bought and totally renovated by the present owners, who own other hotels tuned into the demands of transatlantic travelers and modern hotel operation. Their domain consists of nine acres behind high walls overlooking Dublin Bay, surrounded by lawns and lofty shade trees, and it's all rather big and busy and sometimes brassy with no fewer than four cocktail bars patronized by both tourists and locals—and, our eagle-eyed scout reports, Burt Lancaster. Despite the turnover, though, diners are served first-rate fare, with the emphasis on fish and lamb, everything garden-fresh, sea-fresh or farm-fresh.

Guest chambers in the New Wing at the rear feature huge four-poster beds with modern mattresses and "the racy overtones of a Lithuanian bordello"; rooms at the front are without four-posters but with terraces and views of the bay. If you want lots of space, ask for the Castle Suite or

68

Victorian Suite in the old wing, both high in the turrets—and very high in tariffs. In fact, at $100-plus begorrah be kidding.

Save yourselves a few dollars. Check into a regular four-poster. Order up room service. Tuck in. You won't even notice the crowds.

Name: Fitzpatrick Castle

Manager: Jim Brindley

Address: Killiney, Dublin

Location: On the Dublin Bay coast, 9 miles from the capital

Telephone: (01) 851533

Telex: 30353 FITZEI

Reps: Irish Tourist Board in the U.S. and Canada

Credit Cards: All major cards

Rooms: 45 plus 2 suites

Meals: Breakfast 7:30–10:30, lunch 12–2:30, afternoon tea on request, dinner 7–11; 3-course dinner for two approx. $25–$30; informal dress; 24-hour room service

Entertainment: Cabaret nightly, jazz Saturday and Sunday

Sports: Indoor heated pool, squash, sauna, tennis, minigolf; golf, sailing and fishing nearby by arrangement

Sightseeing: Dublin

P.S. No daytrippers, but busloads of people come for the cabaret

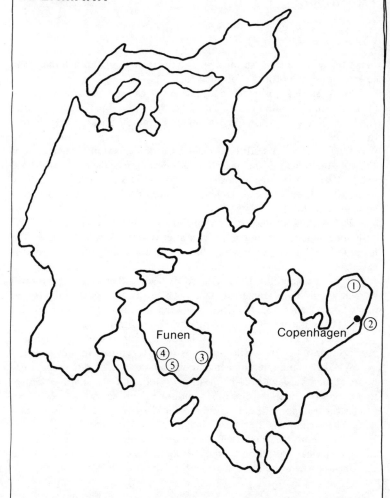

DENMARK

DENMARK

Funen

Copenhagen

1. Store Kro
2. 71 Nyhavn Hotel
3. Hotel Hesselet
4. Falsled Kro
5. Steensgaard Herregardspension

Store Kro
Fredensborg

♔ ✗ $$

Make this your home base when you go castle-hopping through the lovely countryside just north of Copenhagen.

You're so close to Fredensborg Castle you can run up to borrow a cup of sugar if need be. And you're just a brief drive from Frederiksborg Castle and from Kronborg Castle in Helsingør (Elsinore), Shakespeare's setting for *Hamlet*.

King Frederik IV built Fredensborg Castle as his summer hideaway in 1723. At the same time he opened an adjourning inn, the *kro* of which we speak. Part of the original hostelry remains. But you don't want to stay there. It's now an annex to the big house across the street, which is where you *do* want to stay.

The Store Kro (*store* means "big," *kro* means "inn") is very popular with honeymooners. Many return year after year to rekindle their fires. The lakeside location is quite idyllic—literally fit for a king. And the food is excellent.

You can take walks through the royal gardens. The queen's guards will probably peer at you from under their big black busbies. But as long as they don't lower their automatic rifles, just keep walking as if you owned the place. That's the way Queen Margrethe II handles it, we're told.

The castle's chapel, a beautiful baroque affair, is open to worshipers every Sunday, but the castle proper is open to visitors in July only.

Whether you appreciate contemporary art or not, plan to spend a few hours at the Louisiana Museum nearby. It's a beautifully conceived gallery that makes the most of its location overlooking the sea. A big sculpture by Calder for instance looks like a ship under full sail because of its location here. The exhibitions are international, and they change frequently.

What about the hotel itself? The rooms are big and airy but they tend to be somewhat pretentious in their appointments. Perhaps it's natural to put on airs when you're right next to a castle. (R.E.S.)

Name: Hotel Frederik IV Store Kro

Owner/Manager: Flemming Ronald Larsen

Address: 3480 Fredensborg

Location: About 30 miles north of Copenhagen, between Hillerød and Helsingør

Telephone:	(03) 28 00 47
Cables:	STOREKRO
Reps:	(None)
Credit Cards:	Visa
Rooms:	38 doubles, 3 suites

Meals: Breakfast 7:15–9, lunch 12–2:30, dinner 6–9; 3-course dinner for two approx. $48–$50; à la carte room service from 7:15 A.M. to 10 P.M.

Entertainment: (None)

Sports: Billiards, skittles, swimming, tennis, golf, horseback riding nearby

Sightseeing: Esrum Lake, Grib Forest, coastal fishing villages

71 Nyhavn Hotel
Copenhagen

WWW X $$

Attention solace seekers! Here's a delightful little hotel which gives you lots and lots of charm, peace and quiet in exchange for a dead-center location.

The 71 Nyhavn Hotel (that's its address as well as its name) sits on Copenhagen's main harbor channel. You hear a distant bell buoy at night instead of raucous cars and motorbikes. Yet you're a mere five-minute walk from New King's Square (Kongens Nytorv) and the start of the Strøget, a shopper's paradise.

If you gaze about in wonderment as you enter, relax: the 71 Nyhavn contains no hotel clichés. The masterminds who designed it began with nothing more than a 200-year-old shell and some remarkably fresh ideas.

Walls are three feet thick. The same enormous Pomeranian pine beams which supported the building through the British bombardment of Copenhagen in 1807 are still holding the place together. Except today they are all exposed, and an inspired part of the decor.

The Nyhaven opened as a hotel in 1971, so everything is fresh and modern. One quibble: the rooms are handsome but very *compact*. Inspect one. If you need lots more space to feel expansive, splurge on one of the suites. They are super special. You can loll about your sitting room on soft

73

glove-leather chairs, watching the hydrofoils come skidding in from Sweden. Stock the tiny refrigerator with Tuborg, wine and cheese. You never know when you'll be overcome with thirst. Bedrooms are done in velvety soft russets and taupes. All are twin bedded—each bed with its own *dyne* (pronounced "doon") comforter to ward off the evening chill.

By all means be downstairs in time to enjoy the groaning board full of breakfast goodies. Copenhagen is a walking town. Eat well, you'll need all your energy. Dig in to the platters of pungent Danish hams and cheeses. Help yourself from pitchers of fresh milk—or take your carafe of strong, strong coffee. And you must have a fresh Danish pastry, perhaps with a bit of that delicious butter.

Dinner is a treat here, too. However, there's a disadvantage to all the popularity—the staff can't handle the crowd. So don't plan to dine during prime time or if a party is being served in the private dining room. Good as the food is, the slow service will turn you churlish. If the place looks crowded, eat out. All Copenhagen awaits you. (R.E.S.)

Name: 71 Nyhavn Hotel

Owner: Arp Hansen

Manager: (Mrs.) Bente Hjorth

Address: DK-1051 Copenhagen K.

Telephone: (01) 11 85 85

Cables/Telex: NYHAVNHOTEL/27558 HYHOT DK

Reps: (None)

Credit Cards: Visa, American Express, Diners Club, Master Charge/ Eurocard, Access

Rooms: 75 doubles, 6 suites

Meals: Breakfast 7–10:30, lunch 12–3, dinner 5:30–10:30; 3-course dinner for two approx. $48–$52; informal dress; room service available for à la carte breakfast only (complimentary breakfast is not available via room service); menu contains English translation

Entertainment: TV and hi-fi in guest rooms, all programs in Danish, naturally

Sports: (None)

Sightseeing: Wonderful, wonderful Copenhagen. Walk 5 minutes to Amalienborg Palace, to Royal Theater. Walk one way to Tivoli, 30 minutes, but taxi back

Hotel Hesselet
Nyborg

WWW XX $$

Wonder of wonders. This touch of the Far East wouldn't surprise you a bit if you found it along the Pacific coastline at Pebble Beach. But coming upon a neo-Japanese hotel in the midst of quaint, quaint Denmark does make you stop and stare in wonderment.

The real surprise is that it's not too exotic for the natives. They took to it even when the serving girls were formally garbed Japanese maidens who giggled nicely but spoke not a word of Danish. The girls returned home to be replaced by attractive young locals who are fluent in many languages.

Today, moneyed Danes, Swedes and Germans keep the Hesselet busy all year round. And they come for two- and three-week vacations—perhaps for the food, perhaps because the 18-hole golf course is one of the best in all Scandinavia.

Another attraction might be the prices. Manager Zwonko Tresoglavic points out that vacation prices here on the island of Funen are generally about 30 percent less than they are in Copenhagen.

Mr. Tresoglavic is a soft-spoken Yugoslav who speaks perfect English. You wonder how anyone so low key can run such a tight ship. There's no trace of untidiness in the housekeeping, no clatter from the kitchen, no raised voices in the halls. Everything works silently and very, very efficiently.

All public rooms are on the ground level: library, dining room, reception room, heated pool, saunas. The Japanese decor stops where the guest rooms begin—on the second floor. They're done in a style that used to be called English traditional. Quite nice, very comfortable—but a bit short on personality.

You pay a premium for rooms looking out on a great greensward of lawn to the sea. The view is sensational. But if you're economizing, you'll appreciate the 85 or so kroners you can save by taking a room facing the woods.

Yale men will snap to attention when they spot the boulla-boulla on the menu. It turns out to be a cream of turtle soup—*real* turtle, not mock. The tournedos of veal with chantarelles is a nice change if you tire of all the fresh seafood on the menu. Save space for dessert. Be sure you try the almond soufflé with fruit and ice cream. You can swim it all off in the pool or the sea tomorrow morning. The service here is exemplary. But then it is in so very many places in northern Europe. The waiters here take pride in giving good service. (R.E.S.)

Name: Hotel Hesselet

Owners: Karl Haustrup, Kaj Wolhardt

Manager: Zwonko Tresoglavic

Address: Christianslundsvej 119, D-5800 Nyborg

Location: At the eastern end of the island of Funen, about 50 miles and a short ferryboat ride from Copenhagen

Telephone: (09) 31 30 29

Cables/Telex: (None)

Reps: (None)

Credit Cards: American Express, Diners Club, Master Charge/Eurocard

Rooms: 43 doubles, 3 suites

Meals: Breakfast 7–12, lunch 12–2:15, dinner 6–9:45; 3-course dinner for two, approx. $44–$46; informal dress; à la carte room service from 7 A.M. to midnight

Entertainment: Television in TV room, taped music in lobby and dining room

Sports: On premises—6 lighted tennis courts, indoor swimming pool, beach at front door, sauna, massage by appointment, 18-hole golf course, horseback riding, billiards, table tennis, miniature golf

Sightseeing: Odense's cathedral and Hans Christian Andersen Museum, Funen Village Open-Air Museum, 1000-year-old Viking ship at Ladby, castles everywhere

Falsled Kro
Millinge

From the road, the Falsled Kro looks like a typical old thatched-roof coaching stop in rural Denmark. But throw open the front door, and you're suddenly somewhere on the sunny Mediterranean. Hot pinks and citrus colors, dazzling white plaster walls, tile floors, contemporary furniture.

Danish purists shudder at this adulteration of the national taste for conservative home decor, but foreign visitors seem pleased by the melange of hot colors and cool ideas. The shocks don't stop with the furnishings either. That sensational cook in the kitchen is French. The most popular beer at the bar is Whitbread.

The Falsled's double rooms are really suites. All have distinctly separated sleeping and sitting quarters. Many have fireplaces. And absolutely all have private entrances from the outside. You needn't go traipsing through the lobby if you're all covered with suntan creams.

There are flowers everywhere. Little pots of them in all the guest rooms. Big bowers of them in all public rooms. The owner's mother comes visiting every other day to change all the arrangements. She brings fresh flowers from her own gardens or picks them in the gardens around the Falsled.

The terrace is open for alfresco dining by candlelight when the weather favors it. Very pretty. But if you're in the dining room proper, you can keep an eye on what seasonings Chef Jean Louis is using for your *homard aux mousserons.* The open kitchen plan here gives you something to look at during conversation lulls. All the game is local—the asparagus and strawberries are home grown, the salmon is smoked in the Falsled's own smokehouse.

Everyone nips in to the bar afterward to sit by the fire and listen to the crackle of birch. The braver souls order a specialty of the house called a *pousse rapier* made with part champagne and part Armagnac.

The Falsled is situated on a snug little cove with a clear view of the fishing boats going out to sea. If you seek some romantic rainy-day adventure you can drive 48 kilometers south to Troense where you can pick wildflowers to put on the grave of Elvira Madigan and her lover. (R.E.S.)

Name: Falsled Kro

Owners/Managers: Sven and Lene Grønlykke

Address: Assensvej 513, 5642 Millinge

Location: On the south shore of the island of Funen, about 30 miles from Odense

Telephone: (09) 68 11 11

Cables/Telex: (None)

Reps: Relais de Campagne Châteaux Hotels

Credit Cards: American Express, Diners Club, Master Charge/Eurocard

Rooms: 9 doubles, 2 singles

Meals: Breakfast 7–10, lunch 12–2, dinner 6:30–9:30; 3-course dinner for two approx. $50–$52; informal to casual dress; room service available for à la carte breakfast only. Waiters will translate.

Entertainment: (None)

Sports: Nearby—beach, tennis, golf, horseback riding, fishing

Sightseeing: (See Hotel Hesselet)

P.S. Closed every Monday, and throughout January and February

Steensgaard Herregardspension
Millinge

WW X $$

You may have to stifle a sudden impulse to bolt and run immediately after you walk in to the Steensgaard. There's no desk, no reception clerk—just a very grand entry hall containing a knight's shining armor and tier upon tier of stuffed animal heads. You'll think you've trespassed into someone's private trophy room. If you ring before you enter, you'll be properly received, shown to your room, and told when the dinner gong will be sounded.

The Steensgaard is run like a big private home. And what a home it is! It's positively baronial—a big half-timbered stone-and-brick affair with beginnings that date back to 1310. There are five salons. And why not? If aristocratic Danes were able to boogie about in a whole strand of elegant sitting rooms, why shouldn't you? Just be sure you don't wear your crepe-soled shoes. They squeak outrageously on these lovingly polished parquet floors.

The lady of the manor, Frau Seidel, will receive you as you enter the dining room for your evening meal. This has got to be the most beautiful room in the place. All reds and pinks and reflected golds. It looks like the setting for a Vermeer painting—complete with side lighting.

Dinner is obligatory here. The Steensgaard won't let you stay unless you dine. But this is a distinct pleasure, not a penalty! The food is prepared with great imagination and skill—beautifully served, too.

The Frau might strike you as being a bit of a valkyrie at first. But that reserve wears away quickly. She is really a charmer, and she's loaded with

78

fascinating facts about the history of the place. Be sure to ask her about the resident ghost. He appears nightly at precisely twenty past midnight, the hour he was murdered here in 1596.

Every guest room in the Steensgaard is different. You might enjoy staying in one called the Count's Room (it has a secret passage to Guess Whose room, now blocked off). Room 4 is the only one with a four-poster bed and a view of the courtyard. The room with the biggest bed and the loveliest view is 15.

Ask for an outside room if you appreciate the countryside: you can see deer frisking about on their little preserve and more feathered friends than you can probably identify. Walking is a big pleasure here. You can take your morning constitutional stalking past old lindens along the brook and down to the old sluice. No one can hear if you choose to whistle or sing as you walk. The Steensgaard offers you twenty-five acres of grounds for browsing. And more beyond the immediate boundaries if you're really ambitious. (R.E.S.)

Steensgaard Herregardspension

Name: Steensgaard Herregardspension

Owner: Peter Hansen

Managers: Inge Seidel, Hermann Niese

Address: DK 5642 Millinge, Funen (Fyn)

Location: In the southwest corner of Funen; nearest town is Faborg, 4 miles away

Telephone: (09) 61 94 90

Cable/Telex: (None)

Reps: (None)

Credit Cards: (None)

Rooms: 15 doubles

Meals: Breakfast 8–9:30, lunch 12:30 sharp, dinner 7 sharp. (Dinner is a *must*, 110 kroner per person over and above room cost; family style, no selections; place card describes your meal in English.) Informal dress; no room service

Entertainment: Taped classical music in dining room during dinner, TV set in lounge, billiards

Sports: Tennis, horseback riding, 25 acres of walking trails; nearby— swimming in sea; golf

For brief reports on other hotels in Denmark turn to the chapter on Added Attractions at the end of this guide.

HOLLAND and BELGIUM

Leeuwarden

Amsterdam

Arnhem

Rotterdam

Brussels

HOLLAND AND BELGIUM

1. Hotel-Restaurant Lauswolt
2. De Wiemsel
3. Pulitzer Hotel
   Hotel de l'Europe
4. Kasteel Neubourg
5. Kasteel Wittem
6. Waterland
7. Auberge De Kieviet
8. Auberge du Moulin Hideux
9. Hôtellerie du Prieuré de Conques
10. Hôtellerie Trôs Marets

Holland

Hotel-Restaurant Lauswolt
Beetsterzwaag

₩✕✕✕$$$

Once you've had your first dinner at the Lauswolt, you'll be more than willing to overlook the genteel seediness of the place. Alas, the bloom has long since left the damasks here. The furniture looks as if it had been collected at Holland-America Line auctions years ago. But, ah, the food.

Cut your fork through a *médallion* of veal—savor the sauce of mushroom, apple and Calvados. Sample some of the *turbot en papillote*. Taste a stalk of tender white asparagus, and rejoice. The Lauswolt has an asparagus festival every spring from the second week in May until St. John's Day, June 24. Believe it or not, the asparagus is cooked in twelve different ways during the festival. Purists will want theirs quickly and simply steamed, of course.

The chef says he cuts a fine line between the heavily sauced specialties of Escoffier and the less fattening saucing methods of *la nouvelle cuisine*. No matter. One whiff of any dish here is enough to make you forget you'd ever heard of calories.

In these northern climes there may be light enough outdoors for a nice stroll after dinner. In early May, dusk seemed to hold on until very close to 10 P.M., and the days were still getting longer. As a matter of fact, you see golfers arriving to tee off here at all sorts of odd hours in the evening.

Don't get lost on your after-dinner walk. There are some 200 acres of land here, half of it farm land and half of it woods and both beautiful. The hotel is an old white mansion, bearing more than a passing resemblance to one you know on Pennsylvania Avenue. The portico in front cries out for at least one Hispano Suiza—all those Mercedes' look somehow out of place.

Guest rooms upstairs are gracious, high-ceilinged affairs with French windows big enough for papal appearances. Once you're settled in, you'll probably stop noticing the really awful orange lampshade, or the pink and blue tile in the bath. Keep in mind that the Lauswolt has big plans for redecorating.

Sit out on the sunny terrace for tea or an afternoon drink. You can

82

watch what's going on down at the swan house or gaze out over acres of
beautiful woods. Mother Nature did the design job out here and you'll find
no fault with it. (R.E.S.)

Name: Hotel-Restaurant Lauswolt

Manager: Hendrick Bouwknegt

Address: Beetsterzwaag, Friesland

Location: North of the IJsselmeer (the former Zuyderzee), a few miles
east of Leeuwarden, about 2 hours by car from Amsterdam

Telephone: (05126)—1245

Cables/Telex: (None)

Reps: Relais de Campagne Châteaux Hotels

Credit Cards: American Express, Diners Club

Rooms: 22 doubles, 1 suite

Meals: Breakfast 7–11; lunch 12–2:30; dinner 6–10; 4-course dinner for
two approx. $50; full room service; menu is in French, waiters will translate

Entertainment: Taped music in lobby, television in TV room, TV can be
rented for rooms

Sports: Two clay tennis courts, 9-hole golf course, swimming pool, sauna

Sightseeing: Picturesque villages around the IJsselmeer (Urk, Giethoorn,
Hindenloopen) and Friesian lakes

De Wiemsel
Ootmarsum

WWWXX$$

Don't be put off by the way De Wiemsel looks from the outside these days.
The landscaping is new and the saplings and shrubbery haven't had time to
fill out and soften the somewhat barren surroundings.

All unsettling thoughts flee once you enter. Someone of consummate
taste has made De Wiemsel into the inn of many happinesses. The comforts   83

are absolutely deluxe, the food is terrific, the appointments are first rate. (All kudos go to the elegant lady who owns the place, Mrs. Van Der Maas.)

The halls aren't mere halls here. They're galleries for beautiful old *kasten*, highboys, carved Christos, flower-filled sleighs and such. Tapers burn in their big brass candleholders at all hours.

Every guest room is a suite. First there's a velvety sitting room, complete with tiny kitchenette for snacks or morning coffee. Beyond is a big, comfortable bedroom. And beyond that is the bath, another two-room affair. The larger bath area contains a tub, a shower and twin sinks. The sinks are Italian and look like big mushrooms. Go through the louvered door to the smaller room in the bath; here you find your bidet and your toilet.

There's a TV set which swivels between the sitting room and bedroom. (You might catch a vintage American movie, but it will be dubbed in German or in Dutch.) Sliding glass doors take you out to your own private terrace. (You may be tempted to dry out your freshly laundered lovelies on this terrace. However, the thought of the soignée Mrs. Van Der Maas finding them there should be enough to deter you.)

Is it fitness you want? Skip down to the exercise room, the sauna, the pool. Stretch out afterward and relax on deck chairs that once were reserved for first-class passengers on the *Nieuw Amsterdam*. If you're smart, you've worked up a good appetite for dinner.

The dining room is a lovely place. It's all silver, brass, velvets and provincial prints—plus fresh zinnias and azaleas everywhere. A beautiful sound emanates from the kitchen once you've given your order—whisks. Simple whisks. No slamming freezers, no clicking microwaves.

Try the brioche filled with creamed shrimp and halibut. Try the thick veal steak garnished with smoked salmon, scrambled egg, and a slice of ham—this sounds like too much but it isn't. Try the *parfait aux myrtilles* for dessert.

And note the service. Food never comes to your table on a plate. Heaven forfend. It is brought from the kitchen in hot silver servers, transferred to warmed plates, and presented to you with the flourish it deserves.

Two competitive hoteliers advised us that De Wiemsel was something special. They were right. It is. (R.E.S.)

Name: De Wiemsel

Owners/Managers: Van Der Maas Family

Address: Winnhofflaan 2, Oootmarsum (Ov.)

Location: In the east of the province of Overijssel, about 2 hours by car from Amsterdam, half-an-hour north of Arnhem; nearest airport—Twente Enschede

Telephone: (05) 419-2155

Cables/Telex: (None)

Reps: (None)

Credit Cards: American Express, Diners Club, Master Charge/Eurocard

Rooms: 32, all suites

Meals: Breakfast 7–11; lunch 12–2:30; dinner 6–10; 3-course dinner for two approx. $40; menus are in Dutch, waiters will translate; à la carte room service available all day

Entertainment: Taped music in lobby and dining room

Sports: On premises—tennis (1 court), swimming, sauna, exercise room, horseback riding, walking trails

Sightseeing: Historic towns (Zwolle, Deventer) and picturesque villages (Staphorst, Paaslo, Ootmarsum, Giethoorn), castles, forests

Pulitzer Hotel
Amsterdam

ꟺꟺ ХХ ＄＄＄

Scene: garden courtyard in the heart of Old Amsterdam. People sip Heineken Beer in the shade of a hundred-year-old chestnut tree, surrounded by grass and greenery and beds of cotoneaster and laburnum. It's rush hour along the canals, but you'd never know it here, listening to the birds and the carillon playing Bach and the Beatles high in the tower of the 300-year-old Westerkerk. A glass-enclosed walkway winds through the garden, linking the two parts of this unique hotel—an enclave of 16 canal houses, back to back on the Prinsengracht and Keizersgracht. They are typical 16th- and 17th-century canal houses, tall and slender with distinctive neck, spout and clock gables—or *halsgevel, tuitgevel* and *klokgevel*. At one time or another they had served as homes, stores, warehouses for the spices brought home by East India Company merchantmen, as workshops for assorted tradesmen—brassfounder, jeweler, stocking dyer, thread spinner, mustard merchant. Numbers 333 and 337 Prinsengracht were once the home of a

85

gentleman by the name of Pieter van Roosevelt, and a neighboring house had been lived in by a friend of John Paul Jones and John Adams. It is just possible therefore that those two distinguished revolutionaries may have stayed in one of these houses, which in more recent years have sheltered latter-day Americans like James Stewart, Danny Kaye and the top brass of American corporations.

But before the first guests could check in, a transformation of monumental proportions took place. The basic structures were protected by Amsterdam's tight historical-preservation laws, and the facades had to remain intact; so over 1 million bricks had to be steam-cleaned and relined; plumbing had to be installed without altering the structural work. Since the original buildings had foundations of pine piles dug into the muddy subsoil, no one had any idea what would happen to the walls if some of these 300-year-old timbers had to be replaced; since windows and doors had to retain their original shapes, drapes and curtains had to be ordered in nonstandard sizes room by room. Many of the rooms retain their original ceiling beams; some have arched warehouse door/windows overlooking the canals; some are neat little attic nooks with rafter ceilings, skylights and a lovely feeling of seclusion.

When the hotel opened in October 1971, its cost per room was much higher than in a new hotel starting from the ground up. But the end result is a very special hotel. The inspiration behind the transformation was an American gentleman called Peter Pulitzer (yes, he *is* related), a handsome fortyish gentleman. One of his many properties in Florida is a Howard Johnson motel, which hardly sounds like the ideal background for someone creating a hotel like his Amsterdam namesake. He had originally intended it to be a HoJo outpost, and when it opened, it was indeed called Howard Johnson. To this day, alas, much of the furnishings still reflect the orange-carpet-white-plastic HoJo decor, but slowly the color schemes and furnishings are being modified, and the newer rooms have stylish decor more in keeping with the hotel's heritage.

Let me just tell you quickly about a few more shortcomings of the Pulitzer, because I don't want to be accused of favoritism on this one (the Pulitzer is my home-from-home, since I visit Amsterdam five or six times a year). Romantic setting and background notwithstanding, the Pulitzer is very popular with business people; while they stay huddled in meeting rooms they do not create distractions, but occasionally, when let loose, they can be somewhat boisterous. Sometimes Gerri and Kees, Amsterdam's favorite bartenders, play their tapes too loudly. In summer, the lobby is often cluttered with the baggage and scrawled posters of tour groups. The waiters are not always attentive and patient (although this has improved recently); on the other hand, considering the odd crazy-maze layout of the hotel, room service can be quite efficient.

But in the end a few drawbacks hardly detract from the special qualities of the place. The gardens. The patio for drinks. The lovely gabled houses. Step out the front door and you're right on pretty Prinsengracht. Turn right, walk a hundred yards and you're at the venerable Westerkerk, where Rembrandt lies buried. To stroll around this part of Amsterdam on a weekend when all the traffic has disappeared is really to experience romantic Europe. And although the Pulitzer is larger than most of the hotels in this guidebook, because of its architecture and layout, its nooks and crannies, you never get the impression of being in a mammoth hotel. Moreover, for a hotel of its size, the management staff under dedicated Fred Egli is highly visible and accessible; if you do have any problems, ask to see Fred, Theo or Fiet, and tell them I sent you. If you're staying here only a couple of nights, almost any room will fill the bill nicely, except perhaps the few facing interior wells. From the point of view of size, airiness and atmosphere, ask for one of the former warehouse rooms overlooking Prinsengracht—unless you're a light sleeper or late riser. The quarters overlooking the Keizersgracht, on the opposite side, tend to be quieter; among the newest here, Room 645 is a charming attic room overlooking the canal, 620 is exceptional, with sky-high ceilings and windows looking out on a Japanese cherry tree in the garden. My favorites are those looking out on the garden, and a few on the ground floor have French windows or Dutch barn doors opening onto small patios. Up in the roof, Room 447 has a gallery loft, 343 has a cupola and beams and faces the garden. All rooms with 54 in the number have beamed ceilings, bare brick walls and overlook the garden, all those with 26 in the number are similar but overlook the canal. There are times, of course, when you have little choice because the Pulitzer is a very popular hotel most of the year. But even if you don't get the room of your choice, you can still enjoy your Heineken or Dutch gin in the garden, listening to the birds and the carillon.

Name: Pulitzer Hotel

Manager: Fred Egli

Address: Prinsengracht 315–331, Amsterdam

Location: In the center of Amsterdam, a five-minute walk from the Royal Palace and Dam Square

Telephone: (020) 228333

Cables/Telex: Pulitzer Amsterdam/16508

Reps: Golden Tulip Worldwide in U.S., Canada and Europe, Robert F. Warner in U.S. and Canada

Credit Cards: All major cards

Rooms:	189 rooms, 8 suites or apartments

Meals: Breakfast 7–11, lunch 12–3, dinner 6–11, "snack card 11–11"; 3-course dinner for two approx. $30; informal dress; room service 7 A.M. to 11 P.M. (all rooms have minibars)

Entertainment: Taped music in bar, radio and color TV in rooms

Sports: (None)

Sightseeing: All of Amsterdam

P.S. Some small business groups in winter, tour groups in summer

Hotel de L'Europe
Amsterdam

WWWXXX$$$

With Dutch flags flying from its towers and scarlet awnings hoisted at every window, Hotel de L'Europe majestically rises at a turn in the Amstel River like some triumphant galleon sailing home from cannonading the Spanish fleet into toothpicks.

For those who prefer classic big old grand-class hotels, it's all of that. Maids on call 24 hours a day. Concierges who can get you anything from seats at the Concertgebouw to umbrellas for Amsterdam's year-round April showers. The shadowy little bar looks designed for plotting overthrows and forming cartels, and the height-of-decadence dining room for Marlene Dietrich and Adolphe Menjou.

Yet there's a nice sense of coming home here, which bigness does not often beget. Unlike even most small hotels, the management does its best to fit you into a favorite room or provide you with a preferred view. If you've stayed here before, you're remembered with bowls of fresh fruit and flowers when you come back. And although most guest rooms are big enough for a coronation, there are some snug little crannies—Room 418 in the tower and 504 tucked under the roof. They are L'Europe's best, and most romantic, bargains with a pigeon's-eye view over the city's spires and tiled rooftops down to the river and the famous old mint tower that chimes the hour.

If you're in the mood for something more expansive (and ex*pen*sive), there are three especially glamorous quarters where nothing but ostrich-feather negligée and velvet smoking jacket will do. Rooms 111, 211 and 311 give you a huge, balconied bay window that juts right out over the river with a two-sided view of it as it flows in from the hinterlands and out to the harbor. What better place to sip your good-night cognacs and watch the candlelit canal boats slide by?

One thing to avoid here is any inside room. At these prices, it is no consolation to end up staring out at a brick wall.

And if you venture down to the hotel's Excelsior restaurant for one Grand Nosh, do so with many guilders in your pocket and a demand for the best seat in the house—a velvet sofa for two, set into a private little niche in the wall with the whole glassy, glittering dining room before you. It's nice to know you can put on the Ritz even when you're *not* at the Ritz. (C.P.)

Name: Hotel de L'Europe

Manager: Pieter E. J. Jennen

Address: Nieuwe Doelenstraat 2-4, Amsterdam

Location: In the center of Amsterdam, between the Royal Palace and Rembrandtsplein

Telephone: (020) 23.48.36

Cables/Telex: 12081 (europ nl)

Reps: BTH Hotels

Credit Cards: American Express, Diners Club, Master Charge/Eurocard, Carte Blanche

Rooms: 79 rooms, 2 suites

Meals: Breakfast 7-10:30, lunch 12:30-2, dinner 7-9:30; dinner for two approx. $100; tie and jacket; full room service 24 hours a day

Entertainment: (None)

Sports: (None)

Sightseeing: All of Amsterdam is at your feet, including the canal boats

Kasteel Neubourg
Gulpen

₩₩XX$$

Down a long driveway lined with trees, across a moat, through a brick portal, into the castle yard and you're instantly in a world of long, long ago. Kasteel Neubourg has been here since 1320, owned by the same family for the last three or four hundred years, and the elderly Countess Marchant et d'Ansebourg, last of her line, lives in one wing of the courtyard. Stride across the stone bridge beside the castle, and you come upon a garden with 2000 roses, and a forest with 79 varieties of trees; a stream courses through the lawns, and you can walk for miles along tree-lined lovers' lanes without ever leaving the estate. Swallows nest in the courtyard eaves. Four kinds of them. If you're around a few days before September 23, you can see them form up in formation to give the nestlings a chance to put in a few training sorties, then on September 23, without fail, every year, off they fly to the south.

In its heyday, Neubourg must have had all the spendor of a mini-Versailles, and even today you can savor some of this grandeur. Sip an aperitif in the Louis XV drawing room in the warm glow from walls padded with leather. Dine in the high-ceilinged salon, its emerald green walls trimmed with gilt curlicues. Tiptoe to bed across hallways spread with *signed* Persian carpets. It's a world of family portraits and Old Dutch Masters, chandeliers and gilded mirrors, delicately carved and painted ceilings, lintels emblazoned with family crest. But be kind: the Kasteel is beginning to show signs of age, so arrive if you can when the chandeliers are ablaze and the gilt glistens and your first impression is a grand one.

Most of the rooms are vast: Room 107 has a corner site overlooking the rose garden, 109 is dominated by a large marble mantelpiece and family portraits; 112, in Louis XIV style, has a cavernous closet for hats and perukes. A few of Neubourg's rooms share bathrooms and toilets, and although they may be a mite threadbare, they are, considering their size and their surroundings, outstanding value for lovers whose sense of romance is greater than their budgets. And with 60 acres of estate you may not be spending too much of your time indoors anyway.

Name: Kasteel Neubourg

Owner: Countess Marchant et d'Ansenbourg

Manager: Wilhem Reuwer

Address: 6271 PL. Gulpen (Limburg)

Location: 10 miles from Maastricht

Telephone: (04450) 1222

Cables/Telex: (None)

Reps: (None)

Credit Cards: (None)

Rooms: 21 rooms

Meals: Breakfast 7–10, no lunch, dinner 6–10; 4-course dinner for two approx. $50; tie and jacket required; room service for breakfast and drinks only

Entertainment: (None)

Sports: 60 acres of private walking trails; nearby—tennis, 9-hole golf, and indoor/outdoor swimming pools

Sightseeing: Castles, manor houses, Gothic churches and catacombs; Maastricht, the oldest fortified city in Holland; the Caves of St. Pietersberg (mentioned in history as early as 50 A.D., and during WWII its 200 miles of tunnels were used to store art treasures, servicemen and escaped prisoners); Valkenburg and its casino; Germany and Belgium are only minutes away

P.S. Closed January and February

Kasteel Wittem
Wittem

WWXX$$

The Van Wittems, knights of Julément, lived here up until the middle of the 14th century; two hundred years later Emperor Charles V stayed here on his way to his coronation at Aix-la-Chapelle; in 1568 William the Silent, Prince of Orange, used the castle as a base during the struggle against the Spanish in the Eighty Years War, and more recently, one of his House of Orange heirs, Queen Juliana, had luncheon here. Despite its long and aristocratic background, there's nothing haughty or forbidding about Wittem—it's just a nice country inn that happens to be in a nice picture-book castle, owned and run—no, *coddled*—by a gentleman whose family has been in the hotel

91

Kasteel Wittem

business for many, many years. I first visited Kasteel Wittem about eight years ago, shortly after it had opened, and liked it there and then; each time I've returned it has improved. The lovely drawing room overlooking the moat has been repaneled with oak (not just any oak, *French* oak), the guest rooms have been freshly renovated. It's a large L-shaped manor house, three stories high with additional rooms up among the eaves; the circular driveway is shaded by elms and beeches, swans float across the moat, and in the meadow just beyond there's a chestnut tree that is so enormous it looks like three separate trees. Rooms 4 and 5 have little oak window seats overlooking the garden; Room 3 overlooks the parking lot (but don't snub it just for that reason, since most dinner guests have driven off by 10 or thereabouts); 2 is a particularly sunny room with three windows overlooking the meadow with the old chestnut tree; Rooms 7 and 8, in the eaves, have high raftered ceilings, peepholes of windows and oak beds. My favorite is Room 6, a circular room with three loopholes in the room itself, and floor-to-ceiling windows in the bathroom, overlooking the moat and swans.

The Wittem's Michelin-starred restaurant is still its crowning glory, an elegant candles-and-crystal backdrop for baronial feasting. Innkeeper Peter Ritzen is a stickler for having only the finest ingredients in his kitchen, to the extent of having fresh produce carted up from the Rungis Market near Paris, and flying Aberdeen Angus beef regularly in from Scotland. The culinary tradition is French (*rouget à la nage aux fines herbes, le papillote de turbot, l'entrecôte aux ciboulettes* are some of the specialities); the wine list is first rate, with many moderately priced half bottles; and cognac and coffee in the oak-paneled lounge top off what should be a perfect evening.

Name: Kasteel Wittem

Owner/Manager: Peter Ritzen

Address: 6286 AA Wittem (Limburg)

Location: In the southeastern corner of Holland, 8 kilometers from Aachen (Aix-la-Chapelle), 30 kilometers from Liège

Telephone: (04450) 1208

Cables/Telex: (None)

Reps: Relais-Chateaux in U.S., Canada and Europe

Credit Cards: American Express, Diners Club, Visa

Rooms: 12 rooms

Meals: Breakfast 8–10:30, lunch 12–2:30, dinner 6–10; 4-course dinner for two approx. $50; dress informal; room service for breakfast and drinks only

Entertainment: Soft taped music in lounge and dining room; color television on request; gambling casino in Valkenburg, ten minutes away

Sports: Walking trails; nearby, indoor and outdoor tennis, golf and riding

Sightseeing: (See Kasteel Neubourg)

"Waterland"
Velsen-Zuid

♛♛♛✗✗✗$$

The garden is a landscaped park in the English style—lawns and pathways, pines, beeches and oaks. Rhododendrons add clusters of color. Larks trill and wood pigeons swoop from beech to oak. Padded loungers and garden chairs are set out on the lawn for any guest who wants morning coffee or afternoon tea alfresco. Incredibly, this oasis of peace is literally two minutes from the highway, 20 minutes from Amsterdam.

Waterland itself is a stately mansion with white facade and green shutters, built during the 18th century when all the land between here and Amsterdam was a lake (hence, the name "Water Land") and the original owner could *sail* to his country estate. Waterland has been owned for several generations by the family of Baroness van Tuyll van Serooskerken, Countess of Limburg Stirum, whose great-grandfather fought against Napoleon at Waterloo. The baroness now lives in the carriage house, having decided, in 1979, to open up her mansion to paying guests and diners, turning the direction over to the youthful Pieter Moret, who has played in Shakespeare at the Salzburg Festival and studied at Cornell University's hotel school. At the party launching the new venture, Waterland's salons were filled, appropriately, with counts, knights, barons, coutouriers and editors.

A dozen Grecian urns filled with geraniums line the steps up to the tall main door, and once you step inside, you're back in the days of the great Amsterdam merchants. The public salons and dining rooms are decorated with museum objets. In the small dining room known as the *Herenkamer*, or "Gentlemen's Room," 18th-century murals by Pieter Boers; in the *Zomerzaal*, or "Summer Room," walls are decorated with hand-blocked French wallpaper and family portraits by Tischbein. Dining tables are dressed with Brussels linen, the silver-plated candlesticks are copies of Louis XV originals in the Louvre, the silverware is the family heirloom Christofle, and the china costly Tischenreuth Echt Kobalt (lovingly tended in the scullery by an old family retainer).

In winter, open fires beneath marble mantelpieces add to the graciousness of the surroundings, fitting backdrop to Waterland's *paupiette de flétan fumé, médaillon de veau en feuillette* and *omelette Rothschild*. The chefs are French, young and advocates of *nouvelle cuisine*; their kitchen had been functioning for only a few months before they had already received high praise from Parisian critics.

There are only four guest rooms here, up a staircase crowned by windows featuring the coat of arms of the Van Tuyll family and an early study for Rodin's "The Kiss." The spacious bedchambers have been left just as they were when they cosseted family and family friends—hand-stitched *mille-couleur* carpets, Florentine chandeliers, Empire escritoires, family portraits and carved mantelpieces. His and hers royal-blue terrycloth bathrobes now hang in the bathrooms—one of the few "hotel" touches.

Here, then, is a gracious alternative for lovers who want to be at the heart of Holland yet stay in tranquil surroundings among trees and flowers and birds.

Name: "Waterland"

Manager: Pieter R. Moret

Address: Rijksweg 116, Velsen-Zuid

Location: About 20 minutes west of Amsterdam, 15 minutes from Schiphol Airport, at the IJmuiden exit on the A9 highway

Telephone: (02550) 23250/1

Telex: 18118 Telan NL

Reps: (None)

Credit Cards: American Express, Diners Club

Rooms: 4

Meals: Breakfast anytime, lunch 12–3, dinner 6–10:30; dinner for two approx. $60; informal (but not casual) dress; room service during dining room hours

Entertainment: Piano player in the salon; casino in Zandvoort (about 15 minutes away by car)

Sports: Walking trails; horseback riding at the bottom of the garden, beach 5 minutes away, tennis and golf nearby

Sightseeing: Beeckensteyn Castle/Museum next door (and once owned by the same Van Tuyll family); the sights of Amsterdam, Haarlem and the Cheese Market at Alkmaar are just minutes away; Grand Prix at Zandvoort (end of August), various flower shows and parades in spring and fall

P.S. Closed in January; some small groups, occasional weddings (but with only four rooms and tables for forty, groups and weddings tend to reserve the entire establishment)

Auberge De Kieviet
Wassenaar

₩XXX$$

So discreet is this hideaway that many of my Dutch friends who've dined at Kieviet don't even know there are half a dozen bedchambers upstairs. The Lapwing Inn is hidden away in a dormitory suburb of The Hague, surrounded by woods, in a garden bright with marigolds and roses and geraniums, with a fountain and a fish pond sheltering beneath a giant bog oak. The auberge itself, whitewashed brick with colorful window boxes and dark wood shingles, is first and foremost a restaurant, a favorite for a quarter of a century with the diplomats and dignitaries who inhabit The Hague. Like the clientele, the decor is international (a sort of contemporary Belle Epoque with rich reds, lots of chrome and wicker and mirrors in seashell frames), but the kitchen staff of Chef Denis Coma is French, and the menu is *nouvelle cuisine*. The Michelin Benelux Guide awards De Kieviet one star and four red forks, and you'll probably agree with this rating when you sit down to a dinner of *feuilleté de champignons, turbot au pamplemousse* (a Coma creation) or *saumon braisé aux herbes de notre jardin* or *poularde de Bressé au vinaîgre*. For dessert, order up another house specialty: *terrine de fruits frais*, a sort of Bavarois with three fruit flavors—*framboise*, mano and kiwi. Choosing a wine may be almost as simple: the *carte des vins* is impressive unless you want only a half bottle, in which case your choice is very limited. But good—a half bottle of Sancerre Clos de la Poussie 1978, for example, will go nicely with your turbot.

If the afternoon is balmy, with the bees buzzing and the larks and, presumably, lapwings singing, have your coffee and cognac on the terrace before heading upstairs to one of the six nests. Each is decorated differently but daintily, each with a flair for colors and patterns and textures. Room 2, for example, is decked out in a blue floral print on walls and ceilings and drapes and bed, with harmonizing blue wicker headboard and rattan chests; Room 5 is done in a darker floral print, with natural bamboo furnishings. Bathrooms have fluffy carpeting and snuggly bathrobes. All in all, a lovely spot to spend a languid afternoon. Spare a thought for everyone else in The Hague, pondering the heavy affairs of the world, as you lapse into your postmeridian snooze in this little lapwing of luxury.

Name: Auberge De Kieviet

Owners/Managers: Luigi and Malon Gandini

Address: 27 Stoeplaan, 2243 Wassenaar

Location: About 10 minutes north of The Hague, just off the main highway to Amsterdam

Telephone: (01751) 79203/79403

Cables/Telex: (None)

Reps: Relais-Château in U.S., Canada and Europe

Credit Cards: American Express

Rooms: 6

Meals: Breakfast anytime after 8, lunch 12–2, dinner 7–9:30; dinner for two approx. $60–$65; tie and jacket "appreciated"; room service for breakfast only

Entertainment: No radio, no TV; night life and casino in The Hague and Scheveningen; horse races nearby.

Sports: Nothing on the premises; miles of beach (including a nudists' beach), golf, tennis, horseback riding and water sports nearby

Sightseeing: The Hague, Leiden, Delft, Rotterdam—and all those museums, historic buildings, antique shops and galleries: Amsterdam is 40 minutes away by car.

P.S.   The restaurant is closed every Monday (but overnight guests can, of course, have breakfast).

Belgium

Auberge du Moulin Hideux
Noirefontaine

WWWXXXSS

You drive down a winding tree-lined roadway until a sharp bend brings you to a white wrought-iron fence and a bridge across a fast-flowing stream. The leafy garden is decked with spring flowers, the lawns dotted with loungechairs; a weeping willow dips into a fish pond, and at the far end, near the duck pond, a pathway leads off into stands of ash and beech trees. Nothing hideous, then, about this setting, the name notwithstanding. "Hideux" probably derives from a corruption of "Y Deux," from the centuries when there were *two* mills here. Not much of the original *moulin* remains, although you'd have to be a master mason to spot the additions tacked on after World War II, when an earlier generation of Lahires converted the old one-story *moulin* into a vintage 3-story auberge, its rough-cast terra-cotta walls topped by a black mansard roof. The stream, the garden, the flowers, 15 acres of grounds and the tree-clad hills all around give the inn an air of restfulness, langour, contentment.

In theory, the surrounding countryside is the loveliest corner of Belgium, in theory Moulin Hideux is the ideal base for excursions along the valleys of the Semois and the Meuse; in reality, you're more likely to say "Who cares?" and find a quiet, shady corner of the garden. Especially once you've dined here. Especially after a luncheon of *mousse de jambon et de bécasse, médaillon de veau printanier* or *truite pochée aux herbes*, followed by selections from the *plateau de fromages* and the *charrette des desserts* (particularly *tarte au sucre*, a regional specialty). Dawdle through all that in the company of a Château Clos Valentin, and you have the makings of a very lazy postmeridian torpor.

This modest little inn, you see, tucked away in this uncrowded corner, is one of the finest restaurants in Belgium. Michelin has awarded it two stars for the past twenty years, and dedicated gourmets regularly undertake the drive from Brussels just to indulge in its polished but relatively conservative cuisine, and the attentive service of Maître d' Jacques and his small team of waiters.

98   The auberge makes no pretence at fluffy luxury. This is a simple

country inn, and Madame Lahire has decorated the 13 rooms in an appropriately rustic, albeit Boudoir Rustic, style, with cheerful fabrics and wallpapers, vitrines with antique porcelain, percale sheets and wool blankets, room phones and minibars; three suites also have television. All the rooms face the gardens but Rooms 14 and 15 are on the ground floor, at the side away from the lawns and parking lot, with their own little patio— and consequently quieter than the others (but, be warned, near the kitchens, in case those exquisite aromas may prove to be too disconcerting).

Name: Auberge du Moulin Hideux

Owners/Managers: Charles and Martine Lahire

Address: 6831 Noirefontaine

Location: In the Ardennes, southeast of Brussels and Dinant, near Bouillon on the French border, a short drive from Sedan in France

Telephone: (061) 46.70.15

Cables/Telex: (None)

Reps: Relais-Chateaux in U.S.A., Canada and Europe

Credit Cards: (None)

Rooms: 10 rooms, 3 apartments

Meals: Breakfast 8:30–11, lunch 12:30–2, dinner 7:30–9:30; dinner for two approx. $100; tie and jacket required; room service for breakfast only (rooms have stocked refrigerators)

Entertainment: Quiet background music in the lounge and dining room; the apartments have television.

Sports: Walking trails on the inn's 15 acres of forest land; trout fishing (bring your own equipment); horseback riding nearby

Hôtellerie du Prieuré de Conques
Herbeumont sur Semois

WWX$$

Save some of your claret. Then after dinner stroll across the stadium-sized lawn toward the river, past the 400-year-old linden tree and a trio of tall pines; halfway down the lawn on your left there's a tiny arbor with one white bench just big enough for twosomes. Settle in, sip your wine, listen to the birds and the stream, sniff the crisp air. Tell each other what a lovely spot you've discovered.

This lovely old building, built in the 14th century as an offshoot of the great Abbey of Orval, was a real praying priory until 1924; later Florimond de Naeyer, a former lumber executive, and a few friends converted the priory into a *hôtellerie*, decorating its halls and rooms in harmony with its heritage, but adding all the expected modern comforts. In the lounge, where you sip your aperitifs under ancient vaulted ceilings, beside an open fire, even the jigsaw puzzle is an Old Flemish Master. Each hallway sports a small, stocked refrigerator, ungainly but convenient, operated on the honor system.

Hostellerie du Prieuré de Conques

Upstairs, corridors are lined with antiques and hung with lanterns; the eleven guest rooms are decorated in country-inn styles—all with pretty print wallpapers, room phones, antique beds with modern mattresses, wall-to-wall carpeting, candies on the bedside table, terry-towel robes in the tiled bathrooms. Rooms on the third floor, up in the eaves, cost a few dollars less, but they are, if anything, more romantic than the larger rooms on the second.

But the main attractions here are the leisurely pace, the friendly service—and the lovely, secluded setting.

Name: Hôtellerie du Prieuré de Conques

Owner/Manager: Florimond de Naeyer

Address: 6803 Herbeumont sur Semois

Location: In the Ardennes, about two hours by car from Brussels, near the Luxembourg border; nearest town is Bouillon.

Telephone: (061) 41.14.17

Cables/Telex: (None)

Reps: Relais-Châteaux in U.S.A., Canada and Europe

Credit Cards: American Express

Rooms: 11 rooms

Meals: Breakfast 8–10, lunch at 1, dinner 8–9; Dinner for two approx. $60–$70; tie and jacket preferred; room service for breakfast only; stocked refrigerators on each stairway landing

Entertainment: Taped music in the lounge

Sports: Walking trails on premises; nearby, pool, tennis and canoeing

Sightseeing: Belgium's château country; in Dinant you'll find medieval religious art, a citadel overlooking the city, an interesting grotto, and casinos; also, the Bastogne Museum commemorating the World War II battle

P.S. Closed January 2 to March 15

Hôtellerie Trôs Marets
Malmédy

₩XXX$$$

The curious name is, according to the owner, Old French for "Marshy Holes" (not "Three Acorns," as a well-known guidebook would have you believe), but from the inn's perch on a hillside above the "hole," or valley, and there's no sign of marsh anywhere. Just trees. Whole hillsides of *sapin, epicéa* and *orme*. The scent of a log fire will probably greet you at the door and you'll be welcomed no less warmly, and in fluent English, by Monsieur Jo Blesgen.

Built in the thirties as a private home, turned into an inn in the fifties, Trôs Marets still retains the feel and flavor of a private home, its rooms put together without benefit of an interior decorator. The guest rooms are homey but comfortably proportioned, and each has a small stocked minibar thoughtfully concealed in custom-designed cabinets. Each bathroom has a pair of terry-towel robes. From rooms 6 and 7 on the upper floor you have the best view of the bosky hillsides, and the latter is designated the Honeymoon Suite because it's all fluffy and pink with a pink baldachin above a double bed. Two rooms at the rear, without view, rent for much less than the others. By the time you read this, a new wing will have been completed, one level lower, with five more rooms and suites, of which the top floor apartment with very private roof deck and log-burning fireplace is the nest to bid for (assuming that one or other of you is a millionaire).

But it's as a restaurant that Trôs Marets has attained its present acclaim, including Michelin stars. Chef Marot (formerly of the renowned Moulin de Mougins and Byblos on the French Riviera) delights diners from far and near with *mousseline de truite, pâté de sole en feuilette* and *tournedos a la moëlle "Facon Vilette"*; for guests with the appetites of trenchermen there's also a 5-course menu, offering a wide choice of dishes, at a rate of roughly $10 per course. And therein lies a certain reluctance to enthuse over Tros Marets. It's very pricey, and there's just a hint of commercialism in the stipulation that "room rates are 50 percent more if guests don't eat one meal a day in the dining room."

Nevertheless, gourmets do laud Trôs Marets, the setting *is* calm, the view pretty; the high prices ensure a degree of selectivity in the clientele, and sky-high prices are probably necessary to justify an indoor pool and sauna in a 12-room hostelry. But at upward of $44 a meal, the background music should be an improvement on "Bless Your Indian Hide." (Remember? *Seven Brides for Seven Brothers?*) At these prices you deserve Von Karajan and the Berlin Philharmonic.

Name: Hôtellerie Trôs Marets

Owners/Managers: M. and Mme. Jo Blesgen

Address: Panorama Albert 1 er, 1 Mont, 4890 Malmédy

Location: In the hills, 5 kilometers from Malmédy, near the German border, just over 2 hours from Brussels

Telephone: (080) 77.19.17 and 77.19.18

Cables/Telex: (None)

Reps: Relais-Châteaux in U.S.A., Canada and Europe

Credit Cards: American Express, Diners Club

Rooms: 8 rooms, 2 suites, 2 apartments

Meals: Breakfast 8:30–11, lunch 12–2, dinner 7–9; dinner for two approx. $80–$100; dress informal; room service during dining room hours

Entertainment: Soft but absurd taped music in dining room

Sports: Indoor swimming pool and sauna on premises; tennis and golf 20 minutes away

Sightseeing: The battlefield and museum of Bastogne; the Mardasson Monument, dedicated to the American troops who fought in 1944 in the Battle of the Bulge; the Ardennes forest and rivers and nearby castles; music festivals in the towns of Stavelot and Spa open in July and August; the yearly carnival of Malmédy; the Belgian Grand Prix at Spa in June

P.S. Closed November 15 to December 23 (check exact closing dates)

For brief reports on other hotels in Holland and Belgium turn to the chapter on Added Attractions at the end of this guide.

GERMANY

1. Parkhotel Fürstenhof
2. Kommende Lage
3. Schlosshotel Lembeck
4. Parkhotel Wasserburg Anholt
5. Alte Thorschenke
6. Schloss Zell
7. Waldhotel Jagdschloss Niederwald
8. Hotel Schwan
9. Burghotel auf Schönburg
10. Zum Ritter
11. Schloss Heinsheim
12. Schlosshotel Friedrichsruhe
13. Hotel Markusturm
14. Hotel Eisenhut
15. Parkhotel Adler
16. Clausing's Posthotel
17. Hotel Alte Post and Hotelvilla

Parkhotel Fürstenhof
Celle

WW XXX $$$

Things are seldom what they seem, even in historic Celle. Walk up to the Fürstenhof, and you assume you're entering a baroque 17th-century mansion. Walk inside and you're suddenly whooshed into another time and place.

The first eye-opener you face is the lobby. You expected something rustic, something Germanic? This reception area looks almost Palladian in its elegance and simplicity. The next surprise is your room. It's very spacious and totally modern. Obviously you begin to wonder how all this is happening within the confines of the old mansion. It isn't.

A modern glass wing has been built to form a quadrangle around the back of the old building. You can sit out here for cocktails or coffee, marveling at how two totally mismatched buildings can work together in such perfect harmony.

The Fürstenhof is run with great punctilio by Horst Brühl. It's a pity he can't be cloned. The best of American hotels can't compare to the Fürstenhof in snap and polish. So enjoy this excellent service while you can. You won't see its like at home.

The dining room is another splendid affair, full of fresh flowers, duck presses and hampers of fruit. If your mouth's not watering when you sit down, it will be when you read the menu.

There are no fewer than five dishes made with duck. There's also a meat you've probably never heard of: heather lamb. Delicious! There's Bürgdorf asparagus. Plus veal, kidneys, beef, fowl. And strawberries Romanoff, or fresh mango with lemon ice for dessert.

This is very special eating. And all of it is surprisingly *light*—not the dumplings and red cabbage you expect of German kitchens. The chef here is an exceptionally gifted young man named Ernst Rissmann; he'll probably be out to meet you after dinner.

There's much to do beyond the hotel. Some 500 timbered houses dating from the 16th, 17th and 18th centures are still standing and still inhabited—all minutes away. The castle is close, too—try to catch a performance concert in the castle theater. It's the oldest existing theater in Germany (circa 1670)—and a jewel.

Celle is famed as the birthplace of Sophie Dorothea. Her son became George II of England and Hanover and her daughter became Queen of Prussia and mother of Frederick the Great. (R.E.S.)

Name: Parkhotel Fürstenhof

Manager: Horst Brühl

Address: 3100 Celle, Hannoversche Strasse 55/56

Location: In northern Germany; find Hannover and Braunschweig on your map, Celle forms the apex of a triangle north of these; autobahns from Hamburg, Bremen, Hannover or Braunschweig lead you to route 3 which takes you directly to Celle

Telephone: (05151) 27051

Cables/Telex: (None)

Reps: Relais-Châteaux in U.S., Canada and Europe; also Gast im Scholss Assn. in Europe

Credit Cards: Diners Club

Rooms: 70 doubles, 2 suites

Meals: Breakfast 6–11, lunch 12–2, dinner 6–10:30; dinner for two approx. $25; dress informal to tie and jacket; room service for breakfast and drinks

Entertainment: Color television in attic TV room, in suites, in guest rooms on request. Spontaneous songfests in beer tavern; people-watching in the cavelike bar

Sports: Heated indoor swimming pool, sauna, massage room

Sightseeing: Historic Celle is at your doorstep; have a guide escort you through the Celle Castle with its beautiful theater, visit the Bomann Museum, the French Gardens, the Latin School; ask how you can identify architecture of the 16th, 17th, 18th centuries for yourself

Kommende Lage
Rieste

WW XX $$

You enter this old crusader's hall through a roughhewn archway, just as the Knights of St. John did some 700 years ago. This was their safehold from an imperfect world. It just might work in the same way for you today.

107

Though the ancient building has gone through many permutations over the centuries, it remains a simple, peaceful sort of place.

If you're really energetic, have one of the New Forest ponies saddled up and brought around for a ride (an odd breed, more horse than pony). Or just stroll over to the Hase River to fish for chub, bream, carp or eel. Elegant willow trees and big old lindens offer lots of shade for outdoor reading.

Most of the verve you find at the Kommende Lage will radiate from the personality of comanager Brenda Prüfer. Her star shines at all hours of the day and night.

She and husband Norbert run the place and do very a very fine job of it indeed. How many American hotels have you visited where the managers grow Bibb lettuce, tomatoes, scallions, dill and marjoram for the table? How many would taste-test scores of different coffee blends with the local water before deciding on the absolutely right blend?

Norbert is German, Brenda is English. They worked together as a team at hotels in England and the south of France before bringing their talents to the Kommende Lage.

The cuisine is supervised by Norbert, who quickly admits that much of his culinary inspiration comes from a long stay in Provence. Try the veal kidneys in Chablis, or the *venison à la creme*. Great stuff.

Guest rooms are rather spartan, but very comfortable—and all with beautiful views. If you want a very special room, ask for the bridal suite. It's up and far away from all other guests. You must climb your own private 18-step spiral staircase to reach this secluded abode. It looks as if it had been a belfry at one time. And it's well worth the climb. (R.E.S.)

Name: Kommende Lage

Managers: Norbert and Brenda Prüfer

Address: 4555 Rieste

Location: In northwestern Germany, twenty minutes north of Osnabrück by car; take Neuenkirchen exit on the Hansa Highway (autobahn between Bremerhaven and Ruhr district)

Telephone: (0 54 64) 6 31

Cables/Telex: (None)

Reps: In Europe, Gast im Schloss Assn.

Credit Cards: (None)

Rooms: 30

Meals: Breakfast 7–10, lunch 12–2:30, dinner 6–10; dinner for two approx. $35; dress informal; no room service

Entertainment: Color television in lounge, in guest rooms on request. On occasion, medieval banquets complete with singing minstrels

Sports: Horseback riding (for experienced riders only), fishing in Hase River, walking; nearby, golf and tennis

Sightseeing: Nearby Osnabrück is in the middle of the Tentoburger Forest where the Roman legions were wiped out in A.D. 9—a turning point in European history; cathedral in Osnabrück is 1000 years old

Schlosshotel Lembeck
Dorsten

♙♙♙✗✗💲

Here's an imposing 12th-century castle where the pair of you can go swashbuckling to your heart's content. Just be sure you visit on weekdays; hoi polloi arrives to do its swashbuckling in large numbers every Saturday and Sunday.

There are only six guest rooms in the castle. Big and quite majestic. They look like sets for an Errol Flynn movie. And they're tremendous bargains to boot. At roughly $40 a night, these rooms must be among the juiciest buys you'll find in Northern Europe.

Ceilings are 20 feet high. The oils on the walls are real. Floors are planked and polished to fare-thee-well. Beds are canopied. Furniture is enormous and old (maybe not the period of the castle, but still very, very old). The rooms even have names like Napoli or Moses. They're all terrific, but Jan und Gretel has a slight edge over the others. Ask for it.

Yes, there is some dross along with the gold here. You'll be hard put to find a soul who speaks anything more than kindergarten English. This won't affect you much unless you're searching for some chitchat about the history of the place.

The other drawback is the crowd of gourmands who show up daily for lunch and dinner. Your living quarters are totally private. If you can just time your meals to avoid the mob scene in the very popular restaurant, you've got it made.

Apart from walking in the lovely gardens, there are no diversions here other than eating, drinking, sleeping and you know what. (R.E.S.)   109

Schlosshotel Lembeck

Name: Schlosshotel Lembeck

Manager: Joseph Selting

Address: 4270 Dorsten 12, Lembeck

Location: In western Germany, not far from the Holland border; find Dorsten on your map, inch up northward until you find Lembeck; off east-west route 58 which connects to north-south autobahns E36 and E3

Telephone: Via Wulfen (0 23 69) 7213-7283

Cables/Telex: (None)

Reps: None in U.S. and Canada; in Europe, Gast im Schloss Assn.

Credit Cards: American Express, Diners Club, Master Charge/Eurocard

Rooms: 6 rooms

Meals: Breakfast 7–10:30, lunch 12–2:30, dinner 6:30–9:30; dinner for two approx. $35; dress informal; no room service

Entertainment: (None)

Sports: Walking through the flower gardens

Sightseeing: (None)

P.S. Be sure to bring along your Say-It-in-German phrasebook; precious little English is spoken here

Parkhotel Wasserburg Anholt
Isselburg

ẄẄX̌X̌$$

Come spin yourself a romantic dream or two at this lovely little castle. It has most of the makings: swans, seclusion, good food and drink, beautiful flower gardens and wooded walks. There's even a small museum.

What it hasn't got is a period interior. The Wasserburg Anholt had to be gutted after World War II. That's when the decorators got hold of it and transmuted the insides into a second-class steamer cabin on a North Sea ferry. Miraculously, the castle has survived these improvements.

You quickly overlook the gaucheries because the Wasserburg Anholt has so much else going for it. Such as food, wonderful food. The manager of the establishment, Heinz Brune, just happens to be the chef de cuisine as well. He runs a tight ship, and he sets a lavish table.

Be guided by Chef Brune's suggestions for dinner. The menu changes every two days—but he often whips up a specialty that isn't on the menu. Snap at the *salmon mousse* if he offers some. He won't reveal what herbs are in the marvelous sauce, but he admits that its piquant bite comes from using yogurt as a liaison.

His veal dishes are very light, very French. And the desserts are shamelessly fattening. If strawberries are in season, go the whole hog and have them in a thick Bavarian cream. You only live once.

You can add fuel to your amatory fires by asking for Room 37, a big favorite with honeymooners. This is a corner room with a little watchtower turret you can climb into when you want to commune with the stars or with your muses. (Be warned there's a stork's nest on top of the tower. You can take this to be a good omen or a terrible one, as you wish.)

If you can't bear to see the common folk poking about the gardens of your private Camelot, don't come on Saturdays or Sundays. The park grounds and the castle museum at Wasserburg Anholt are open to the public; weekends tend to be crowded. (R.E.S.)

Name: Parkhotel Wasserburg Anholt

Owner: Fürst Zu Salm-Salm

Manager: Heinz Brune

Address: 4294 Isselburg

Location: In western Germany, almost sitting on the Dutch border; find

111

Bocholt on your map, trace your way west to Isselburg; very close to autobahn E36

Telephone: (02874) 2044

Cables/Telex: (None)

Reps: In Europe, Gast im Schloss Assn.

Credit Cards: American Express, Diners Club, Master Charge/Eurocard

Rooms: 24 doubles, 1 suite

Meals: Breakfast 7–10:30, lunch 12–2:30, dinner 6:30–9:30; dinner for two approx. $35; dress informal; room service for breakfast and drinks

Entertainment: Color television in lounge

Sports: Strolling through formal gardens; nearby, 9 hole golf course

Sightseeing: Museum and art gallery on the premises

Alte Thorschenke
Cochem

W X $ $

Lots of hotels claim to be local landmarks. This one proves its point with a front wall that actually adjoins one of the ancient town gates. Step behind that typically tilty, flower-festooned, half-timbered outside wall, and you'll be greeted in the small lobby by a tall suit of armor, a mélange of antiques and a remarkable steep, carved, curved staircase whose dark burnished wood dates back to the inn's beginnings in 1332. No further doubt about it—this inn is *historic*.

And in spite of a busy location in the heart of one of the prettiest (hence most popular) of the castle-topped villages bordering the steep banks of the Mosel River, the hotel has managed to hold on to its charm. Wind your way up the old staircase, and you may find yourself sleeping beneath a carved wooden canopy or in a colorful bed with hand-painted head- and footboards. The furnishings vary, but all of the rooms have pretty printed wallpapers with coordinated draperies, handsome tall chiffoniers for your clothes and a comfortable sitting area. You may even get the corner room where Napoleon once spent the night. Just be sure to request a room in the old wing, since modernism is beginning to make its standardized way into some of the most recently renovated parts of the hotel. The renovation does

112

mean an elevator, however, if you're not keen on climbing those stairs.

As you might expect here in the heart of Mosel wine country, the wine list is prodigious, and you'll note a number of culinary awards sharing space with the hunting trophies on the dining-room wall. The schnitzel here is as pink and tender as you'll find anywhere, and the game is excellent. The room itself might be called "country formal"—plaid drapes, old-fashioned lamps and a high-timbered ceiling.

When weather permits, you can move out of doors to the corner terrace and watch the world go by as you dine. Have your after-dinner drink at one of the nearby cafés along the riverfront, then wend your way back hand-in-hand through the crooked streets to wind up a historic night together. (E.B.)

Name: Alte Thorschenke

Owner: H. Trimborn

Manager: G. Schultz

Address: Bruckenstrasse, D559, Cochem

Location: Along the banks of the Mosel River approximately 40 miles south of Koblenz on route 49; boat cruises operate south from Koblenz or heading north from Trier or Bernkastel from mid-May to mid-October

Telephone: (02651) 7059

Cables/Telex: (None)

Reps: (None)

Credit Cards: American Express, Diners Club, Visa, Master Charge/ Eurocard

Rooms: 52 rooms

Meals: Breakfast 7–10:30, lunch 12–3, dinner 6–10; dinner for two approx. $38; tie and jacket preferred; room service for breakfast 7–12, drinks anytime; outdoor terrace

Entertainment: (None)

Sports: (None)

Sightseeing: Cochem Burg (the old castle in the hills above town, rebuilt in 14th-century style and richly furnished; open Easter to end of October); the Mosel Valley, miles of picturesque driving along the river canyoned between steep vineyards. Within an hour's drive are Koblenz, with its Old Town and historic churches, and Trier, "capital" of Roman antiquities in

Germany (see the Porta Nigra gate, imperial baths, cathedrals, the basilica and gardens of Constantine the Great, the Rhineland Museum).

P.S. Some small tour groups

Schloss Zell
Zell

♨ ✗ $ $

Schloss Zell is something of a surprise. After all, who'd expect to find a small castle tucked away behind a vine-covered garden right on a main street of town?

Of course, there wasn't much around to block the view when the Archbishop of Trier decided to build himself a summer place here back in 1490. The town of Zell has grown up, but the castle is much as it always was, turrets and all, one of the oldest intact buildings in the Mosel area. It was acquired and turned into a hotel 30 years ago by Herr Jakob Bohn, an elderly gentleman whose love of preservation is surpassed only by his yen for acquiring antiques. So when you enter the parlor, with its beams and old fireplace and tall cut-velvet chairs, you'll be facing a high-backed settee of gilt and leather initialed "J"—a gift from Napoleon to his empress, Josephine. And when you climb the stairs, you'll find a minimuseum of German history on the walls in Herr Bohn's collection of antique metal fireplace plates depicting scenes from the ages—Bible scenes, medieval times, the Renaissance and the Reformation. (There's also a collection of slate fossils interspersed with the plates, in case you happen to be a secret fossilizer.)

If you become friendly with your host, he may also invite you into the family chambers to see his pewter collection, a 400-year-old carving of Oberon, protector of the vineyards, and the lovely old gilt altar that belonged to the archbishop.

As you might expect, the ten bedrooms here are also Old World and antique-filled. Ask for room 1 if you want the round turret room once occupied by one of the Emperors Maximilian. Room 7, the Little Tower, is just that—a small turret separated from the main building by a balcony. It's flowery white chintz interior often serves as a romantic bridal suite.

Steep vineyards still climb the hill behind the castle, and you can sample some of the local crop under a vine-covered arbor in the front garden. The two dining rooms off the parlor are on the dark and formal side

114

but brightened with flowers and plants and shiny brass chandeliers.

It may not be the setting you expected for a castle, but it's a fine, history-laden home base for exploring the beautiful Mosel Valley. (E.B.)

Name: Schloss Zell

Owner/Manager: Jakob Bohn

Address: Hotel Schloss Zell, Zell

Location: On the banks of the Mosel approximately halfway between Koblenz and Trier, on route 53

Telephone: (06542) 4084

Cables/Telex: (None)

Reps: (None)

Credit Cards: (None)

Rooms: 10 rooms

Meals: Breakfast 8–10, lunch 12–2, dinner 6–10; dinner for two approx. $15; informal; no room service; outdoor terrace for drinks

Entertainment: (None)

Sports: (None)

Sightseeing: (See Alte Thorschenke Hotel in the Mosel Valley)

P.S. This is the home of the original Zeller Schwartze Katz (Zell Black Cat) wines. Ask for a sample from the castle's own vineyards.

Waldhotel Jagdschloss Niederwald
Assmannshausen

The front yard is a nature preserve, the back is rolling lawns looking down on a nonstop panorama of the Rhine Valley. The Duke of Nassau certainly knew what he was doing when he built his hunting lodge in the woodlands high above the river back in the 1700s. When the gracious cream-colored structure with its black shutters and roof burned in 1921, the German

115

government decided it was too pleasant a place to lose so the stately manor house was rebuilt line for line outside, while the inside was redone, making for a surprisingly modern interior in a traditional setting. In recent years, it's been leased out and run as a hotel, a quiet spot conveniently located just above Rudesheim, the crowded wine-tasting and boat-tour center of the Rhine.

The furnishings here are functional modern, comfortable but nothing memorable. But the setting is something else. You could spend hours gazing at the landscape from the glassed-in "winter garden" that stretches the length of the hotel. Stroll outdoors and watch the baby deer on the grounds. Have lunch on the terrace. Take the chair lift up to the sky-high Niederwald monument or down to the colorful wine village of Assmannshausen. Just two miles down the road in Rudesheim you can sign on for a day-cruise up the Rhine or visit the Drosselgasse, a street of Weinstuben and merrymaking, day and night.

When you've had enough of the music and sampled enough wine, you can return to your serene and silent hilltop hideaway.

Be forewarned—all that space and beauty attracts business conferences. But that really just means you have the grounds to yourself all day. And after dinner, who cares who's down in the dining room? (E.B.)

Name: Waldhotel Jagdschloss Niederwald

Owner/Manager: Egon Dirschinger

Address: Auf dem Niederwald, 6220 Rudesheim

Location: In the tiny village of Assmannshausen, just outside Rudesheim on route 42 along the right bank of the Rhine

Telephone: (06722) 2515, 2367

Cable: Jagdschloss Rudesheim

Telex: 42152

Reps: (None)

Credit Cards: (None)

Rooms: 54 rooms, 1 suite

Meals: Breakfast 7–10, lunch 11:30–2:30, dinner 6:30–9:30; dinner for two approx. $50; informal; no room service; outdoor terrace in season

Entertainment: (None)

Sports: Nothing other than hiking in the nearby countryside

116 **Sightseeing:** Niederwald Monument, Germania statue commemorating

reestablishment of the German empire in 1871, reached by auto or by cable car from Assmannshausen, offers beautiful panorama of the Rhine Valley. For Rudesheim diversions, see Hotel Schwan

P.S. Expect small business groups and tours. Pool and steam baths due to be added in 1980. Hotel is closed December through March.

Hotel Schwan
Östrich/ Winkel on the Rhine

WXX$$

Prop up the pillows and you can set up your own watch on the Rhine. The Hotel Schwan, a picture-postcard inn whose tile-roofed, timbered, vine-covered facade once inspired Goethe to poetry, has been around since 1628, when it was a stage post on the Rhine road. For 300 years it has been run proudly by the Winkel family, and the sixth generation is presently enrolled in hotel school in Lausanne. It remains a nice spot for river gazing, even though the road in front is a lot busier than when the carriages used to roll by. The rooms are pleasant, beds usually tucked into curtained alcoves, leaving an airy separate sitting area. There's a very special round tower room done up in whites and florals, with *seven* windows looking out on the view.

The owners grow their own wine here, shoot their own game, catch their own trout and serve it all in dignified flower-filled dining rooms—or better yet, on a big outdoor terrace looking out to the river.

Altogether, there's much to recommend the Schwan, but only with a word of caution. With a location just minutes from tourist-filled Rudesheim, where Rhine cruises and wine-tastings proliferate, the Schwan has taken to specializing in two-day tours of the area—some wine sampling in their own cellars, a boat ride up the river, a night on the town—all very pleasant, but likely to make for crowds in the summer. And that road can get pretty noisy in season, too. You're a lot more likely to wax poetic about the Schwan if you can visit during spring or fall. (E.B)

Name: Hotel Schwan

Owner/Managers: Familie Winkel-Wenckstern

Address: 6227 Oestrich/ Winkel

117

Location: On the right bank of the Rhine, approx. five miles east of Rudesheim on route 42

Telephone: (06723) 3001

Cable: SchwanHotel

Telex: 42146

Reps: (None)

Credit Cards: American Express, Diners Club, Visa

Rooms: 55 rooms, 3 suites

Meals: Breakfast 7–10, lunch 12–2, dinner 6–10; dinner for two approx. $30; tie and jacket requested; room service for breakfast; outdoor terrace overlooking the Rhine for summer dining and drinks

Entertainment: Occasional wine tastings

Sports: (None)

Sightseeing: In Rudesheim, Rhine cruises, wine tastings and entertainment on the Drosselgasse, Bromserberg wine museum; scenic drives along the Rhine, lots of old castles to explore between Rudesheim-Bingen and Koblenz (most scenic route is the Rhinegoldstrasse off route 9 on the left bank; watch for signposts showing a castle and glass of wine; most spectacular section is between St. Goar and Bacharach)

P.S. *Lots* of tours during the summer; closed December and January

Burghotel auf Schönburg
Oberwesel on the Rhine

♛♛♛✗✗$$

This is *it* —the ultimate castle. A million miles above the river—towers and ramparts, drawbridge and arches, the whole thing.

Schönburg means "beautiful fortress" and that's just what it was 1000 years ago when it was built as a fortress towering over the Rhine. A Roman stronghold, it was later occupied by the Franks, housed the beloved Barbarossa, and was part of centuries of European history until the whole place went up in flames, plundered by the French in the so-called Orleans or Reunion Wars of 1689. For 200 years it lay in ruins until along came Major

118

J. J. Oakley Rhinelander, a New York banker who, as his name suggests, was a descendant of a local family. The major bought the place, and every year from 1885 to 1920 he would arrive by ship for a two-month stay to oversee the castle's restoration, greeted by gun salutes, flying flags and a welcoming party led by the mayor. Two million gold marks later, the job was done, right down to the lovely chapel, where many local couples come today to be married.

In 1951 a son of the major sold the castle back to the town. One portion was turned into what must be the world's most atmospheric youth hostel. Then 22 years ago another wing, totally separate, was converted into a small hotel by Hans Huttl, a local vineyard owner who's done the place over with style and a sense of romance. Follow the passages, and you'll find that each chamber has a name and personality of its own. Perhaps you'd like to sleep in Prinzesszimmer in a curtained Himmelbett, an old four-poster bed. The rooms are shaped by the beams and walls of the old castle, furnished with antiques, carved chests and chairs, lanterns, even an occasional old spinning wheel. Outside your leaded window there's an eagle's-eye view of the Rhine at one of its steepest and most spectacular points near the famous Lorelei rock.

You can enjoy the same spectacular view in the outdoor restaurant, a kind of turret where luncheons and snacks are served. In the intimate dining room, you'll eat by candlelight, seated in carved wooden chairs, admiring the weapons, ancient stove plates and pewter pieces on the walls while you wait for one of the house specialties, whiskey steak or pepper steak. Consult Herr Huttl about the wine list—he's an expert. Incidentally, he's also a collector, and if you care to bring along a bottle of your best local dry white wine, he'll trade for two of his favorite Rhine varieties.

Enjoy your dinner and your wine, then wind your way back down the passage to that cushy curtained bed. You'll even find a note from your host on the pillow wishing you a pleasant night. Remember—only 10 rooms here, and they fill up far in advance, so you'll have to write early to reserve a place at the Schönburg. It's worth it. It isn't every night you can play prince and princess in a real live castle. (E.B.)

Name: Burghotel auf Schönburg

Owner/Manager: Hans Huttl

Address: 6532 Oberwesel/Rhein

Location: High above the village overlooking the Rhine—follow signs in town (Oberwesel is on the left bank of the river on route 9).

Telephone: (06744) 8198

Cables/Telex: (None)

Reps: (None)

Credit Cards: (None)

Rooms: 10 rooms

Meals: Breakfast 7–10, lunch 12–2, dinner 6–9, dinner for two approx. $60; dress informal; no room service, snacks served from noon to 10 P.M.; outdoor terrace dining in season

Entertainment: (None)

Sports: (None)

Sightseeing: Church of Our Lady *(Liebfrauenkirche),* Gothic structure with interesting altarpieces; Burg Schönburg, a total of three castles (one containing the hotel) protected by a wall, with main terrace commanding the Rhine, the village and the miles of river scenery (for Rhine cruises and drives, see Hotel Schwan)

P.S. Remember—early reservations are a necessity. Closed December through February

Zum Ritter
Heidelberg

W ✗✗ $$

It's right there on the official old city walking tour: "Hotel Ritter, built in 1592 by the French cloth merchant Charles Belier, a Huguenot refugee. This was the only patrician dwelling to survive the city's destruction in 1693. It took its present name from the knight St. George whose figure crowns the Renaissance facade."

Chances are you're going to want to see Heidelberg, in spite of all those tour coaches with the same idea in mind, and the Ritter, with its mellowed stone, carved and curlicued facade, is a choice home base here for a lot of reasons, beginning with all that history. The central location, too, on the *Hauptstrasse,* is a big plus in a city that's meant for exploring on foot—and it also means that you can get out early before the crowds come, retreat for a beer or lunch or whatever when the crunch gets to you, then return later in the afternoon for a second look after the buses have gone home. It's only a couple of blocks to see the *Glockenspiel* when it chimes at six and the pedestrian shopping section starts a few feet from the hotel door.

Once inside you'll find a peaceful escape from the crowds. You may wonder about the lack of a lobby, but it proves to be an advantage since the sitting areas are placed on each upstairs floor, away from the public. On the first floor, for example, you can relax in baronial chairs around a knight-size table, surrounded by choice antiques including a charming old cradle.

Upstairs there's an old fireplace of rust-color stone, beamed ceilings and comfortable rustic-style chairs and a sofa on an oriental rug.

The hallways are unusually pleasant because all the bedroom doors are painted in scroll and flower designs. The rooms are relatively simple, but with fresh hand-painted furniture in a country style reminiscent of American Pennsylvania-Dutch motifs.

The dining room on the main floor looks just like old Heidelberg should look—vaulted ceilings, old swords, arched leaded windows. The *Ritterstube* (Knight's Room) is especially cozy with beams, dark furniture and a stone carving of a knight riding to battle above an ornate stone fireplace. Order the knight's plate, and it will be served on an old pewter platter. Breast of chicken in wine sauce served with asparagus tips and mushrooms from the nearby woods is another Ritter treat.

For another kind of old Heidelberg atmosphere, step next door to the *Bierstube.* You'll have a hard time finding anyone resembling the Student Prince, but there's no shortage of students and their good spirits, their *Gemütlichkeit,* are contagious. (E.B.)

Name: Hotel Zum Ritter

Owners/Managers: Margarete and Georg Kuchelmeister

Address: Hauptstrasse 178, 6900 Heidelberg 1

Location: Take Heidelberg exit off E4 or route 27 along the Neckar River. Hauptstrasse, the main street of the old city, bans all traffic during the day; park in one of the garages on the edge of town.

Telephone: (06221) 24272, 20203

Cables: Rith D

Telex: 46-1506

Reps: (None)

Credit Cards: American Express, Diners Club, Visa

Rooms: 35 rooms, 2 suites

Meals: Breakfast 7–10, lunch 12–3, dinner 6–10, dinner for two anywhere $25–$60; dress informal; room service for breakfast only

Entertainment: (None)

Sports: (None)

Sightseeing: All the sights of the beautiful old university town: grocers' stalls on the Marktplatz, Church of the Holy Spirit, Knights' Mansion, University Library, Electoral Palatinate Museum, Students' Gaol, convivial beer halls; famous castle and gardens towering above the town, Philosopher's Way across the river for exceptional views (for castles along the Neckar, see Schloss Heinsheim)

Schloss Heinsheim
Bad Rappenau

W X X $$

They come from miles around to be married in the little round chapel on the grounds here—and that tells you a lot about the atmosphere of the Heinsheim.

Tucked away in this tiny village is a wealthy family's gracious country estate. It was built in the 1730s and is still in the same family, but they've turned it into a hotel so that you can enjoy the place along with them.

The one-time carriage house now boasts outdoor tables and chairs on a gravel patterned patio under a shaded arcade. It has been modernized inside, has a cozy rustic reception room centered around a white open-hearth fireplace and a variety of handsome dining rooms.

But it's the old house that has the real charm, its steep roof dotted with chimneys, its little gable windows with lots of shutters, and the pots of plants all around the semicircular stone stairs and geraniums spilling off the tiny second-floor balcony. The rooms here are spacious with chandeliers and big mirrors, floor-to-ceiling drapes and cozy down quilts on the beds, and they all come equipped with minibars. You can relax in country elegance in the grand sitting room on the main floor. Beyond the door a manicured lawn runs down to a small swimming pool. Back near the main house is the chapel, its simple white interior the kind that inspires romance.

The menu at the Heinsheim runs on for pages. Like so many places in the countryside, the specialties are fresh-caught game and fish, and everything is prepared with care.

The Schloss Heinsheim is located just a few minutes off the autobahn right on the Neckar River, and the road along the river is dotted with castles all the way to Heidelberg. It's an ideal detour for a pleasant night in the country, followed by a day of castle hopping on your way to the old city. (E.B.)

Name: Hotel Schloss Heinsheim

Owners/Managers: Philipp and Monica von Racknitz

Address: 6927 Bad Rappenau 4, Heinsheim

Location: Take Bad Rappenau exit off E 12, continue north to Heinsheim; hotel is on town's main street. From Heidelberg, follow route 37 to 27 along the Neckar River to Heinsheim

Telephone: (97264) 1045, 1046

Cables/Telex: (None)

Reps: (None)

Credit Cards: (None)

Rooms: 40 rooms

Meals: Breakfast 7–10, lunch 12–2:30, dinner 6–9:45; dinner for two approx. $30; dress informal; no room service; outdoor terrace

Entertainment: (None)

Sports: Small outdoor swimming pool

Sightseeing: Hornberg, Hirschhorn and Dilsberg castles on route 27 along the Neckar toward Heidelberg (for Heidelberg itself, see Hotel Zum Ritter

P.S. Very little English spoken here

Schlosshotel Friedrichsruhe
Friedrichsruhe

₩₩XXX$$

The first thing you notice are the birds, twittering away fortissimo, calling your attention to the glorious quiet of the place.

You may wonder a bit about that name "schloss" when you arrive at   123 the gatehouse to register, since the timbered building with its modern additions doesn't look much like anyone's notion of a castle. But wait. Walk around the corner, and there it is. Not your towers-and-turrets type of castle, but something that might be at home in French château country— stark white walls, gabled red roof, elaborate stone carving high over the columned doorway, formally shaped potted trees along the front and a formal garden for a front yard.

Friedrichsruhe was a summer residence built for Prince Johann Friedrich back in 1712, which accounts for its parks and woods setting. In 1969 it was turned into a full resort, a place that's going to tempt you to settle in for a while. It's located about midway between Rothenburg and Heidelberg, so it's possible to combine day trips to the cities with relaxing on the green lawns, swimming indoors or out, playing a set of tennis or a round of golf, then reviving your weary muscles in the sauna.

And as if that weren't enough incentive to stay around, the hotel is widely noted for its fine cuisine. Only the freshest foods will do for fussy manager Lothar Eiermann: every dish is lovingly cooked to order by a kitchen staff of 18, and Eiermann deliberately restricts the number of groups he will accept at the dining room so that the quality of the food won't suffer. Game and fresh-caught trout are specialties, but if you happen to fancy calves liver, wait until you taste what they do with it here.

Even breakfast is a treat, with big-stemmed goblets of fresh orange juice, a spread of cold meats and cheeses, lots of fresh-baked rolls and soft German pretzels, homemade jellies served in brightly painted pottery crocks. It's all served in a charming "winter garden," all windows to let the outdoor gardens and lawns right in. There's a big terrace, too, for outdoor dining when the weather is good.

Where to sleep is the dilemma here. The new wing off the old carriage house has been done in light rustic woods; they're modern, attractive and many have balconies and terraces looking out on the lovely grounds. But how can you pass up that castle, with the great old tear-drop chandelier, the curved tufted furniture, gilt mirrors and columns in the downstairs sitting room, the aristocratic rooms upstairs where you might be sleeping under a carved ceiling and a crystal chandelier in a handsome antique bed?

Which way is better, rustic or romantic? Maybe you'll just have to ask the management to let you sample each. (E.B.)

Name: Schlosshotel Friedrichsruhe

Owner: Fürst Kraft zu Hohenlohe-Öhringen

Manager: Lother Eiermann

Address: 7111 Friedrichsruhe

Location: About midway between Rothenburg and Heidelberg. Take Öhringen exit off Autobahn E12, continue past Öhringen to Friedrichsruhe.

Telephone: (07941) 7078

Cable: (None)

Telex: 07-4498

Reps: Relais-Châteaux in U.S., Canada and Europe

Credit Cards: American Express, Diners Club, Master Charge/Eurocard

Rooms: 48 rooms, 6 suites, 2 villas

Meals: Breakfast 6–12, lunch 12–2:30, dinner 6–10; dinner for two approx. $50; tie and jacket optional though dining room is rather formal; room service for drinks only; outdoor terrace for dining in season

Entertainment: TV in some rooms: TV room for guests

Sports: Tennis, indoor and outdoor swimming, golf (9 holes), hiking, sauna

Sightseeing: About an hour's drive to Rothenburg (see Hotel Eisenhut) or Heidelberg (see Hotel Zum Ritter)

P.S. Some groups, but held to a minimum. Dining room slated for redecorating in 1980

Hotel Markusturm
Rothenburg

WX$$

It's not as lavish as its more prestigious neighbor, the Eisenhut, but the Markusturm has its own history to boast about. The old facade was constructed out of the city's first fortified walls back in 1264, and though there's been a lot of modernizing, the dark old wooden stairway and antique furnishings, the art displayed on the walls, do maintain a measure of medieval charm.

The hotel has stretched to encompass two neighboring townhouses. It has a new modern kitchen area, an enclosed garden and a spacious sauna for guests. There's a TV room downstairs, and free parking (no small matter in crowded Rothenburg).

Most of the bedrooms are traditional in style, with printed papers and matching formal window arrangements. If you want something a bit special (and specially priced), ask for one of the four "heaven beds," beautiful old carved bedsteads with head and footboards that extend up into a scalloped wooden canopy.

Meals are served in an informal dining room with attractive hanging lamps over each table or in a paneled room done up in velvets with lots of greenery. There's also a *Weinstube,* all red leather.

All in all, it's a pleasant place, in keeping with its surroundings—and good value for the money. (E.B.)

Name: Hotel Markusturm

Owner/Manager: Marianne Berger

Address: Rodergasse 1, 8803 Rothenburg

Location: 62 miles from Wurzburg on route 25, the "Romantic Road", 100 miles east of Frankfurt

Telephone: (09861) 2370

Cable/Telex: (None)

Reps: (None)

Credit Cards: American Express

Rooms: 30 rooms

Meals: Breakfast 7–10, lunch 11:30–2, dinner 6–9; dinner for two approx. $22.50; informal; no room service

Entertainment: Taped music in dining room, TV room, sauna

Sports: (None)

Sightseeing: (See Hotel Eisenhut)

P.S. Closed January through March

126

Hotel Eisenhut
Rothenburg

WWWXXX$$

The entry is spectacular—soaring dark paneled ceilings, baronial chairs, stone pillars, gilded statues and a grand stairway. And that's only the start of what's in store.

Everything here seems slightly larger than life. The Eisenhut was part of the history of Germany's best-preserved medieval walled city, remains very much a part of the local atmosphere today, yet it's a refuge from Rothenburg's crowded cobblestone streets, with its terraces and gardens turned to the peaceful hills beyond.

Located on the Herrengasse, the old city's best address, the Eisenhut is actually composed of three former patrician homes joined together into a rambling whole, plus a recently acquired fourth house just across the way. The oldest of the buildings, the one now housing that impressive entry, was once a small 12th-century chapel, and you can still see one of the old gothic iron doors to the left of the reception desk. In time it became the home of one of the town's leading families, then in 1876 passed on to Georg Eisenhut, who turned it into a small inn where he sold the wines he cultivated in the Tauber valley. As Rothenburg's charms became more widely known, more visitors came and the hotel prospered and grew. Today it is owned by Mrs. Georg Pirner, granddaughter of the founder, and her touch is conspicuous throughout the hotel, in the beautifully planted garden and in the elaborate decor of the rooms.

Since in the days gone by the large family bedrooms faced the street and the servants used to be relegated to the back of the house, the front rooms here are enormous, really almost suites, with large sitting areas. To compensate, however, the rear rooms have big picture windows and, in some cases, balconies looking out at the surrounding valley. It's a difficult choice, but wherever you face, you can be assured of unusually colorful surroundings personally chosen by Mrs. Pirner. No two of the 85 rooms are remotely alike—or like rooms you've seen anywhere else. "Opulent" is an apt word. You may find yourself in a tailored setting, all red and blue plaids. Or in soft tones of violet with lace and ribbons and butterflies all around. Or surrounded by dramatic dark greens and maroons. Or in a mirrored setting of gold and white and crimson. If you want something really different, there's the "stork's nest"—a duplex with a winding stairway.

Back downstairs, you'll find an appropriately grand sitting room chock full of oversize antiques. Take a look at the glass-topped table in the corner, and you'll see signatures of some of the hotel's former guests, including Sir

Winston Churchill and the former Shah of Iran. Above the table along the wall is a collection of sketches of the city, donated by the large local artist's colony out of affection for the old hotel.

Breakfast is served in a former courtyard two stories high, now enclosed but still with its old wooden columns and balustrades. The large paneled dining room is done in mauves and florals, and it opens to a spacious terrace where you can dine on a nice day to the peaceful accompaniment of a trickling fountain in the garden below. Take the stairs down to the garden and you can relax on an old-fashioned glider-swing, a million miles away in feeling from the town that's really just outside the door.

Take in the marvelous old streets and buildings of Rothenburg, visit the irresistible wooden toy store across the street, then come back home to the Eisenhut to get away from it all in medieval luxury. (E.B.)

Name: Hotel Eisenhut

Owner: Frau Georg Pirner

Manager: K. L. Prusse

Address: Herrengasse 3–7, D-8803, Rothenburg

Location: 62 miles from Wurzburg on route 25, the Romantic Road; 100 miles from Frankfurt

Telephone: (09861) 2041

Cable: eisenhuthotel

Telex: 61367

Reps: Steigenberger Reservation Service and Relais-Châteaux in U.S., Canada and Europe

Credit Cards: American Express, Diners Club, Visa

Rooms: 85 rooms, 2 suites

Meals: Breakfast, 7–11, lunch 12–2:30, dinner 6:30–9:30; dinner for two approx. $40; tie and jacket preferred; room service available for all meals, outdoor dining in season

Entertainment: TV in a few rooms, music with dinner

Sports: (None)

Sightseeing: The medieval walled city of Rothenburg is steeped in the 16th century—see the Town Hall, Baumeisterhaus, Burggarten, St. James, 128 (St. Jakob Kirche) with its 1504 Riemenschneider altarpiece, the Hospital, the Ramparts, St. Wolfgang's and the Franciscan church, and the town museum in a former Dominican convent. Rothenburg is on the Romantic Road, 207 miles of medieval towns and rolling pastoral scenery from Wurzburg to Fussen, where you can connect with the German Alpine Road (Alpenstrasse).

Parkhotel Adler
Hinterzarten

WWWWXXXX$$$

It's been called "an aristocratic of the continent," and "one of the beauty queens of Germany." When you see the Parkhotel Adler, you'll understand why it inspires superlatives.

Everything here says "class": the filigree lamppost out front, the welcoming stone basket planters brimming over with flowers at the door, the graceful yellow building with its distinctive sloped roofline and curving balconies, the spacious double salon inside that extends to a semicircular windowed wall looking out at the grounds. Even the town of Hinterzarten is special, with its domed baroque church and picturesque homes. It would be a delightful place to stay no matter where it was located, but as luck would have it, the Adler is in the heart of that glorious area known as the Black Forest, and it is that serene mountain and woodland setting that truly sets it apart.

In a country full of historic inns, this one stands out. Once known as the Adler royal domain, some 198 acres of woods and meadows with a rural tavern, it is mentioned in documents as far back as the 12th century. (Hinterzarten was part of Austria then and until the 1870s, which accounts for the Austrian heraldic double-eagle on the inn sign.)

Marie Antoinette stopped here on her journey from Vienna to Paris to marry the Dauphin of France in 1770—in fact, the road through the Hollental Valley was first built for her journey. Marie Louise, Empress of France, also stayed over on her way back to Vienna after the downfall of her husband Napoleon.

The 300-year-old rustic Black Forest house where they slept still stands, separated from the main house by a flower-filled outdoor terrace. But today the hotel has grown into a deluxe resort with every kind of facility: an enormous all-weather, glass-enclosed swimming pool; a fitness

129

center for exercise, baths and massage; indoor and outdoor tennis; seven acres of park surrounded by 72 acres of forest for walking; a wild deer park; an outdoor exercise course; a bowling green; even a private shopping center right on the premises. And that's just for warm weather. In the winter there are ski lifts, a skating rink, curling, sleigh rides and a toboggan run.

Some things haven't changed, however. The Riesterer family is still in charge, as it has been for the past fourteen generations, and they still make sure that their guests are treated royally. Your room will be large and furnished in traditional style—velvet drapes, antiques, curved sofas. There's a big walk-in closet for your things, a soft terry robe and bubble bath waiting for you next to the tub in the bathroom. The minibar enclosed in a handsome wood cabinet not only contains the usual drinks and snacks but also *fresh* orange juice, white grape juice, champagne and boxes of salted almonds.

If you choose the expensive new wing, you'll be enjoying the most luxurious lodgings imaginable—huge quarters in restful brown and rose tones with wraparound terraces big enough to entertain your 50 best friends, an entire wall of closets, and two bathrooms per room so that no one need ever be inconvenienced for a moment. There's even a private wall safe for your jewels.

At dinner time you can choose from no less than six dining rooms. They're actually all one complex, but each has been done in a totally different style, so that one night you can have stucco walls and beams and a forest-green color scheme, the next you can move into a low-ceilinged soft blue room next door where there are lace curtains, red carnations on the tables, little pleated lamp shades and little pots of flowers in front of the leaded windows. The main dining room is large and formal; it adjoins the bar and dance floor where there's live music every night, tea dancing on the weekends.

As for the food, let's just point out that the hotel has won awards from four separate French culinary societies, as well as being a member of the Gastronomische Akademie Deutschlands.

All of the lodgings and restaurants, the pool and fitness center are connected by an underground passageway, so you need never worry about the weather. And there's a pleasant plaid TV room downstairs, if you want to catch up with the outside world.

But why would you want to bother about reality when you've found the Adler? In spite of all those facilities, you're never overwhelmed here; and while there's everything to do, it's equally pleasant to do nothing, just sit back and get some sun, admire the extraordinary scenery and the stylishly dressed guests (queens, diplomats, sportsmen—everyone who is *anyone* has been here). Or take a walk around the grounds and into the woods with the lederhosened Germans.

Hinterzarten is a spa, by the way, where some people come to ease their

Parkhotel Adler

chronic complaints by taking the waters and breathing the healthy mountain air. The only thing *you're* likely to complain about here is leaving. (E.B.)

Name: Parkhotel Adler

Owner/Manager: Helmut Riesterer

Address: Adlerweg, D 7824 Hinterzarten

Location: Take Freiburg exit off E4, follow signs to Titisee for 17 miles to Hinterzarten (nearest airport, *Zurich*, 60 miles)

Telephone: (07652) 711, 717

Cables: Adlerhotel

Telex: 07-72692

Reps: Relais-Châteaux in U.S., Canada and Europe

Credit Cards: American Express, Diners Club, Visa

Rooms: 90 rooms, 19 suites

Meals: Breakfast 7–11, lunch 12–2:30, dinner 7–9:30; dinner for two approx. $30; jacket suggested for dinner; room service 24 hours; outdoor dining in season

Entertainment: Dinner music and dancing nightly, tea dancing on weekends, occasional shows, TV lounge

Sports: Heated indoor pool, sauna, solarium, masseur, bowling, tennis, boccie, fitness trail, hiking paths, wild deer park, fishing, stables, gymnasium and exercise room; in winter, skiing, ice skating, curling, sleigh rides, tobogganing, golf nearby

Sightseeing: St. Peter Baroque Church, drives into the forest, Lake Titisee, Lake Schluchsee, Freiburg (Cathedral, Augustine Museum, Swabian Gate)

P.S. Some conferences, but you probably won't know it

Clausing's Posthotel
Garmisch

♛♛✗✗$$

Enough pictures have been taken of the Zugspitze through the round post-horn sign of Clausing's Posthotel to keep Kodak stock soaring for years.

If you haven't been to the German Alps yet, you should know that the Zugspitze is the highest and most imposing point, and it towers over the town of Garmisch like an ever-present, awe-inspiring guardian. Almost as much of a landmark is the Posthotel, which has been an inn in the center of town since 1624. The pink facade with its scalloped roof line and carved figures was familiar to generations of skiers and mountain climbers long before the Olympics brought fame to Garmisch, and the glassed-in terrace in front always was and still is the best people-watching spot in town.

The Clausing family has been in charge here since 1891 and they've left their mark on the hotel in various ways. One Clausing was the proud inventor of the first Berliner Weisse, a kind of strawberry-flavored beer, and it's a house specialty, served in an enormous footed goblet. Another was a photographer, and his outstanding shots of the Alps line the hallways. The latest son to take over, a handsome young man in his 20s, seems determined not to let progress spoil the traditional Bavarian atmosphere of his hotel. He's added a discotheque, for example, but he placed it around the corner from the building, so that the only music you need hear at night remains the old Bavarian oom-pah, from the Bierstube. The Posthotel's low ceilings, arched hallways, gaily painted beams, pastel frescoes and religious carvings all remain, all carefully maintained. There are several dining rooms—one with fat round pillars, a variety of hanging post horns and tapestries on the walls, another with lots of pewter and pretty embroidered tablecloths, still another with high ceilings, big beams and an enormous wrought-iron candelabra—and all have kept their old-fashioned look.

The bedchambers are old-fashioned, too, big and comfortable but with those convenient modern minibars. Young Herr Clausing says the rooms are slated for remodeling, but is seems safe to assume he won't let them give way to anonymous modern. The choicest rooms, of course, are the ones that look out at the mountains.

Garmisch is a place to visit year around, for skiing, hiking, sailing, swimming or sunning in the fresh mountain air. Whatever your pleasure, here's the hotel that will put you right in the heart of things. (E.B.)

Name: Clausing's Posthotel

Owner/Manager: Heinrich Clausing

Address: Marienplatz 12, 8100 Garmisch-Partenkirchen

Location: In the heart of Garmisch village off the German Alpenstrasse, about 112 miles from Lindau

Telephone: (08821) 58071, 58072

Cables/Telex: (None)

Reps: (None)

Credit Cards: American Express, Diners Club

Rooms: 30 rooms

Meals: Breakfast 6:30–10, lunch 12–2:30, dinner 6–9:30; dinner for two approx. $20; dress informal; room service and snacks available all day; outdoor terrace (enclosed in winter)

Entertainment: "Oom-pah" band in the bar, discotheque

Sports: Skiing, skating, tobogganing, curling nearby; hiking and lake swimming nearby in summer.

Sightseeing: Cablecar to the Zugspitze (highest point in the German Alps), ski and skating stadiums, Old Church (alte Kirche) in Garmisch, St. Anthony's sanctuary and park in Partenkirchen; "Mad Ludwig's" Linderhof castle at Oberammergau

Hotel Alte Post and Hotelvilla
Wangen

♛♛ ✕✕ $$

This one is a sleeper—the town, the hotel, and most specially, the Hotelvilla.

Wangen seems just another of those many dots on the map, but since it's located just above the start of the German Alpenstrasse, it's a place you could choose to spend the night before setting out to drive through the mountains. If you do, you'll discover a delightful small nontouristy baroque city, still with its old walls and painted towers leading into the town. In the Postplatz, one of the old squares, there's a grilled gate that leads to the Alte Post. It doesn't look like much from the outside, obscured by a grocery store, but walk through that gate and up the marble stairs and you'll find as elegant a small hotel as you've seen anywhere.

The *alte* "old" in the name refers to the inn's beginnings back in 1409. It was made into a modern hotel in 1945, then it was totally renovated by the Viele family in 1975, and decorated with real flair by Frau Viele. Husband Werner and son are in turn responsible for the excellent food you'll be served in the dining room here. The furnishings are appropriately baroque, a mélange of wooden and upholstered pieces, painted chests, crystal chandeliers, formal drapes centered with delicate white lace curtains. Most of the bedrooms are fairly formal in feeling, but a few are done with fresh hand-painted country wooden pieces. Even the halls here have been beautifully done—big and wide with deep red carpeting, white walls lined with antiques, beams, chandeliers and flowers.

The hotel is a charmer, but wait until you see the villa, located just a few minutes away in a woodsy residential section of town. Again, it has been done over with Frau Viele's unerring good taste, this time a bit more rustic in feeling but still the epitome of elegance. You can have an enormous old-world bedroom with a sitting area of comfortable sofas and chairs, plus a balcony looking out at three sets of Alps—Swiss, German and Austrian— spread out in Cinerama before you. Downstairs is an apartment that just might be one of Germany's biggest hotel bargains—$80 (or thereabouts) a night for three rooms plus bath, a luxurious living room with a semicircular glass wall looking out at all those multinational Alps, a cozy den, a bedroom and every convenience, right down to a dumbwaiter in the wall next to the bed. When you're ready for breakfast, just pick up the phone, and they'll send the tray down via the dumbwaiter without ever a knock on the door to interrupt you.

It's just the sort of place you hope you'll discover in Europe, a true hideaway. Who could blame you if you change your plans and decide to settle in here for a few days? To explore Lake Constance a few miles down the road. Or take a few forays into the Alps. Or maybe just sit on the terrace and hold hands while you do a little mountain gazing. (E.B.)

Name: Hotel Alte Post and Hotelvilla

Owners/Managers: Werner and Luise Viele

Address: 7988 Wangen (Allgau), Postplatz 2

Location: On route 18, 10 miles north of Lindau, 20 minutes from Lake Constance, 10 minutes from the start of the Alpenstrasse (Alpine Road); nearest airport, Zurich

Telephone: (07522) 4014

Cables/Telex: (None)

Reps: (None)

Credit Cards: American Express, Diners Club, Visa

Rooms: 30 rooms, 3 suites

Meals: Breakfast 7–10, lunch 12–2, dinner 6–10; dinner for two approx. $20; informal dress; room service all day

Entertainment: TV in lounge and in some rooms

Sports: (None)

Sightseeing: Lindau (see the Municipal Museum, Hauptstrasse with picturesque Alpine houses, the harbor, boat rides on Lake Constance); forays into the Alps; painted town gates and baroque architecture in Wangen

For brief reports on other hotels in Germany turn to the chapter on Added Attractions at the end of this guide.

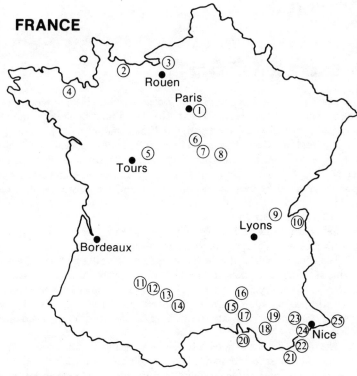

FRANCE

FRANCE

Rouen

Paris ①

Tours ⑤

Lyons

Bordeaux

Nice

1. Hôtel Ritz
   Hôtel de l'Université
   L'Hotel
   Hôtel Lutèce
   La Résidence du Bois
2. Château d'Audrieu
3. Auberge de Vieux Puits
4. Manoir du Vaumadeuc
5. Château d'Artigny
   Domaine des Hauts de Loire
   La Tortinière
6. Hôtellerie du Bas-Bréau
7. Auberge des Templiers
8. L'Hôtellerie de la Poste
   Hôtellerie du Moulin des Ruats
   Chez La Mère Blanc
   Hôtel de la Verniaz
   Hôtel Les Prés Fleuris
   L'Auberge du Père Bise
11. Moulin du Roc

12. Le Vieux Logis
13. Le Métairie
14. Château de Mercuès
15. Hôtellerie le Prieuré
16. Château de Rochegude
17. L'Auberge de Noves
18. Le Mas d'Entremont
19. Le Mas des Herbes Blanches
20. L'Oustau de Baumanière
21. Hôtel Byblos
22. Hôtel du Cap
23. Château du Domaine St.-Martin
    Le Mas d'Artigny
    Auberge Le Hameau
24. Le Cagnard
25. Hôtel La Voile d'Or
    L'Hôtellerie du Château
    de la Chèvre d'or
    Hôtel Le Cap Estel
    Hôtel Le Vistaero

Hôtel Ritz
Paris

♛♛♛✗✗✗$$$

"You have reached the height of your profession," said the courtesan, "as I have in mine." "Alas," replied César Ritz, "with far less pleasure and far more trouble than you have experienced, mademoiselle."

The peak for César Ritz was The Perfect Hotel. His ideal was a place where guests would feel they were in a home away from home. Since the guests he had in mind happened to be kings and queens, archdukes and counts, the hotel he created was, and is, one of the most elegant in the world.

What is the Ritz like?

Let's put it this way. If you're staying at the Ritz, there's no point going to Versailles unless you're interested in landscape gardening.

The Ritz is a palace of chandeliers and mirrors, silks and satins, grand marble stairways and costly carpets. You don't walk through the Ritz so much as make a royal progress. Tall double doors open onto sumptuous salon after salon, with even taller windows looking onto courtyards and flooding the rooms with the airiness of a conservatory in a country mansion.

The main part of the hotel, which was originally the town house of the Duke of Lauzun, who commanded the French cavalry at Yorktown, faces the handsomely proportioned Place Vendôme. It's connected to a second wing on the Rue Cambon by a long corridor lined with showcases displaying the temptations of the haute couturiers around the corner.

The man who created this palace-away-from-palace was the thirteenth child of a Swiss shepherd (the crest on the hotel's notepaper is a replica of the crest on the family stove).

César Ritz left school at thirteen, and elected to make his way in the world as a waiter. His first boss told him, in one of those inept but resoundingly pompous prophecies sometimes inflicted on the younger generation, that he had absolutely no talent for the hotel business. Whereupon Ritz became the best waiter in Europe, graduated to the grandest restaurants, and was soon the darling of Europe's pleasure-bent royalty. The Prince of Wales once told him: "Where you go, Ritz, we will follow." And follow they did. Since the Ritz opened its double doors in 1898, the guest list has included kings (Bulgaria, Yugoslavia, Portugal), grand dukes and archdukes, maharajahs (Jaipur and Cooch Behar), three generations of Aga Khans, a succession of Rockefellers, Vanderbilts, and F. Scotts and Zeldas.

138

At first, guests were probably attracted by the luxuries and comforts. (The Ritz was the first hotel in the world to have bath and shower in every room, at a time when chambermaids brought in large copper tubs and jugs of lukewarm water.) But what has kept them coming back year after year, and in some cases actually moving in for good, is the service.

It was a basic principle of César Ritz that the hotel would spare no expense to maintain its standards of luxury and service. When he wanted the best chef, he went out and got the great Auguste Escoffier. When he needed a craftsman with special skills to maintain the *patine décoratif* in one of the rooms, which is now a national monument, he hired one of the half dozen or so craftsmen with this skill, and the hotel to this day has one of these craftsmen on its staff full-time.

Before you arrive in your room, it's checked out by an army of technicians. An electrician checks the light bulbs. A plumber tests the faucets. A painter covers over finger marks. A varnisher tests the drawers. A housekeeper checks the towels on the warming rack, and replaces the coat hangers the previous guest tucked into his souvenir bag. An assistant manager double-checks the lot. And, just in case, another assistant manager escorts you to your room. From this you may have gathered that the Ritz has an unusually big staff. Most deluxe hotels, not merely first class but *deluxe* hotels, have a staff-to-guest ratio of one and one-half to one; at the Ritz, the figure is two to one, calculated for peak hours in peak seasons. If you arrive off-peak, the ratio may be four to one. You command these servants, not by telephone, but from a panel of buttons beside your bed. There are four buttons—valet, chambermaid, sommelier/waiter and *service privé*. (The *privé* is perfectly innocent, it simply connects directly with the room of your personal servant if you bring him or her along.) You can rustle up the same team while sitting in your bathtub, and you could probably receive them at one time in that spacious room ("A bathroom should always be a *room*," was another of Ritz's tenets). It's unlikely that you'll ever have to wait more than short minutes for a response to your button pressing or to receive your champagne or breakfast. The Ritz puts so much emphasis on room service that there are often more waiters than meals.

It's this kind of service and attention to detail that makes the Ritz the perfect hotel. Oddly enough, the man who created this ideal was with the hotel only four years. But in that time, César Ritz established himself as the most legendary figure in the hotel world.

Until recently, his ideals were carried on by his son, Charles Ritz, and a team of managers and servants dedicated to the Ritz. One quarter of the Ritz staff has been there 25 years or more. Those who leave often end up running successful hotels elsewhere. Throughout France you'll meet owners and managers proud to have put in a stint at the Ritz and chefs proud to have scraped a potato within ladle distance of the great Escoffier. But no matter how hard they may try, their hotels can never quite measure up. The Ritz is still the Ritz.

And the Ritz Bar is still the Ritz Bar.

There are three bars in the hotel, but the one near the entrance on the Rue Cambon is the Ritz Bar frequented by F. Scott Fitzgerald and his protégé, Ernest Hemingway. This is where Zelda got tiddly, where Garbo eluded the crowd, and where Churchill sipped the hotel's private 1858 cognac. It's still one of the smart places to meet in Paris, and you may be surprised who gets tiddly there these days.

If the cuisine at the Ritz is not so exalted as it was in the day when Escoffier ruled the kitchen, the hotel restaurant is still a magnificent place to dine. A modest lunch can easily take on the aura of a state banquet at the Elysëe Palace. The hotel's grill room, l'Espadon, rates one star in Michelin, which puts it among the elite of hotel restaurants in Paris.

The archdukes are gone. The kings are on budgets. The splendors of the Ritz are now accessible to us all. All of us (all of *you*), that is, who can afford $150 and up for a night of splendor. On the other hand, at least once in a lifetime everyone should sample life at the Ritz. Breakfast in bed served on Haviland china. Afternoon tea with Limoges china. Rich damask drapes and crystal chandeliers. Big red terry-towel bathrobes. Giant tubs. *Crêpes Roxelane* (lemon soufflé wrapped in a crêpe and served with fresh raspberry sauce) in the garden restaurant beneath sun umbrellas, surrounded by fountains and flowers en masse.

Some readers may wonder what a 186-room hotel in the heart of Paris is doing in a guidebook on hideaways, but the truth is once you ensconce yourselves in a hushed chamber facing the courtyard you could be miles out in the country. At the same time, a suite facing the Place Vendôme is not to be sniffed at. Here is one of the most beautifully proportioned cityscapes in the world, and you can look out of your tall windows on the boutiques of Schiaparelli, Van Cleef & Arpels, Boucheron and Patek-Philippe, with a branch of Banque Rothschild close at hand. A courtesan at the peak of her profession could ask no more.

Name: Hôtel Ritz

Managers: Frank Klein

Address: 15 Place Vendome, 75041 Paris

Location: On one of the most elegant squares in Paris, within walking distance of the Louvre and the Champs Elysées

Telephone: 260.38.30

140 **Cables/Telex:** Ritzotel/220262

Reps: HRI in U.S.A. and Canada, HRI and Relais-Châteaux in Europe

Credit Cards: American Express, Diners Club, Master Charge/Eurocard, Access

Rooms: 120 rooms, 46 suites

Meals: Breakfast anytime, lunch 12–3, dinner 7–11; dinner for two approx. $60; jacket required; room service around the clock, but only drinks and snacks after midnight

Entertainment: Television in some rooms, otherwise on request

Sports: (None)

Sightseeing: Paris

P.S. Free underground parking; no conventions or tour groups

P.P.S. As these words were being written, the mighty Hotel Ritz was being acquired by "Arab interests." These anonymous interests have, naturally, vowed to preserve the Ritz as the Ritz; and since it is a national monument, their hands are partly tied. However, they *have* changed manager. Otherwise, we must wait and see, with some apprehension. Muzak at the Ritz? *Mon Dieu!*

Hôtel de l'Université
Paris

♦$$

Until fairly recently the Left Bank could offer no really satisfactory moderately priced hotels above the "frumpy" level. Now there's the Hôtel de l'Université. It's on the Rue de l'Université, a three-minute stroll from the *quais* along the Seine, seven minutes from the Louvre, and a couple of quick blocks to the intellectuals' and swingers' corner of the Boulevard St. Germain, the Café aux Deux Magots, Café de Flore, Le Drugstore, and Brasserie Lipp.

L'Université is a result of La Grande Toilette of Le Grand Charles (the citywide face lift ordained by then President de Gaulle). It's a completely renovated hotel in an elegant *hôtel*, or Parisian townhouse. There's an antique store at the entrance, so you won't be surprised to find the interior furnished with period pieces. In one corner of the lobby, there's a tall clock that's been ticking off the hours for a hundred years or more, and a tapestry that's more or less 300 years old.

141

The lobby looks on to a miniature glass-enclosed courtyard, where the birds sing after a spring shower. Behind an elevator the size of a refrigerator, there's a snug lounge and writing room furnished with elegant chairs and desks.

L'Université is a small hotel—just 30 rooms with bath or shower. But each one is a miniature masterpiece. A typical double is done in grays and white, with wall-to-wall carpeting of tapestry-gold, bronze-colored draperies, a mammoth mahogany wardrobe, and a rocking chair. The bathrooms have double washbasins, bathtub, and shower. The rooms on the top floor have small terraces that look across the inimitable rooftops of Paris, every garret like a set for *La Bohème*.

Each room is a different size and shape, and each is decorated in its own style. One room is laced with hand-hewn ceiling beams. Another is encased in Louis XV paneling.

As far as we can tell, the rooms are well soundproofed, and apart from some traffic noise at the front, this is, for Paris, an oasis.

The hotel is filled with little touches that show you the management takes its business seriously. There are 17 hangers in the wardrobe, a stack of thick white towels, soap by Roger & Gallet; afternoon tea is served on silver trays, in a tea set of English ironstone.

There's no restaurant. But in the vaulted cellar of the hotel, you'll find a private bottle club—open to just 100 members and the guests of the hotel. Anyway, don't worry about the absence of a restaurant. It's no disadvantage in a neighborhood where every store that's not an antique shop or boutique is a restaurant. And who'd want to eat in a hotel with *ten* one-star restaurants just around the corner?

Name:	Hôtel de l'Université
Manager:	Hélène Bergman
Address:	22 Rue de l'Université, 75007 Paris
Location:	On the Left Bank, two blocks from the Blvd. St. Germain and its cafés
Telephone:	261.09.39
Cables/Telex:	260717 Orem 310/Univerotel
Reps:	(None)
Credit Cards:	(None)
Rooms:	29 rooms, 1 suite
Meals:	Breakfast 7–11, afternoon tea is the only other meal served; drinks are available from room service during the day.

Entertainment: (None)

Sports: (None)

Sightseeing: Paris

P.S. Parking? Allow 20–30 minutes to find a spot.

L'Hôtel
Paris

WWWXX $$$

Walk as far as the black-marble circle in the foyer. Stop. Look up. And there you have one of the most dazzling sights in Paris: a pure white tunnel twinkling with chandeliers and soaring straight up to a round glass roof six floors above. That's L'Hôtel, probably the most delicious place you will ever hang your hat.

A dozen or so years ago, a flamboyant French actor named Guy-Louis Duboucheron bought what had once been the ice house of a baronial 17th-century estate and later became the frowsy little fleabag where Oscar Wilde lived his last days. M. Duboucheron quickly set about turning it into the silk purse of all hoteldom. He has, as anyone can see, succeeded handsomely.

No two rooms at L'Hôtel look alike. The one thing they all have in common is their Fall of Rome marbled and mirrored bathrooms, complete with heated towels, sunken tubs, and vast vanity mirror studded with enough frosted light bulbs to satisfy the biggest ego MGM ever built a dressing room for.

Wherever you look in L'Hôtel you're greeted by some tiny touch designed to make life just a shade more bearable.

Like jugs of freshly cut roses all over your room. Thick pink and blue linen sheets that are changed every day. Matching terry-cloth robes. Closets that light up when you open the doors. And hideaway refrigerators stocked with Cliquot Brut. On the table beside your bed is a small leather book. Instead of pages, it has buttons. One for disco. One for Mozart. One for music-to-love-somebody-by. Push and your choice comes floating out of hidden speakers around the bed.

Nothing, of course, is perfect. And at L'Hôtel it's the service that isn't. The entire staff, from the *gamine* who hands you your key to the headwaiter who pops your cork, look and act like escapees from the Cannes film

143

festival—self-absorbed, offhand, and just a shade above it all when you complain that you can't get a call through the switchboard or your laundry hasn't come back and you're leaving town in an hour.

But in a big-city hotel, when you're away most of the day—and night—service isn't quite so crucial as at a resort hotel where you're plugged into the life-support system all the time. Our advice is to suffer the staff bravely and ask for Room 36.

Here, Duboucheron has shimmeringly re-created the boudoir of one of the twenties' most fatal femmes fatales—Mistinguet. You step into a tiny foyer and just beyond, resplendent on a crimson-carpeted platform, is a gigantic, fur-covered bed—the very one the lady herself once owned. White fur rugs undulate off the bed and onto wall-to-wall carpet. Bed, chairs, tables, all belonged to her, and everything is made of reflecting glass. A narcissist's dream. You can see yourselves from a thousand different angles.

But if you missed being a member of the Me Generation, you might prefer Room 16, done in the style of Oscar Wilde's time and taste. The opulent, yet masculine, fin-de-siècle furniture was imported from England, and is surrounded by dark, glowing brocade. Room 22 is entirely red velvet—walls, beds, draperies, doors, floors. Room 40 sports purple wall-to-wall carpeting and red silk moiré walls. Wild, but it works, as does every other inch of decor M. Duboucheron puts his hand to. (Except for his own bigger-than-life portrait hanging over the bar downstairs, which belongs in one of the curiosity shops on Rue Jacob a block away.)

But when in the mood for really grand gestures, skip the smaller quarters and reserve L'Hôtel's penthouse apartment (Apartment 25). Its brick terrace looks out over window boxes full of flowers, past a lavender-blossomed tree winking with miniature lights, and across the rooftops of Paris. Both sitting and dining rooms are done in restrained silks and velvets and tasteful antiques. The kitchen cabinets are full of good silver and china. The bedroom is tiny and full of bed. There are tropical plants and bowls of hothouse flowers everywhere—and a maid at your beck and call. Or you can have an entire little house within the hotel (Apartment 55), consisting of two bedrooms, salon, bathroom, separate shower and terrace.

As for where else to go in L'Hôtel, there's a bar-lounge, which is a mile of red-velvet sofa opposite a baby grand and a 250-year-old tree growing straight through the roof. Beyond, you'll find a red-velvety cave of a dining room with fountain and vaulted ceiling. For breakfast, you can descend to the real *cave*, which is a nice way the French have of saying "cellar." Except that few other cellars in Paris are as romantic as this. A maze of tiny vaulted chambers carved out of stone. You may find yourselves concentrating more on each other than on the *café et croissants*. In which case, you can dash back to your room and order champagne, lunch and dinner sent up (there's 24-hour-a-day room service).

L'Hôtel, of course, is not everybody's cup of tea. It's a little too miniscule and a little too precious for some, but if it passes the test with Hepburn, Minelli, Streisand and several hundred Rothschilds, who knows? You may be able to take it for a few days yourself. (C.P.)

Name: L'Hôtel

Owner: Guy-Louis Duboucheron

Manager: Phillipe Feutré

Address: 13 Rue des Beaux-Arts, Paris 5

Location: Left Bank near St. Germain des Prés

Telephone: (1) 325.27.22

Cables/Telex: 270870

Reps: (None)

Credit Cards: (None)

Number of Rooms: 25 rooms and 2 suites

Meals: Breakfast 7:30–all day, lunch 12–7, dinner 7:30–1 A.M.; dinner for two approx. $50; casual; room service 24 hours a day for anything you want.

Entertainment: Piano bar; color TV in every room

Sports: (None)

Sightseeing: All of Paris

P.S. Leave your car elsewhere

Hôtel Lutèce
Paris

W$$

Maybe Patton and Montgomery never knew it, but ideal headquarters for any latter-day invasion of Paris is in Nôtre Dame's backyard with one foot next to the Right Bank's *grande luxe* and the other beside the Left Bank's mouldering charm.

145

That would put you right in the middle of the Seine on the Ile St. Louis, a sliver of very precious earth and tight-little-island home to some of Paris's most formidable celebrities.

All told, the island probably doesn't cover as much acreage as Macy's. Yet sandwiched into its historic old streets are dozens of pint-size restaurants and bars, plus charcuteries, patisseries, etc., plus three small hotels all owned by the same innkeeper. Of the three, only one can pass as comfortable—with private baths and passingly good service and maintenance. But Lutèce is no mini-Ritz. It was, after all, built three centuries ago, and just five years ago it was a tumbledown pension.

Since then it's been put back together, spruced up, and outfitted with modern tiled baths, telephones, elevator and breakfast in bed. All this for $45 a night is not bad when you consider that a glass of lemon juice and Perrier at a nearby outdoor café costs $3 and a gin-and-tonic at the Crillon is $7.

True, the colors are garish, the service well-meaning but spotty, and the clatter from the street at 5:00 A.M. deafening. But the place does have an easygoing charm. Just off the lobby there's a refrigerator full of ice and Perrier; you're trusted to take what you need and tell whoever totes up your bill before you leave. You can use it to chill a bottle of wine or a pâté from the irresistible shop across the street. Breakfast is brought to your bedside every morning, and the lobby with its venerable hearth and tiles is a friendly place to rendezvous with friends.

These days, however, $45 shelter doesn't, alas, deliver much more than that—shelter. Colors clash. Rugs are frayed. Bathrooms fall far short of spotless. Don't expect to find a place to park your car within hiking distance. Or maids who magically know when you're in or out without ever knocking or crashing in at the wrong moment. Or thick towels.

But, then, consider the alternatives. It's up to you what you can and can't live without. I, for one, would rather sacrifice a three-star dinner and spend the difference on a three-star hotel room. If nothing else, it lasts longer. (C.P.)

Name: Hôtel Lutèce

Owner/Manager: M. Buffat

Address: 65 Rue St. Louis en L'Ile, Paris 4

Location: Directly behind Nôtre Dame

Telephone: (1) 326.23.52

Cables/Telex: (None)

146 **Reps:** (None)

Credit Cards:	(None)
Rooms:	23
Meals:	7:30–1 (served in room), bar next door open 7–1 A.M.
Entertainment:	(None)
Sports:	(None)
Sightseeing:	Paris
P.S.	Parking hopeless

La Résidence du Bois
Paris

WW XX $$$

Surprise. Right in the middle of Paris sits a peaceful, unpeopled little garden full of geraniums, and right in the middle of the geraniums sits a hotel full of tall, sunny windows and lovely antiques.

Instead of pavement, your room looks out on a forest of lilacs. Instead of the grumble of traffic, you wake up to bird songs. Yet you never feel the least bit isolated. A four-minute walk through the park takes you to Avenue Victor Hugo and a mile of fashionable antique and clothes shops. A ten-minute cab ride lands you at Maxim's, Hermès, the Louvre, or the Opéra.

Résidence du Bois started life 300 years ago as a palatial Parisian manor house. Some years ago, it was totally redone inside. Its burnishings and furnishings are comfortable and attractive, if just a shade flashy.

Each of the Résidence's 20 rooms is done differently, and has a bright, modern tiled bath. Apartment 25 gives you your own private entrance from the court to a pretty salon that can be used for writing, entertaining or snoozing. A curving, carpeted stairway leads to a pink-and-gray bedroom overlooking the garden.

Room 23 is a particularly posh little haven with a stone balcony over the garden. The bedroom also faces on the garden, and the sitting room gives you a view of a leisurely street scene rarely ruffled by anything more aggressive than a bicycle.

Rooms 21–24 (from $26) are also exceptionally pleasant. They're all large, airy, and look out on the garden. But the Residence's best bargain is a

147

small, snug room (Room 12) nestled behind the lilacs and done in cheering yellows and blues.

La Résidence has no official restaurant. You tell the maître d' where you feel like dining (in a huge salon with a blazing fireplace, in the bar, in the garden, or in your room), and that's your restaurant for the evening. The food is basic, but good. And this is the only place we know in Paris where the chef will whip up your favorite dish for you (send the recipe in advance if it requires complicated ingredients).

You won't see armadas of Alfa Romeos pulling up to the door or countesses and film stars swooping in and out. But after the hurly-burly of a day—or night—in Paris, your nerve endings will thank you for getting them back to this leafy little island of calm. (C.P.)

Name: La Résidence du Bois

Owners/Managers: M. and Mme. Henri Desponts

Address: 16 Rue Chalgrin, 75116 Paris

Location: One block from l'Étoile (Place General de Gaulle) on the far side of the Champs Elysées, near Bois de Boulogne

Telephone: 500.50.59

Cables/Telex: Resiboisotel

Reps: Relais-Châteaux in U.S., Canada and Europe

Credit Cards: (None)

Rooms: 17 rooms, 3 suites

Meals: Breakfast anytime, lunch 1–2:30, dinner 7:30–9:30 (in the courtyard in summer); dress informal; full room service by day, but drinks and snacks only in evening hours

Entertainment: Color television in the rooms, bar and lounge with Vivaldi-type taped music

Sports: Nearby—swimming, tennis and boating on the Bois de Boulogne

Sightseeing: Paris

P.S.   Some, but not all, of the staff speak English. The hotel takes no tour or convention groups. Parking will be a problem unless you use the garage up the street, which is expensive.

Château d'Audrieu

Audrieu

♥ ✗ $$$

Two acres of beige gravel surrounded by two acres of beige château may not be your idea of the world's warmest spot to lay your head after a long day's trek through Calvados country. But don't let all that stoniness put you off. The warmth and the welcome are inside this vast ancestral home, presided over by a couple whose pride in Audrieu comes naturally. After all, it's been in the family for nine centuries now—ever since William the Conqueror made a gift of it to a doughty Viking named Percy for helping William do the conquering. As a direct descendant of Percy, the present Baron of Audrieu can tell you about every shot that's been fired here since the Hundred Years War, including 27 direct hits it took during WWII.

Although some changes have been made, Audrieu is probably as close as you can come to seeing a medieval château still working the way it did centuries ago.

Just past the garden wall stands a forest of 400-year-old oaks, beeches, chestnuts and sycamores. Cows and donkeys graze the lawns of the main house undisturbed. Workmen from the tiny town that over the centuries has accumulated around the manor house quietly tend the orchards and gardens and smokehouse that keep Audrieu's kitchen stocked with fresh fruit and vegetables, Calvados, homemade bread, and smoked salmon and hams.

In fact, dinner here probably isn't very different now from the hogshead-and-venison-haunch bashes that the Percy clan was throwing 30 or 40 generations ago. The wine may be a shade drier and the sauces more refined, but the chef still relies on what the estate and the neighboring sea can give him. Fresh *saumon papillotte,* for instance, and a shishkabob of mussels, ham and bacon. There's a marvelous salad of four greens topped by four tiny mounds of different seafood.

The view from the dining room, through seven-foot-high casement windows, still faces the sunset on one side and the forest on the other. A huge stone fireplace chases out the evening chill. And as you weave your way back to your room, remember to duck the giant crossbeams, sliced 400 years ago from the oaks whose heirs now fill Audrieu's private forest.

The guest rooms in the main house are comfortable if not *grande luxe.* The introduction of steam heat has cracked and warped the beautiful old paneling, and those antiques didn't come from the Rue du Faubourg St. Honoré. But suite 2 is quite grand with cavernous marble fireplace, high white-beamed ceiling, and a big French-windowed bath that lets you watch the cows as you take your bath.

149

Among the nicest rooms are 14 with a view of the garden and all the attic rooms, which come in small, medium, and large and are tucked cozily under the beams with tiny garret windows and ceilings slanting abruptly down to the floor.

But the most romantic accommodations at Audrieu were yet to come when we were there. Fifteen tons of hay had recently been removed from the stable to make room for next year's guests, and in their place a charming series of rooms was taking shape—each just about big enough for a couple of spirited Shetland ponies. Of the three upstairs stable rooms, two are to be done in rattan furniture imported from the Philippines and the third will be Art Deco. Downstairs, the rooms are more traditional: antiques, linen walls, floral cottons at every window, each of which is an arched expanse of glass the width of the entire room.

In case all this makes you forget where you really are, note the nameplate on the wall, honoring the last permanent guest. Her name was Mollie. (C.P.)

Name: Château d'Audrieu

Owners/Managers: M. and Mme. Livry-Level

Address: 14250 Audrieu (Calvados)

Location: Midway between Caen' and Bayeux

Telephone: (31) 78.21.52

Cables/Telex: Chamco Caen 170234

Reps: Two World Tours

Credit Cards: American Express

Rooms: 18 rooms, 4 suites

Meals: Breakfast: 8–10:30, lunch: 12:30–1:30, dinner 7:30–9; approx. 85 francs; tie and jacket preferred; room service for breakfast and drinks

---

Entertainment: Chamber groups on special weekends in November, December, March

---

Sports: Heated pool and walking trails; beaches, fishing, and tennis nearby

---

Sightseeing: WWII's famous landing beaches (Normandy, Omaha); the tapestries of Bayeux; the distinctive golden-stoned châteaux of Calvados (Brécy, Manneville, Fontaine-Henri, etc.); the Abbey of St. Gabriel

---

P.S. Closed December 20 to March 1, and on Wednesdays during off season only breakfast is served

---

Auberge du Vieux Puits

Pont-Audemer

W X X $

Now that even the remotest country inns have discovered the joys of charging Paris prices, here is a charmingly creaky, crooked little exception where the best room in the house was only eighty francs at the time of this writing. Yes, *eighty francs*—when that's what they're getting for a bottle of not very good Beaujolais in not very good restaurants all over France these days.

But Auberge du Vieux Puits ("inn of the old well") is more than a bargain. It's a time capsule filled to its historic rafters with three centuries of French provincial charm. So *this* is what all those quainte "olde innes" from Connecticut to Carmel, California, have been imitating for the last two hundred years—whether they know it or not!

Auberge du Vieux Puits

Although the town it's in is of no particular distinction, it's close enough to the *autoroute* from Paris to Caen to be a logical stopover for anyone traveling west. Outside, Puits (pronounced more or less *pweet*) is pure Normandy (crisscross timbered walls under tiled roofs, casement windows with wide blue shutters, window boxes spilling over with geraniums).

Built in 1630, everything is on a smaller-than-life scale and at topsy-turvy angles that send floors and ceilings skittering off in unexpected dips and curves. Two tiny dining rooms are dominated by ancient low-hanging beams and the crackle of burning logs in the fireplace. The guest rooms are in a separate little house of their own tucked quietly away beside the inner courtyard. The only wakeup sounds you'll hear are from the local church tower every morning at seven.

There are just eight guest rooms, each barely big enough for a downy double bed. Some have full bath; others have everything but a toilet, which—in grand French tradition—is five hops down the hall. The sheets are the thickest and snowiest linen this side of the Hôtel Ritz, and your breakfast of steaming café au lait, fresh croissants, and homemade jam is brought on a tray and tucked under your chin while you're still blissfully under the covers.

As at any small, family-owned inn, one of the small joys of staying here is the warmth of the welcome. Having inherited Puits and its treasures from a father who spent his life hunting antiques and welcoming travelers to his hearth, the present owner carries on the tradition.

He sees to it that his restaurant keeps the Michelin star it won so long ago with hearty country cooking that makes the most of what the landscape has to offer: duck, rabbit, trout—and, of course, Calvados.

He'll also explain the mysterious workings of his 18th century "coffin" clocks, tell you the history of a rare set of "patron" dishes, and happily show you his huge collection of *rats de cave* (for more details, book a room immediately).

For those who prefer their stopovers less authentic, there's another so-called Normandy inn nearby, where the real thing has been re-created à la Beverly Hills. Le Petit Coq aux Champs in Campigny offers slightly more sophisticated food than Puits, complete with heated swimming pool, pseudo antiques, and huge lounges festooned with miles of naugahyde and glass. The rooms are bigger, the grounds more spacious, but the charm is as manufactured as the mock thatch roof. (C.P.)

Name: Auberge du Vieux Puits

Manager/Owner: Jacques Foltz

Address: 10 Rue Notre-Dame du Pre, 27500 Pont-Audemer (Eure)

Location: On the Risle River, between Rouen and Caen, about 35 miles southwest of the former, 45 northeast of the latter

Telephone: 16 (32) 41.01.48

Cables/Telex: (None)

Reps: (None)

Credit Cards: (None)

Rooms: 8

Meals: Breakfast 8–9:30, lunch 12–2, dinner 7:30–9; dinner for two approx. $40; tie and jacket; room service breakfast only

Entertainment: None, but there's a casino in Deauville, 20 miles away

Sports: None at the inn, but tennis, pool and horseback riding nearby

Sightseeing: Old Rouen (cathedral, monument to Joan of Arc, Rue de Grosse Horloge etc.,), Honfleur, Trouville, Deauville, World War II beaches

P.S. Closed December 20 to January 20 and June 26 to July 5

Manoir du Vaumadeuc
Pléven-Plancoët

WW XX $$

In America, pigeons coo; in France they *roucoulent*. At Vaumadeuc, the *roucoulement* of snowy-white fantailed pigeons wakes you for a breakfast of piping hot chocolate, brioches fresh from the bakery in the village, butter and cream fresh from the farm across the fence.

The Manor of Vaumadeuc was built in the sixteenth century by a local squire for his bride, and named for the dreamy Vale of Madeuc that slopes away from the back door to the edge of the forest. Its present personality comes from its owner, the Vicomtesse de Pontbriand. Her husband was a colonel in the French army and together they traveled widely, collecting antiques and objets d'art for the manor. Three years ago, the manor was restored and renovated, but the essential character and charm of the place remain.

It's typically Breton in its granitey grandeur, but in the warm summer   153 of Brittany the facade softens when the vine of the virgin blooms across its stones, almost concealing the diminutive Gothic entrance. If the exterior seems austere, the interior is sumptuous. The rooms are spacious and ceilinged with old beams.

In the main salon, a fifteenth-century Flemish tapestry looks down on a Renaissance chest and an enormous table which was once the top of a Louis XIV billiard table. At one end there's a massive fireplace, and since the French love the smell of a wood fire and since Vaumadeuc is surrounded by forest, there's usually a fire blazing in the evening—an invitation to settle down in one of the armchairs, with a glass of Armagnac.

The dining room is dominated by another fine Flemish tapestry, a wrought-iron chandelier, and a console table of yellow Brocatel marble. Even the radiators are concealed beneath slabs of Brocatel.

There are nine bedrooms at Vaumadeuc, each decorated in a different style, and much too luxurious for an overnight stop. All the bedrooms have fireplaces, dressing tables, and writing desks. The bathrooms have toweling robes, and even here, out in the countryside of Brittany, the soap is by Madame Rochas, the bath salts by Elizabeth Arden.

You reach the bedrooms up a wide, dove-gray granite stairway, and along a red-carpeted corridor. To the right at the top of the stairs is the grandest bedroom at Vaumadeuc—Room 6. You enter it through a heavy oaken door, proceed onto a short gallery with a carved wooden balustrade, and there below is a room the size of a theater lobby. It has a large double bed, Dutch Renaissance chest, and a desk covered with bibelots and bric-a-brac. The chairs are Louis XIV, and on each side of the fireplace are two red *chauffeuses,* or warming stools, from the time of Louis XV.

Our second favorite room at Vaumadeuc is the library, a gracious room with seventeenth-century wood paneling. It really was the library at one time, and the wall opposite the fireplace is still massed with 500 leather-bound volumes, some of them printed in the 1600s. In the evening, the maids transform the library into a bedroom simply by pulling out the red-velveteen sofa and making it into your *grand lit.*

There are two guest cottages in the courtyard. The snuggest one faces the Rose Garden, and in the morning you can join the birds for breakfast among the blossoms.

Vaumadeuc is a place where people come for solitude. Occasionally a herd of cattle shuffles up the road, and once a day the *boulanger* drives up in his old Citröen to deliver *baguettes.* Otherwise the only sounds at Vaumadeuc are the *roucoulement* and flurry of the pigeons.

Name: Manoir de Vaumadeuc

Owner/Manager: The Vicomtesse de Pontbriand

Address: 22130 Pléven/Plancoët (Côtes-du-Nord)

Location: On a country road, between Dinan and St. Brieuc, somewhere in the heart of Brittany, surrounded by a park of 250 acres of forest and heath; 12 miles from the coast, 20 miles from the airport at Dinard (Din*ard*, not Din*an*)

Telephone: (36) 27.14.67

Cables/Telex: (None)

Reps: Relais-Châteaux in U.S., Canada and Europe

Credit Cards: American Express

Rooms: 9

Meals: Breakfast 8–10, lunch 12:30–2, dinner 8–9; 3-course dinner for two approx. $55–$60; tie and jacket; room service 8 A.M.–10 P.M., drinks and snacks only

Entertainment: Taped music in lounge

Sports: Nearby—tennis, golf, beaches, fishing, riding

Sightseeing: Britanny, the Emerald Coast, Dinard (resort), Cancale (fishing village), Cape Finisterre; Mont St. Michel is about an hour away by car; castles at Dinan and Hunaudaie; folk festivals (including local "Fest Noz" in summer).

P.S. Closed mid-January to mid-March; absolutely no groups or conventions; not suitable for children

Château d'Artigny
Montbazon

WW XX $$$$

A perfumer's nose is a sensitive thing, so when Francois Coty of the perfume firm built his dream house, he commanded his architect to put the kitchens upstairs so the cooking smells would pass over his head. His dream house is now a luxury hotel—and his kitchens some of the most unusual bedrooms in France.

From its perch above the River Indre, about seven miles south of   155

Tours, the château looks across a sweep of idyllic pastures and woods and a zig and a zag of the river. Although cheek by jowl with the historic châteaux of the Loire, d'Artigny is just a baby—built in the 1930s in imitation of a grander age. And it is, indeed, very grand. Some would say haughty.

When you stride through the tall French doors, you know you're in a rich man's house. Polished, pure-white limestone rises on all sides. Gleaming sky-high French windows send sunlight splashing across the magnificent grand stairway. The dining-room floor is marble inlaid with brass. The drawing room has delicately carved wood paneling and row on row of early editions of Voltaire, Molière, and Balzac. Upstairs, yet another dazzling drawing room, above which M. Coty himself smiles down at you from a portrait that stretches about half a mile around the cupola and includes his best friends, his wife and his wife's lover.

But if you're looking for something slightly snugger, try the kitchen. It is now Room 30, a milky-white marble hideaway with a 15-foot domed ceiling, huge porthole windows, and French doors that open to a view of other grand châteaux in the distance.

Then there's the pastry kitchen, now Room 31. The sitting room is pink Russian marble, both walls and floor. And, of course, the table where the chefs once rolled their pastry dough is properly marble, too.

D'Artigny's most romantic rooms are on the third floor. This is a maze of corridors, turrets and turns. To get to Room 45, for instance, you go up a little flight of stairs, down another, then up a private red-carpeted stairway to a room tucked under the eaves. There's a double bed at one end and a porthole window looking directly down on an old mill stream, complete with waterfall. You get a view of the river again from Room 22, which has a canopied bed and tiled floor.

Most spectacular of all, though, are the rooms in d'Artigny's chapel. The pious can relax—it's been deconsecrated. But the soaring windows and carved columns remain. In one apartment here, two noble stone columns climb through the middle of the sitting room to the bedroom above. The bathroom is down a flight of steps, the bedroom up a spiral staircase, and upstairs again is another bath, surrounded by columns and plinths, where you can pretend you're Caligula-cum-concubine. Apartment 74, also in the chapel, has its own staircase leading to a maze of white columns interspersed with twin beds, a velvet sofa, Louis XIV chairs and tables, and an inlaid desk. An archway leads to a private glass-sided terrace overlooking the forest.

There's also a cozy little gatehouse on the grounds. Ask for the room on the first floor—it's like having a country cottage all to yourself. Room service down there is nearly as prompt as it is at the château. And just down the road is a small country house called Port Moulin. It has eight guest rooms, its own lawns and gardens, and a stream rushing under a bridge into the Indre. You can hear the river from your bed and in the morning take your breakfast tray over to a tiny island for a secluded picnic.

The dining room at d'Artigny is appropriately grandiose, and so is the menu. Sea bass braised with seaweed and thinly sliced breast of duck in red wine sauce have won it a Michelin star, and waiting for you in the cellar are 25,000 bottles of wine, including some of the fine local Chinons.

Some weekends, you can attend a chamber concert in the grand salon. Surrounded by the gilt and mirrors and chandeliers, you may find yourself developing a Louis XV complex, and although Mozart can't be there, you will have famous pianists, violinists and flutists tinkling away for you. When the last note dies, head for the heated swimming pool or a stroll through the 40-acre park. The management has thoughtfully marked three paths: "Tranquil" (15 minutes), "Undulating" (25 minutes), and "Sportive" (40 minutes). Our advice is take "Undulating" and you'll have a little left over for a fast set of tennis the next morning. (C.P.)

Name: Château d'Artigny

Owner: René Traversac

Manager: Alain Rabier

Address: Route d'Azay-le-Rideau, 37250 Montbazon

Location: Eight miles from Tours

Telephone: (47) 26.24.24

Cables/Telex: 750 900

Reps: (None)

Credit Cards: American Express

Rooms: 36 rooms, 20 suites

Meals: Breakfast 7–12, lunch 12–2, dinner 7:30–9:15; approx. $60; tie and jacket; full room service

Entertainment: (None)

Sports: Heated swimming pool; 2 tennis courts (floodlit at night); walking trails; golf and horseback riding nearby

Sightseeing: The historic châteaux of the Loire such as Chinon, Chenonceaux, Azay-le-Rideau, Chambord, Amboise along with their forests and parks (Chambord, for instance, sits in a park larger than Paris); guided tours and *son et lumière* in season

P.S. Closed late November to January 15

157

Domaine des Hauts de Loire
Onzain

WWXX$$$

Of all the château-hotels in the Loire Valley, this is the most gracefully renovated and furnished. Each guest room is as meticulously art-directed as one of those too-good-to-be-true museum re-creations. Yet it's done in a comfortable country style you'll have no more trouble living with than the dashing 18th-century count who used the place as hunting lodge and hideaway.

Because it was built for sporting purposes and not for growing a huge 18th-century family tree, the scale of the place is pleasantly small. A Lilliputian staircase spirals up and around a brick-and-beamed tower from the first floor's paneled and parqueted grand salons. You step into your room and wonder why Goldilocks isn't lying in the middle of that big, puffy bed, surrounded by gleaming old attic beams slanting from ceiling to floor. Fresh floral cottons hang at the casement window. The view, naturally, is the perfect swan mirrored in the perfect pond.

Talk about detail. You catch the same fresh-faced pink from the curtains showing up in the embroidery on the hem of the sheets, in the tiles in the exquisite bath, and finally inside the beautiful old pine cupboard that serves as closet and is as lovingly furnished as the room itself, with fabric walls and matching quilted hangers.

If only the same loving care went into the food and the management of the place. Neither the food nor the maître d' comes close to the standards of a good French dining room. And it takes far too long to get bills totted up and luggage carried down. It could be that the couple who own and run Hauts de Loire—and are still in the middle of renovating other buildings on the estate—will get their act together eventually, or hire someone to do it for them.

Nonetheless, it's definitely worth a stop on your tour of the château country. It's hard to choose a "best" room. My two candidates would be Rooms 14 and 16, the latter because of its private little winding staircase within the tower. French doors open onto a balcony overlooking endless lawns and vineyards. The antiques are splendid and the carpeting velvety wall-to-wall. Room 14 puts you in a feathery double bed under a skylight, looking out at a castle chimney.

But whichever room you're given, ask if you can't see some of the others—such minor masterpieces make a worthwhile tour in themselves—even without any *son et lumière*. (C.P.)

158

Name: Domaine des Hauts de Loire

Owners/Managers: M. and Mme. Bonnigal

Address: 41150 Onzain

Location: Midway between Blois and Tours

Telephone: (54) 79.72.57

Cables/Telex: (None)

Reps: (None)

Credit Cards: American Express, Diners Club

Number of Rooms: 14 rooms and 2 suites

Meals: Breakfast 8–10, lunch 12–2, dinner 7:30–8:30; approx. $40; tie and jacket; room service anytime for breakfast, drinks, snacks

Entertainment: (None)

Sports: Rowboating and fishing in the lake

Sightseeing: (See Château d'Artigny)

La Tortinière
Montbazon

WWXX$$$

This hilltop and this view of the river were the inspirations for the story "The Sleeping Beauty." Much later the same hilltop and the same view inspired a rich Frenchman to build himself a *belle-époque* manor house here—complete with towers, fairytale stone cottage, and a stable wreathed in wisteria. Now you can spend the night in this enchanted hideaway and dream your own dreams.

When you wake up, pad down to the heated swimming pool. Or take a horse for a canter by the riverside. But save a few ergs for burning up after dark.

First, there's La Tortinière's cheerfully trellised restaurant. Among the specialties of a new but talented chef are *sandre*, a delicate white river fish, poached in white wine; poached salmon with a creamy sorrel sauce; pâté of fresh garden vegetables; and a local oddity, *matelote d'oeuf*, a sort of egg ragout flavored with red wine, mushrooms, and pork; for dessert, don't

159

miss the fresh raspberries heated in a skillet with almonds, cream, and raspberry brandy.

Then, defying all laws of gravity, pick yourself up and catch the late-late *son et lumière* show at Chenonceau, Chambord or Villandry. These are among the grandest of France's grands châteaux in the Loire Valley. And La Tortinière sits right in the middle of them. Wherever you wander, the extravagant folly of some long-lost king or queen or courtier rises up before you. Some of the châteaux are still lived in, but most of the best have been turned into French National Monuments. So now, for a few centimes you can picnic in the same royal glade where Henri II promised Diane de Poitiers that Chenonceaux would be hers forever. (Alas, the promise only lasted as long as Henri did. Then his widow tossed the beautiful Diane out and moved herself into what is still probably the most romantic house west of the Taj Mahal.)

Back at La Tortinière, you'll find all sorts of romantic spots even Henri would have loved. For instance, take an apartment (12) in the tower and you'll have an apricot-velvet Roman bed in your sitting room and a small, sunny bedroom with river view. Or curl up in Room 25, which is usually reserved for wedding nights. Behind a filmy white curtain lies a big bed with a window on each side. One peeks out through the treetops and a parade of old stone turrets on the roof. The other presents you with the river and miles of green and orange trees. The bath is small, tiled and immaculate.

Another sybaritic little suite in the main house is Room 2. Eight-foot-tall windows in the sitting room overlook the dining terrace and a bend of the river beyond. And there's a lovely old tiled bath just off the bedroom.

The most peaceful place of all to stay, though, is in the stable. The original tenants would have a hard time guessing this used to be home. It's now two duplex suites and three other guest rooms. Suite 21 has a snug sitting room and wood-burning fireplace. Upstairs is a bedroom laced with old beams and downy twin beds. There's a modern bathroom on one side and a terrace on the other. Suite 22 has a sitting room downstairs and a staircase leading to a pine-ceilinged bedroom with twin beds and a marvelous vanity corner, all delicate curtains and soft lights. The bath is pink and white tiles, and French doors take you out to a miniscule white terrace.

For seekers of true privacy, however, there's a cottage just on the other side of the main gate. It once belonged to the gardener, but now it looks more like quarters for a pair of amorous Martians. The upstairs consists of a huge beamed sitting-TV room and just off it stands a gigantic round white Thing the owner swears is not a UFO but a super-romantic bed. To go with it there's a shiny modern bath, refrigerator and balcony.

The charm of this storybook manor house lies in more than its towers and turrets. Mme. Olivereau-Capron has lovingly pampered every nook and cranny of the place as if she'd lived here all her life. Which she has. She inherited it from her parents and can't help treating her guests as especially favored friends in her own home. Which, of course, you are. Of all the hotels in the Loire this, for our money, is the warmest and most welcoming.

Come in the spring or fall and miss the humidity and the busloads of tourists who swarm to see châteaux. It will still be warm enough in mid-October to take a dip in the pool. (C.P.)

Name: La Tortinière

Owner/Manager: Mme. Denise Olivereau-Capron

Address: 37250 Montbazon

Location: 6 miles from Tours

Telephone: (47) 26.00.19

Cables/Telex: Boy 750806 162Y

Reps: (None)

Credit Cards: American Express and Diners Club

Rooms: 14 rooms and 7 suites

Meals: Breakfast 8–11, no lunch, dinner 7:30–8:30; dinner for two approx. $60–$65; tie and jacket; room service for breakfast and drinks

Entertainment: (None)

Sports: Heated pool, walking trails; horseback riding and golf nearby

Sightseeing: (See under Château d'Artigny)

P.S. Closed December 1 to February 1

Hôtellerie du Bas-Bréau
Barbizon

♔♔♔✗✗✗$$$

A long line of famous Frenchmen have weekended in this quaint neck of the woods just forty minutes from Paris. It started with kings and courtiers, who came for the stag hunts and liked the neighborhood so much they left it the Royal Forest and the palace at Fountainbleau. Then came the   161 landscapists whose dreamy style got its name from the town of Barbizon. And more recently, Bardot, Montand, Moreau and even César Ritz (when he wanted to take a vacation from his own nice little hotel in Paris). The attraction these days is neither the deer nor the painterly sunlight. It's a humble Hansel-and-Gretel village inn that will cost you, for a brief stay, roughly what Louis XIV spent on his annual budget.

There are, of course, compensations. For instance, a wine cellar of 85,000 bottles, some so old their labels have disintegrated and even the owner doesn't know their exact age. "Somewhere in the late 1800s," he says of one, which is unusually dry and flinty for a Bordeaux Blanc, yet costs less than a so-so '79. And after dinner, there's a 1930 Grand Bas-Armagnac. One small snifter of the stuff is $18. Or you can help owner Jean-Pierre Fava deplete his stock of 67 bottles of 1930 Calvados—the last 67 bottles of it left in the world.

While the service in many of France's three-star restaurants has been sliding steadily, sloppily downhill, Bas-Bréau's stays stubbornly the same. Flawless. You enter a perfect still life of fresh-cut flowers and snowy table linen. Every copper dish, skillet, pitcher and poacher that shows its face has been given a relentless ten-minute polishing that morning—and every morning of its life. Spotless black-tied waiters come and go like acolytes at a high mass. And over it all presides the meticulous M. Fava.

He is one of that endangered species—the innkeeper who, night and day, lives, breathes and watches over every inch of the inn like a mother hen with a dozen Fabergé eggs. Not one spoonful of one meal is served that Fava's eye isn't on it. And long after you've succumbed to your last brandy and tottered off to bed, he's at the market—from 2 A.M. to dawn—personally choosing every last filet of sole and asparagus spear.

If you think Michelin never gets its stars mixed up, compare a meal at Bas-Bréau (one star) with dinner at Allard or Tour d'Argent (three).

As for what makes Bas-Bréau a pet stopover for so many of the world's fattest cats, it's another case of simple perfectionism. There must be hundreds, even thousands, of country inns in France as picturesque, but this is the gleaming little model for all the others to live up to.

Bas-Bréau's gardens are tended by five full-time gardeners. A footman is always at your beck and call. The kitchen will bring anything from iced Perrier to *aiguillettes de canard au vinaigre de la champagne* to your room 24 hours a day. Every room is superbly done, often with fabric walls, enviable antiques, and magnificent tiled baths.

With a nightingale singing to you from the chestnut trees and a sea of delphiniums bursting beneath your casement window, who knows? You may even cease to care what the bill is going to be. (C.P.)

Name: Hôtellerie du Bas-Bréau

Owner/Manager: Jean-Pierre Fava

Address: Barbizon (77 Seine-et-Marne)

Location: In the center of town

Telephone: (1) 066.40.05

Cables/Telex: 690953

Reps: Two World Tours in New York

Credit Cards: American Express, Master Charge/Eurocard

Rooms: 12 rooms, 7 suites

Meals: Breakfast anytime, lunch 12–2:30, dinner 8–9:30; 3-course dinner for two approx. $90; tie and jacket; full room service 24 hours a day

Entertainment: (None)

Sports: Across the road in the Forest of Fountainbleau, there are miles of walking-jogging trails and horseback riding. There's also an excellent 18-hole golf course nearby and fishing and sailing in the Seine.

Sightseeing: The town of Barbizon has been preserved just as it was when Millet and Rousseau were painting there. Their ateliers are open to the public along with a clutch of tiny dusty museums. The Château and Forest of Fountainbleau; Château Vaux le Vicomte; Morey-sur-Loing

P.S. Sometimes closed for a month in early winter

Auberge des Templiers
Les Bézards

WWWXXXX$$$

Templiers is for enjoying the simple pleasures. A snug thatched roof. A soft, wide bed. A warm welcome. A cool pool.

But don't let the less simple pastimes go unsampled. For instance, sip a Lafite-Rothschild 1868 with your *coeur de filet de boeuf au coulis de trufles*. The wine will cost you $800 or thereabouts—but it *has* lived five or six times longer than you have. Or attend one of Templiers' wild-boar barbecues by the swimming pool. Hamburgers will never taste the same. 163

At first glance, Templiers is deceivingly rustic, perhaps because it was once a stagecoach stop. But don't let all that ivy and thatch fool you. You won't have to rough it here. In fact, this is one of the most sumptuous little watering places in France. With superb food and a wine cellar to match.

The bar is a marvelous beamy old room glowing with brass chandeliers and a hearth full of blazing oak. Every last candlestick and tile and beam has been polished and pampered with a perfectionist's fond eye. The mantel and the bar are decked with huge copper tubs full of wheat and dried marsh flowers that look as if they'd been arranged at Max Schling's. A Chopin nocturne comes discreetly purling out from behind crimson-covered walls. The drinks are mixed to perfection. The service is faultless.

In the dining room, there is one cozy alcove just big enough for three— you, your companion and a bottle of champagne. Be sure to ask for it on an evening when dinner is by candlelight.

Templiers' guest rooms are scattered around 12 grassy acres at the edge of the Forest of Orléans. You can stay in the main house within easy reach of food and wine. Or in a brand new pavilion by the pool. Or in a thatch-roofed cottage with pure white, windowed towers and a log fire crackling at the foot of your bed.

Our choice is the thatch cottage (*chaumière* in French).

The tiniest tower room, for instance, is completely round with a silk-walled foyer, weathered old beams, and a glistening carriage lamp to see you safely into bed. Or choose a larger room that's all velvet draperies and bedspreads. Every room at Templiers is furnished with shiny new reproductions so faithful to the original antiques that it's hard to believe Marie Antoinette didn't dally in your bed.

Every bathroom is done with totally different tiles and wallpaper, all in impeccable taste.

Gourmets flock here in fall, the season for dining off France's legendary game. The forest next door to the inn is leaping with rabbit, deer, wild boar, woodcock, pheasant and partridge. And M. Depée, Templiers' dead-eye owner, keeps the kitchen stocked with the best the forest has to offer.

You'll discover that nearly all the inns where food, service and ambience are outstandingly good have one simple thing in common: an owner (or owners) who, no matter how prosperous and famous he is, still does all the shopping for the kitchen himself and oversees every tiny detail of every meal that's served. We can scarcely think of a single really great inn in France where this isn't true.

At Templiers, while the owner is out shooting your dinner, his mother (one of France's very few lady chefs with two stars from Michelin) is at the market, prodding artichokes and snapping asparagus and beans to make certain they're tender enough for you.

There's nothing of special interest in the country around Templiers.

But it's a natural stopping-off place for anyone headed for the South of France, the Alps, the vineyards of Burgundy and the Loire, or the châteaux of the Loire, which begin nearby. You can count on the weather here to be warm and reasonably sunny from late April to mid-October. And the pool is heated whenever there's a chill in the air. (C.P.)

Name: Auberge des Templiers

Owners/Managers: M. and Mme. Jacques Depée

Address: 45290 Les Bézards-Boismorands (Loiret)

Location: About 80 miles south of Paris on Route Nationale 7 (Route Bleue) which goes from Paris to the Riviera

Telephone: (38) 31.80.01

Cables/Telex: Templotel/708998F

Reps: Relais-Châteaux in U.S., Canada and Europe

Credit Cards: American Express

Rooms: 21 rooms, 4 suites

Meals: Breakfast 7–12, lunch 12–2 (grill by the pool in summer), dinner 7:45–9:30; 3-course dinner for two approx. $60–$70; tie and jacket required; room service during dining room hours

Entertainment: Soft music in the lounge, television in some rooms

Sports: Two tennis courts and heated swimming pool; nearby there is golf, horseback riding, hunting, shooting and walking the trails in the Forest of Orléans

Sightseeing: Chateau la Bussiere (Museum of Fishing) and the châteaux and cathedrals of the Loire, the beautiful Chateau and Forest of Fountainebleau, the vineyards of the Loire (e.g. Pouilly) and Burgundy, wine festivals and the Forest of Orleans

P.S. Closed mid-January to mid-February; very small conventions are permitted.

P.P.S. I.K. would like to add a few words to what C.P. has written above. I revisited Auberge des Templiers recently and found it even better than I had remembered. Lunch there was one of the most gratifying meals ever, especially the local salmon smoked over wood right there at the auberge, accompanied by a Sancerre Chavignol Les Monts Damnes, a local vintage. But it wasn't simply the high level of the cuisine, it was also the impeccable dining room, and the dedicated service. If you have problems with the menu

165

or your French here, call over the maître d'hôtel; don't let his fluent French fool you—his name is Stewart Cunningham, he comes from Edinburgh and he'll take very good care of you.

L'Hôtellerie de la Poste
Avallon

WWWXXXX$$$

Most hotelkeepers in France are gleefully proud of their *livres d'ors*—the golden books in which guests record their names and praises. Not so René Hure at La Poste. "Too dangerous," he claims. "Perhaps a husband arrives this week with a lady friend and next month her husband arrives with his. . . ." Probably a wise precaution because La Poste is as cozy a trysting place today as it has been for two and a half centuries. If there were a golden book, however, it would be a Burke's Peerage of romantics: Richard Burton and Elizabeth Taylor, Jean-Paul Belmondo, Gilbert Becaud, Salvador Dali, counts, kings, queens, emperors and assorted eastern potentates in bullet-proof Cadillacs.

Of all its guests the inn is proudest of Napoleon. La Poste was already a hundred years old when the Emperor made a triumphal entry into Avallon on his way back from exile in Elba, just one hundred days before Waterloo. Years later, a youthful John F. Kennedy stopped off here and slept in Napoleon's room, in the single bed beneath a little silken canopy (thereby sacrificing the convenience of a private bathroom).

La Poste owes its eminence to two facts. Because of its location on the main highway out of Paris to Switzerland and the Mediterranean, La Poste has always been a popular relay—but not for old stagecoaches; "only the Cadillacs of stagecoaches." It's a comfortable morning's drive from Paris. You can breakfast at the Ritz or Crillon, drive down through Fontainebleau and pull into the courtyard of La Poste in time for lunch.

The second fact is that La Poste is one of the legendary restaurants of France. Wherever you travel in France, you will find that the best waiters and chefs have probably been trained in one of three places: with the late Ferdinand Point in Vienne, at the Ritz in Paris, or with René Hure in Avallon.

You may be surprised, therefore, when you see how small the dining room is—about twenty tables, plus a few tables in the courtyard when the weather is balmy.

The dining room is elegantly furnished, in keeping with the atmosphere of the inn, and the main wall facing the courtyard is dominated by a massive mellow-hued tapestry of strutting birds in an arcadian park. At the foot of the steps leading down to the restaurant, there's a quiet table for two with a banquette seat—the perfect spot for a loving couple. If you want this table, reserve it early because the restaurant attracts many diners in addition to guests staying at the inn.

We asked M. Hure to plan our meal. Here's his choice.

First, *les amusettes de l'hôtellerie* (roughly translated, the whimsies of the inn). The waiter brought us *pâté de brochet mousseline de cresson*. Follow by *brioche de foie gras*. Followed by *cassolette de queues d'écrevisses*. Followed by *tartelette de ris de veau a l'ancienne*. A prodigious start. For the main course M. Hure's recommendations were *filet d'agneau et petits légumes*, and *poulet de Bresse en civet aux vieux Bourgogne*, a complex version of this most aristocratic of chickens. Burgundian dishes like these leave little room for dessert. We had been looking forward, sustained by memories from a previous visit, to a portion of La Poste's succulent *dolce Borghese*; instead, we settled for *sorbet cassis*, sherbet drenched in the black currant liqueur of Burgundy.

Since this is Burgundy, and since that region's vineyard owners appreciate La Poste's food and have been regular customers through several generations, the inn has one of the finest cellars in France. It stocks about 600 different *types* of wine, from *têtes de cuvées* to unassuming *vins du pays* (but not *too* unassuming, this being Burgundy). If you're feeling especially ardent, you may want to sample a Romanée-Conti 1945 or a Pauillac Château Lafite Rothschild 1964, both around the $100 mark. There's a Santenay Graviers of 1895 which is "no longer particularly good but still interesting"—and fairly inexpensive. If your budget is more restrained than your yearnings, La Poste has a wide selection of moderately priced wines—such as a Chablis Abbaye 1967 or a Pouilly Fuissé 1967.

The proper way to conclude a dinner in Burgundy is with a glass of marc. Be warned. Marc is not soda pop. It's made from the residue that's left after the wine is pressed. After you've quenched the flames, there's not much to do in Avallon except retire to your room and enjoy *les amusettes des lits*.

There are thirty rooms at the Hôtellerie de la Poste and they are all decorated the way you would expect them to be in an old inn catering to a sophisticated clientele. Napoleon/JFK's room is the only one without private bath. It's in the main building, facing the main street. We suggest that you avoid the rooms facing the street if you're a late sleeper (which in a French provincial town means that you're still in bed after seven).

Ask for a room overlooking the narrow cobbled courtyard. Some rooms have private entrances (a delicate touch in a trysting place). Room 23 has a snug little sitting room; but our favorite at La Poste is the cottage at the end of the courtyard, on the edge of the garden. Facing the garden, there's a terrace where you can breakfast with the birds, and a small sitting room with a handsomely polished campaign chest; up a pair of steps, there's a voluminous bed covered with a satin comforter and topped with a silken canopy. The furniture is in the style of Louis XIV—which, come to think of it, was already antique when Napoleon dropped in. Most of the rooms have lock-ups for your car, usually right under your room—one of the advantages of staying in an old staging post.

Avallon is a walled town on a hill above a writhing gorge. It has a history, but not enough of one to entice you to spend much time seeking it out. Its main attraction, apart from La Poste, is that it is convenient as an excursion center for the surrounding countryside—the vineyards of Burgundy, and the hilly region of Morvan, with its forests of oak and ash and pine, and the game for the table at La Poste. You'll find plenty of historical and picturesque spots, châteaux, abbeys, fortified villages and lakes. The great vineyards of Burgundy—Pommard, Vougeot and Romanée-Conti—are in the area around Beaune, which is about half an hour by car from Avallon. You can visit most of these *vignobles* and sample the wine; in September and October you can watch the harvest and the pressing.

Name:	L'Hôtellerie de la Poste
Owner/Manager:	M. René Hure
Address:	Place Vauban, 89200 Avallon (Yonne/Bourgogne)
Location:	121 miles southeast of Paris on Route Nationale 6
Telephone:	(86) 34.06.12
Cables/Telex:	Hotelposte Avallon
Reps:	Relais-Châteaux in U.S., Canada and Europe
Credit Cards:	(None)
Rooms:	25 rooms, 5 suites
Meals:	Breakfast 7–11, lunch 12–3, dinner 7:30–10; dinner for two approx. $40–$45; tie and jacket required; room service during breakfast hours only
Entertainment:	(None)
Sports:	None on the premises, but tennis and a pool two kilometers away
Sightseeing:	Avallon itself has Roman ruins, fortified walls and old cobbled streets and its own museum, but it's also an excellent base for

visiting the surrounding historic towns with their castles and vineyards

P.S. Closed for the months of December and January; no tours or conventions

Hôtellerie du Moulin des Ruats
Avallon

It's *très rustique*—a centuries-old, vine-covered mill beside a swiftly flowing river—but on a Saturday afternoon the parking lot begins to fill early with Porsches, Lancias and Peugeots from Paris. Some of the newly arrived couples go strolling hand-in-hand along the country road among the oaks and birches; others seem to disappear upstairs, to be followed shortly thereafter by white-jacketed waiters with ice buckets, champagne and a couple of goblets.

Hôtellerie du Moulin des Ruats

The moulin is not one of the great kitchens of Burgundy but its woodsy, unpretentious dining room has an ambitious menu from which you can chart a formidable meal: say, *jambon cru du pays, truite au bleu beurre blanc crème du Major Thompson* or *caille des dombes sur canapes,* then *côte du boeuf grillé vigneronne* (for twosomes), to be followed by *tarte aux mirabelles, crêpes des Ruats* (that is, with pineapple and cream) or *soufflé Glacé au café.* The wine list is loyal to the *vins du pays,* from an Aligote at $8 to Chambertins at ten times that amount. There's also a reasonable selection of half bottles.

The Ruat rooms are pleasantly country-innish, with period chairs and chests, bright wallpapers matching bedspreads. There are a couple of attractive rooms (23 and 24) in the adjoining annex; Room 1, facing the road, has a small wooden balcony covered with vine of the virgin; Room 6 among the eaves and rafters also has a small balcony, without vines and facing the River Cousin. Most guests, in fact, ask for a room overlooking the Cousin, but don't be deterred if you're offered one facing the roadway— it's hardly a major highway, and once your maid closes the shutters on your window you won't hear a single Porsche or Lancia.

Name: Hôtellerie du Moulin des Ruats

Owners/Managers: M. and Mme. Francis Bertier

Address: Vallee du Cousin, 89200 Avallon (Yonne/Bourgogne)

Location: A couple of miles from Avallon beside a rushing stream.

Telephone: (86) 34.07.14

Cables/Telex: (None)

Reps: Relais-Châteaux in U.S., Canada and Europe

Credit Cards: American Express, Master Charge/Eurocard

Rooms: 21 rooms, 13 with private bath

Meals: Breakfast from 7:30 on, lunch 12–2, dinner 7–9; dinner for two approx. $50; dress informal; room service for breakfast and drinks only

Entertainment: (None)

Sports: (None)

Sightseeing: (See Hôtellerie de la Poste)

P.S. Closed the last Sunday in October through the first Saturday in March; the inn looks its best from May on, when the *vigne vierge* is leafy and the garden is filled with roses and begonias

Chez La Mère Blanc
Vonnas

W XXX $$

Your first sight of Chez La Mère Blanc suggests a relatively modern operation, but in fact Georges and Jacqueline Blanc are the fourth generation of the family to work here. Since the 1880s, La Mère Blanc has probably been the sole reason for coming to Vonnas, a quiet village of some 5000 souls, well off the beaten track; its solitary claim to fame these days seems to be that its flower gardens earned it the title of number one garden village in the European Common Market in 1978. Over the years, the restaurant/hotel has evolved, expanded, tacked on, modernized (the latest addition—a gleaming new $150,000 kitchen, which you can inspect on your way to the dining room—hence the deceptive exterior).

But there's nothing deceptive about the cuisine (it rates two stars in the Michelin Guide), so work up a Burgundian appetite and order as follows: *foie gras d'oie marine au vieux porto* et *petite terrine d'artichaut, fricassée de poularde de Bresse au vin de Julienas et aux champignons sauvages*, followed by a nibble or two from the selection of twenty or so *fromages frais et affinés*, followed by a nibble or three from *le grand assortiment des desserts*. That's the 110 franc menu. A la carte, begin with *petite tarte aux poireaux et aux oignons blancs* (outstanding), then *poularde a la crème a la façon de La Mère Blanc* (exceptional), followed by et cetera. The selection of 450 wines includes, in addition to 14 Meursaults and 24 Volnay vintages, some surprisingly inexpensive half bottles—such as the Mâcon Viré Clos du Chapitre at roughly $7.

La Mère Blanc would be a good introduction to 2-star dining: the quality is there, but there's nothing overwhelming about the place. Georges and Jacqueline Blanc are young and charming, the dining-room staff is polite and attentive, and they'll take time to explain the *spécialités de la maison*. In the cooler months, dinner is served in a handsome 22-table room dominated by a wall-to-wall Flemish tapestry, ornate gilt mirrors, a monumental stone fireplace and enormous vases brimming with fresh flowers; in summer, you dine on the terrace beside the stream.

Not all the Blanc greenbacks have been lavished on the kitchen; the guest rooms, are, in their modest way, lavish, a combination of modern comforts (some rooms come equipped with trouser pressers, some have color TV) and period furnishings. The bathrooms are almost sybaritic, with armrests in the tubs, Worth soap, L'Air du Temps bath oil, fluffy towels and fluffy white bathrobes. Despite that modest exterior, then, Chez La Mère Blanc is quite a classy little place. Jean-Louis Trintignant and Richard Burton are two of the celebrities whose signed caricatures decorate

171

the walls of the lounge. And where else have you found a country restaurant with a logo *"crée par Raymond Loewy"*?

Name: Chez La Mère Blanc

Owners/Managers: M. and Mme. Georges Blanc

Address: 01540 Vonnas (Ain)

Location: 40 miles northeast of Lyon, between Mâcon and Bourg-en-Bresse, in the heart of Burgundy

Telephone: (74) 50.00.10

Cables/Telex: Geblanc/380776

Reps: Relaix-Châteaux in U.S., Canada and Europe

Credit Cards: American Express, Diners Club

Rooms: 16 rooms, 2 suites

Meals: Breakfast 7–12, lunch 12–2, dinner 7:30–9:30; 3-course dinner for two $50 and up; dress informal; room service for breakfast and drinks only

Entertainment: Television in rooms

Sports: Heated swimming pool; nearby—tennis, riding (5 kms) and golf (10 kms)

Sightseeing: Churches and castles and the fabulous vineyards of Burgundy

P.S. Closed for the month of January and every Wednesday and Thursday at lunchtime; no groups or tours

---

Hôtel de la Verniaz
Evian-les-Bains

♔ ✗✗ $$$

When you walk through the vine-covered archway and into the leafy courtyard, just about the first thing you see is a huge outdoor rotisserie, which tells you that the emphasis here is on dining. The second feature you see is a circular tower which houses a bar decked out, surprisingly, with plaids and other Scottish motifs. Behind it, in what was once the coach house, you'll find the formal flower-decorated dining room and *la rôtisserie de l'hiver,* or winter rotisserie; but in warm weather (which apparently occurs more often than you might think here) tables and chairs are set out among the tulips or roses, beneath the chestnut and linden trees. The advantage of the terrace is that you can enjoy your *filet de Charolais à la brioche* and a bottle of Pomerol without having to listen to "Stormy Weather" on the tape deck. The guest rooms at La Verniaz are located at various points throughout the garden, among the flower beds and pool and tennis court. Those in the coach house, above the dining room, should have the best view, but, alas, power cables and telephone poles clutter up the scenery. Twenty-eight of the forty rooms are housed in the main lodge, a three-story structure with a facade of balconies in slender columns, the corridors lined with French hunting prints, the double doors padded to keep sounds out—or in. Rooms at the rear look out on trees and cost a few dollars less; rooms at the front, on the second and third floors, have the best views of lake and hills. Room 70 on the third floor has a raftered ceiling, an enormous antique wardrobe and an oddly shaped corner bathroom—but the most romantic room is a dollhouse chalet called Liseron, very snug, with heart shaped windows in the bathroom and a sundeck overlooking the pool. It's also the most expensive room in the hotel.

Room rates are probably higher than the rooms merit, but the menu prices are reasonable—and you will find a pleasant garden and lots of fresh air.

Name: Hôtel de la Verniaz

Owners/Managers: Marcel Verdier Family

Address: 74500 Evian-les-Bains (Haute-Savoie)

Location: In the hills, about 15 minutes from the shore of Lake Geneva, one hour from Geneva

Telephone: (50) 750490

Telex: 385715

Reps: Relais-Châteaux in U.S., Canada and Europe

Credit Cards: American Express, Diners Club, Carte Blanche, Master Charge/Eurocard

Rooms: 40, in two main buildings and 4 chalets

Meals: Breakfast from 7:30, lunch 12-2, dinner 7:30-9, in the patio when the sun shines; dinner for two approx. $40-$45; informal dress; room service for breakfast only (all rooms have minibars)

Entertainment: TV room, billiards; casino in Evian

Sports: Tennis court, swimming pool, sauna, massage; indoor driving range for golfers; horseback riding across the street; golf, watersports, winter sports nearby

Sightseeing: Boat trips on Lake Geneva; Montreux and Geneva, the Alps

P.S.   Closed December and January; no tour groups, but some small seminars in the off-season

Hôtel Les Prés Fleuris
Evian

♛✗$$$

You're higher here than at La Verniaz, and from the terrace among the fruit trees you have a sweeping view of Lake Geneva. Cowbells tinkle in the pastures, pear and cherry trees grow in the orchard, white-flowered knotweed climbs the walls, and the meadows are, as the name says, abloom with flowers. Likewise the interior. Flowers (some plastic, though) and greenery (fresh) everywhere. This hundred-year-old farmhouse combines the folksy charm of a farm with the upholstered comforts of a salon—a happy blending of tile-topped tables and cut-velvet sofas, antique coal bunkers with modern plate-glass windows eager to take in the view. The dozen guest rooms are divided between the original chalet-style farmhouse and a newer wing, all with double *and* twin beds, small lounge area, color TV, minibar, room phones and loggias large enough for breakfasting. Farmyard animals in silver, ceramic, copper and wood decorate the dining room, which is highly regarded in these parts. Georges Demonceau is chef de cuisine; Mme. Demonceau runs the hotel—and the beehives in the garden. If you're looking for a very quiet, unpretentious, take-it-easy kind of place, the Flowery Meadows might be your ideal.

Name: Hôtel Les Prés Fleuris

Owners/Managers: M. and Mme. Demonceau-Frossard

174   **Address:**   74500 Evian-les-Bains (Haute Savoie)

Location: Half a mile above Evian, about 5 very winding miles from town on Route 24 to Thollon Grand Roc

Telephone: (50) 752914

Cables/Telex: (None)

Reps: Relais-Châteaux in U.S., Canada and Europe

Credit Cards: American Express, Diners, Carte Bleu, Eurocheque

Rooms: 12

Meals: Breakfast from 8, lunch 12–2:30, dinner 7–9:30; (on the terrace when the sun shines) dinner for two approx. $38–$42; informal dress; room service for breakfast only (minibars in the rooms)

Entertainment: Color TV in the rooms

Sports: Walking trails from the garden; other sports in Evian

Sightseeing: (See Hôtel de la Verniaz)

P.S. Closed mid-October to the end of March; "curative waters from the Evian spa can be delivered every morning before seven"

L'Auberge du Père Bise
Talloires

♥♥♥♥✕✕✕✕$$$$

When you throw open the shutters of your room at the auberge, you look out upon a scene so sublime it seems to be nature's answer to a Mozart violin sonata. Across Lake Annecy, the Alps rise from the rippling waters to peaks with a frosting of snow. On the left, the Château du Duingt squats on its rocky island. By the edge of the lawn, where the willow reaches down to tickle the lake, a swan is drifting around waiting for the tidbits it knows will come sooner or later. If ever there was a setting designed for lovers, this is it.

But your delights don't end there. When you come down for meals, you dine on the terrace beneath linden trees, or in one of the loveliest dining rooms we've ever seen. It's an airy place, with floor-to-ceiling windows, against one wall of beautifully carved wood with tinted casement windows; you are somehow blinded by sun, bowls of fresh flowers, sparkling silverware and table linen whiter than the swan out on the lake. The auberge

175

is one of the shrines of French gastronomy, rated with three stars in the Guide Michelin. Gourmets and gourmands and other discerning travelers detour to this corner of Haute Savoie just to dine at Père Bise. The Rothschilds—Guy, Edmond and Elie—stop off here on their way to their ski resort at Megève; the conferees of Geneva drive over for lunch or dinner; the Comte de Certau, lucky fellow, crosses over from Château Duingt; Brigitte Bardot, Gina Lollobrigida and Charles Aznavour drop in now and then; other hungry people have set out from Paris or Amsterdam or London or New York—with the single goal of dining at Père Bise.

Many of them have been coming here since the original Père Bise opened his auberge sixty years ago. Now that the line of succession has passed via son and daughter-in-law to the present chef, François Bise, and his wife, they still come. A few of them may nod their heads nostalgically and say things aren't what they were in the old days, and one or two of them may leap for each new issue of Michelin to see if François has retained his three stars. François Bise is determined to maintain the reputation of the restaurant. And why shouldn't he? Since he was a toddler this has been his world. He learned about cooking at the knees of *grand-père* and papa and all the great gourmets who came there to dine. He learned about wine by listening to the conversations of the owners of France's great vineyards when they sat around over brandy discussing *cuvées, vendanges*, and *soutirage*. Three stars or two stars, the auberge is worth a detour.

We dined off fresh asparagus with a *mousseline* sauce, and until you've tasted asparagus in a restaurant like Père Bise you have no idea how voluptuous it can be; *mousse de foie de volaille au xérès; carré d'agneau*; a selection of cheeses from the groaning cheese board—Reblochon, Chèvre de Montagne, Rigotte and Pont l'Évêque (the swan's favorite, by the way, is Chabouchon). After the cheeses, the waiters bring you two platefuls of petits fours—*secs* and *glacés*—about two dozen goodies on the plates; taste one and you have no choice but to polish them off. In most restaurants back home, petits fours such as these would have been the highlights of the meal.

One of the outstanding dishes of this region is *omble-chevalier*—a fish from the mountain streams and lakes, in texture and flavor somewhere between a trout and a salmon. At Père Bise, they prepare it braised in port and cream, in aspic with a *sauce vermeille*, or poached with *sauce Nantua*. Plan your vacation properly, and you can have your *omble* all of those ways. If you pick your season carefully, you can also descend on Père Bise for partridge fed on vine leaves, hare cooked *à la royale*, young chicken braised with fresh *morilles* (the forest mushrooms Madame du Barry used to serve Louis XV, to renew his interest), and *volaille Souvaroff*, which you must order one hour in advance—chicken stuffed with chopped foie gras and truffles, sprinkled with cognac, and cooked in a casserole sealed with a strip of dough.

176   The desserts at Père Bise match the surrounding Alps in splendor.

We'll taunt you with just three—*frangipane ambassadeur Grand Marnier*, which is a fluffy cream oozing with Grand Marnier; *mille-feuille Marzolaine bois joli* is layer upon layer of paper thin pastry with chocolate; and the *soufflé Rothschild Grand Marnier* (how grand to visit a three-star restaurant and find a soufflé named for you; somehow *soufflé Keown* does not have quite the proper ring).

We had a Morey St. Denis Clos de la Roche 1970 with dinner, but the next day at lunch we chose a beguiling Cheval Blanc on the recommendation of M. Bise. His own favorites from his superb stock include Château Margaux 1947, a Palmer 1966, and a 1953 Latour. His cellar also stocks a wine you don't see on too many wine lists; in fact you may not even see a bottle at Père Bise since he is allowed only 36 bottles a year, and *that's* as a special favor. It's a Haut-Brion Blanc.

Take a peek into Père Bise's kitchen; you probably wouldn't want to work there because the copperware, stainless steel and tiles are so gleaming if you dropped a crumb on the floor, we're sure Père Bise would throw you in the lake.

There are now two dozen rooms at Père Bise, a few in the main building above the dining room, the remainder in annexes in the garden. They're all different, all much plusher than you might expect in a country inn, even a country inn with three Michelin stars. We happened to prefer the old style French Provincial rooms, but there's no denying that the new decor adds up to a collection of very cozy love nests. The largest rooms are in the main building, and of these you might prefer La Tour, which has a small sitting area with TV, wooden rafters and wooden stairs. Le Nant Sec has rustic modern furnishings and a large wooden balcony overlooking the lake dock; La Baie has a view of the lake; Le Roc de Chene, a corner room with windows on two sides, is furnished in the style of Louis XV and the TV is concealed in a boudoir table. The suites in the pavilion across the garden are rather grand, with concealed TV and Telefunken radios in paneled closets, bedside controls for lights and electric window shades. Suite 28 comes in shades of lavender, blue and lilac.

Obviously, you can get lazy in a place like this. It's very easy to lapse into a routine of breakfast, lounge chair, lunch, siesta, dinner, bed, which has a lot to be said for it. Go for a swim in the lake. Or rent a rowboat and race the swans.

Name: L'Auberge du Père Bise

Owners/Managers: François and Charlyne Bise

Address: 74290 Talloires (Haute Savoie)

Location: On the shores of Lake Annecy, about 8 miles south of the town of Annecy, about 1½ hours by car from Geneva

Telephone:	(50) 447201
Telex:	385812
Reps:	Relais-Châteaux in U.S., Canada and Europe
Credit Cards:	American Express, Diners Club
Rooms:	24, including 6 suites

Meals: Breakfast 7–11, lunch 12–2:30, dinner 7:30–9:30; on the terrace when the weather is right; dinner for two approx. $80–$90; tie and jacket preferred; room service for breakfast only (all rooms have minibars)

Entertainment: TV in rooms, casino in Annecy

Sports: Tennis (4 courts), beach, golf, horseback riding, boating, watersports—all nearby

Sightseeing: Lake Annecy, boat trips on lake, Old Annecy, Château of Montrottier, the mountains, Geneva

P.S. Closed November to January

Moulin du Roc
Champagnac de Belair

WWWXX$$

After two hundred years of jostling with each other, the Mill of the Rock and the fertile soil of Périgord seem to have reached a state of détente: in winter, the mill stands out, the simplicity of its sturdy gray walls clearly defined; but from spring on the mill all but disappears in an embrace of vines and hedgegrows, jonquils and begonias and the sun-dappled leafiness of *tilleul, peuplier* and *ormeau*. It's an enchanted setting this, with the River Dronne flowing by, a delight for all the senses. For the eye, the honest proportions of the mill, the mottled texture of its stone walls and wooden shutters. For the ear, the chirping of the birds, the purl of the mill stream. For the nose, the fragrance of roses and geraniums and freshly mown grass. Indoors, the enchantment begins all over again. Of all the ancient mills we've seen converted into inns, few have been transformed with quite so much charm, flair and whimsy. The backdrop of native stone and sturdy wooden beams is accented with splashes of flowers and cheery fabrics. Cogwheels, bellows, copper vats and other paraphernalia of the oil-pressing

178

Moulin du Roc

mechanism have been recast as plant holders or coffee tables, or, simply, objets, and the centerpiece of the salon is a vitrine displaying the actual mill wheel. In the dining room, the beam-and-stone setting is softened by hand-sewn antique tapestry curtains, oriental rugs and an ornate bronze pendulum clock. Tables for twosomes have been set aside in quiet corners, set with flowers and candles and gleaming napery.

Each of the five guest rooms is different, but each creates a charming environment with hand-carved chests and *ciel de lit*, dainty lace and copper pots, tapestries and paintings, TV, minibars and telephones have been concealed in antique armoires and commodes. Some people may find the rooms small, but for lovers curled up on bed they're romantic as fairytales. Which one you choose may depend on the view. Orge overlooks the bridge across the Dronne; Ble peeps out at reeds, the cascade and *peupliers* across   179 the river. Pop your head out of the window of Mais and you look directly down on the water wheel. The magicians who created the Mill on the Rock, the Gardillous, are a congenial, youngish couple with a background of innkeeping but no special training in decorating. Just natural flair. Solange Gardillou doubles as chef de cuisine while her husband runs the restaurant (her *truite aux cèpes* is highly recommended). The role of Moon, the lumbering St. Bernard, is less certain.

The Moulin au Roc is an admirable base for touring the countryside of the Dordogne, but you're excused if you never venture beyond the vein-covered gate. Sit in the garden and dream. Sniff the roses. Listen to the mill stream. Sip a glass of champagne in the gazebo. This is, to paraphrase Wordsworth, a place to loaf and invite the soul.

Name: Moulin du Roc

Owners/Managers: M. and Mme. Gardillou

Address: 24530 Champagnac de Belair (Dordogne)

Location: On Route D83, about 45 miles southwest of Limoges, about 75 miles northeast of Bordeaux, near a town called Brantôme

---

Telephone: (53) 548036

Telex: Chacoper 57335 Roc

Reps: Relais-Châteaux in U.S., Canada and Europe

Credit Cards: American Express

Rooms: 5

Meals: Breakfast 8–9:30, lunch 12:30–1:30, dinner 8–9; dinner for two approx. $35–$40; tie and jacket; room service for breakfast only (stocked minibars in all rooms)

Entertainment: TV in guest rooms, soft classical music in lounge

---

Sports: Walking through the forest and along the river, bikes and rowboats; swimming pool, tennis and horseback riding nearby

---

Sightseeing: The abbey in Brantome, boat trips through Brantome's canals, grotto at Vilan; the Foire aux Montois at Champagnac (August)

P.S. Closed November 1–December 20; "not too keen on children"; M. Gardillou speaks some English, the staff somewhat less, but since everyone is so hospitable, so concerned, you should have few problems with language. Moon responds to a scratch behind the ear, regardless of the language.

Le Vieux Logis
Trémolat

ŵŵ✗$$

The Dordogne, that bucolic corner of Central France, is about as uncrowded as any region in the land, and Trémolat is as uncrowded as any village in the Dordogne. Narrow streets zigzag past *boulangerie* and *boucherie*, a somber Romanesque church dominates the town square with its war memorial. Walk two streets and you're back among the fields and orchards. Le Vieux Logis, just off the square, blends in discreetly with this setting. *Vigne vierge* covers the old stone walls, moss ages the rust-colored tiles. Flowers blossom, birds chatter, a rivulet trickles through the garden between the lawn and the weathered *jeu d'eaux*. The trees that tower over the roof tiles are a couple of hundred years old if they're a day, but they're mere saplings compared with the house itself. This old Périgord farmhouse, and its cottages in the garden, have been in the Giraudel family for some five hundred years. When the reigning Mme. Giraudel-Desord converted the dwellings to a hotel a quarter of a century ago, she didn't have to rush out and buy furniture. It was all there. To this day, you sit on, sleep in and dine off family heirlooms. Only the tiled bathrooms are new (a few have showers only, by the way). Each is furnished differently, of course, but all in a style that can only be identified as Farmhouse Cozy, with carpeting, big comfy beds, print wallpapers and, of course, antique chests and commodes. Room 4, one of the prettiest, has a four-poster bed, oak washstand and a minibar. Look around and choose your room before settling in, if you have a chance, but just to stay in Le Vieux Logis, in any room is to plop yourselves into *la vie de campagne*.

Name: Le Vieux Logis et ses Logis des Champs

Owner/Manager: Mme. Giraudel-Destord

Address: 24510 Trémolat (Dordogne)

Location: In Périgord, on the back roads between Bergerac and Sarlat, on the north bank of the River Dordogne, where it makes a great loop known as *Le Cingle de Trémolat*, about 75 miles due east of Bordeaux

Telephone: (53) 618006

Telex: 570418

Reps: Relais-Châteaux in U.S., Canada and Europe

Credit Cards: American Express

Rooms: 14, including 3 suites, in the main building and a garden annex

Meals: Breakfast 7–10, lunch 12–2, dinner 7–9; dinner for two approx. $35–$40; informal dress; room service for breakfast only (or cold plates on request)

Entertainment: A log fire. Birds. Conversation

Sports: Nearby—tennis, horseback riding, sailing

Sightseeing: Castles (more than a thousand of them), old churches and churchyards (by the hundreds), caves (dozens); Museum of Prehistory at Les Eyzies; Drama Festival at Sarlat (July and August), International Music Festival of Gourdon and Quercy (July and August)

P.S. Closed January and February (and the restaurant is closed also in November and December except to overnight guests)

La Métairie
Mauzac

WX$$

A typical old Périgord farmhouse, with vine-clad beige stone and tall, steeply angled russet roof, it's been weathering on its hilltop above the Dordogne now for almost 400 years. Fifteen years ago it was renovated and transformed into a charming country-house hotel. At first glance it looks like a stable, and when you step into the tiny lobby, sure enough the hat stand is draped with riding gear. The family's. There are no riding facilities at La Métairie itself, but the equestrian Vignerons will show you where to rent horses in the neighborhood. The lounge gives off a lovely rustic effect with its beamed ceilings, log-burning fireplace and stone stairway, and the guest rooms are furnished in dainty French Provincial style with pastoral-print wallpapers and mahogany beds. Room 11 is probably the simplest but the most charming, with a big bed set into an alcove under the ancient wooden beams (the tiled bathroom has shower only, no bath). Another attractive love nest is the apartment, with its own discreet entrance and own terrace overlooking a plum tree. The remaining score of guests have to settle for an attractive communal terrace overlooking the valley, a restful place to have breakfast or sip noontime drinks. In the evening, you can sample local dishes prepared by the Alsatian chef, and sample one of the local wines—such as a Pecharmant from Bergerac.

182

It's a shame that La Métairie and Le Vieux Logis are located within a couple of miles of each other. How you choose between them I don't know—unless you want a swimming pool in the yard, in which case you make a dive for La Métairie.

Name: La Métairie

Owner/Manager: Madame Vigneron

Address: Mauzac, 24150 Lalinde (Dordogne)

Location: Like Le Vieux Logis (above), on the north bank of the Dordogne, between Bergerac and Le Bugue, near the intersections of routes C301 and C303

Telephone: (53) 615047

Cables/Telex: (None)

Reps: Relais-Châteaux in U.S., Canada and Europe

Credit Cards: American Express

Rooms: 11

Meals: Breakfast 8–9:30, lunch 12:30–2, dinner 7:30–9; dinner for two approx. $40; dress—*correcte*, that is, tie and jackets for gentlemen at dinner; room service for breakfast and drinks only

Entertainment: (None)

Sports: Swimming pool; tennis, horseback riding and sailing nearby

Sightseeing: (See Le Vieux Logis)

P.S. Closed November to Easter; it helps to speak some French here

Château de Mercuès
near Cahors

♛♛♛✕✕$$$

This is a real once-upon-a-time place, where Pelléas and Melisande wouldn't look out of place dallying in the garden. Once upon a time, the Château of Mercuès was the home of the bishops of Cahors. Once upon another time, during the 16th-century's wars of religion, it was the scene of a brutal battle. It couldn't have been an easy place to attack. The castle crowns a hill that rises abruptly from the banks of the River Lot. In its present peaceful role as a hotel, Mercuès is surrounded by a garden filled with cedars, pines, crabapple trees and in the month of June 600 prize roses. The spacious terrace has a majestic view over the valley of the Lot, and at one end it dips down to a second terrace with a secluded Olympic-sized swimming pool. Beyond that, 50 acres of forest invite you to walk and picnic among medieval statues, fountains and wells. The castle's chapel, with 300-year-old stained-glass windows, has been converted into a meeting room; the former guard room and dungeon is now a bar and lounge; and the bishops' drawing room is now a bar looking out on the garden with the cedars, pines and crabapple trees.

There are 23 rooms at Mercuès, and one of them is so romantic it towers above the others—literally. It's one of the most fascinating rooms in France, and a favorite nook for honeymooning daughters of princes and occasionally for reigning queens. Suite 11 is all spiral stairways, oaken doors, turrets, crenellations and *archières*. The bedroom is in the turret, a case for a square bed in a round room, almost totally enclosed with draperies. Above the bed, among the old beams, there's a large glass panel which opens upward at the press of a switch to reveal the naked beams and joists of the peak of the tower.

Suite 11 is, of course, rather expensive. If you want something more modest, a chamber for the courtier rather than the prince, try Room 10. It's an enormous bedroom-cum-sitting room, with sofa and desk, and an equally spacious bathroom built into one of the towers, retaining the roughhewn stones of the original wall. Here you can bathe in the round, sink into the bubbles and reach for your soap from a shelf that's 300 years old if it's a day.

In the smaller turret over by the chapel, Suite 13 has a compact sitting room and a bedroom with a window directly over the frothing weir 400 feet below; in the distance, the landscape is a checkerboard of cornfields, farmyards, and pastures with statuesque cattle. You get the same view from the bathtub.

Suite 8 is small but daintily posh, with its own stairway up to the

Its sitting room has a huge stone fireplace; one flight up, you have a cozy round bedroom with a window over the weir.

Geographically, the Château of Mercuès is in the region of Lot in the province of Guienne; gastronomically, it's in the heart of Truffle Land. If you never quite understood the mystique of the truffle, here's where to find out what the fuss is all about.

The Mercuès menu lists no fewer than eight different dishes featuring the fabulous *truffe*. If you were so inclined you could have truffle soup, truffle appetizers, truffles for the main dish. Not even the most zealous Guienner would go that far. To sample the truffle unadorned, order *truffe á gros sel* (you can make it your main dish if you want); the waiter will then bring you something that looks like a black golf ball, with a pile of coarse salt on one side and warm walnut oil on the other. The flavor is subtle to the point of evasiveness, but if you find it, positively unique. If the mystery of truffles eludes you, don't despair; the chefs at Mercuès also know their way around the classic dishes of French cuisine.

There's another specialty of the region you should sample at Mercuès—the Black Wines of Cahors. They get their name from their deep red hue, and they're something of a legend beyond their own region because they don't travel well.

Besides the big swimming pool, the château has Ping-Pong and *pétanque* (France's boccie), and five miles away there are facilities for riding, with some superb trails over the scraggy moors known as *carrigues*.

Cahors, which is only five miles from the château, is a historic town on a loop of the Lot, and is famous for its Valentre Bridge and 13th-century cathedral of St. Étienne. It's also close to some of the great grottoes with prehistoric remains, and to the shrine of Rocamadour. During the summer months, there are several *son-et-lumière* productions in the neighborhood.

The Château of Mercuès has been a hotel since 1966 and the place is spotless; but there are still a few rough spots in its service and a few lapses in its decor (like the peculiar soldier models on the walls of the dining room). It's also a shade overpriced. But if money is no object, don't let a few dollars stand between you and Camelot.

Name: Château de Mercuès

Manager: André Souiller

Address: 46000 Mercuès, Cahors (Lot)

Location: In the heart of France, just off Route Nationale 20, between Limoges and Toulouse, about 8 miles from Cahors

Telephone: (65) 360001

Telex: 520602

Reps: Relais-Châteaux in U.S., Canada and Europe

Credit Cards: American Express

Rooms: 23

Meals: Breakfast from 7:30, lunch 12:30–2:30, dinner 7:30–8:30; dinner for two approx. $90; informal dress; no room service

Entertainment: TV room

Sports: Two tennis courts, swimming pool; horseback riding nearby

Sightseeing: In Cahors, the cathedral and Valentre Bridge; village of St. Circq Lapopie and castle Bonaguil; grottoes at Rocamadour, Sarlat, Les Eyzies and Padirac

P.S. Closed January through March; some small seminars in the off-season

Hôtellerie le Prieuré
Villeneuve-lez-Avignon

ᗯᗯ💥💥 $$$

The parking lot is screened from the garden and tennis courts by trees, you walk to the reception desk through a rose arbor, and lunch is served in the courtyard beneath a 150-year-old plane tree. Le Prieuré was built in the 14th century for a wealthy cardinal, Arnand de Via, and since then it has seen service as priory, private school, boarding house for artists, and now in its new guise as a luxury hotel. Credit for the transformation goes to the Mille family, most recently Jacques and Marie-France, a warm, hospitable couple who have brought the hotel to its present luxurious state. Half the guest rooms are in a new 4-story wing beside the swimming pool, but many romantics prefer the older rooms, filled with period furnishings befitting a former cardinal's residence. All of them now have minibars and air-conditioning, most of them have also color TV and private wall safes. The newer rooms are semisuites, with comfy armchairs and sturdy coffee tables, tiled floors and scatter rugs (the upper floors are best, away from the pool sounds); of the rooms in the original wing, Room 5, above the courtyard, is particularly spacious, 9, a smaller room (less expensive, too) has a blue-tiled bathroom up five marble steps; 11 is large and overlooks the red-tiled roofs of the town.

186

Villeneuve-lez-Avignon is an interesting little backwater in its own right, with its historic fort, the Tower of Philip the Fair, ancient churches and winding streets, and panoramic views of Avignon just across the river.

Name: Hôtellerie le Prieuré

Owners/Managers: Jacques and Marie-France Mille

Address: 7 Place du Chapitre, 30400 Villeneuve-Lez-Avignon (Gard)

Location: Just across the river from Avignon, 3 hours south of Lyon, 1 hour north of Marseille.

Telephone: (90) 25.18.20

Cables/Telex: Prieuré Avignon/431.042

Reps: Relais-Châteaux in U.S., Canada and Europe

Credit Cards: American Express, Master Charge/Eurocard, Visa

Rooms: 22 rooms, 7 suites

Meals: Breakfast 7:30–11, lunch 12–2, dinner 7–9:30 (served in the courtyard in warm weather); dinner for two approx. $60–$70; dress informal; room service during dining room hours

Entertainment: In Avignon—cafés, nightclubs, concerts, recitals

Sports: Pool, two quick-drying tennis courts; nearby, horseback riding

Sightseeing: In Villeneuve-lez-Avignon, the Tower of Phillip the Fair, the medieval Fort André (superb view of Avignon from its crenellated ramparts and towers), La Chartreuse de Val de Benédiction, once a Carthusian abbey; in Avignon, Le Petit Palais Museum, Calvet Museum, Palace of the Popes, where summer drama festivals are now held; nearby, Roman ruins in Arles, Nîmes, St.-Remy and Orange, Fontaine-de-Vaucluse (remembered for the poet Petrarch and his adored Laura), Châteauneuf-du-Pape vineyards; music festivals in Aix and Orange; jazz festival in Salon-en-Provence

P.S. Closed November 1–end of February; some small tour groups; lunch guests may use the swimming pool (especially on weekends, which usually means families)

Château de Rochegude
Rochegude

WWXX $$$

Have the chef pack you a picnic basket for lunch and find yourself a mossy rendezvous in Rochegude's 35 acres of private park. (If you climb long enough and high enough, you can picnic in the ruins of an ancient temple of love.)

You may want to mosey farther afield among the Roman ruins in the hills beyond. Or just spend your afternoon dipping into the chateau's huge Roman pool.

Earlier owners of this 900-year-old castle gave it sweeping stone terraces, cobbled courtyards, and sky-high halls and bedchambers. The incumbent has made some nice additions of his own. Crystal chandeliers and antique furniture dating from the Renaissance to Napoleon III. And large, luxurious bathrooms. And quite a good restaurant, which prides itself on its crayfish, trout braised in champagne, and *pintadeau* (a tiny game bird of exceptionally subtle flavor).

The 26 rooms and apartments have names, not numbers. Chinon is one of the most prepossessing rooms, with its 16-foot ceilings and mirrored walls. Amboise has a great marble fireplace and a tiled bathroom that opens onto a terrace. You can take your morning bath alfresco while you listen to the choirboys practicing below. Our favorite, though, is Laetitia. Not so much for the room (which is pleasant, but unspectacular) as for the terrace—one of the biggest and grandest we've seen. At one end of it, there's the vestige of a wall that was partly destroyed in some medieval war; it makes a marvelously private nook for having drinks and soaking up the view of the valley beyond. At the other end, an enormous stone fountain of Neptune splutters and splashes for you. Very soothing when the lights are out and you're unwinding after a busy day.

Rochegude is a handy stopping-off place on your way to the Côte d'Azur. We recommend arriving in time for a swim, a snooze in the sun and dinner. A few hours' sleep and breakfast will send you on your way, and you can be on the Riviera by lunchtime. (C.P.)

Name:	Château de Rochegude
Owner:	Fernand Galibert
Manager:	André M. Chabert
Address:	26130 Rochegude (Drôme)

Location: Just east of the Autoroute du Soleil, 10 miles north of Orange at the junction of routes D117 and D8

Telephone: (75) 048188

Telex: 345661

Reps: Relais-Châteaux in U.S., Canada and Europe

Credit Cards: American Express, Diners Club, Master Charge/Eurocard

Rooms: 26, including 4 suites (all with air-conditioning)

Meals: Breakfast 8–11, lunch 12:30–1:30, dinner 7:30–9:30; dinner for two approx. $55; tie and jacket; room service for breakfast and dinner

Entertainment: TV room

Sports: Tennis court (lighted), swimming pool, walking trails; horseback riding nearby

Sightseeing: Roman Museum in Orange and Vaison-la-Romaine, Le Maison de Fabre in Serignan, Roman theaters in Orange and Vaison, Pont du Gard in Nîmes, Grignan Castle, festivals in Orange and Avignon

P.S. Closed November 1 to March 1; taped music in lounge and dining room

L'Auberge de Noves
Noves

♔♔♔ ✗✗✗ $$$

Here's another snoozy stopover on the way to the Côte d'Azur, where you can get reacquainted with the long-lost joys of doing absolutely nothing. Nothing but dabbling in the swimming pool. And gazing across blue-green hills to the ruined turrets of Châteaurenard. And eating. And eating. And eating.

Michelin's merry men have blessed the Auberge de Noves with two stars, which is a mighty show of approval. After all, there are only 60 or so two-star restaurants in all of France.

Consider some of the reasons for Noves' two: Lobster soufflé. Fresh truffles stuffed with *foie gras*, rolled in ham, and cooked in a pastry. Baby chicken *(pousinette)* baked in cream sauce with truffles. Praline mousse

189

whipped with raisins and rum and awash with hot chocolate sauce.

Twenty-five thousand bottles lie waiting in the wine cellar. For those with uncompromising taste buds, the inn has plenty of Château Margaux '29s and Lafite '28s. But M. Lalleman, the owner, will probably suggest a private-label Châteauneuf de Pape from the region since you won't get a better one anywhere in France (and, indeed, some of them you may not find elsewhere—Domaine Ott, Bellet Château Cremat, Lapalette Château Simone.

As for the service, it's good if not great.

The dining room has a giant fireplace and one long wall of scene-stealing windows. But the place to dine is the terrace, where you sit high on a windy hill with miles of Impressionist blues and greens and golds spread out before you.

Inside, there's a refreshing openness of doors and windows that lets the outdoors come breezing right in. The main salon is steeped in cool marble and tropical plants. Beyond, in the reception room, is an aviary atwitter with a rainbow of tiny birds.

You'll find less flora and fauna in the guest rooms, but there's the same airiness and informality. And they're all luxurious.

Our favorite one is Room 5. Another—all velvet and paneling—has a long tiled terrace and a lovely view. Inside, you push a button and remote-control blinds move up or down to suit you. This way, you needn't lift more than a finger to watch the sun set (or rise) from your downy velvet bed.

The best months to stop at Noves are April, May and October (the four in between often turn out hot and always crowded).

Name: L'Auberge de Noves

Owners/Managers: The Lalleman family

Address: 13550 Noves (Bouches-du-Rhône)

Location: In the country about 10 minutes south of Avignon (near the Avignon Sud exit from the A7)

Telephone: (90) 94.19.21

Cables/Telex: Auberno 43.13.12F

Reps: Relais-Château in U.S., Canada and Europe

Credit Cards: American Express, Master Charge,/Eurocard, Visa

Rooms: 23 rooms

Meals: Breakfast 7:15 on, lunch 12–2:30, dinner 7–9:30; dinner for two approx. $60–$70; tie and jacket required at dinner; room service for breakfast and drinks and snacks

Entertainment: Television in some of the rooms

Sports: Heated swimming pool (usable year-around); tennis and horse-back riding 10 minutes away (and a new tennis court's planned for the inn)

Sightseeing: (See Hôtellerie Le Prieuré and Le Mas d'Entremont)

P.S. Closed January and February; seminars of 14–15 persons are accepted, but no tour groups.

Le Mas d'Entremont
Aix-en-Provence

W X $ $

This is the ideal spot if you're planning a visit to the Aix-en-Provence Festival—three summers from now. During the festival (and for most of July and August) the nine rooms and five villas here are booked years in advance, and it's easy to see why. The inn is built in the style of a typical Provençal *mas*, or country house, with terra-cotta walls, curved rust-colored roof tiles, and tiled patios among gardens of pine and cypress and olive trees. The nine rooms in the main building, each with a terrace, are tastefully furnished in the style of Provence, with antiques and paintings and handwoven fabrics. But it's the bungalows that are the real eye-openers: wonderful weathered wooden doors from Majorca and Corsica. The owner has thoughtfully added wrought-iron doors as a bonus, to let the breezes flow in. Each room is designed with antiques, custom-designed wrought-iron wall lamps and table lamps, handwoven fabrics that offset the modern addenda like color TV, direct-dial telephones, tiled bathrooms and full kitchens—all for the price you'd pay for a regular room in many hotels nearby.

The inn opened in 1960, the bungalows were added in 1977/78 but already the pleasures of D'Entremont have become cherished by a discerning and secretive clientele. In addition there are pleasant hilltop gardens, a large pool with fountains (floodlit in summer evenings), quiet patios and an attractive dining room in stylish rustic manner (*moëlle de boeuf en brioche sauce bordelaise, civet de porcelet, brochette d'agneau grillé* are among the specialities). The location is ideal, too, on a breeze-cooled hill just outside town, surrounded by enough tall trees to block out the sounds from Route Nationale 7. Even if you're not here for the festival, it's still an ideal spot.

Name:	Le Mas d'Entremont
Owners/Managers:	François and Valérie Marignane
Address:	Route d'Avignon, 13100 Aix-en-Provence (Provence)
Location:	Two kilometers north of town, just off Route Nationale 7.
Telephone:	(42) 23.45.32
Cables/Telex:	(None)
Reps:	(None)
Rooms:	9 rooms, 5 villas
Meals:	Breakfast 7:30–10, lunch 12–2, dinner 7–9; dinner for two approx. $35; dress informal; room service for drinks only, but the villas have full kitchens.
Entertainment:	(None)
Sports:	Pool in the garden; nearby—tennis, golf and horseback riding
Sightseeing:	Excavations (Entremont was the site of the first settlement in Aix); the atelier of Paul Cézanne, the Flemish tapestries and primitive triptych in the Cathedral of St. Sauveur, Granet Museum, Tapestry Museum, the Fondation Vasarely, a museum and experimental center begun by the modern artist Vasarely, and the charming tree-lined, café-lined avenue known as Cours Mirabeau
P.S.	Closed November 1 through March 15

Le Mas des Herbes Blanches
Joucas

It's built in the style of a Provencal *mas*, rough-cut stone upon rough-cut stone, topped off with a roof of curving rust-colored slates, and surrounded by fields of grapevines and apricot and cherry trees. In the spring, the gritty ground around the *mas* is whitened by flowering herbs, *les herbes blanches.* Each room, in turn, is named for a Provencal herb—La Sarriette, Le Thym, and so on—and your key comes attached to a sachet of the appropriate herb.

There are nice touches in the stylized-rustic guest rooms (the inn is only five or six years old, so everything is fresh and new), and each has a small loggia, television, radio, telephone and desk. Lounges and dining room have beamed ramada-style ceilings and stone fireplaces. The food is good (seasonal fare, but not necessarily *du terroirs—carré d'agneau grillé aux herbes, saumon frais a l'oseille, feuilleté d'asperges*). The service is efficient if unenthsiastic. But the view across orchard and vineyard to the Luberon hills is pure Provencal. This is a place to visit if you're looking for calm and quiet in comfortable surroundings. Preferably when the garden is white with *les herbes blanches.*

Name: Le Mas des Herbes Blanches

Owner/Manager: Claude Revel

Address: 84220 Joucas (Vaucluse)

Location: About 25 miles east of Avignon, a few miles from Gordes or Apt, on highway D102A

Telephone: (90) 72.00.74

Cables/Telex: (None)

Reps: Relais-Châteaux in U.S., Canada and Europe

Credit Cards: American Express

Rooms: 14 rooms

Meals: Breakfast 8–10:30, lunch 12:30–1:30, dinner 7:30–8:30; dinner for two approx. $60; dress casual; room service during meal hours; minibars in the rooms

Entertainment: Radios in the rooms

Sports: Swimming pool; horseback riding nearby

Sightseeing: The picturesque countryside of Luberon and the walled villages of Gordes and Roussillon and Fontaine-de-Vaucluse

P.S. Closed November 15 to March 1

France

L'Oustau de Baumanière
Les Baux-de-Provence

WWWW XXXX $$$$

In the Middle Ages, when Europe was setting aside its old barbaric ways in favor of something more civilized, Les Baux was renowned for its *cours d'amour*. Troubadours from all over France came to these Courts of Love to compete for the favors of the most beautiful ladies of Provence. If these favors were poetic and platonic rather than passionate, so much the better; even so there were occasions when a husband resented the conduct of a troubadour, and more than one of these medieval Bob Dylans found himself leaving Les Baux by the most direct route—down the cliff.

The town rides high on a saddle of the Alpilles, those foothills where the Alps make one last lunge before sinking into the flatness of the Camargue. At first sight, Les Baux is a grizzly graybeard of a town; its castle has long since been shattered, but the village itself still has its old town hall, its churches and its strange houses carved into the side of the hills, many of which have been restored by artists and artisans, and now house art galleries, boutiques and restaurants.

From the town's Place St. Vincent you get a dramatic view of the countryside below. The hills around here are blanched and gnarled, with grotesque facelike shapes—a sort of cadaverous Mount Rushmore. Beneath the town, to the left, is the Valley of the Fountain, and to the right, the Valley of the Inferno. Apparently Dante came here and was inspired to write his *Inferno*.

If this be Inferno, let's sin. Because here is one of the supreme restaurants of France—L'Oustau de Baumanière. The genius who transformed this unlikely spot into a gastronomic shrine almost 40 years ago is Raymond Thuilier. He was until that time the president of the largest insurance company in France, but he decided to quit the world of commerce, retire to this curious spot—and become a chef. So he bought a 16th-century olive mill and opened the Oustau de Baumanière. Today, a spry, twinkly-eyed octogenarian, Raymond Thuilier dons his chef's apron (he refuses to wear the traditional *toque*), supervises his kitchen, personally prepares the sauces that have helped earn three Michelin stars for something like a quarter of a century, and still finds time to greet his guests during the course of a meal.

Since Les Baux is off the beaten track, Raymond Thuilier also turned his olive mill into a hotel so that diners could linger over their meals (and, of course, be on the spot to return for lunch next day). This in turn became so popular that he expanded by buying up various villas and manors throughout the *Vallon des Fontaines*, and now a visit to Baumanière is like staying in the *Vallon des Thuiliers*, a comfortable estate with guest houses scattered throughout the property. The Oustau itself fits nine rooms into its sturdy walls, all of them looking onto a terrace above the dining room, then over the swimming pool and garden to the valley. Five more rooms nestle in Le Manoir two hundred yards down the valley, three in La Residence in its own secluded garden, eight in Carita between the stables and the peach orchard. There are, in addition, 15 rooms in Cabro d'Or, part of the Thuilier bailiwick but more or less as a separate hotel and restaurant (which has its own Michelin star). The rooms at Cabro d'Or are smaller (and—as we discovered when a few giggles at midnight had the elderly couple next to us banging on the wall with a walking stick—the walls are thinner) but staying here and dining here is less expensive, since Raymond Thuilier built Cabro d'Or specifically so that younger, less affluent lovers could get a taste of *la vie douce*, checking into Cabro d'Or but making an occasional foray to the grand dining room at the mill.

Otherwise, where you stay at Baumanière here depends on what's available, since regular guests have their favorite rooms and there are *always* regular guests in residence. If you take the trouble to request a particular room in advance, here are a few suggestions: in Le Manoir, Rooms 15 (twin beds beneath a green-and-pink brocade baldachin) or 18 (double bed, golden decor, window looking out on a pine tree); in La Résidence, two attractive apartments with television and minibar. If you're staying in La Carita's Room 25, you can step from a silken-canopied bed across a private arbor covered with vines and into the Carita swimming pool. Room 26 at La Carita also has a canopied bed, and a sunny sitting room with oriental rugs and fabric walls.

In the Oustau itself, guests who had the foresight, or good fortune, to snare Room 2 can stumble upstairs from their feasting and tumble into a canopied double bed in white tambour, beside an old stone fireplace the height of a troubadour and a black-tiled bathroom with a circular shower. In Apartment 3, the bathroom has stained-glass windows, the sitting room features a 17th century tapestry depicting various forms of bucolic high jinks, and a private entrance leads directly to the pool.

Most of the rooms throughout Baumanière are hung with paintings, mostly still lifes and flowers, signed "R. Thuilier." The same. Raymond Thuilier, corporation president, *aubergiste, saucier par excellence*, horseman and mayor of Les Baux, is also an accomplished artist whose works fetch thousands of dollars in esteemed Paris galleries. You'll also find his initials in the dining room on the colorful abstract tablecloths, designed by Thuilier and woven (no pennypinching here) by Porthault. The main dining room of Baumanière was the actual olive mill, and the well where the olives were scrubbed is now filled with fresh flowers from the restaurant's own gardens (one of the waiters creates the superb floral displays in his spare time). The table beside the well is officially Table 1, for our money the most romantic setting in the room, and Maître d'Hôtel Serge Meloni will try to seat you there if he can; but any table in this gourmet shrine is welcome, and in any case during *la belle saison* you will be dining out of doors on the terrace, beneath the trees, beside the bank of flowers, with the town of Les Baux floating floodlit above you.

The menu at Baumanière is more specialized than at most continental restaurants. The Thuilier principle seems to be to concentrate on a few dishes and *excel*. And what he excels in most is lamb, the young lamb of Provençal—"at least but not more than six weeks old . . . no less than four, not more than five kilos. . . ." It takes top billing on the menu: *gigot d'agneau au poivre vert, gigot d'agnelet en croute* and *selle d'agneau à la broche*—all of them lovers' dishes prepared for a minimum of two people. Another dinner at Baumanière might consist of *mousseline d'omble-chevalier, caneton aux pommes*, a portion of Livarot or Camembert, to be topped off with *crêpes soufflées Baumanière* (that is, a Grand Marnier soufflé in the form of crepes, with vanilla cream and apricot sauce). No, not topped off, because your waiter will then bring you a selection of petit fours which are themselves miniature masterpieces—*pralines, trouffe aux chocolat, marron chocolat, orangettes, petit banquette*.

Baumanière is one of the few restaurants that still has a *sommelier*, the stately René Boxberger in his *tablier de cuir*, who has been here since opening day pondering a wine list of wide-ranging tastes and a *cave* that accommodates 50,000 bottles.

There are those who claim that Baumanière is not what it used to be, that the staff has become too smug, that the place is overpriced. Maybe it's *not* what it used to be, but for those who never knew it in its younger days, it is still exceptional, and grandson Jean-André Chariel is being groomed to continue the family tradition. The staff is, to be sure, very proper and professional, and some people may confuse this with smugness, but Serge Meloni is an unusually gracious maître d'hôtel (his English is fluent), and if you ask M. Boxberger to recommend a wine, he is as likely to suggest a modest *vin du pays*—a Chateauneuf du Pape or a Côte du Rhône most likely—as a costly Pommard or Montrachet. (One small carping note, however: the table cards offering Baumanière wines for sale strikes a discordantly commercial note in such surroundings.)

Of course Baumanière is expensive, but you still get value for your money, all things considered (one of which has to be the enormous cost of running an operation such as this in a remote location such as this, where all the staff must be housed by the hotel). Certainly people who can afford this kind of high living are still attracted to it—the former Shah of Iran who helicoptered in a few years ago, Queen Elizabeth who took over the entire establishment for a couple of days in 1972. If neither of them can be considered arbiters of *haute cuisine*, other dedicated gourmets still flock to

M. Thuilier's domain. These days, too, you'll find more younger devotees and lovers staying there. Models, movie people, up-and-coming executives. Be sure you join them. Baumanière is the kind of soufflé you should sample at least once in a love affair.

Name: L'Oustau de Baumanière

Owner: Raymond Thuilier

Manager: Jean-André Chariel

Address: 13520 Maussane (Bouches-du-Rhône)

Location: 20 miles south of Avignon, 45 minutes from Marseille's Marignane airport

Telephone: (90) 97.33.07

Telex: Baucabro 420203

Reps: Relais-Châteaux in U.S., Canada and Europe

Credit Cards: American Express, Diners Club, Master Charge/Eurocard, Carte Blanche, Bankamericard, Visa

Rooms: 25 rooms and suites in four buildings

Meals: Breakfast anytime, lunch 12:15–2:30, dinner 7–9:30/10; dinner for two approx. $100–$110; tie and jacket preferred; room service for breakfast only (minibars in some rooms)

Entertainment: Television in the rooms

Sports: One tennis court, two swimming pools (one very large), walking trails and a riding stable with 20 horses

Sightseeing: Les Baux, the Valley of the Inferno, the Roman ruins at Arles, Nîmes and St. Rémy, the walled city of Avignon; festivals of music, drama or jazz at Aix-en-Provence, Avignon and Salon-de-Provence

P.S. Closed for the month of February; some small seminars in the off-season, but usually not intrusive

Hôtel Byblos
St.-Tropez

♔♔♔♔✗✗ $$$$

A Lebanese zillionaire landed in St.-Tropez fourteen years ago and built the jet-set version of an Arabian Nights resort. It glides up and down on a dozen different levels, and it's laced with inner hallways and outer staircases like the glittering twists and turns of some space-age Casbah—full of filtered sunlight and surprises.

Turn a corner and a tiny window gives you a peepshow of sun-bleached hills and sea. Turn another and you find yourself face to face with the monumental stone gates of an early Christian catacomb. Miniature waterfalls splash at you on your way to the pool. The floors are paved with magnificent modern ceramics. A staircase turns out to be a Picasso-like portrait of 80 staring faces, all done in ceramics. Even the fire extinguishers are works of art. Byblos cost its creator, who has since gone home to Lebanon, a cool 16 million francs, or about $50,000 a room.

Every guest room is a playground full of French and Middle Eastern antiques, liberally laced with extravagant 20th-century touches.

You might like the suite (157) that Bardot always chooses. It's hard to tell where the bed ends and the floor begins. Both are a sea of shaggy white fur. The bed is low and as wide as it is long, which is 6½ feet, with three pillows. The rest of the furniture is traditional Knoll: marble-top tables and tulip and womb chairs. There's also a sitting-room with a pair of Roman beds beside an antique fireplace. But the most sybaritic spot of all is the bathroom—an uninhibited expanse of pink marble and floor-to-ceiling mirrors opposite a bathtub just big enough for two, nestling in its own marble nook.

Altogether, there are 60 guest rooms at Byblos. All give you a view of the pool and the sea, which is a ten-minute amble away. Many have fireplaces and balconies, and all the rooms on the second floor have bathrooms with sunken tubs.

Then there are the three extraordinary rooms on the top floor. Each has an outsized double bed, a velvet couch for two, and a private terrace that turns into your own personal wading pool. Switch on the tap, lie back—and all of a sudden you're up to your bikini in cool, clear water. Nobody can see you, and all *you* can see is sky, red-tiled roofs, and water trickling over your companion's toes.

There are also some interesting split-level apartments. Like Apartment 353, which has a spiral staircase that takes you up to jumbo twin beds on a balcony overlooking a sitting room with a snug Mediterranean-style fireplace full of pine logs for chill nights.

Another (202) has a sitting room with a view of the pool. The balcony is crossed with 300-year-old beams above a roomy four-poster bed and windows that look down to the hotel's blossomy inner court.

Byblos is the only hotel we've found in France with "bachelor" rooms for loving singles. Meaning that they have much bigger beds than twin size—and much lower rates than double rooms. But rules are rules even in France, and couples aren't allowed to book bachelor rooms. Nevertheless, if the bachelor ends up with company, no one seems to mind.

There's plenty at Byblos to keep you busy and bronzed. The free-form fantasyland known as the swimming pool takes you under a low-hanging balcony that belongs to the bar. Order up something cooling as you splash by. Then take a turn underwater around a huge sun-tanning platform that rises up out of the pool and produces soft music from way down in the watery depths. As you surface, look up and you'll see a sexy sculpture of the mythological Leda rapturously enfolded by her loving swan. Probably more than any other one thing, this little piece of granite characterizes the out-and-out hedonism of this remarkable hotel.

Just beyond the pool is a solarium wrapped with wisteria. Slip out of your suit and into the sun. The gallant pool boy will protect you from onlookers. Your only other cover is a forest of flowers, bamboo, and cypress. So skip the solarium if you're shy.

Nighttime diversions include a friendly little bar, a high-decibel discotheque with a dance floor the size of a hula hoop, and an underground nightclub—huge and dark with flashing lights, well-known singers and top rock groups.

(Liquid Note: If you like Pimm's Cup, this is the place to have one. It is magnificently constructed with mint, lemon, orange, a knot of cucumber rind, and two large grapes that taste as if they'd been soaking in cognac for about 200 years.)

St.-Tropez has reportedly turned into a summer circus of trippers and gawkers, who come clamoring to see celebrities at play. Some say it got swallowed up by the 20th century, and the unspoiled little fishing village that once charmed the world-weary and blasé couldn't charm a garter snake anymore.

Right. And wrong.

In high season (July to mid-September), it's about as unspoiled as the boardwalk at Coney Island. Hundreds of Beautiful People, in Alfas and Lamborghinis, and thousands of *un*-Beautiful People, in polyester toreadors and wraparound shades, arrive. Hotel space, dining space, beach space, breathing space all disappear. And so does St.-Tropez.

Then, when the weather turns cool and crisp and the sun stays out until eight o'clock every night, something wonderful happens. Most of the BP and *all* of the un-BP miraculously dematerialize, and the real St.-Tropez resurfaces. And the same is true from March to July.

You can stroll cobbly little streets down to the harbor at night and never hear anything louder than a bell buoy. The bright little village cafés hugging each other all along the waterfront still welcome you with the pop of corks and sea-salted Gallic laughter. But the people you meet are more likely to be trawlers than trippers.

Of course, there are enough $20,000 sports cars whizzing around town to keep you on your toes—and you'll find most of them parked outside Byblos.

Don't be afraid to make friends. A lot of Byblos guests keep their own cabin cruisers sitting in the harbor, because the best beaches are down the coast five or ten miles. So it's nice to be able to hitch a ride. Otherwise you have to rent a boat or go by car.

(Beach Note: West of St.-Tropez, where the vineyards stop and the sand starts, the beach is divided into lots of little beaches, most of them owned by the restaurants attached to them. One is called Liberty Beach— you'll know it when you get there, because nobody wears a bathing suit. You're welcome to join the fun, or keep walking until you come to a restaurant called La Voile Rouge (The Red Sail). It's the first topless one we've seen where it's the *customers* who are topless. No pretty girl is expected to dine in more than her bikini bottoms, and by the time you read this, even those may be optional.

The food at Byblos is pleasant, but be sure to go prowling the town in search of local specialties. There isn't a stuffy, pretentious restaurant to be found. Just breezy indoor and outdoor cafés with aromatic Provençal cooking and platters of fish and shellfish that couldn't be fresher.

Above all, don't let St.-Tropez's reputation for going gaudy keep you away. Go at the right time, stay at the right place, and you won't find another spot on the Côte d'Azur you love better. (C.P.)

Name:	Hôtel Byblos
Manager:	Claude Maret
Address:	Avenue Paul-Signac, 83990 St.-Tropez (Var)
Location:	At the western end of the Côte d'Azur, 1½ hours by car from Nice Airport, on a hillside a few blocks from the center of town
Telephone:	(94) 970004
Cables/Telex:	Byblos Sttropez/Byblos 46015F
Reps:	(None)
Credit Cards:	"Most"
Rooms:	60, including 15 duplex apartments

Meals: Breakfast anytime, lunch/dinner noon to 1 A.M., indoors or poolside; dinner for two approx. $60; tie and jacket "frowned upon"; room service around the clock (cold meals only after midnight)

Entertainment: Piano/guitarist in dining room, Cap du Roi nightclub/disco (one of the best on the Cote d'Azur), underwater music in the pool

Sports: Pool, sauna, massage; tennis, beach, golf, horseback riding and watersports nearby

Sightseeing: Musée de l'Annunciade (Impressionist paintings), Citadel in town; Bravade (folk festival which has been running consecutively for over 400 years) three days in mid-May

P.S. Closed November to mid-December; very few children, some small seminars in winter; when checking in "the one who signs should be the one who pays"

Hôtel du Cap
Cap d'Antibes

ẆẆẆ✗✗✗$$$

For the price you and I and lesser mortals would like to pay for a room, the Hôtel du Cap guests fork out for a beach cabana and lounger. Not only is the expense a mere incidental for most of them, they reserve their favorite cabanas when they reserve their favorite rooms, in many cases year after year. Only an exceptional hotel could carry it off, and by any yardstick the Du Cap seems to be just such a hotel.

It sits on one of the choicest spots along the entire Mediterranean—in a natural park at the tip of Cap d'Antibes, with a daydreamlike panorama that takes in the azure Golfe-Juan, Ile de Lérins, the Croisette of Cannes and the hills of the Esterel. Its cabanas and loungers rest not on beach but on rocks twenty feet above the sea, and the great swimming pool of its Club Nautique, attached to the renowned Eden Roc Pavilion, has been blasted from basalt and rock. From the pool, a long cobbled driveway lined with pines leads up an incline to the châteaulike hotel, its canteloupe facade topped by a blue mansard roof. It's a setting from a very romantic movie, and you've seen it many times as the backdrop for fashion and champagne ads. Since it opened over a hundred years ago, the hotel has hosted everyone who is or was someone. In older days—when the Prince of Wales and English lords, grand dukes and bejeweled countesses, Carnegies and Mellons stayed here—Du Cap was a winter resort, but since the twenties and the F. Scott Fitzgeralds it has been a summer resort. In fact, in 1925 Fitzgerald wrote in a letter back home (the spellings and punctuation are his): "No one at Antibes this summer except me, Zelda, The Valentinos, the Murphy's, Mistinguet, Rex Ingram, Dos Passos, the Macleishes, Charles Bracket, E. Philips Openheim, Mannes the violinist, ex-Premier Orlando— just a real place to rough it and escape from all the world." Sometimes, though, it was hard for other guests to escape the Fitzgeralds. They put on one of their tiresome show-off acts here in 1927, when Zelda whipped off her lace panties, handed them to a friend who instantly jumped fully clothed into the sea (lace panties have that effect on some people), and Alexander Woolcott took off all his clothes and lumbered through the elegant lobby. You *might* see some high jinks here during the Cannes Film Festival (assuming you can get near the place) but it seems to welcome a more sedate crowd nowadays.

It is, heaven knows, romantic. The great driveway sweeping down to the sea. The one-star Eden Roc restaurant, its terrace perched on the rocks with moon and stars as a backdrop. The tennis courts tucked away among the pine trees. The masses of tropical flowers. The sheer stylishness of the place.

The Hôtel du Cap changed hands a few years ago, and its new Swiss owners have promised not to change a thing, although one of the first things they did was build a new 3-story wing of rooms beside the main entrance, which adds nothing to your entrance. Try to avoid these rooms. If you're going to all the trouble and expense of staying at the Hôtel du Cap, you might as well go whole hog and plump for a room facing the park and the sea. And don't forget to reserve your cabana. There are only 28 to go around.

Name: Hôtel du Cap

Manager: J-C Irondelle

Address: 06604 Antibes (Alpes-Maritime)

Location: Beside the sea, at the tip of Cap d'Antibes, 6 miles from Cannes, 15 from Nice Airport

---

Telephone: (93) 613901

Cables/Telex: Capotel Antibes/470763

Reps: HRI in U.S., Canada and Europe

---

202 **Credit Cards:** (None)

Rooms: 105, plus 10 suites

Meals: Breakfast from 7, lunch 12:30–3, dinner 8–10, on the terrace of Eden Roc Pavilion; dinner for two approx. $55–$60; informal but stylish dress, and men are expected to wear jackets but not ties at dinner; 24-hour room service, full meals during dining room hours

Entertainment: Night life and casinos along the coast; TV lounge, in rooms on request

Sports: 4 tennis courts, heated seawater swimming pool, waterskiing, pedalos, sailing, snorkeling, diving, wind surfing; golf and horseback riding nearby

Sightseeing: The Picasso Museum in Antibes; otherwise, all the sights of the Côte d'Azur

P.S. Closed mid-October to Easter; reservations almost impossible to come by during Cannes Film Festival (May) and during July and August

Château du Domaine St.-Martin
Vence

♛♛♛✕✕✕$$$$

This is a heavenly spot where you can linger over breakfast on a balcony with a 70-mile view across the hills of the Côte d'Azur, or swim in a heart-shaped pool beneath elderly olive trees, or wander through the Vale of Roses and pluck a *Rosa gallica* for your lover.

Domaine St.-Martin is a hilltop estate above the old town of Vence which in turn sits on a hilltop above St.-Paul-de-Vence which in turn sits on a hilltop above Cannes. The Domaine is 15 minutes from the sea and an hour from the Alps (if you time your visit precisely, you can snow ski in the morning and water ski in the afternoon). It's close enough to Cannes and Nice and Cap d'Antibes to be part of the Riviera revelry, yet secluded enough on its hill to give you peace and solitude when you want them.

The hotel consists of a tower that was once part of a Commandery of the Order of Knights Templar, an old portico and drawbridge, and a terrace which dates back to Roman times and is now a National Monument. These relics were purchased in the 1930s by a wealthy French industrialist who built around them a massive mansion for his retirement; but as often happens with tycoons, he couldn't adjust to the inertia of retirement, so he decided to turn his mansion into a hotel. Not the moneymaking kind of hotel, but a place where he could welcome guests as though they were his own friends dropping in for a weekend. The friendly atmosphere is now carried on by his son, M. Daniel Genève, and the hotel's director, Mlle. Brunet.

One of the first things you notice is that your room has a name rather than a number, and it's filled with antiques from the family's private collection.

In the main salon downstairs, there's signed Louis XVI escritoire; the bar has a splendid Flemish tapestry (which cost a thousand dollars just to restore); the men's room and the ladies' room are identified not with the usual signs, but with appropriate miniature paintings from the nineteenth century. Take a close look at the needlepoint upholstery of the chairs and chaises in the public rooms. There's nothing antique about them; in fact, every miniscule *point* was stitched by the present owner or his mother.

There are 29 rooms and apartments at Domaine St.-Martin, and most of them have fine views over the valley or the hills. The bathrooms are often larger than most hotel rooms, and they all have towel robes you can snuggle into. However, one or two of the rooms deserve a special mention.

In the old tower, the room on the ground floor has a high vaulted window that opens right out onto the terrace that's a national monument. The other two rooms in the tower are smaller, but they both get plenty of sun and they have tiny balconies; they're also less expensive than most of the other rooms.

Next to the main building there's a small villa called Papa Maman. The upstairs suite belongs to the proprietor, but the ground floor is a stunning apartment for guests. The sitting room has a Persian rug, superb antiques and panoramic windows that embrace the full expanse of countryside. The bathroom is 200 square feet of sparkling tiles, with a large glass door leading to a 30-foot terrace that runs roughly north to south and beckons the sun from dawn to dusk. You can step from tub to terrace without so much as a glance at your towel. Or bikini.

Up on the hillside above the hotel, at the top of a private road that winds up through terraced fields, there are five cottages, designed in the style of the traditional Provençal bastide, with squat towers and red-tiled roofs. The cottages have 50-foot tiled terraces with the finest vista of all— the valley and the sea *and* the château itself, down between the cherry trees and almond trees. The sitting rooms of the cottages blend modern and antique furniture (with some collectors' items, like an Alsatian marriage *armoire* of the 19th century). The circular dressing room has a refrigerator stocked with champagne, Scotch, beer, mineral water and soft drinks (the prices are posted in the refrigerator door). You can have dinner served in the privacy of your room.

The dining room at Château du Domaine St.-Martin is a terrace enclosed from floor to ceiling with glass, but the spectacular view probably won't distract you from your food, because the cuisine at the Domaine is on a par with everything else. Marc Chagall sometimes drives over for lunch when he can drag himself away from his canvases.

If we were back there now, we'd probably order *foie d'oie frais à la gelée de porto* (made right there in the hotel kitchen) or *terrine de canard* (which also makes a wonderful snack for a picnic) or *loup en papillote.*

Ask for your coffee to be served out on the open terrace where you can sit beneath a parasol and decide on the afternoon's pleasures. The tennis court, behind the heart-shaped pool, is in tip-top condition, and there are golf and skeet shooting a few miles away. Or you can drift through the Domaine's 30 acres of gardens and park, past the two farms that keep it supplied with fresh milk, fresh cream, fresh eggs, fresh fruit and fresh barbe-de-bouc. Take a peek into the pool with a score of trout and a scurry of crayfish. Sniff the blooms in the Vale of Roses (they're so beautiful, they're shipped to chic flower shops of Paris, rather than pulped for the local perfume industry).

If you climb the craggy hill above the hotel, chances are you'll be alone with yourselves and the larks. If you go by car farther up the valley, you come to the rugged foothills of the Alps and the Grand Canyon de Verdon (not as dramatic as *the* Grand Canyon, but worth a visit).

The town of Vence itself, whose cramped and walled old section you can see from your balcony at the hotel, is picturesque. Its Chapel of the Rosary was designed and decorated by Henri Matisse; its Galerie des Arts has works by Picasso, Chagall, Dufy, Derain, Buffet, Vlaminck, Carzou and Modigliani. If you visit Vence on March 27, you can pelt blossoms at each other during the local Battle of Flowers. (The hotel is a convenient base for all the flower festivals of the Riviera—Mimosa, Lemon, Grape, Rhododendron, Olive Oil, Jasmine, Edelweiss and Lavender.)

St.-Paul-de-Vence is also paradise for art lovers. Dine on the terrace of the famous Colombe d'Or (the Golden Dove) with plain old white doves circling overhead and an original Léger mural at your elbow; take a stroll through the interior dining room and admire its collection of original paintings by many of the greats who were lured here by the skies of the Côte d'Azur; continue to the swimming pool at the rear and you'll see an original Calder mobile ready to plunge into the cool waters. When you leave Colombe d'Or, forget your car and walk up the hill to the little white church for a look at Tintoretto's "Saint Catherine of Alexandria." Then take the road to the left of the church and continue up the hill (it's quite a walk but what's the rush?) to the Fondation Maeght, one of the most sensuous museums we've ever visited; it's in a garden where mimosa and other flowers mingle with marble and metal sculptures.

Most visitors to the Riviera hurry headlong along the lower Corniche   205 and never get up into the hills. Don't get caught in the rush. Turn off at Cagnes on to Route D2 and drive up through St.-Paul-de-Vence and Vence to the Château du Domaine St.-Martin. You won't be disappointed.

Name: Château du Domaine St.-Martin

Owners: The Genevè Family

Manager: Mlle. Andrée Brunet

Address: 06140 Vence (Alpes-Maritimes)

Location: On a spectacular hillside overlooking the town of Vence, 15 miles from Nice airport

Telephone: (93) 58.02.02

Cables/Telex: Domartin/470282F

Reps: Relais-Châteaux in U.S., Canada and Europe

Credit Cards: American Express, Master Charge/Eurocard

Rooms: 19 rooms, 10 villas .

Meals: Breakfast 7–12, lunch 12–2:30, dinner 8–9:30; dinner for two approx. $60; tie and jacket required; room service during meal hours (the villas have their own minibars for drinks)

Entertainment: Television in the villas, but not in the rooms

Sports: Tennis court, swimming pools (heated April to November) and Ping-Pong on premises; golf, riding and water sports nearby

Sightseeing: The Fondation Maeght in Vence has works by Giacometti, Braque, Chagall and Kandinsky; the Matisse Chapel (Chapelle du Rosaire) in Vence and the 12th-century church in St.-Paul-de-Vence with paintings by Tintoretto; the Ramparts of St. Paul-de-Vence

P.S. Closed December and January

Le Mas d'Artigny
St.-Paul-de-Vence

WWXX $$$$

Suites with private plunge pools are not unknown in the Caribbean and Mexico, but this new hilltop palace may be the first with private pools on the Côte d'Azur. It's the Mediterranean cousin of the Château d'Artigny on the Loire, and outpoints the latter on luxury if not in elegance. I recall, on a visit to Château d'Artigny ten years ago, owner René Traversac showing me architect's renderings of an ambitious new project in the South of France; I assumed it was just a pipe dream, but I was wrong and here is the *mas*, with its 21 hilltop pools and secluded patios, and already boasting a Michelin star in its dining room. Mas d'Artigny is still only a few years old, hasn't had a chance to weather, and it's maybe too big and stark for this location, but it certainly is quite a hotel.

It's not quite what the yardsticks spelled out at the beginning of this guidebook might lead you to expect; more mass than *mas*, it appears in these pages mainly because of its pool suites. Each suite has sitting room, bedroom, dressing room, floor-to-ceiling windows with electric shutters operated from your bedside; bathrooms have twin vanities, separate toilet, oval bathtubs, separate circular showers, color TV, and two patios—one shaded, one in the sun. Each patio pool is enclosed by hedgerows so you can't see the cars parked at the foot of the lawn—or your neighbor sybarites. The regular rooms are almost as luxurious, with furniture that echoes either Provence or the Caribbean.

Guests who don't have private plunge pools, or prefer an audience, can cavort in an enormous indoor/outdoor pool beneath the panoramic windows of the dining salon.

Name: Le Mas d'Artigny

Manager: Jean-Claude Scordel

Address: 06570 St.-Paul-de-Vence (Alpes-Maritimes)

Location: In the hills above St.-Paul-de-Vence, 10 miles from Nice airport

Telephone: (93) 32.84.54

Cables/Telex: Artimas/470601F

Reps: Relais-Châteaux in U.S., Canada and Europe

Credit Cards: American Express

207

Rooms:	49 rooms and 24 villas including 21 apartments with pool, all air-conditioned

Meals: Breakfast 7–11, lunch 12:30–2:30, dinner 7:30–9:30/10; dinner for two approx. $45–$55; tie and jacket required; room service 7A.M.–10P.M.

Entertainment: TV in some, but not all, of the rooms

Sports: Tennis court, swimming pools (heated April to November) and Ping-Pong on premises; golf, riding and water sports nearby

Sightseeing: (See Château du Domaine St.-Martin)

P.S. No tour groups (or very few of them) but some business seminars

Auberge Le Hameau
St.-Paul-de-Vence

This is a peaceful place of rambling courtyards, quiet patios, stone paths and archways and sunlight filtering through vine arbors. You can have breakfast or drinks in the sun-dappled courtyard beneath the arbors, or somewhere in the gardens among the palm, cherry and orange trees. The setting is typically Provençal, and the interior decor matches it pleasantly— from the rustic lounge with tiled floor and fireplace, to the beamed ceilings in the guest rooms. All 13 rooms are different. Room 12 is right above the roadway (but not noisy), with beamed ceiling and a view across the valley; Room 9 has a more constricted view but more charm; and over near the dovecote at the end of the garden there's a new split-level studio. Le Hameau's main attraction though may be its rates (most rooms are less than $35) and the warm welcome of manager Xavier Huvelin.

Name: Auberge Le Hameau

Manager: Xavier Huvelin

Address: Route de La Colle-sur-Loup Longs, 06570 St.-Paul-de-Vence

Location: In the hills, about 12 miles from Nice

Telephone: (93) 32.80.24

Cables/Telex:	(None)

Cables/Telex: (None)

Reps: (None)

Credit Cards: American Express

Rooms: 13

Meals: Breakfast only, in your room or beneath the vine arbor, 8–10; light snacks on request for lunch or dinner

Entertainment: TV in, alas, the lounge

Sports: Nothing in the hotel; beach, tennis, golf, horseback riding, water sports nearby

Sightseeing: (See Domaine du St.-Martin)

P.S. Closed December 1–15; you won't hear much English spoken here

Le Cagnard
Haut-de-Cagnes

WWXX$$

Haut-de-Cagnes is another of those extraordinary perched villages you find on hilltops all along the Riviera—rugged ramparts growing out of the hillside, rising in terraces to the turreted tower of some medieval fortress. In the case of Haut-de-Cagnes, the castle is a former stronghold of the Grimaldis (Prince Rainier of Monaco's family). Like most of its counterparts, Haut-de-Cagnes is home to artists (Renoir lived here, Modigliani in the valley below), artisans and sculptors, its narrow winding streets lined with galleries and boutiques. But what sets this perched village apart is its night life. The main square, Place du Château, is encircled with restaurants, terrace cages and nightclubs. Swingers drive up here from Nice, Monte Carlo and Cap d'Antibes; where they find a place to park is a mystery, how they manage to negotiate these steep streets after an evening on the town is still more of a mystery. The smart thing to do is check into Le Cagnard, in a quiet corner away from the hubbub. The restaurant has been modeled from the former guardroom of the Grimaldi Castle, and the guest rooms have been added from various homes in the adjoining buildings. You enter through a narrow door, step down a narrow stone stairway to a cubicle-sized reception office leading to a vaulted dining room with fading

209

murals and a huge fireplace at one end. In the evening, with taper candles gleaming on the wine glasses and silverware, with fresh flowers on the tables and logs sparkling in the great stone fireplace, it's magical. A new dining terrrace has been added in a glass-enclosed terrace, more popular in the summer months. Here you can linger for hours over Chef Barel's specialties—*foie gras frais de canard, daurade grillé au feu du bois avec Pastis,* or *filet de boeuf Charolais à la Carême,* followed by a selection of 24 cheeses and a dozen pastries. The 14 guest rooms and suites are much sprightlier and more charming than you might expect to find within these solid 13th-century walls. They're all different, recently renovated, and they all have gleaming tiled bathrooms, comfortable beds, period furniture. A few also have loggias. Room 7 looks out on the red rooftops of the town, 3 surveys the hills and dales to the Chateau Villeneuve-Loubet, and 8 is the favorite of French writers and literati. But the cream of the crop are the apartments set into the ramparts. Like La Petite Maison, a duplex with bedroom up a curving flight of tiled steps and a very private terrace with pots of geraniums, looking out on laurel and almond trees. Apartment 16 has a working fireplace in the corner (the maid will set it for you), a big double bed on the gallery above. These apartments also have minibars, color TV and bathrobes. Even the Grimaldis never had it so good.

Name: Le Cagnard

Owners/Managers: M. and Mme. Barel

Address: 06800 Cagnes-sur-Mer (Alpes-Maritimes)

Location: In Haut-de-Cagnes (Upper Cagnes), a medieval hill town 5 minutes from the center of Cagnes-by-the-Sea and 10 minutes from Nice airport

Telephone: (93) 20.73.21

Cables/Telex: (None)

Reps: Relais-Châteaux in U.S., Canada and Europe

Credit Cards: American Express, Diners Club

Rooms: 14 rooms, some with balcony, and 4 suites

Meals: Breakfast from 7:30 on, lunch 12:30–2:30, dinner 7:30–10:30, served on the terrace in summertime; dinner for two approx. $65–$75; dress informal; room service for breakfast only

Entertainment: Television is available in some rooms; nightclubs and discotheques in the village

Sports: Tennis, golf, riding and water sports nearby

Sightseeing: The castle built in 1309 by Raynier Grimaldi, Lord of Monaco and Admiral of France; the Renoir Museum with a few of the artist's works

P.S. Closed November 15–December 15; some very small tours are accepted; it helps to speak some French here, but Mme. Barel will greet you warmly

Hôtel La Voile d'Or
Cap Ferrat

₩₩₩✗✗✗$$$$

Cap Ferrat is probably one of the most valuable chunks of real estate in Europe. Still green, interspersed with secluded villas among cypress and pine, it's home to successful novelists, movie stars and bankers. The tiny harbor and marina at St.-Jean-Cap-Ferrat is liberally flecked with hundred-foot yachts. David Niven and Rex Harrison have been known to stop in for drinks, Lauren Bacall, Metropolitan Opera star James McCracken and many celebrities have stayed here. Not surprisingly. There's so much luxury all around—and so much attention to creating a beautiful ambience for the clientele.

The Hotel Golden Sail rises six floors above the jetty and the bobbing fishing boats and fishermen mending their nets. The entrance is only a modest doorway, belying all the plushness that delights the eye as you walk through the lounge and dining room and terrace until you come to a large swimming pool built above the shore. The family of Jean and François Lorenzi are in the construction business, so when he built his dream hotel about 15 years ago, he was able to lavish on it marble and glass and crystal. Local craftsmen were called in to design and weave the rich fabrics for windows, beds and chairs. Provençal-style chests and headboards were custom-crafted for the guest rooms, all of which have big marble bathrooms with twin vanities and fluffy bathrobes. Jean Lorenzi even had a special red rose, "Sonya," created for his hotel and Sonyas appear daily on the dining-room tables.

When the new harbor was built a few years ago, the hotel added a few rooms right above the dock. They have something of the feel of cabins on a cruise ship. All windows are double glazed, so you won't be kept awake by the comings and goings of yacht people. In any case, the yachts may not use

211

power before 8 A.M. And what a view you get from the windows and balconies! Most hotels on the Riviera look out to sea, but half the rooms here look *inland*, so that guests can sip their aperitifs as they watch the sun set behind the hills, and dine with the twinkling lights of Beaulieu and Eze as the backdrop. (Rooms on the garden side cost a few dollars less.)

Meals are served on a beautiful terrace beneath golden-tinted awnings. Butterflies flit by, birds sing, cool breezes waft in from the sea. To add to the pleasure of the experience, the Voile d'Or kitchen has a Michelin star. There are few lovelier places along the entire coast to sample *fricassee de St.-Pierre aux petits légumes et au cerfeuil* or *daurade royale aux tomates et citrons confit*. Dollar for dollar, chandelier for chandelier, you get exceptional value here—especially in the off-season—everything except July through September.

Name: Hôtel La Voile d'Or

Owners/Managers: Jean and François Lorenzi

Address: 06290 St.-Jean-Cap-Ferrat (Alpes-Maritime)

Location: On the waterfront, about halfway between Monte Carlo and Nice

Telephone: (93) 011313

Telex: 470317F

Reps (None)

Credit Cards: (None)

Rooms: 44 rooms and 6 suites (most with balconies, all with air-conditioning)

Meals: Breakfast anytime, lunch 1–2:15, dinner 8–10:30, on the terrace or indoors; dinner for two approx. $65–$75; tie and jacket recommended at dinner; room service, no extra charge, during dining room hours

Entertainment: TV room (in rooms on request), casino at Monte Carlo

Sports: Two swimming pools (one freshwater, one seawater), waterskiing and scuba diving; tennis, golf, beach, horseback riding nearby

Sightseeing: In town, the Rothschild Museum; otherwise, the Riviera (see Domaine du St.-Martin or Vistaero)

P.S. Closed November 1 to February 1; few children, small meetings in off-season (up to 25)

L'Hôtellerie du Château de la Chèvre d'Or
Eze Village

ance

WW XX $$$

Walt Disney came here once for a sandwich and stayed for two weeks. It's easy to see how a place like this would appeal to the master of fantasy. Even Snow White's Droopy would be compelled to raise an eyebrow at the sight of Eze Village perched on its pointed hill. It sits 1500 precipitous feet above the Mediterranean on the Moyenne Corniche, the middle of the three serpentine highways that link Nice and Italy. Eze Village is a fortified village with a history going back more than two thousand years, but until a few years ago, it was no more than a ghost village. Then it was rediscovered by a group of artists, an American pianist, a Swedish prince and assorted French and American millionaires. They redeveloped the village, turning old houses into studios and dramatic summer homes, and the cluster of buildings on the edge of the cliff into the Hôtellerie du Château de la Chèvre d'Or, the Hotel of the Castle of the Golden Goat.

This is no place to arrive with a trunk load of luggage. To visit Eze Village you have to leave your car in the parking lot beneath the town walls and enter through the fortified gate. From there, you have to walk up and along and down cobbled alleyways to the hotel. The hotel porter will, of course, carry your luggage, but trunk loads of the stuff won't make you too popular unless you're a generous tipper.

There are only ten rooms in the hotel, and you should make a point of staying in one of the four rooms that overlook the sea. The best one is Room 9, which has a private terrace, totally remote from the rest of the world. Room 4 is a split-level duplex right at the edge of the cliff.

The next choice should be 10, which is brand new with beamed ceilings and stucco walls; downstairs, you have a sitting room with tiled floor, casement windows and a small refrigerator; upstairs, there's a bedroom with a balcony and gleaming tiled bathroom.

Right on the edge of the village, where it comes to a point, there's a swimming pool and terrace. The pool can be covered in half a dozen strokes, although it took the workmen two years to gouge it from the rock. What it lacks in size it makes up for in drama. On the right is St.-Jean-Cap-Ferrat, one of the Riviera's poshest resorts. Directly below—out of sight beneath the hillside that tumbles to the sea in clumps of sea pine, olive trees, chestnut trees and mimosa—is Eze-Bord-de-Mer. Over to the left, on the ridge of the neighboring hill and hiding in a grove of trees, is the pink mansion of a millionaire, and just below it, the pink chapel he built specially for the wedding of his son to an Italian princess. Down by the edge of the sea, there's another grandiose mansion, with a pathway leading out to a swimming pool on a private promontory. It's that kind of neighborhood.

You get the same stunning view as you nibble on *rouget en papillote* or *escalopes de loup* in the Michelin-starred dining room. The best time to dine here is at lunch; in the evening, the lights sparkle along the coast and twinkle out on Cap Ferrat, but you're more likely to see your own reflection in the windows, and you'll have to suffer through endless tapes of mindless, inappropriate pops. The Chèvre d'Or is a feudal affair with great stone walls and beamed ceilings. The setting may put you off your guard when the waiter inquires if you'd like to try the specialty of the house, Pipi de Chèvre. It's concocted right there on the edge of the bar in a tall crystal pitcher with a spigot, filled with kumquats, lemon and orange slices, sprigs of herbs, all left there for five or six years to flavor the basis of the drink—the iniquitous *marc*. Try it by all means, but don't tell us the name didn't warn you.

We don't know what Walt Disney did here for two weeks. If he was looking for inspiration, there are probably few places more likely to unleash the mind on flights of fancy. When Friedrich Wilhelm Nietzsche walked down the mule path, a two-mile trip to the sea, he was inspired to sit down and write *Thus Spake Zarathustra.*

Spend a day exploring the village itself. From the Chèvre d'Or everything in the village seems to be up—up the alleyway to the main gate, up the stepped streets to the 15th century chapel with the mosaic of pebbles, up to the House of the Penitents, up to the ruined château, where you'll find a garden of cacti and succulents. Along the way you can stop off in various studios and restaurants to fortify you. When you get back down, you may want to reward yourself with fresh mussels and beer at the wall-side restaurant unhappily known as À Votre Eze—at your "ease." Get it?

Take the Moyenne Corniche and the Grande Corniche to another precarious medieval village called La Turbie, where you'll find one of the most important Roman ruins in Europe, and the Hôtellerie Jérome, a modest one-star restaurant which is, we're told, where Princess Grace and Prince Rainier go for candlelight dinners. Or jump into your car, twist your way down to Beaulieu for cocktails, over to Villefranche for dinner, then off to Monte Carlo for an hour or two at the tables. As we were saying, it's that kind of neighborhood.

Name: Hôtellerie Château de la Chèvre d'Or

Owner/Manager: Bruno Ingold

Address: 06360 Eze Village (Alpes-Maritime)

Location: On the Moyenne Corniche, between Monte Carlo and Nice, about 10 miles from Nice airport

Telephone:	(93) 411212

Cables/Telex: Chevredor/470673 OREM 903

Reps: Relais-Châteaux in U.S., Canada and Europe

Credit Cards; American Express, Diners Club

Rooms: 6 rooms and 3 suites

Meals: Breakfast 7:30–11, lunch 12:30–3, dinner 7:30–10; dinner for two approx. $55–$65; informal dress; room service for breakfast only

Entertainment: The view

Sports: Small swimming pool; everything else nearby

Sightseeing: Eze Village and the view from the tropical garden above the hotel; the Côte d'Azur

P.S. Closed December and January

Hôtel Le Cap Estel
Eze-Bord-de-Mer

♛♛♛ЖЖЖ$$$$

Sixty years ago, a wily Russian countess packed up her icons and emeralds and jumped on a train out of St. Petersburg in the nick of time. The Bolsheviks got there shortly afterward. Her next stop was the Cote d'Azur, where she sold a few of the family emeralds and started dreaming up something worthy of a countess. Cap Estel is the result.

She built her pure-white villa just off the Corniche, which takes you from Monte Carlo to Nice. A towering gate of black-and-gold wrought iron stands by the highway to mark the entrance. You drive down and down through an immaculate private park of royal palms and tropical flowers. Then there it is—a dream house to outdazzle all dream houses.

Cap Estel is ringed with tiers and tiers of sunny terraces (every guest room has one) from rooftop to garden. The main terrace sweeps around the house to give you a glorious view of the Mediterranean, then suddenly opens into a huge white stone staircase. You find yourself watching for an explosion of Scott Fitzgerald characters in dinner jackets and scarlet voile racing down the stairs and through the palms to dive, champagne in hand, blithely into the sea.

215

The entire villa with its gardens and fountain and beaches and pools is built on a jut of land surrounded by the Mediterranean on three sides. The outdoor swimming pool lies out at the very tip. The winter pool is underneath, covered, heated and equipped with a jet stream.

Cap Estel's owner, Robert Squarciafichi, is no laissez-faire kind of innkeeper. Whatever you want you get. Fast. Box seats at the opera in Monte Carlo. A Rolls and driver to take you there. A speedboat or a 60-foot yawl to sail along the coast for the day. A vibrating massager—either man or machine (the hotel provides both, in your room or at the sauna baths).

Even the *rocks* at Cap Estel have been thoughtfully flattened and contoured so when you come up from the sea you can stretch out on a warm, smooth perch by the water on *padded* loungers.

There are 45 rooms and apartments and a private cottage to choose from. Each one is superbly furnished, and gives you a terrace and a clear

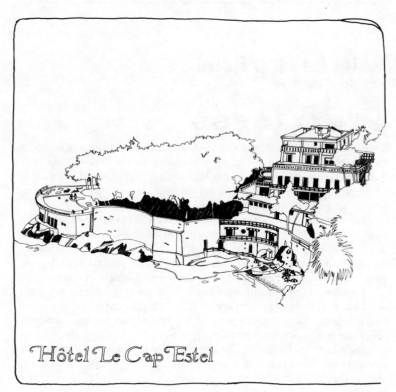

Hôtel Le Cap Estel

view out to sea. A typical apartment is done entirely in mustard silk and cocoa velvet with a gigantic bath of pink marble.

Or you can rent your own little cottage a few steps from the main house. The whole roof is your private terrace, and the Mediterranean is your front yard.

The three most fascinating accommodations at this resort are hewn right out of the gray-stone seawall surrounding the estate. You walk down a stone stairway from the garden to what looks like the deck of a superluxury yacht. It turns out to be the terrace for three guest rooms inside the wall. Follow a mahogany passageway and you come to the Mayflower, the Santa Maria and Room X. All three are paneled in mahogany ship's planking and furnished exactly like cabins in a seagoing yacht. Your portholes look directly down onto sand and sea. You can park your car on the roof and your Sailfish under the front door. For swimmers, snorkelers, skin and scuba divers, and just plain sun worshipers, nothing could be closer to heaven. Just ask and the hotel will have scuba gear delivered to your door. You can spear yourself a sea wolf for lunch, or simply spend the morning gliding through clouds and clouds of colorful fish.

With the Casino at Monte Carlo just a five-minute drive away, you should have no trouble finding ways to fill your evenings with fun and games. But before you try your luck, fortify yourself with some of Cap Estel's adventuresome cooking.

You might start with *les oeufs pochés Grand Duc,* which translates as a poached egg inside a flaky pastry filled with shrimp, truffles and asparagus tips, covered with Mornay sauce.

Then on to the bouillabaisse full of fish freshly scooped from the Mediterranean that morning.

Or sample the rock lobster (*langouste*), which the chef does no fewer than *five* different ways—including a curried version with shallots, rice and truffles flambéed in cognac. Nor is the sea wolf (*loup*) to be missed. Don't let the name intimidate you. It's a deliciously subtle fish almost like sea bass, and Cap Estel's kitchen prepares it with fennel, tarragon, shallots, butter, cream and truffles.

And then there are the hotel barbecues out under the palm trees, beside a fountained reflecting pool. Gold-headed tame pheasants march up and down, keeping an eye on the proceedings. Sea breezes air-condition everything. And if you can think of a more idyllic way to spend a summer evening, let us know. (C.P.)

Name: Hôtel Le Cap Estel

Owner/Manager: Robert Squarciafichi

Address: 06360 Eze-Bord-de-Mer (Alpes-Maritime)   217

Location: Between Nice and Monte Carlo, between the road and the sea, 10 miles from Nice airport, a few miles from the railroad stations at Eze and Beaulieu

Telephone: (93) 015054

Telex: 470305 Capstel

Reps: (None)

Credit Cards: Master Charge/Eurocard

Rooms: 38 rooms and 7 suites (all air-conditioned)

Meals: Breakfast anytime, lunch 1–3, dinner for two on the elegant terrace in *la belle saison*; dinner for two approx. $65; tie-and-jacket in the evening; room service for breakfast and drinks only

Entertainment: TV in rooms, casino in Monte Carlo

Sports: Two seawater pools (1 indoors), pebbly beach; water sports by arrangement; tennis, golf and horseback riding nearby

Sightseeing: The Côte d'Azur (see Le Vistaero and Domaine du St.-Martin)

P.S.   Closed November 1–February 1; some small seminars in off-season

Hôtel Le Vistaero
Roquebrune-Cap-Martin

ᙠᙠ ✕✕ $$$

As you're breezing along the Grande Corniche east from Monte Carlo, you'll spot a titanic gray precipice high above you in the distance. There seems to be something perched out on the tip of it. Is it a bird? Is it Princess Grace? Or are you slightly hung over?

No. You're getting your first glimpse of Vistaero.

The second glimpse—from inside—is even more spectacular. Through a wall of glass you see Monaco to the right, the Italian Riviera to the left, and a thousand feet below is the deep blue sea; while all around you stands the simple glass-and-poured concrete splendor of one of France's most imaginative modern hotels.

218

The dining room is a huge expanse of windows, fresh flowers and fountained pool (for looking at, not swimming in).

The pool that *is* for swimming lies sunning itself on the rocks about a hundred feet below the hotel. You zoom down to it in a special elevator and sunbathe on a spit of granite overlooking the tennis clubs and grand old hotels and new high-rises of Monte Carlo.

Vistaero's most lavish quarters are three suites with sun-washed, floor-to-ceiling windows that stretch around the room to give you 700 square feet of awesome view. One suite is done in Scandinavian modern. The other two are furnished with beachy bamboo chairs and tables and canopied double bed. Their terraces are screened from view so no one can catch you getting an overall tan. The standard rooms are all different (because of the wedge shape mostly) and all decorated with paintings or prints from the private collection of the new owner—Max Grundig of electronics fame.

The national summer sport in this part of the world seems to be fireworks—and the championships are held right outside your window, every weekend during the season. Suddenly, the sky is carumphing with Roman candles, pinwheels, fizgigs, skyrockets and enough cannon crackers to wake Napoleon. To watch all hell break loose, all you have to do is raise the blinds and prop up your pillows.

For daytime sports, Vistaero has two beaches with cabanas just a five-minute drive down from the hotel. Nearby, there are public golf and tennis—and in Monte Carlo, sailboats and speedboats for rent.

Like any Côte d'Azur hotel worth its salt, Vistaero is very crowded from July to September 15. The best times to go are from mid-May to July and mid-September to October. Before and after that, the air is likely to be chilly, because the hotel sits so high and unprotected from the wind. (C.P.)

Name: Hôtel Le Vistaero

Owner: Max Grundig Foundation

Manager: Kenny Boone

Address: 06190 Roquebrune (Alpes-Maritime)

Location: Between Monaco and Menton, 1000 feet above the Mediterranean, on the Roquebrune-Cap Martin Grande Corniche, at the Monaco exit of Autoroute A8

Telephone: (93) 350150

Cables/Telex: Vista Hotel/461021

Reps: Robert F. Warner and Relais-Châteaux in U.S. and Canada, Relais-Châteaux in Europe

Credit Cards: American Express, Diners Club

Rooms: 29, including 3 suites

Meals: Breakfast 7:15–11, lunch 12–2:30, dinner 7:30–9:45; dinner for two approx. $50–$60; informal dress; room service during dining room hours (minibars in all rooms for drinks)

Entertainment: TV in rooms, casino in Monte Carlo

Sports: *Piscine aérienne*—or small hillside swimming pool, accessible by steep steps; tennis at Monte Carlo Country Club, beach and water sports at Monte Carlo, horseback riding and golf (at Mont Angel, a course dating from the turn of the century) in the hills

Sightseeing: Typical medieval villages like Roquebrune, Eze and La Turbie; the Côte d'Azur; Grand Prix at Monte Carlo

P.S.   Very few children, tours or groups

For brief reports on other hotels in France turn to the chapter on Added Attractions at the end of this guide.

AUSTRIA

Vienna

① ②
③
Salzburg

④
⑤ ⑥ Innsbruck

SWITZERLAND

⑧
● Zurich
Lucerne ●
⑨ ⑦ ⑩
⑪

Geneva ●

⑬
⑫ ⑭

1. Hotel Schloss Mönchstein
2. Hotel Goldener Hirsch
3. Hotel Schloss Fuschl
4. Hotel Goldener Adler
5. Schlosshotel Igls
6. Hotel Grünwalderhof
7. Hotel Hirschen
8. Hotels Drachenburg, Waaghaus and Garni
9. Le Vieux Manoir
10. Hotel Château Gütsch
11. The Grand Hotel
12. Hotel Monte Rosa
13. Hotel Alex
14. Hôtellerie Tenne

AUSTRIA AND SWITZERLAND

Austria

Hotel Schloss Mönchstein
Salzburg

WW ֎ XX $$$

"How late do we serve breakfast? Oh, you may be served anytime you wish. Just sleep in tomorrow if you like."

That's very much the spirit of things at Schloss Mönchstein, a vine-covered villa hidden away high above the city of Salzburg. Unless you happen to have an uncle or a friend who's an Austrian count, this is probably the closest you'll come to staying at a private estate with a personal staff to tend to your needs.

Mönchstein Castle was built in 1358 atop the Mönchsberg, the mountain in the heart of the city, as a retreat for the guests of the Archbishop of Salzburg. In the 1800s, after a lift was built down the mountain, the castle became more easily accessible and served as a home for several prominent citizens of the city. It became a hotel in 1948 and ten years later it was taken over by the present owner, Baron von Mierka, who lives right next door and seems determined to continue the old tradition of treating his visitors like guests in a castle. What could be nicer, especially when all the delights of Salzburg are just an elevator ride away?

There are only 12 rooms here, one reason why the staff has the time to pamper you, and everything is set up to make you feel you are in a home, not a hotel. If you arrive by car or taxi, winding your way around the hairpin turns up the mountain to the gate, you'll be greeted by a velvety lawn dotted with perfect tiny formal garden beds and just two pairs of chairs set out to catch the sun. A statue of an archer points the way to the manor, a tall tile-roofed tan building wrapped in greenery, with gables and turrets pointing every which way as though not to miss a single angle of the lofty view. All aound you are trees and flowers and blissful silence.

Now, you say you're thirsty and would like a drink? Just mention it to the desk. They'll rush one to you, on a silver tray, to the lawn or the tiny shaded terrace or the all-white mirrored alcove on the main floor or the large elaborately decorated sitting room on the second floor.

Or, of course, to your own room, most likely a spacious Old World bedroom with a comfortable private sitting area in front of the windows—

222

tables and chairs and perhaps a caned settee or a sofa with a tufted back. Some of the rooms are tucked around the corner of the building and have private entrances; some of the smaller third-floor rooms have interesting ceilings because of the unusual roof lines of the house; and most of them have crystal chandeliers. The choicest, of course, look out at the city, but it's hard to fault the alternative view of gardens and woodland. Wherever you are, they've thought of everything for your comfort, from the satin comforters on the bed to the miniature satin pin cushion fitted out with needles, thread and thimble.

There's a wonderful elevator that you open with a big brass key, with just about enough space for the two of you. There are only four tables for breakfast on the terrace, just five tables in the impressive red-and-black dining room, and always the staff remains just the right side of hovering. They seem to care here whether you've *really* had a nice day or *really* enjoyed your meal.

For breakfast you'll be served croissants and hard rolls, cheese and meats and jam. At dinner you can order à la carte or choose the four-course daily menu which goes for about $20. A typical menu might be prosciutto and melon, consommé, schnitzel and fresh fruit cup. It's nicely prepared, if not inspired, but chances are you'll be dining out anyway since you're certainly going to want to spend some time exploring Salzburg. Have dinner in the city, perhaps take in one of the many concerts around town, then come back to your "private" villa to look down on the twinkling lights below and the twinkling stars above. (E.B.)

Name: Hotel Schloss Mönchstein

Owner/Manager: Baron Karl Mierka

Address: Mönchsberg 26, A-5020 Salzburg

Location: On the mountain just above the city (take the marked turn left off Muhner Hauptstrasse just north of the center of the city)

Telephone: (06222) 41363-66

Cable: Mönchsteinhotel Salzburg

Reps: (None)

Credit Cards: American Express, Diners Club

Rooms: 12

Meals: Breakfast anytime, lunch 12–2, dinner 7–9; dinner for two approx. $40; informal dress; room service all day; drinks and breakfast served on outdoor terrace

Entertainment: None in hotel; casino 5 minutes away on foot

Sports: Tennis court, walks in nearby woods

Sightseeing: The delightful city: Hohensalzburg fortress, 17th-century Dom (cathedral), St. Peter's Church, Franciscans' Church, Getreidegasse with its wrought-iron shop signs, Alte Markt for spice bouquets. Mozart's birthplace and residence, the Residenz, Mirabell Gardens; music festivals at Easter and July–August, concerts at Schloss Mirabell; Heilbrunn Castle just outside the city; outstanding views from Winkler Cafe atop the Mönchsberg

P.S.   Closed mid-October to mid-April

Hotel Goldener Hirsch
Salzburg

♛♛Ⅹ$$$

If you perform at the Salzburg Festival, you probably stay here during rehearsals since the distance from Golden Stag to stage door is only a hundred bounds. If you're opera buffs, you will most likely follow a local tradition and sup here after the performance, when the dining room and adjoining Bratwurstherzl *stube* overflow with elegant couples in full fig. But if you're simply seekers after romantic inns redolent with charm and breeding, you may still choose the Goldener Hirsch.

It's been a staging post or *stube* or hotel in some form or another for almost 800 years—which means it was an old timer even when Wolfgang Amadeus Mozart was born a few doors away. In those days it was a very basic establishment (today's dining room was once the stable), but when the Walderdorff family took over, they polished up the gold, so to speak, and turned it into a deluxe spot. The Goldener Hirsch, now two buildings around two courtyards, was renovated from top to bottom in 1972, but it still retains the ambience of Alte Salzburg—and the courtly hospitality of the ever-attentive Count Walderdorff. From Getreidegasse, you enter a low arched door in the peach-colored facade. A tiny lobby leads to a colorful bar brightened by a skylight, then into the spacious dining room with its low, vaulted ceiling. Young waiters, dressed in green hunting jackets and white ankle-length aprons, are eager to show off their English, deft at

224

transporting trayloads of food, meticulous at serving your *Zwiebelrost-braten mit Bratkartoffeln* or *Rehrücken mit Preiselbeeren.*

Although it's smack in the heart of Salzburg activity (at any time of the year, festival or no festival), the Goldener Hirsch is relatively quiet, since all rooms have double-glazed windows and many of them (the singers' favorites) are located around the inner courtyard. Guest rooms are furnished with antiques or Tyrolean farmhouse furnishings, augmented by modern accessories and tiled bathrooms. Room 35, for example, is decorated in Old Salzburg colors with hand-carved antique chest and a sleeping alcove with a double bed. Other popular rooms are 7 (overlooking Getreidegasse) and 17 (overlooking the courtyard), while the two apartments are snapped up by singers who want more spacious surroundings to stretch out in between rehearsals.

Name: Hotel Goldener Hirsch

Manager: Count Johannes Walderforff

Address: 37 Getreidegasse, A-5020 Salzburg

Location: In the center of town, on the street where Mozart was born

Telephone: (06222) 41511

Cables/Telex: Goldenhirsch/62967 Hirsch

Reps: Robert F. Warner and AIHR in U.S. and Canada

Credit Cards: American Express, Diners Club, Master Charge/Eurocard

Rooms: 52, including 2 apartments

Meals: Breakfast 7–11, lunch 11:30–2:30, dinner 6:30–9:30 (to 1 A.M. during the Festival); dinner for two approx. $35–$40 (about half that in the Bratwurstherzl); informal dress, but tie and jacket after performances during the Festival; full room service during dining room hours

Entertainment: TV on request; casino up the hill; concerts and recitals throughout the year in theaters and castles

Sports: None in the hotel; tennis, golf, horseback riding, walking, winter sports nearby

Sightseeing: (See Hotel Schloss Mönchstein)

P.S.   Book far ahead for the period of the Easter Festival and the Salzburg Festival (July/August), but there's plenty to do in the area outside of those times

Hotel Schloss Fuschl
Salzburg-Hof

♔♔♔♔ ✕✕✕ $$$$

It sits at the hilly tip of a promontory, its square turret and high-pointed roof rising above Lake Fuschel, surrounded by 34 acres of lawns and flowers and pines. With the becalmed lake below and the sheltering ring of mountains and meadows all around, this is quintessential Salzkammergut. There are millions of people around the world, though, who think of it as quintessential *Sound of Music*, since Schloss Fuschl made a guest appearance in that movie (with the result that the road from Salzburg to the schloss is sometimes filled with special *Sound of Music* sightseeing tours).

Fuschl was built 500 years ago as a hunting lodge by the Archbishops of Salzburg and through its crested doorway there has been a steady parade of the high-and-mighty of history—from Emperor Maximilian I to Nikita Khrushchev and Anwar Sadat. When the castle was taken over a few years ago by Germany's Grundig Foundation, hundreds of thousands of dollars were injected for improvements, but the money has been spent discreetly, and the castle still feels more like an aristocrat's home than a hotel. Walls are lined with hunting trophies (all neatly tagged and numbered) and portraits of the archbishops (ditto). The lounge bar is a striking room with open fire, fluted ceilings and oriental rugs. Every guest room (most of them with double beds) has at least one antique piece—secretaire, commode or armoire—but overall the gracious furnishings follow the styles of Louis XIV or XV. Assuming you have a choice (with only 20 rooms in the main building and a loyal clientele, there may be few options), we suggest you put in a bid for one of the following: Room 17, a corner room overlooking the lake; 3, on the 3rd floor overlooking the lake, with a fireplace and original oil paintings; 5, a maroon-and-green boudoir on the 2nd floor, also with a great view; 8, with feminine decor and a view of the garden and mountain; or 22, a corner room with a small balcony. The prize accommodation is suite 7, another corner salon with four viewful windows, palatial bathroom/dressing room, pewter chandeliers, an original painting above the bed. It's priced, shall we say, audaciously; but since this is where Messrs. Sadat and Nehru, Clark Gable and pianist Alexis Weissenberg have bunked down, this room is in demand, regardless of the rate (something like $200 a night). There are also a dozen rooms in an annex in the garden. Annex, indeed. The Jägerhaus, as it's called, is a typically Tyrolean chalet, with most rooms decorated in colorful Tyrolean style. Anywhere but at Fuschl these rooms would be tops, so don't hesitate about staying here, if the schloss itself is full. The three cottages by the lake have their own kitchens. Many musicians and celebrities choose them for their privacy, but few of them bother to use the kitchens since the schloss chefs set such a high standard. Game all year. Fish from the lake.

The hotel's own smokehouse supplies the kitchen with *Rauchertforelle* (smoked trout) and *Hirschschinken geräuchert* (smoked deer ham), which, with melon, makes an ideal beginning to lunch on the orange-awning terrace overlooking the lake. Follow that with *Fuschlseerenke auf Fenchelstangen gebraten mit Pernod flambiert* (that is, Lake Fuschl pike cooked in fennel and flamed with Pernod) and fresh berries grown without the help of chemicals at the farm up the hill. In the cooler months, meals are served in the Winter Garden. During the Salzburg Festival, the castle serves a postopera supper for its guests. They are to be envied. The true romantics among them rent the Fuschl Rolls, which drops them at the door of the Festspielhaus; after the performance, the chauffeur is waiting to whisk them back to the schloss, down the long driveway now lighted by torches, up the old stone door with the crest of the archbishops. In the candlelit dining salon *Rauchertforelle* and champagne are the perfect finale.

Name: Hotel Schloss Fuschl

Manager: Uwe Zeilerbauer

Address: 5322 Hof Salzburg

Location: About half an hour by car from Salzburg; alert the hotel in advance and they will send a Rolls-Royce or Mercedes to pick you up (about $30).

Telephone: (06229) 253

Telex: 63454

Reps: Robert F. Warner and Relais-Château in U.S. and Canada, Relais-Château in Europe

Credit Cards: American Express, Diners Club, Master Charge/Euro-card/Access

Rooms: 64, with 18 rooms and 6 suites in the main castle, 12 in the Jägerhaus, and 6 more in 3 self-contained cottages by the edge of the lake

Meals: Breakfast anytime, lunch 12–3, dinner 7–9, plus a postopera supper 10–midnight during the Festival; lunch on the terrace in summer; 3-course dinner for two approx. $50–$55; tie and jacket; full room service to 9 P.M.

Entertainment: TV in lounge (in rooms on request), taped music (mostly Mozart) in the lounge and dining room; concerts and casino in Salzburg

Sports: Tennis court (with a curious, interlocking plastic surface), indoor 227

marble swimming pool, sauna massage, beach and sundeck beside the lake, 9-hole golf course, walking trails (2 hours of lakeside paths), rowboats, electric power boats, wind-surfers, fishing, rifle range, bowling alley; horseback riding nearby

Sightseeing: Hunting Museum on hotel grounds; the Salzkammergut and its lakes, the White Horse Inn at Wolfgangsee, cogwheel railway up Schaffenberg; Salzburg (See also Goldener Hirsch)

P.S. Closed November through March; some small tour groups

Hotel Goldener Adler
Innsbruck

WX$$

Innsbruck is not exactly the kind of town one might call romantic, but how can you ignore an inn that goes back some four hundred years and has hosted, among others, Goethe, Heine, Ludwig I of Bavaria and Chancellor Metternich. In fact, so many historic personages have visited the Goldener Adler that its oldest visitors' books are now in the Goethe Archives in Weimar.

First, Innsbruck. All that fancy publicity the town got when it hosted the winter Olympics might lead you to believe it's some kind of idyllic Alpine town, but the reality is a joyless jumble of concrete, one-way streets and too much traffic. When you get there, head straight for *Altstadt*, the Old City, a picturesque maze of squiggly streets, odd facades and, in summer, sidewalk cafés. Step through one of these cafés, under mammoth gray arches, and you enter the tiny lobby of the Golden Eagle, just as Goethe and Ludwig and all those others did in centuries gone by. The first two floors are dedicated to eating and drinking and *Gemultlichkeit*, tourist attractions in their own right (but not necessarily "touristy," with the exception of the Goethe Stube and its nightly yodeling). Portraits of Emperor Joseph II, the Empress Maria Theresa, Goethe and Schiller line the walls, together with manuscripts and documents with famous signatures. But for some unaccountable reason, the corridors of the upper floors are lined with framed prints of veteran tramcars of Glasgow Corporation, vehicles I can remember from my youthful days.

The guest rooms have all been renovated in recent years. The older rooms are all furnished and decorated differently: Room 205, for example, has Spanish antique furnishings (wood and leather chairs, carved wooden

228

headboard); the Franz Josef Room comes with settee, armchairs and a baroque wardrobe; the Heinrich Heine Room features pine walls, ceilings and closets. Rooms on the top floor are newer, less ambitious, following typical Chalet Modern style of pine paneling, low-slung beds with *duvets.* All rooms come with bath and shower, telephone and FM radio.

The Golden Eagle's four restaurants offer guests a choice of dining atmosphere. The two "classier" rooms, on the second floor, are designed for hotel guests, but you'll probably prefer the two on the ground floor, intended for the general public. Both have more local flavor—the Batzenhäusl being the simpler of the two, the Goethe Stube entertaining diners with Tyrolean music, amplified to a degree that might send Goethe, were he to return, screaming across the Inns Bruck.

Name: Hotel Goldener Adler

Manager: Karl Pokorny

Address: 6 Herzog-Friedrichstrasse, A-6020 Innsbruck, Tyrol

Location: In the Old City, a few yards from the bridge on the River Inn that gives the town its name; in a pedestrian-only section, so park as close to the bridge as you can

Telephone: (05222) 26334

Cables: Goldener Adler Innsbruck

Reps: American International Hotel Representatives in U.S., Wolfe International in Canada

Credit Cards: American Express, Diners Club, Visa, Carte Blanche

Rooms: 37

Meals: Buffet breakfast 7–10, lunch and dinner 11 A.M. to midnight in one of four restaurants; dinner for two approx. $20–$25 (but you can eat informally for less); informal dress; room service for drinks only

Entertainment: Amplified Tyrolean music and yodelers every evening in the Goethe Stube, from 8 to 1

Sports: Nothing at the hotel, everything in the surroundings; free bus to ski slopes in winter

Sightseeing: The historic buildings of Old Innsbruck—the 18th century imperial palace, the Hofburg; Cathedral of St. Jacob; Ambras Castle; Tyrolean Folk Museum; Regional Museum; cable cars up to mountaintops; various music festivals, recitals throughout the summer on the 15th-century wooden organ in the Silver Chapel of the Hofkirche

Schlosshotel Igls
Igls

WWWXXX$$$

Where did you last encounter a cozy 17-room inn with its own indoor/outdoor swimming pool? At the end of a corridor lined with antiques and bas-reliefs?

Schloss Igls is not, as its name might lead you to expect, some centuries old fortress but a big cheery Victorian mansion with a curvaceous white facade, curly gables and a steep dark-hued roof with dormers and turrets. A white stone wall encircles a large garden with spacious lawns, with stone tables and chairs set out beneath the oaks and firs. A pair of Porsches and a Lancia are parked in the driveway, and a handful of guests are reading on padded loungers on a pleasant blue-and-white veranda. There's a sense of quiet contentment about the place. The mansion sits at the edge of town, 2700 feet above sea level, 1500 above the valley, surrounded by Tyrolean mountains. Until a few years ago it was a private home, but then it was converted by Fred and Annedore Beck into a stylish country-house hotel offering "exceptional comfort for the fastidious." It's something of a hobby for them, which is very nice indeed for the guests since this means it's not run on the cost-conscious lines of commercial hotels. This doesn't mean that the Becks are not professional hoteliers. Far from it. They also own the Sporthotel Igls up in the village (very attractive in its own lively ski-resort way) but the mansion is where they have fun, lavishing on it their collection of antiques and heirlooms. apart from the small reception desk and the bar in the lounge, you could be walking into a private home, and you'll probably find a welcoming log fire burning in the wood-paneled lounge.

Annedore Beck, a classy lady who skis, plays golf and drives the Lancia, designed the decor. It may not be to everyone's taste (it has a certain heady Viennese-waltz gaiety about it), but there are certainly several attractive love nests here. Every room comes equipped with stereo radio, color television, telephone, bathroom scales, clothes brush and needle-and-thread kits, but otherwise they are all different. Some are decorated in Biedermeier style, some are Tyrolean, others Viennese, a few Decorator Extravagant. Our favorites are Room 32 (double bed, breakfast nook, custom-made inlaid tables and doors), 24 (*three* corner windows), 17 (lots

Schlosshotel Igls

of windows and a balcony), 12 (L-shaped with the bed in an alcove, crowned by a vaulted ceiling in blue floral wallpaper, and with a balcony to catch the morning sun) and 25 (large sitting room with a small circular bedroom and turret windows). The grandest guest chamber in the Igls is Room 21, which has an enormous sitting room and tiny balcony, and a few steps down to a circular bedroom.

The Igls dining room, on the other hand, is conservative, its wood paneling and porthole windows giving the impression of a salon of the emperor's yacht. The tables are set with Hutschenreuther china, large crystal goblets with a floating rose—even the toothpicks come in a silver case.

Schloss Igls, in other words, is a place to spend a comfy, pampered, oh-so-restful weekend. Fresh alpine air. A swim in the pool. Sunbathing on the lawn. Lunch on the veranda. A stroll, a siesta. Aperitifs on one of the stone benches beneath the oaks and firs as you watch the sun set on the peaks behind Innsbruck. Dinner. Cognac in the lounge, beside the baroque carved fireplace. Later, perhaps, muffled giggles in Schloss Igls.

Name: Schlosshotel Igls

Manager: Klaus Ledwinka

Address: A-6080 Igls, Tyrol

Location:	In the hills above Innsbruck, about ten minutes away by car
Telephone:	(05222) 7241
Telex:	053314
Reps:	(None)
Credit Cards:	American Express, Visa, Diners Club, Bankamericard
Rooms:	17

Meals: Breakfast 7–11, lunch 12–2 (on the veranda in summer), dinner 7–9; dinner for two approx. $22–$25; informal dress ("but no blue jeans"); full room service during dining room hours, drinks and snacks around the clock

Entertainment: TV in rooms, taped music in lounge; bars and lounges just up the street in the village (including 5 o'clock tea dancing in season), other night spots in Innsbruck

Sports: Indoor/outdoor heated pool, sauna massage; Rejuvenation Center at nearby Sporthotel Igls (same owners); tennis, golf, horseback riding, rowing, walking, hiking, winter sports nearby

Sightseeing: Cable car up to 7145-foot-high Patscherkofl (see also Goldener Adler in Innsbruck)

P.S. Closed November (and possibly also for a few weeks in spring); some small ("very small") seminars in spring and fall

Hotel Grünwalderhof
Patsch bei Igls

This is pretty much the kind of country inn you would expect to find in the Tyrol. Chalet lines with steep overhanging roof. Walls painted with bright murals of hunting scenes. A forest preserve across the roadway, pastures filled with gentian in spring, and across the valley a 180-degree panorama of peaks and glaciers, with here and there a tiny red steeple peeking from between the birches and firs.

The Green Wood Farm dates from the 15th century (although most of what you see here today is 18th century) and it has been in the same family for more than 150 years. Not any family, mark you. The present *graf*, or count, comes from a long line of Thurn und Taxis, hereditary Postmasters General of Tyrol for centuries until the demise of the monarchy at the beginning of this century. They converted this old hunting lodge on the old Roman post road into a hotel about 50 years ago, and the present count has been running it since the 1960s.

On a recent visit the clientele seemed to be less postmaster general than mailman, but the place has a pleasantly informal, rustic feel. Hunting prints and trophies line the walls, antiques range from hand-carved Tyrolean chests to an old cashier's desk with slate top. The snug *Stube*, with its wood-paneled walls and fancy murals, must be one of the most authentic in Austria. The guest rooms are traditional country-home style, with rustic wood furnishings and (in most cases) low cot-type beds. A few are decorated with Biedermeier pieces, a few have balconies. Ask to see a few rooms before checking in, but specify in advance that you'd like a room facing the valley and the mountains and the glaciers. It's the kind of view you come to Austria to admire.

Name: Hotel Grünwalderhof

Owner/Manager: Franz Graf Thurn und Taxis

Address: A-6082 Patsch bei Igls, Tirol

Location: In the mountains above Innsbruck, about 10 minutes from the Brenner Autobahn linking Germany and Italy

Telephone: (05222) 73404

Cables/Telex: (None)

Reps: (None)

Credit Cards: Diners Club

Rooms: 30, most with private baths

Meals: Breakfast 7:30–10, lunch 12–2, dinner 7–9; dinner for two approx. $12–$15; informal dress; room service during dining room hours

Entertainment: TV room, occasional folklore shows; bars and discos in Igls (five minutes away) and Innsbruck (15 minutes away)

Sports: Outdoor and indoor pools, sauna, sun room, exercise room, walking trails and cross-country skiing through adjoining nature park; tennis, golf, horseback riding, walking, hiking and winter sports nearby

Sightseeing: (See Hôtel Goldener Adler, Innsbruck)

P.S. Closed September to Christmas and mid-March to May

Switzerland

Hotel Hirschen
Langnau

♕ ✕✕✕ $

You've probably admired pictures of those fabulous Swiss farmhouses with the dipping rooflines and the painted flowers on the eaves. Now you can sleep in one—and with gourmet meals, no less, even in these rural surroundings.

The place is Hotel Hirschen in Langnau, the heart of the cheese-making Emmental Valley between Lucerne and Bern. The proprietors, Maria and Walter Birkhauser, took over the 500-plus-years-old inn some years ago after a long stint in Puerto Rico, where Walter's culinary prowess helped make the Swiss Chalet one of San Juan's best continental restaurants. He's still wearing his chef's toque, still busy tending to the kitchen, which now draws crowds to the hotel's simple dining room where Maria reigns as gracious hostess.

There's nothing pretentious about the Hirschen, so don't expect frills. But you can expect starched linen tablecloths, simple lace curtains at the window, fresh flowers and well-prepared food. As for wine, ask to see the cavernous wine cellar, or to have a tasting there on barrel-top seats around a table made from a giant bellows. (When you see the thickness of the cellar walls, you'll understand how the building has survived so well.)

Upstairs there are comfortable beds, pleasant flowered curtains, and plump pillows and comforters. Only four of the double rooms have private baths, but the bathroom down the hall is spotless.

The Hirschen may not be everyone's idea of romantic, but it's just the kind of typical local inn to give you a true feel for the country, situated in a picturesque but non-touristy town, run with pride by nice people. And that has a kind of romance all its own. (E.B.)

Name: Hotel Hirschen

Owners/Managers: Walter and Maria Birkhauser

Address: 3550 Langnau

Location: Midway between Bern and Lucerne on highway T10

Telephone: (035) 2 15 17

Cables/Telex: (None)

Reps: (None)

Credit Cards: American Express

Rooms: 16 rooms, only 4 with private bathroom

Meals: Breakfast 7–10, lunch 12–2, dinner 6–9; dinner for two approx. $35; informal dress; no room service; outdoor terrace

Entertainment: TV in lounge; occasional wine tastings in cellar

Sports: (None)

Sightseeing: Emmental Valley, picturesque cheese-making center; Bern and Lucerne, each less than an hour's drive (for Lucerne sights, see Château Gutsch)

Hotels Drachenburg, Waaghaus and Garni
Gottlieben

WWXX$

The bell you hear in the morning isn't an alarm clock, just a contented Swiss cow somewhere in the valley below.

Here in Gottlieben you're in a sort of pastoral Swiss Brigadoon, a town so tiny you could pass by and never know you'd been there, a peaceful place where people keep cows in their backyards. Yet it's the home of three of the most idyllic hotels you're likely to find.

They all belong to the same people, the Martin-Hummel family, who started the whole thing about 100 years ago when they took over the old timbered Waaghaus, or Weigh House, a rustic inn on the River Rhine. They fixed it up, added a flower-bedecked terrace on the waterfront and made it so appealing that people from Zurich began finding their way to Gottlieben. Then things started to grow.

In 1953 the Martin-Hummels acquired the old Drachenburg across the road, another picture-postcard contender with painted shutters, window

235

boxes and rounded timbered turrets topped with fat domes. A neighboring hotel was annexed onto the Waaghaus in 1966 and in 1979 the Garni was remodeled and added to the group. This is just one of the town's many historic houses, but it has been done up into a cozy, almost luxurious little place, a decorator's delight—fabric walls matching the bedspread and drapes, polished mahogany furniture, custom-built-in chests to match, hand-painted bathroom tiles, big thick color-coordinated towels. The old radiators are screened by window seats, the mini-bars built into cabinets, every room comes with the latest in radios and digital clocks.

Decor and comfort vary from building to building. (The bedrooms in some are more old-fashioned, with brocaded walls, canopies and that sort of thing, those in the Drachenburg more elaborate) but everything has been done with an obviously artistic eye. The upstairs Waaghaus dining room with its painted wooden chandeliers, windows on all sides topped with a scalloped flowered valance and matching drapes, is extraordinarily fresh and appealing. Even the flower arrangements are done with care, each one a perfect color-coordinated small bouquet.

Back at the Drachenburg you'll dine in a rustic room with timbered walls, beamed ceilings and brick floors. The breakfast room is a sunny glass-walled spot looking out onto a courtyard, drinks are served in a grand salon where sets of elegant sofas and chairs have been clustered around individual serving tables.

There's an equal amount of attention lavished on the food. The chef often recommends his *médaillon de veau*, very tender, served in a cream sauce topped with wild mushrooms, garnished with homemade noodles and fresh baby peas. For dessert, the *parfait Grand Marnier* sprinkled with finely grated Swiss chocolate is nothing short of *parfait*.

It will take you just above five minutes to walk around Gottlieben, but during that time you'll see homes dating back to the 13th century, still occupied and perfectly maintained—a working weaver, a couple of antique shops. Otherwise, you enjoy simple pleasures—peace and tranquillity, a walk in the woods, a ride on the river, a chance to unwind. (E.B.)

Name: Hotels Drachenburg, Waaghaus and Garni

Owners/Managers: The Martin-Hummel Family

Address: CH8274 Gottlieben TG

Location: About an hour north of Zurich; 2 miles from Constance (Konstanz) on the banks of the Rhine just before it widens into Lake Constance. From Zurich, take E17 to Winterthur, N7 to Frauenfeld, then follow signs to Konstanz until you see turnoff for Gottlieben.

236   **Telephone:** (072) 69 14 14

Cables/Telex: (None)

Reps: (None)

Credit Cards: Master Charge, Visa

Rooms: 60 rooms, 4 suites

Meals: Breakfast 7–10, lunch 11:30–2, dinner 6–9; dinner for two approx. $22; informal dress; room service for breakfast only; outdoor terrace in season

Entertainment: (None)

Sports: Hiking, water sports, tennis, golf nearby

Sightseeing: Boat rides on Lake Constance, craftsmen, antique shops, old homes in Gottlieben; Konstanz (the port, the Basilica, old City Hall, Rosgarten Museum, Konzilgebaude, boat excursion to Mainau Island)

P.S. Off-season, Gottlieben is a rare find, but it is becoming better known and gets busy in the summer months. All year round you have to be prepared for the Sunday onslaught when everyone and his grandmother comes to town for dinner and a walk in the country

Le Vieux Manoir
Murten-Meyriez

♛♛✗✗✗$$

Suppose you were a French aristocrat-general planning to build a rustic retreat in Switzerland. First, you'd probably want to find yourself a lake, one with restful views of surrounding hills. Then it might be nice to be near to a very special kind of village, one you could look forward to returning to year after year.

With luck, you might come up with Le Vieux Manoir, a stone, stucco and timber country home with green lawns and gardens running right down to the water's edge. Built as an aristocrat's country home, it later served as a school, then became a hotel in 1956, retaining its placid air but adding a glassed-in dining gallery to open up the vista of blue water, white sails and the green vineyards of Mount Sully off in the distance.

The town of Murten is a tiny gem, a village that preserves its medieval walls, winding streets and arcaded walkways, adds overflowing flower

237

boxes and provides plenty of little sidewalk cafés for soaking up the atmosphere. A nice place to come home to, indeed.

Today it's primarily the food that keeps people coming back to Le Vieux Manoir. Located just at the beginning of the French-speaking part of Switzerland, the hotel boasts cuisine that is definitely French and very highly regarded, a favorite for many Bern residents who make the drive to Murten when they want to get away from it all. Even breakfast is memorable here—fresh squeezed juice *and* fresh grapefruit sections, buttery croissants, homemade yogurt in stemmed glasses, a gigantic wedge of local cheese and a long loaf of French bread to go with it.

Le Vieux Manoir is not a formal place. There are no lounges, but the bedrooms are particularly pleasant. Room 3, papered in a soft blue-and-periwinkle flowered print, has a fringed canopied bed, pillows and comforter edged in hand embroidery, long windows and a Dutch door leading to a terrace overlooking the lake. To help put you in a properly romantic mood, there is even a heart carved in the headboard.

Room 15 is bigger, a huge corner room with hardwood floors, an oriental rug and two big carved wooden beds pushed together. Or you might prefer 28, facing the lake, with flocked wallpapers—or 21, with walls, headboard and drapes all in matching tapestry stripes.

You'll sleep and eat well here in the country in a quiet hideaway that's just 20 minutes from busy Bern. (E.B.)

Name: Le Vieux Manoir

Owner/Manager: Hans O. Scherrer

Address: CH-3281, Murten-Meyriez

Location: 20-minute drive from Bern; follow signs to Fribourg or Neuchâtel, turn off on Murten road. Meyriez is less than a mile beyond, on a lake.

Telephone: (037) 71 12 83

Cables: (None)

Telex: 36442

Reps: (None)

Credit Cards: American Express, Diners Club

Rooms: 23 rooms

Meals: Breakfast 7–11:30, lunch 12–2, dinner 6–9:30; dinner for two approx. $35; room service available all day

238 **Entertainment:** (None)

Sports: Public swimming pool next door, tennis and riding nearby

Sightseeing: Tiny medieval walled city of Murten; Fribourg, Bern and Gruyere are close enough for easy day excursions

P.S.   Closed November through January

Hotel Château Gütsch
Lucerne

ŴŴ XX $$

From the town it's a fairytale white castle with a gingerbread tower, perched high in the hills. Take the cable car to the hotel and it's Lucerne that becomes the fantasy, a toy town of spires, tile roofs and miniature houses clustered along the lake. Beyond the city the lake widens, fills with tiny sailboats and yachts. And beyond *that*, the Alps, still covered with snow even while you're sunning yourselves beside the pool.

The Gütsch has carefully preserved its old medieval atmosphere to make things even more romantic for latter-day knights and their ladies. You enter under a wooden canopy decorated with armor and weapons, pass into an entry hall with more weapons and painted figures of knights, and, of course, the *de rigeur* suit of armor standing to welcome you.

To the right is the salon, an enormous room elegantly done in scarlets, blues and golds, filled with period furniture, tapestries, and a striking blown-glass chandelier. One entire wall is windows, and there's that view again. Walk on into a smaller adjoining room where, seated in a mighty carved chair much like a throne, you could catch a bit of TV—if you could keep your eyes away from the vista below.

Upstairs, the rooms vary but you can count on finding antiques and fine reproductions, usually in French Provincial or Swiss Baroque style. Room 21, for example, is done in tones of silver and red with floor-to-ceiling drapes, a padded leather bedstead, a massive carved wardrobe with handsome brass locks, a more delicate writing table with a leather upholstered straight-back chair, and tall glass doors leading to the terrace.

Next door you can have a room in light blue and white with a big Italian carved wooden bed, and right down the hall there's another room in greens and golds with a ruffled canopy on the bed and oriental rugs on the floor. The deluxe duplex suites with beams and spiral stairs, hidden off in a corner off the main floor, are worth splurging for a terrace and that

239

incomparable view. Each has a minibar stocked with refreshments and a radio to supply soft music.

The château building dates back to the 14th century when it served as a watchtower for the town. It was destroyed in a fire in the 1870s, then rebuilt in its present ornate style, but you can't help but sense the original medieval spirit of the place when you head into the underground stone passage that takes you to the dining room. It's a surprisingly rustic room, with hand-hewn supporting beams and ceiling and a stairway to the balcony made of logs that look as though they came straight from the forest, bark and all. But come nighttime and candlelight, it's magically transformed. The city lights up below, there's music to dine and dance by, even a lady selling long-stemmed roses. Just be sure to reserve your table in advance, as this is a popular spot with all Lucerne visitors who want to see the panorama from the Gütsch.

Everyone's been to the Gütsch, from Queen Victoria to Alfred Hitchcock. If you're a romantic at heart, by all means add your name to the list. (E.B.)

Name:	Hotel Château Gütsch
Owner:	Fritz Furler
Manager:	P. Wallimann
Address:	P.O. Box CH-6000, Lucerne 3

Location: Atop the hills overlooking the city, reached by auto or private cable car from the old city

Telephone:	(041) 23 38 83
Cables:	Fuhot CH
Telex:	78233
Reps:	Utell, Inc.

Credit Cards: American Express, Diners Club, Master Charge/Euro-card, Visa

Rooms: 40 rooms

Meals: Breakfast 7–10, lunch 12–2, dinner 7–10; dinner for two approx. $48; tie and jacket required; room service for breakfast and snacks; outdoor terrace overlooking the city

Entertainment: TV lounge, dinner music and dancing

Sports: Outdoor pool, walking trails, tennis available at sister hotel Carlton Tivoli in town

240

Sightseeing: The old city, Kongresshaus, Panorama, Lion Monument, Glacier Garden, Swiss Transport Museum, Musegg Fortifications, Kapell Bridge, Old Town Hall, Stiftskirche, St. Xavier's Church, Franciscan Church, Lido Beach, Museum of Swiss Folk Costumes, Swiss Museum for Bread and Pastry; rowing regattas, casino, International Festival of Music in summer, Municipal Theater in winter; one hour from Zurich, within easy drives of scenic lake country

P.S. Be sure to make reservations in advance for dinner

The Grand Hotel
Bürgenstock

♕♕♕ ✗✗ $$$$

The porter carts your bags to the piazza, where you board the funicular for the slow, steep ride down to the dock. There you catch the ferry for the sail across Lake Lucerne to Lucerne. As you pull away from the dock, look up, up and up the mountainside until vaguely on the hilltop you can see the outlines of one of the unique resorts of Switzerland.

The Bürgenstock Estate is 500 acres of pine-clad arête, 1500 feet above the lake, another thousand above the sea, and covered with more than a hundred types of trees, masses of flowers and 8000 rose bushes. On the side opposite the lake the ridge sweeps down to a picture-postcard Alpine valley and beyond that to the distant peaks of the Bernese Alps.

The hundred-year-old Grand Hotel is one unit of what is essentially a mountaintop resort village. A self-contained village at that, with its own power station, water supply, fire department, construction plant and workshops for carpenters, masons, electricians and ironmongers. There are two other hotels (the Palace, which accommodates more seminars than you want to mingle with, and the Park, which is about to be remodeled from top to bottom and will have to wait until a later edition); eight restaurants and snackbars; a pretty little white chapel built by a countess; a two-hundred-year-old wooden granary which can be pressed into service as a discotheque; and a few private homes which will make you *Lederhosen* green with envy. Plus a quartet of boutiques. Not the customary postcard-and-cuckoo-clock type of boutique but branches of famed jewelers Bucherer and Gubelin, clothiers Grieder and Fein Kaller. When you are shown to your room, in fact, you will be presented with envelopes containing the current Gubelin and Bucherer catalogs. Over the years, 241 apparently, the Grand has been accustomed to catering to a well-heeled clientele of movie stars (Audrey Hepburn, Sean Connery) and statesmen (Konrad Adenauer, Hubert Humphrey), although it's currently patronized more by wealthy industrialists. Just like the owner.

This remarkable gentlemen, Fritz Frey, is something of a Swiss Renaissance man: tycoon (calcium carbide, electrical and electronic factories, one of which built the mechanism for the cable car between Manhattan's East Side and the Roosevelt Island complex); controller of one of the Swiss central banks, director of another; flower lover (he has written a book called *My Friends the Flowers*); and art collector. And how! His private collection has been valued at $10 million, and most of his 130-odd paintings and tapestries hang in the Bürgenstock hotels. In the Grand alone, a Bernard Buffet hangs in the lobby, a Rubens in the reading room, a Lely in the drawing room, a Nicolaes Maes in the dining room. And so on. Not surprisingly, Fritz Frey considers Bürgenstock something of a hobby (although there's nothing casual about the operation) and he simply pumps the mountaintop profits back into the mountaintop. Currently he and his son Peter are developing a new health center and indoor tennis complex. The new health center is located beside a large hilltop pool shaped approximately like Lake Lucerne, and if you happen to be here on a day when the sun is shining, you can dine poolside from an elaborate buffet of 31 dishes—from *choufleur en salade avec persil* to *langue de boeuf* and *entrecôte*.

The pool, like the other sporting facilities up here, is reserved for hotel guests. An important point. Because although Bürgenstock is a private estate, in Switzerland the mountains are for everyone, and a trip up to Bürgenstock is a cherished treat for people living or vacationing in Lucerne and the surrounding towns. You *may* arrive with hordes of daytrippers or weekends or holidays, but the hotel facilities are strictly for the guests—and that includes the dining room, the great terrace high above the lake, the swimming pool and the tennis courts. For seclusion, stay put in the hotel or pool until the evening, when the mountaintop quiets down again and you can once more hear the cowbells in the pasture.

When you make your reservation at the Grand, ask for a room facing the lake. There's no surcharge because the view to the *rear*, across the Alpine meadows and Alpine peaks, would be considered premium view in any hotel less fortunately endowed. If you can afford to plump down the fee, check into one of the Junior Suites (108, 208 and 308, on the corner, are particularly spacious). Some guests (the late Konrad Adenauer among them) prefer the 20-room annex linked to the main hotel by a covered walkway, and right at the edge of the mountainside.

Most of the Grand's rooms have small balconies and French Traditional furnishings. All rooms have crystal chandeliers (the Frey interests include one of the largest electrical supply companies in

Switzerland). Avoid, if you can, Rooms 104 and 107, which are above the lounge and therefore subject to the amplified thumping of the resident combo. The beat goes on late into the night, even during July and August when the Grand seems to be inhabited by old timers who look barely able to shuffle let alone tango. On the other hand, in their gracious gowns (a different one for each night of their stay) they add a nostalgic Last Year at Marienbad, end-of-an-era touch to the place. You'll find a younger clientele (though hardly hard-core swingers) in spring and fall. May, June and September are good months to visit Bürgenstock, although in this foothill-of-the-Alps location, the weather is unpredictable to say the least.

Assuming you have fine weather, you'll find yourselves in glorious surroundings. The view from the terrace is the classic breathtaking panorama—to be enjoyed at leisure during afternoon tea or over aperitifs—with the lake far below and the cloud-wrapped peak of Mount Pilatus (remember the James Bond movie?) off to your left. An audacious walkway among the pines, up and around a still higher peak, brings you after 25 minutes, if you don't stop every five minutes to look over the edge (or grip the railings), to the world's highest outdoor elevator, which sweeps you up the cliff face to Hammetschwand. Here you'll find a rustic chalet café with coffee and pastries to steady your nerves, observation points with panoramas of seven lakes, and the start of a walking trail back down to the hotel (about two hours, they say, top to bottom). Other trails lead through woods and valley, and there's a crafty, tilted 9-hole golf course presided over by a personable English pro, Grahame Denny. If you've come to Bürgenstock by car, and don't mind the 15-minute obstacle course down to the valley floor, the Grand is also a wonderfully central location for excursions to Zurich, Interlaken and Bern. Buy yourselves a pair of Swiss Holiday Cards and you can roam at will on funiculars, ferryboats and trains (you could easily spend a rewarding vacation just taking trips on the lake below, going ashore here and there for wine and wurst).

If may be, of course, that the unpredictable weather will rustle up some mist and cloud, and the setting becomes even more dramatic. And if heavens open up and the rain pours down, you can always retire to your comfy room and curl up with your Bucherer and Gubelin catalogs.

Name: The Grand Hotel, Bürgenstock Hotel Estate

Owners/Managers: The Frey Family

Address: CH-6366 Bürgenstock (in winter, Hirschmattstrasse 30, CH-6003, Lucerne)

Location: About 20 minutes by road from Lucerne (follow the signs Interlaken/Engelberg and watch carefully for the exit—the *second* exit just after you leave the tunnel); or by ferryboat from the dock across the street from Lucerne Central Station, then by funicular up the hill (alert the hotel and they'll send a porter to cope with your luggage)

Telephone: (041) 621212/641122

Cables/Telex: Freyhotel Bürgenstock/78462 bueho

Reps: HRI in U.S. and Canada

Credit Cards: American Express

Rooms: 211, including 12 suites, in three hotels

Meals: Breakfast anytime, lunch 11 A.M.–11 P.M., dinner to 11 (meals are available in 8 restaurants, in addition to a poolside buffet when the sun shines); dinner for two approx. $50–$60 in the Grand, but much less in the restaurants; tie and jacket in the Grand, informal elsewhere; 24-hour room service

Entertainment: Dancing to a combo in the lounge, movie shows twice a week (mostly in English), disco (occasionally), TV in lounge (in rooms on request)

Sports: 2 clay courts, swimming pool at hotel, beach at lake, 9-hole golf course (small green fee), massage, 6 miles of marked hiking trails

Sightseeing: Museums (Swiss Transport, Richard Wagner, Swiss Folklore, etc.), Planetarium, Glacier Gardens, old city walls and wooden bridge—all in Lucerne (see also Chateau Gütsch); trips up Mount Pilatus and Mount Rigi; evening boat rides on lake; Lucerne Festival mid-August to September 8 (1979 programs included the Berlin Philharmonic, the Boston Symphony, Cleveland Orchestra, Israel Philharmonic, Von Karajan, Mehta, Maazel, Ozawa, Fischer-Dieskau and several Swiss performers)

P.S. Closed mid-October to beginning of May; no groups or conventions at the Grand, although there may be some at the Palace and Park

Hotel Monte Rosa
Zermatt

When the first alpinists came to Zermatt at the turn of the century, lured by the challenging configurations of the mighty Matterhorn, they stayed here at the Monte Rosa. Later, for the first stretch of their hike from the valley

up to the village 5,300 feet above sea level, they built a cogwheel railway, trains that still haul visitors up from Brig. Now there's a roadway up through the valley, but it doesn't go quite as far as Zermatt, which still manages to remain a car-free village. Horse-drawn carriages (sleighs in winter) and electric carts greet visitors at the train station, and it's one of these horse-drawn vehicles that will convey you up through the main street to the Monte Rosa.

This 7-story hostelry is the oldest in Zermatt, alpinists still hold their reunions here, and the owners (Seiler Hotels) have taken considerable care to maintain the turn-of-the-century atmosphere in the public rooms. The pine walls of the *salon de lecture* are lined with sepia photographs of the early alpinists, while other walls throughout the hotel are decorated with signed photos of later guests such as Winston Churchill, the King of Malaysia, a former Archbishop of Canterbury and Charles Bronson. The dining room is maybe a bit stuffy for an alpine resort, even with its fancy ceiling and gilt mirrors, although some clients may be attracted by the private dining salon usually reserved for visiting royalty. The guest rooms, too, are turn-of-the-century in flavor, with modern facilities like tiled bathrooms (at least in the double rooms), minibars, double doors and double-glazed windows.

The ambience, in other words, is more turn-of-the-century than ski resort, but it's a pleasant spot for a couple of nights.

Zermatt is essentially a winter resort, but it's also very popular in summer. Come here for fresh air and mountain trips rather than total relaxation.

Name: Hotel Monte Rosa

Manager: Urs Keller

Address: 3920 Zermatt

Location: In the Center of town, about 5 minutes by horse-drawn carriage or sleigh from the station; to get to Zermatt take the cogwheel railway from Brig (or the road to Tasch, 3 miles away, then by train to Zermatt)

Telephone: (028) 671922

Cables/Telex: Monterosa/38328 moros ch

Reps: HRI and Utell in U.S., Canada and Europe

Credit Cards: American Express, Diners Club, Visa, Master Charge/Eurocard

Rooms: 63

Meals: Breakfast 7–10, lunch 12:30–1:30, dinner 7–8:30; dinner for two approx. $27–$30; informal; room service 7 A.M. to 8:30 P.M. (and all rooms have minibars)

Entertainment: TV room, taped music in lounge

Sports: Free entrance to indoor pool, sauna and massage at sister hotel, the Mont Cervin; tennis nearby, plus hiking ("best and longest network of hiking trails—approx. 250 miles—in the Alps") and winter sports

Sightseeing: Trips by cog railway up to the Gornergrat; "the highest cable car ride in Europe," a ride on the new underground funicular; Alpine Museum; Chamber Music Festival (first two weeks in August), Folk Costume and Music Show (mid-August)

P.S.   Closed for 2 weeks after Easter, plus October and November

Hotel Alex
Zermatt

₩ X $$$

Here's one of the most unusual hôtels in the Alps, a pampering, cosseting snuggery that's virtually hand-built by the eponymous Alex—Alex Perren. Like his father before him, he was a Matterhorn guide, but when he took a tumble 15 years ago and lost a limb, he decided to take up innkeeping instead. With a vengeance. He never stops adding (15 deluxe new suites in a new wing in 1979) and improving what was there before.

The Alex is all sturdy timbers, wood paneling, hand-carved ceilings, hand-painted headboards, with heavy bronze doors on the suites. Gisella Perren designed many of the fabrics and a stained-glass mural depicting a climb up the Matterhorn. All 70 rooms have balconies and plush bathrooms, five of them have fireplaces, and there's one spectacular suite, the Flick Flat, with raftered ceiling, stone fireplace, flokati rugs, decorative ceiling and fancy royal-blue bathrooms.

The lounges and Alex Grill are popular gathering spots for sports enthusiasts from other hotels in town, and you can expect an air of conviviality here. (Sometimes, it's reported, you can also expect a certain amount of grumpiness from the staff, but it doesn't seem to deter the hotel's devoted regulars.)

We would probably be more enthusiastic about the Alex if it were situated on a pristine slope with a pristine view above the village, rather

246

than up an alley behind the cog railway terminal (which is hardly, of course, a Grand Central).

Name:	Hotel Alex
Owners/Managers:	Alex and Gisella Perren
Address:	3920 Zermatt
Location:	A few yards from the railroad station
Telephone:	(028) 671726
Cables:	Alexhotel
Reps:	(None)
Credit Cards:	American Express
Rooms:	70, including 40 suites

Meals: Breakfast 7–11, lunch/dinner noon to 4 A.M.; dinner for two approx. $25–$30; informal dress; round-the-clock room service

Entertainment: TV in guest rooms; bars and discos in town; taped music in dining room

Sports: Indoor tennis (extra charge); 2 squash courts (extra charge), spectacular indoor free-form swimming pool, sauna, massage, exercise room; walking, hiking, winter sports nearby

Sightseeing: (See Hotel Monte Rosa)

P.S. Closed mid-May to mid-June and mid-October–end of November; some ski groups in winter

Hôtellerie Tenne
Zermatt

₩X$$$

Another typical chalet-style hotel, this time beside the terminal for the cog railway going *up* the mountains to Gornergrat (no problem with noise, though, since the last train leaves at 6). It's another attractive hotel, with exteriors of old barn siding, decorated with colorful escutcheons and window boxes. The lobby, with walls of cherry wood, has a coffered ceiling

247

decorated with *näif* panels depicting winter sports scenes, painted by one of the young Stöpfers. Guest chambers have less personality, but they're all snug and comfortable, with down comforters, cheerful bedspreads and drapes, and double-glazed windows to block out sound and keep in heat. Half the rooms have hand-hewn wooden balconies, and some of them have views of the Matterhorn's peak.

The Tenne's *Stube*-restaurant, with wooden beams and wood-burning fires, boasts a Chaîne des Rôtisseurs shield, so the menu leans to French cuisine rather than traditional fondue and *raclette*.

Name: Hôtellerie Tenne

Owners/Managers: The Stopfer Family

Address: 3920 Zermatt

Location: Two minutes from the cog-rail terminal, on the edge of town

Telephone: (028) 671801

Cables/Telex: (None)

Reps: (None)

Credit Cards: American Express, Diners Club, Visa

Rooms: 30

Meals: Breakfast 7–11, lunch 12–2, dinner 7–10/11; dinner for two approx. $30–$35; casual dress; full room service during dining room hours

Entertainment: TV lounge, taped music in lounge and dining room (organ music live in winter)

Sports: Tennis, walking, hiking, winter sports nearby

Sightseeing: Mountain trips by cogwheel train or cable car

P.S. Closed May (and maybe part of June) plus October and November

---

For brief reports on other hotels in Austria and Switzerland turn to the chapter on Added Attractions at the end of this guide.

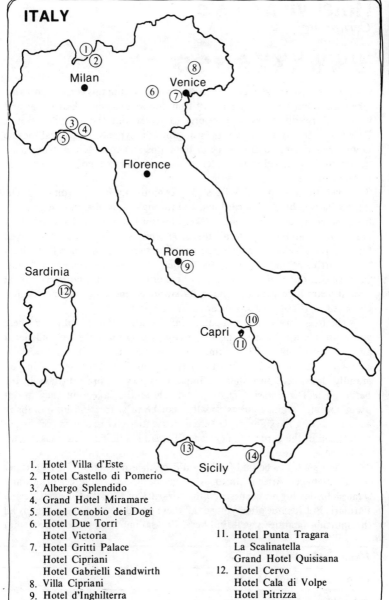

ITALY

ITALY

Milan

Venice

Sardinia

Florence

Rome

Capri

Sicily

1. Hotel Villa d'Este
2. Hotel Castello di Pomerio
3. Albergo Splendido
4. Grand Hotel Miramare
5. Hotel Cenobio dei Dogi
6. Hotel Due Torri
   Hotel Victoria
7. Hotel Gritti Palace
   Hotel Cipriani
   Hotel Gabrielli Sandwirth
8. Villa Cipriani
9. Hotel d'Inghilterra
   Hotel Lord Byron
10. Hotel San Pietro
11. Hotel Punta Tragara
    La Scalinatella
    Grand Hotel Quisisana
12. Hotel Cervo
    Hotel Cala di Volpe
    Hotel Pitrizza
13. Villa Igiea Grand Hotel
14. San Domenico Palace Hotel

Hotel Villa d'Este
Cernobbio

WWW XXX $$$$

Only a fairytale or ballet could get away with a setting this corny. A dreamy lake with mountains soaring almost from the water's edge. A driveway and walls and twenty acres of parkland to screen out the everyday world. Pathways winding through stands of pine and cypress. A magical mosaic monument leading to an avenue of fountains and cascades. A promenade beside the lake, shaded by linden trees. A swimming pool and sundeck floating in the lake.

Even the very name, Villa d'Este, conjours up tales of romance. The great villa was built for a cardinal, and throughout its 400-year span it has been owned by, among others, a duke, a marquis, a count and a ballerina. A czarina came all the way from Russia to spend two months here and stayed for two years. When the widowed ballerina remarried a general, she built mock fortresses and towers in the garden—to keep her general at home. Princess Caroline of Brunswick-Wolfenbüttel, wife of George IV, spent several years here with her young Italian lover and had a statue, "Venus Crowned by Eros," set up in her private apartments.

The five-story villa is still palatial and opulent, the sort of place where you acquire a mantle of grandeur just by striding through its chandeliered and columned halls. The dining room is majestic, with a large glass-enclosed veranda for enjoying the view as you dine. The guest rooms are grandly decorated, furnished in Impero style, with brass fittings in the bathrooms. The choicest chambers overlook the lake, but they are at premium, and regular guests usually manage to snap them up months in advance during the summer. Other cognoscenti prefer to stay in the wing at the far end of the garden, the Queen of England building, which has its own concierge.

There's a lot to be said for Villa d'Este: the loyal staff (roughly one per room); manager Arrigo Mario, who has been welcoming celebrities and semicelebrities for a dozen years; the wizardry of Chef de Cuisine Luciana Parolari. But it's not often you get all these grand hotel attractions *plus* all the sporting facilities you'll find here. Parasailing? Canoeing? Kite flying?

Name: Hotel Villa D'Este

Manager: Arrigo Mario

Address: 22010 Cernobbio (Como)

Location: On the western shore of Lake Como, about 15 minutes north of the town of Como, 45 minutes from Milan

Telephone: (22010) 512471 or 511471

Telex: 38025 Villeste

Reps: HRI in U.S., Canada and Europe

Credit Cards: American Express

Rooms: 200, including 18 suites, in two lakeside villas

Meals: Breakfast 7–11, lunch 12–3 (on the terrace in summer), dinner 8–10; dinner for two approx. $40–$45; tie and jacket; room service from 7 A.M. to 11 P.M., and all rooms have minibars

Entertainment: Piano bar, discotheque (in the sports center), TV room; casino on Lake Lugano, across the border in Switzerland but just half an hour away by car

Sports: Tennis (6 courts, 2 lighted), 2 swimming pools (one covered, one floating in the lake—and a separate pool for children), sauna and massage, exercise room, 18-hole golf course (private, but 7 miles away), 1700-yard parcure course, canoeing, rowboats, parasailing, kite flying, waterskiing— everything but sauna and massage no extra charge

Sightseeing: Cornaccina Island for picnics, boat trips on the lake

P.S. Closed November through March; a few small tour groups, a few dozen day trippers on weekends, some seminars (40–50 people) in the off-season; May, June and October are uncrowded and pleasant

Hotel Castello di Pomerio
Pomerio d'Erba

WⵖX$$

As a *castello* it's a few centuries old (its history goes all the way back to the son of Charlemagne), as a hotel it's less than five. Between times it served at one point as a silk factory, and the old mulberry tree that fed the silkworms still stands, albeit precariously, in the cobbled courtyard. Many of the implements of silk manufacturing have been pressed into service as furniture or decoration—old looms into frames for bathroom mirrors or antique headboards. In the garden, hand-hewn logs form a bridge leading to the pool, surrounded by old wooden troughs filled with flowers, and an

251

antique bellows decorates the barbecue corner.

It's all very ingenious and picturesque, a deft blend of chunky stone-and-timber with fluffy contemporary comforts, carved stone capitals and panels of glass, 14th-century frescoes and 20th-century metal sculptures and Vasarely lithographs.

Half the rooms are located in the main *castello*, and a more recent selection in the chatelaine's house in the garden across the road. They're all attractive. In the garden wing, decor is Victorian, and some of the rooms have french doors opening onto the tree-shaded lawn. Life is quieter, more secluded over there. But to get the true flavor of the *castello* you'll probably prefer a room in the main building; six of them have galleries with wooden stairs leading up to sleeping lofts, and they all have modern tiled bathrooms and minibars.

Other attractions at Pomerio are the intimate rustic dining rooms, the library/billiard room and the contemporary flair of the lounge (even with the ungaínly ultramod television set perched on the bar).

As you look around, it's hard to visualize that only a few years ago the castle was such a ruin that the Italian government didn't even bother to list it as a national monument. Lita Donati and her Milanese colleagues (an architect, a professor and an antiques dealer) have wrought a minor miracle, even if Signora Donati has to hang a larger-than-life photo of her 4-year-old grandson in the lobby because that's "the only way she gets to see him nowadays." Grandma's loss, guests' gain. Guests like the chic young Milanese couples fill the lounge on weekends—or the young German who confided to his colleague as they passed through the lobby: *"Es war eine schöne Nacht mit einer Blonden."*

Name: Hotel Castello di Pomerio

Owner/Manager: Lita Donati

Address: Via Como 5, Pomerio D'Erba (Como)

Location: In the hills, on the road from Erba to Como, 10 miles east of Lake Como, 25 miles north of Milan

Telephone: (031) 611516

Telex: Pomerio 380463

Reps: Relais-Châteaux in U.S., Canada and Europe

Credit Cards: American Express, Diners Club

Rooms: 50, in the *castello* itself and the garden wing across the road

Meals: Breakfast 7:30–10, lunch 12:30–2:30, dinner 7:30–10; dinner for two approx. $45–$50; informal; room service during dining room hours,

252

and rooms in the main building have minibars

Entertainment: Piano bar in lounge, TV in same lounge

Sports: 2 tennis courts, heated swimming pool (covered pool promised), sauna, boccie; walking and hiking nearby

Sightseeing: Museum of pre-Roman Civilization in Como; all of Milan; panoramic view from Alpe de Valle Bova ("on a clear day you can see Milan Cathedral"); Grand Prix at Monza

P.S. Some small seminar-type meetings in the off-season

Albergo Splendido
Portofino

♛♛ ✕✕ $$$

The Fine Port itself is so romantic (even in the rain) it would be worth visiting even if you had to sleep in a *pensione* . But you don't—you have the Splendid Inn, one cove short of the harbor.

It sits halfway up a hill that's so steep and twisty tour buses pass it by, just beneath the villa once owned by Portofino-phile Rex Harrison. Its pink-and-canteloupe facade rises from terraced Mediterranean gardens overhung with pines and palms, mimosa and orange trees, with a vine arbor to shade the terrace. Originally a private villa when built at the turn of the century, the Splendido was expanded at the end of the first World War and converted into a hotel. Since then hosts of celebrities have wound their way up that winding driveway—Humphrey Bogart, President Roosevelt, Ava Gardner, Raf Vallone and Groucho Marx, whose entry in the visitors' book says "Wonderful place, wonderful people." Still on the whole, true, and celebrities still make their way here.

But the *albergo* has, like Italy itself, seen more glorious days. You almost get the impression that apart from installing a highly regarded manager, Tito Pinchetti, the insurance company that owns the place is not quite sure what to do with it next. The indoor dining room is a bore, and despite all the flourish and wheeling around of carts, the food offers little compensation. (A minor problem this, since you can always nip into town and dine on a terrace beside the water.)The lounges are comfortable, but for some reason the bar is decorated with murals of West Point and Niagara— hardly what you've come to Portofino to see. The guest rooms vary considerably. Those on the first floor have vine-covered terraces, those on

253

the second and third floors have terraces or balconies large enough for tête-à-tête breakfasts. Rooms on the top floor are tiny, all but two of the *albergo's* rooms face the sea. But avoid rooms with connecting doors unless you get your kicks from listening to the couple next door buttering their breakfast toast.

In other words, Albergo Semi-Splendid. But that's no reason for staying away. Its faded elegance does have a certain charm, the view across the garden and the Golfo Tigullio is endlessly rewarding. Lunch on the awning-shaded terrace, with the birds singing like prima donnas and the scent of orange and mimosa in the air, is the kind of romantic scene you come to Italy to enjoy.

And, of course, Portofino is just around the corner.

Name: Albergo Splendido

Manager: Tito Pinchetti

Address: Viale Baratta 13, 16034 Portofino

Location: Near the tip of the Portofino Peninsula, about 20 miles east of Genoa (take the Rapallo exit from the Autostrada)

Telephone: (0185) 69195

Cables/Telex: Splendido/Splendid 331057

Reps: Relais-Châteaux in U.S., Canada and Europe

Credit Cards: Visa

Rooms: 55, including 12 suites

Meals: Breakfast 7:30–10, lunch 12:30–2:30, dinner 7:30–9:45, on the terrace in summer; dinner for two approx. $40–$45; tie and jacket in winter, informal in summer; room service during dining room hours (most rooms also have minibars)

Entertainment: Piano bar in summer, TV room, TV in suites

Sports: Tennis (1 court, lighted, $1 an hour), heated swimming pool, sauna, massage; water sports nearby

Sightseeing: Castello Brown (14th-century fortress with museum, exhibitions, art shows); boat trips and footpaths to nearby villages; Spring Festival (last Sunday in March), Festival of San Giorgio (April 25); also excursions to Genoa (½ hour), Pisa (1 hour), Lucca (1 hour)

P.S. Closed January 11 to March 9; a few group tours or seminars in the off-season; May, June, September and October are the best times to visit

Grand Hotel Miramare
Santa Margherita Ligure

♙✗$$$

It's not so grand in size (a manageable 73 rooms) but it manages to maintain much of the style of the turn of the century, when it first opened its shutters on the dazzling Ligurian coast. Public rooms are high ceilinged and deep piled; the dining room is pristine and bright (air-conditioned in season); each floor has spacious halls and corridors. The guest rooms retain their double doors and polished wood floors, but with modern additions like television, radio, telephone (with bathroom extension), air-conditioning and double-glazed windows. Half the rooms face a Mediterranean garden, ablossom with camellias and rhododendrons, and shaded by palm and laurel trees; the other rooms face the sea—but even with the double-glazing, and with the air-conditioning working, some people may find this side too noisy on weekends and prefer the quieter garden side. Rates are the same, and garden rooms have balconies as a bonus.

Santa Margherita Ligure itself is a lovely spot, with yachts and boat-building yards sharing the curving palm-lined shore with sun worshippers and vacationers from Italy and the rest of Europe. It's quieter, they say, than San Remo or Rapallo, but still with plenty of restaurants, cafes and clubs to keep live wires occupied. And the Miramare is the kind of hotel people come back to year after year—including Middle Eastern potentates, Italian movie stars and regular romantics come to enjoy the *mira di mare*.

Name: Grand Hotel Miramare

Manager: Adalberto Gigli

Address: 16038 Santa Maria Ligure

Location: On the Italian Riviera, about 25 minutes from Genoa, 10 minutes from Portofino

Telephone: (0185) 87014

Cables/Telex: Miramare/270437

Reps: HRI in U.S., Canada and Europe, Steigenberg in Europe

Credit Cards: American Express, Visa

Rooms: 73, including suites

Meals: Breakfast 7–10:30, lunch 12:45–2:15, (poolside buffet 1–3), dinner 7:45–9:15; dinner for two approx. $40–$45; informal dress; room service from 7 A.M. to 9:15 P.M. (minibars in rooms)

Entertainment: Disco in the cellar (separate entrance), soft taped music in the lounge, TV in rooms, cafes and bars in town

---

Sports: Heated seawater pool, beach across the road (loungers included in the room rate), sauna, massage, waterskiing; tennis courts to come; tennis, golf, horseback riding, sailing and motorboats nearby

---

Sightseeing: (See Albergo Splendido, Portofino)

P.S.   Closed November 1 through December 23; separate dining room for children; some small seminar conventions in off-season

---

Hotel Cenobio dei Dogi
Camogli

₩ 🍴🍴 💲💲

When the doges of Genoa built their seaside "retreat" a few centuries ago, they selected one of the most stunning yet beautiful spots, a lush pine- and cypress-clad hill rising abruptly from the rocky shore of the Golfo Paradiso. Their L-shaped palazzo, complete with pink-and-white chapel, is now the nucleus of a modern hotel, run by the third generation of DeFerraris. The sea spreads out on one side, the hilly park on the other; a huge swimming pool fills a terrace above the rocks, stone paths lead down to pebbly beaches with loungers and cabanas.

Of the 82 rooms, the largest are in a newer, 5-story wing behind the pool, but the most charming rooms, with parquet floors and period furnishings, are in the original palazzo—and of these the choicest are Rooms 32, 33, 35, (each with a large terrace), and 11, 14, 15, 20 and 21 which face the sea.

If you don't snare a room with a view (just over half of them face the sea), you can enjoy the panorama of fishing village and gulf from the big-windowed large dining rooms and lounge (from which you can also peer through portholes into the swimming pools). The courtyard gardens, planted with hydrangea, rhododendrons and geraniums, interspersed with statuary that once belonged to the doges, help isolate you from the town.

Camogli itself is a curious place, a town stacked up in a deep ravine at the edge of the sea. The corner opposite the hotel is fairly nondescript, but at the lower levels Camogli is a bastion of skinny 7-story and 8-story houses, all pink and green or orange or magenta, curving around the harbor and ending in a seaside church and castle. No cars are allowed into the port area, where you'll find the usual tempting collection of *trattorie*, terrace cafés and boutiques. Camogli may be less well-known than Portofino, but in its funky way it's just as picturesque. Only a few miles separate the two ports, and ferryboats will take you from one to the other to compare notes.

Name: Hotel Cenobio dei Dogi

Owner/Manager: Massimo de Ferrari

Address: Camogli, Genoa

Location: On the Golfo Paradiso, 15 miles east of Genoa

Telephone: (0185) 770041

Cables/Telex: Cenobio Camogli/21116

Reps: (None)

Credit Cards: (None)

Rooms: 82

Meals: Breakfast 7:30–10:30, lunch 12:30–2, dinner 7:45–9; dinner for two approx. $30–$35; informal dress; room service from 7:30 A.M. to 9 P.M.

Entertainment: TV lounge, disco every Saturday in July and August; cafés and bars in town, 5 minutes away

Sports: Lighted tennis court ($5 an hour), large heated seawater pool, pebbly beach, cabanas and loungers (extra), 20 minutes of walking trails through the pine, palm and cypress trees; golf, horseback riding and watersports nearby

Sightseeing: Maritime Museum; hill towns and villages, old churches and castles; Blessing of the Fleet (2nd Sunday in May); boat rides to Portofino; Genoa

P.S. Closed November, some small groups during the off-season

Hotel Due Torri
Verona

WW XX $$$

More travelers would probably pick and choose their rooms before settling in if every hotel were as considerate as the Due Torri. Here you select your room right at the reception desk—from a panel of color slides. You have a choice of 15 different styles popular in the 18th and 19th centuries. Vittoriana. Ask for Room 88. Luigi Filippo? Check into 87. Your tastes run to Biedermeier's briarwood veneers and *naïf* landscape murals? Rooms 15 or 18 will fit the bill. And so on. And thereby hangs an explanation.

The original Two Towers was built back in the 14th century as the official guest house for the Lords of Verona, the Scaglieri Family. Generations later it was turned into a coaching inn, apparently *the* place to stay in Verona. A plaque in the lobby records that "Wolfgango Amadeo Mozart" stayed here in January 1770; and it seems to have been the southern equivalent of Innsbruck's Goldener Adler for travelers tackling the Brenner Pass across the Alps, since the guest lists of both hotels have many names in common—Goethe, Heine, Maria Theresa to name a few. The Due Torri finally closed in 1882, the building went through years of maltreatment, before being bought by Dr. Enrico Wallner and reopening as a deluxe hotel in 1958. An antique dealer and a restorer by profession, Wallner resolved to fill his new Due Torri with the furnishings in vogue when it closed in 1882. Hence the Vittoriana, Luiggi Filippo and so on.

All of which makes it a most unusual hotel. As a historic treasure, the basic structure had to remain intact. The former courtyard, where guests dismounted from their horses or carriages, is now a vast lobby/lounge, with marble floors, marble columns and arches, frescoes and an airy, artificial ceiling with authentic 17th-century paintings depicting the signs of the zodiac—from a hotelier's point of view, a complete waste of space, but for guests it creates a feeling of spaciousness and grandeur. In addition each of the floors has its own spacious lounge filled with family antiques—chinoiserie, a lacquered hurdy-gurdy, antique lace and "grandmotherly things." Even the TV lounge sports a collection of precious teapots and coffeepots.

What you have, then, is a very elegant, deluxe 19th-century hostelry, but with modern facilities, double-glazed windows and sound-insulated walls. The crystal bedside lamps have dimmer switches to create a romantic glow, each room seems to have a large mirror that can be moved and tilted to suit every whim, and stocked minibars put vino and *spumante* on tap for the right moment.

Manager Raimondo Giavarrini, fortyish, urbane and multilingual, is dedicated to running a deluxe operation with thoughtful old-style service. In the evening, for example, the chambermaid not only turns down your bed, but dims the lights and places your slippers (facing in the right direction) on a drugget carefully placed beside the bed.

If there's a shortcoming at the Due Torri, it's the restaurant, a split-level salon with a low-ceilinged *galleria* on top. The tables are well spaced and attractive, the food is tasty, but the service (unless it has changed, which is quite likely) is more appropriate to a Panamanian cruise ship than a deluxe hotel. But that's not a real drawback since there are so many romantic restaurants and terrace cafés within a couple of blocks of the hotel.

In any case, a deluxe hotel in Verona (and this is the only one) costs several dollars less than a deluxe hotel elsewhere in Italy—and a *lot* less than in Venice, for example, which can easily be accommodated in a day's outing from the Due Torri.

Name: Hotel Due Torri

Manager: Raimondo Giavarrini

Address: Piazza San Anastasia 4, 37100 Verona

Location: In the heart of the old city, near the Duomo and facing the church of S. Anastasia

Telephone: (045) 34130

Cables/Telex: Duetorri Verona/480524 Duetor

Reps: Robert F. Warner in the U.S. and Canada, William R. Galley Associates, London

Credit Cards: American Express, Diners, Master Charge/Eurocard

Rooms: 100, including 14 suites

Meals: Breakfast 7–11, lunch 12–2:30, dinner 7:30–9:30; dinner for two approx. $36–$40; tie and jacket during the opera festival, informal otherwise; room service during dining room hours, drinks around the clock (but all rooms have minibars)

Entertainment: Combo and dancing in the boîte downstairs, two TV lounges, terrace cafés around the corner

Sports: (None)

Sightseeing: Castelvecchio (paintings and sculpture), Museum of Natural History, Museum of Africa, Roman Arena, Piazza dei Signori, San Zeno Maggiore (Romanesque churches, one on top of the other); Romeo's

259

"tomb," Juliet's "tomb", the view from Castel San Pietro; Opera Festival in the Arena (July); nearby—Lake Garda, Vicenza, Mantua and Venice

P.S. There are a few cramped parking spaces (and an eagle-eyed attendant) at the door, a parking garage three minutes away

Hotel Victoria
Verona

WW$$

We doubt if you'll find a breakfast room like this one anywhere. Not just because it looks more like a smart restaurant, but because the circular "wells" in the middle of the floor look down on mosaics dating from 300 A.D. and portions of the original Roman walls.

This theatrical touch is typical of this unique hotel, a deft and tasteful fusing of the new and the very, very old in what was once a 14th-century palazzo. The rugged beams and bare brick of bygone centuries are now augmented in the lobby by rough-cast concrete and circular skylights. In the lounge, dark beams and natural stone are complemented by wood-and-leather armchairs and marble floors echoing the pattern of the Roman mosaics.

Even some of the guest rooms incorporate fragments of authentic Roman mosaic, yet each of the 45 rooms is handsomely contemporary in styling and comforts, with soft blue-gray carpeting, air-conditioning, radios, direct-dial telephones, modish TV sets, concealed strip lighting and concealed minibars.

The Victoria welcomed its first guests in the spring of 1979, although it took the owners, Assicurazione Cattolica, and *architetto* Dottore Cecchini six years to bring about the transformation. Fortunately for Verona their efforts were victorious.

Name:	Hotel Victoria
Manager:	Rodolfo Zema
Address:	Via Adua 8, 37100 Verona
Location:	In the heart of the old city, a short walk from the Arena
Telephone:	(145) 590566
Telex:	431109

260

Reps: (None)

Credit Cards: American Express, Bankamericard

Rooms: 45

Meals: Breakfast only 7–11, in the breakfast room or guest rooms; minibars in all rooms

Entertainment: Brazilian group with electronic organ in lounge, quiet taped music in lounge and lobby

Sports: (None)

Sightseeing: (See Hotel Due Torri)

P.S. Underground garage ($6 for 24 hours)

Hotel Gritti Palace
Venice

WＷWＷWＷXXXXＳＳＳＳ

Pity the poor rich who come to Venice and have to choose between the Cipriani and the Gritti! There's something to be said for escaping from the touristy hubbub to an island retreat like the Cipriani. On the other hand, what could be more romantic than staying at the Gritti? In a palace. Right on the Grand Canal. With a planter-screened terrace restaurant at gondola level. With gleaming private launches to whisk you across the lagoon to the tennis courts and golf course and the casino. With the presence of Venice everywhere. The Gritti was the favored hideaway of Queen Elizabeth, Princess Margaret, Charlie Chaplin, General de Gaulle, Paul Newman. Maria Callas and Joan Sutherland stayed here while performing at the Teatro la Fenice. Writers from Somerset Maugham to the ubiquitous Ernest Hemingway have sought inspiration here.

The Gritti became a palace-hotel just after World War I, in time for the great American discovery of Europe, and after all those eventful years and traipsing tourists, it remains a splendid place. The public rooms glow with well-being, reflected in gilt-framed mirrors and polished glass. Walls are hung with artworks—white-and-gilt decorative tile murals with maps of Europe and Venice, ceramic tiles from Bassano, 18th-century engravings after the style of Guardi and Canaletto. CIGA Hotels, the owners, spend $150,000 a year just to keep the artworks and paintwork in spanking   261 condition. Its courtly manager, Nicola Passante, formerly of the prestigious Grand Hotel in Rome, directs a loyal staff that still seems to cherish old-style innkeeping (it's probably one of the few hotels where the valets rather than the maids clean the bathtubs). Each room is different; some have damask sofas, some antique tables and sideboards, some beautiful parquet floors. "Corner room on the canal" is the customary command, so the four corner rooms are usually the most difficult to snare. Other regular guests prefer the quieter rooms on the *side* canals (the hotel is screened from the pedestrian traffic by alleys that lead nowhere).

The grandest accommodations are the Princess Margaret Suite, the Doge's Suite, and the Hemingway Suite, where, it is said, a large part of *Across the River and into the Trees* was written. Don't believe it. Not even the most blindly dedicated scribe could concentrate in such exquisite surroundings. Not with all those gondolas beckoning outside the window. Not with all Venice at your feet. Write your best-sellers elsewhere, then spend your royalties in Venice. Solve the where-to-stay dilemma as follows: a few nights at the Gritti Palace to luxuriate in the city at first hand, followed by a few more nights at the Cipriani to savor the afterglow.

Name:	Hotel Gritti Palace
Manager:	Nicola Passante
Address:	Campo Santa Maria del Giglio 2467, 30123 Venice
Location:	On the Grand Canal, near the Giglio *vaporetto* stop, about 10 minutes from the railroad station, 25 minutes from the airport by water taxi (uniformed staff will meet you at either location on request)
Telephone:	(041) 26044
Telex:	410125
Reps:	CIGA Hotels in U.S., Canada and Europe
Credit Cards:	"All major cards"
Rooms:	97, including 16 suites
Meals:	Breakfast from 6:30 on, lunch 12:30–3:30, dinner 7:30–midnight, both served on the canalside terrace (reservations recommended, even for hotel guests); dinner for two approx. $60; informal by day, tie and jacket in the evening; room service during dining room hours, drinks and snacks around the clock, and all rooms have minibars
Entertainment:	TV room; cafés and bars nearby; private launch to sister CIGA hotels on the Lido for discos and casino
Sports:	On the Lido, at CIGA hotels—swimming pool (free of charge),

tennis courts and golf course (special rates and charge privileges)

Sightseeing: Everything in Venice is within walking distance; also boat trips to San Michele, San Francisco del Deserto, Locanada; history of art courses in the hotel in spring, Cooking School in July and August

P.S.   May be closed mid-November to early March

Hotel Cipriani
Venice

♛♛♛♛ ✗✗✗✗ $$$

Here you may well have the best of all possible worlds. Part Venice, part Caribbean, part yacht; resort by day, grand hotel when the chandeliers glisten.

It's a private little world all on its own, on the island of Giudecca, off-shore from the Piazza San Marco, yet only four minutes by private launch from all the excitement of the canals, churches, *campi* and cafés. You breakfast on the terrace beneath the white-and-coffee lathe awnings, beside clumps of ortensia and rhododendron. As the bells of San Giorgio Maggiore chime 9, you walk to the private jetty to board the yacht "tender" and skim across the lagoon. At four minutes past 9 you step ashore at the Piazza San Marco, abuzz for a morning of exploration. When the heat and the crowds (and, perhaps, the pungent presence of the canals) begin to pall, you return to the *fondamento* once more to board your launch with brass fittings, lace-curtained windows and the words "Hotel Cipriani" embla-zoned on the gleaming mahongany hull. Back at your resort, a quick swim before lunch in the only pool in Venice (Olympic size, "pure lightly saltwater heated to 75 degrees F"). The lightest of *cannelloni* at Del Gabbiano, the Seagull Club's new poolside restaurant. An hour in the sun. A siesta. Come sundown you're refreshed and dressed, ready for *aperitivi* in the piano bar, until you are led to your table on the terrace by the distinguished Maître d'Hôtel Rodolfo Martinuzzi, who for years performed the same service for queens, presidents and cardinals at the Grand Hotel in Rome. Build your meal around the *tagliolini verdi gratinati al prosciutto* (it's almost a cliché to recommend such a famous dish, but recommend we do). Fill your glasses with Venegazzie Riserva di Casa, Conte Loredan. Candles flicker. The lights of the Lido glisten on the lagoon. It's almost too romantic for words.

But sobering words are what you are about to get. You can't have all 263 this tootling back and forth across the lagoon, all this pampering service, all these gardens filled with tulips and magnolia and ortensia, an Olympic-size pool, poolside waiters with uniforms like a guard of honor,—you can't, as we say, have all this without paying mightily for it. Especially in a waterlogged city like Venice, which has its own unique inflationary problems. The least expensive quarters here (overlooking the garden at the rear) will set you back more than a hundred dollars, even in the off-season; the grandest suites are $300 and up. But if you were smart enough to put your money in gold in 1977, or you own a Turin, you can afford some of the most stunning rooms in Italy. Like one of the apartments butting right onto the lagoon, with four windows to gulp in the view and swirls of lace curtaining to filter the sun. The choicest one has Venetian flourishes like painted headboards, painted ceiling and chairs with gold-leaf trim. It was once an heiress' home.

The newest nests are the so-called Cabana Suites, near the pool. Big fluffy double beds float on pedestals; bedside buttons activate a glass-covered coffee table which unfolds while a Grundig color TV rises like Venus from her shell. Some of these Cabana Suites (there are only seven) have bathrooms with tinted wall-to-wall mirrors, circular bathtubs and bamboo screens that roll back to reveal a tinted glass panel peeking into the bedroom (we haven't tried it, but it may be possible to watch the performance on television without leaving the tub).

The remaining Cipriani rooms vary considerably—from new Junior Suites on the fourth floor with very private balconies indented in the roof line to the original 1958 rooms, slightly traditional woody-brown rooms which have a certain yachtlike charm. (The reason for the wide variety of accommodations and styles here is explained by the fact that the hotel was built in 1958 by Giuseppe Cipriani of Harry's Bar fame; a few years ago it was bought by an organization with the unpromising name SeaContainers Inc., whose driving force is a youngish American of, presumably, romantic inclinations, now living in London. Not content with creating a conglomerate and buying up beautiful hotels, he competes with struggling travel writers by publishing his own guidebook to the restaurants and shops of London.)

Even with its Campanile-high prices, the Cipriani's regular guests come back year after year (in some cases they've been coming for ten years). Three days is the average stay of the average guest (as if there could possibly be anything average about Herbert von Karajan, Paul McCartney and the Duke of Bedford, to name just three from the Cipriani guest list), and three nights is really the minimum you need to do justice to the Cipriani-Venice magic.

After dinner, when you've drained your last glass of Venegazzie, take the launch once more across the lagoon. With luck you'll have a full moon.

But even without it the shimmering spectacle of the floodlit city is stupendous. The filigreed Palace of the Doges. The Palladian pomp of the churches. The floating city they call "la Serenissima." This is perhaps the best of all possible sights.

Name: Hotel Cipriani

Manager: Dottore Natale Rusconi

Address: Giudecca 10, 30123 Venice

Location: On the island of Giudecca, 4 minutes from Piazza San Marco by private launch, 15 minutes from the station or 30 from the airport by water taxi (and you can arrange to have a uniformed attendant meet you)

Telephone: (041) 85068

Cables/Telex: Hotel Cipriani Venezia/410162 Ciprve

Reps: In the U.S. and Canada, Robert F. Warner, HRI and Relais-Château; in Europe, Relais-Château, HRI, and Fairways and Swinford (London)

Credit Cards: American Express

Rooms: 100, including 14 suites

Meals: Breakfast from 7 on, lunch 12–2:30 (on the pool terrace or lagoon terrace), dinner 7:30–10:30/11 (indoors or outdoors, but reservations are essential—even for guests); dinner for two approx. $50–$55; tie and jacket in the evening; full room service during dining room hours, snack menu thereafter, and several rooms have minibars

Entertainment: Piano bar in lounge, TV room (sets also in some suites); cafés and discotheques a short launch ride away

Sports: Olympic-size seawater pool, walks among the quiet piazzas and churches of Giudecca, tennis court to follow; tennis, golf, beach, horseback riding, water sports on Lido (launch from 10 A.M. to 4:30 P.M., free of charge)

Sightseeing: (See Gritti Palace)

P.S.   Closed from January 6 to mid-March ; top level seminars (up to 20) in off-season; "advance booking is … essential at Easter and July through September." If you come by car, follow the signs for Piazzale Roma and head for Mini-Rent Cars, who will park your car, get you to a water taxi, then have your car waiting for you when you return.

Hotel Gabrielli Sandwirth
Venice

Another historic palace, another very Venetian setting—right on the Riva degli Schiavoni, the Quay of the Slavs, that runs along the Canale San Marco east from the Piazza San Marco.

At the private entrance on the side canal, you step ashore from your gondola and walk through a rose garden with a 14th-century fountain depicting the Archangel Gabriel. From the marble-floored lobby with its decorative beamed ceiling you step through a Gothic arch into an umber-colored patio with grilles on the windows and a Mediterranean oak towering above the tiles. It's the kind of secluded courtyard you might find anywhere in Venice, but in fact it's the Gabrielli Sandwirth's restaurant. On the fifth floor there's also a rooftop sun deck with drinks-only service, and a panorama of lagoon, churches, cruise ships and canals.

The Gabrielli Sandwirth is now in the third generation of Perkhofers (grandfather Perkhofer came from Austria, hence the un-Italian name), and the guest rooms have evolved over the years rather than being all color-coordinated by a master decorator. They vary considerably. Some are done in elegant Liberti style, with colorful Venetian chandeliers. Others are plain jane with highly polished floors and functional furnishings. One of the attractions of this friendly hotel is that one-third of the rooms overlook the canal and lagoon. Of these Room 124 is one of the prizes in Venice—right above the main entrance, with a curvaceous wrought-iron balcony trimmed with geraniums. Perfect for a *serenata*. All the rooms on the third floor, the *piano nobile* where the gentry lived, have high ceilings, but Rooms 334 and 336 also have balconies facing the lagoon. Likewise, a pair of corner rooms 521 and 522—from which you can wave at the passing gondolas.

Most of the guest rooms have twin washbasins ("otherwise when a lady is in the bathroom the gentleman cannot shave"); and probably *all* of the rooms would have private bathrooms, if the Perkhofers hadn't learned an interesting lesson last time they embarked on a modernization plan. By the time they had installed extra bathtubs, washbasins and toilets, the additional weight caused the hotel to start to sink. The Perkhofers had to spend an additional $100,000 to shore it up again. That's one of the perils of owning a hotel in Venice.

Name: Hotel Gabrielli Sandwirth

Owners/Managers: The Perkhofer Family

Address: Riva degli Schiavoni, 30123 Venice

Location: On the "waterfront," facing the lagoon, at Imbarcadero 17, if you arrive by *vaporetto*, or, if you arrive by water taxi or gondola, at a private jetty round the corner (in which case you don't have to tip an official porter to carry your luggage across the way to the hotel)

Telephone: (041) 31580

Cables/Telex: Gabrielliehotel/410228

Reps: In the U.S., Interhotels (Port Jefferson Station, New York)

Credit Cards: "All major cards"

Rooms: 120 (90 with private bathrooms)

Meals: Breakfast 7–11, lunch 12–2, dinner 7:30–9:30, in the patio; dinner for two approx. $40–$45; informal dress; room service for breakfast only (and 50 of the rooms have minibars)

Entertainment: (None)

Sports: (None)

Sightseeing: All the sights of Venice are within walking distance

P.S.   Closed November 10 to 2 weeks before Easter

Hotel Gabrielli Sandwirth

Villa Cipriani
Asolo

♛♛♛✗✗ $$

White flowers garland the old well in the middle of the garden. A hundred pink roses clamber up a wall. Pomegranate and cypress trees shade garden chairs and loungers. *Olea fragrans* perfumes the air. Worn steps lead down to a grove of olive trees where an old gardener gets on with his pruning, oblivious to everyone. From the Villa Cipriani terrace you look down on red-tiled roofs and flowery gardens. In the opposite direction, through the cypress trees you can glimpse more red-tiled roofs and an ochre campanile. Across the valley, another hilltop is dominated by the classical facade of an abandoned mansion that once belonged to an aristocrat—his summer home since it faces north, which is connected by a tunnel through the hill to his winter home, which faces south. It's the classic arcadian scene poets hymn and artists paint.

Asolo is the perfect little Italian hill town, and over the years it has been home to Robert Browning and Elizabeth Barrett Browning, writers, artists, romantics. A Texan couple live in the villa once owned by tragedienne Eleonora Duse. Dame Freya Stark, the English archaeologist/explorer/writer, lives just a few doors up from the Cipriani. The hotel itself has been hideaway to Marcello Mastroianni, Graham Sutherland, Catherine Deneuve and Joan Sutherland, who came here to give a recital in the castle's Eleonora Duse Theater.

The Villa Cipriani was originally the Villa Galanti, built back in the 17th century; but it has been a hotel for only a few years. It's owned by CIGA Hotels, but the restaurant is run by graduates of Harry's Bar in Venice and its renowned owner, Giuseppe Cipriani. Hence the name. (Dining is one of the delights at the Villa Cipriani—the restaurant merits a star in the Michelin Guide to Italy. Try the *la braciola di vitello all'griglia, risotto all'Asolo* or *il filetto all'Duse* and you'll know why.)

The Cipriani's 24 guest rooms are comfortable, in a country villa sort of way—period furnishings, polished wood floors, high ceilings, fresh flowers, although some have ungainly air-cooling units stuck in the windows. The choicest rooms are 101, 120 and 103, which have large terraces overlooking either the valley or the town (if you'd like to stay in one you'd better think about sending off your reservation now). Ten of the rooms are in an annex at the far end of the garden, all very attractive, a few with french doors leading directly to a tiny secluded garden beneath a cherry tree, with geraniums and hydrangeas in pots, and wild roses embracing a Grecian pillar.

Take any room here. You come to the Villa Cipriani not for the wall-

Villa Cipriani

to-wall plush but for serenity. Breakfast in bed. A spot of sightseeing. A snooze in the garden among the lilac and plumbago. A spot of *cannelloni* for lunch. A siesta. A stroll into town for Cinzano in one of the terrace cafés in the piazza. A Bellini (peach juice and sparkling wine) on the terrace.

After dinner, take what's left of your Bianco Soave della Cantine Soave and sip it in the garden. Beneath the stars. Beside the old well with the white flowers.

Name: Villa Cipriani

Manager: Sandro Matassini

Address: Via Canova 298, 31011 Asolo (Treviso)

Location: In the hills, about an hour north of Venice's Marco Polo Airport (by arrangement the hotel will send a limousine to meet you—about $35 to $40); by car, follow the signs to Castelfranco or Cittadella.

Telephone: (0423) 52166

Telex: 411060

Reps: CIGA Hotels in U.S., Canada and Europe

Credit Cards: "All major cards"

Rooms: 32

Meals: Breakfast anytime, lunch 12–2:30, dinner 7:30–10; dinner for two approx. $42–$45; informal; full room service during dining room hours, drinks and snacks around the clock

Entertainment: TV room; cafés and bars in town; concerts and recitals in castle throughout the year (first-rank performers)

Sports: Tennis, golf and horseback riding nearby

Sightseeing: Castle of Queen Cornaro, Cathedral, Tomb of Eleonora Duse; excursions to stately homes in nearby towns—villas Venete, Foscari, Barbaro, Rinaldi and half a dozen others

P.S. Parking garage (free) across the street

Hotel d'Inghilterra
Rome

♛♛$$$

Sir Alec Guinness and ballerina Carla Fracci check in here when they're in Rome. Hemingway and Anatole France have stayed here, and in the two hundred years since a hotel first opened its doors at 14 Mouth of the Lion Street, it has hosted kings and at least one pope, Pius IX, who dropped in "precisely on 2nd of July, 1855" to visit the King of Portugal, as well as poets, musicians, sculptors and philosophers. Not surprisingly, since this has traditionally been a district of Rome popular with intellectuals, many of whom have gathered at the even more venerable Café Greco, around the corner on Via Condotti. The Hotel England's doors lead to a small lobby with black marble floors and cozy lounges furnished with antiques and white drapes embellished with the Inghilterra crest. No two rooms are alike, but each is highlighted by period furnishings and antiques, some of which, like the building, also go back to the 17th century. Rooms on the fifth floor have big balconies overlooking tiled rooftops and artists' lofts. Room 254 is

considered the Honeymooners' Suite, entered through double doors between restored frescoes. The Inghilterra staff is friendly and courteous, and long-serving concierges Luigi and Paolo will direct you to the best eating places in the neighborhood. One of the attractions of the Inghilterra for many guests is its convenient location: the Borghese Gardens, the Forum and the Colosseum are all within easy walking distance. And just around the corner you have the Spanish Steps, the boutiques on the Via Condotti—and the inimitable Café Greco.

Name: Hotel d'Inghilterra

Manager: Patrice Hanhart

Address: Via Bocca di Leone 14, 00187 Rome

Location: One block from the fashionable boutiques of Via Condotti, near the Spanish Steps

Telephone: (06) 6781151

Cables/Telex: HotingItaly/6145552

Reps: (None)

Credit Cards: American Express, Visa, Diners Club

Rooms: 105 rooms, including 2 Royal Suites and 4 Presidential Suites (some air-conditioned, extra charge)

Meals: Breakfast only 6–11 A.M.; snack bar to 11 P.M.; room service (drinks and snacks) from 6 A.M. to 11 P.M.; (some rooms also have minibars)

Entertainment: (None—TV on request, extra charge)

Sports: (None)

P.S. Limited parking nearby; no through traffic on Via Bocca di Leone

Hotel Lord Byron
Rome

WWWXX $$$

Here's one of the most stylish small hotels in Rome. It's located in the Parioli district, to the north of the Borghese Gardens, a slight detour from the tourist path yet only half a mile from Via Veneto. This patrician villa was converted into a hotel in 1962 by Amadeo Ottaviani who is always in attendance to welcome his cosmopolitan clientele—Italian actors and bankers as well as a sprinkling of Europeans and Americans of all ages. The exterior gives you no clue to the chic contemporary styling of the interior. It's a decorator's delight, although some people might find it in places a touch too "QE 2." Decor in the public rooms features chrome, high gloss, tinted glass and indirect lighting. The guest rooms are extremely comfortable (individually controlled air-conditioning, phones, minibars, radios, TV), but again, in some cases the decor is less than restful. Since each room is different, maybe you'd better have a look around first, if you plan to settle in for an extended stay. Otherwise, ask for one of the rooms (there are only a few) with a balcony overlooking the Borghese Gardens. For many guests (many of whom come back year after year) the highlight of their stay is lunch or dinner in the hotel's intime patio restaurant, Le Jardin.

Name: Hotel Lord Byron

Owner/Manager: Amadeo Ottaviani

Address: Via G. de Notaris 5, 00197 Rome

Location: In a quiet, exclusive residential district, just to the north of the Villa Borghese

Telephone: (06) 3609541

Cables/Telex: Lordbyronotel/62217

Reps: Scott Calder International in U.S.; Utell International in Canada and Europe; Relais-Châteaux in U.S., Canada and Europe

Credit Cards: American Express, Visa, Diner's Club

Rooms: 54 rooms, including 7 suites

Meals: Breakfast 7–10:30; lunch 12:30–3; dinner 7:30–10, in the Garden Restaurant; dinner for two approx. $40–$45; tie and jacket preferred but not essential; room service (snacks and drinks) around-the-clock

Entertainment:	Piano bar
Sports:	(None)

Hotel San Pietro
Positano

♛♛♛♛✗✗✗$$$$

When in 1967 Carlo Cinque decided to turn his cliff-top villa into a hotel, he took on a task that would have daunted lesser men. Rooms had to be blasted out of a rock cliff that drops precipitously into the Bay of Salerno. It took one year just to make the 80-meter elevator shaft down to the beach, three years to finish the job.

But for Carlo Cinque it was a labor of love and his hang-the-expense bravura has created one of the most dazzlingly beautiful and comfortable hotels on the Mediterranean coast.

Everywhere you look, there's something to delight the eye: handsome, polished antique furniture; Veronese marble staircases with swirling wrought-iron handrails; chunky, hand-painted crockery from a local pottery; exuberantly decorated tiles; so many marigolds, salvias, hibiscus, dahlias, zinnias, roses and bougainvillea vines that it takes two full-time gardeners to look after them. The lounge sparkles with bright white walls, a glistening tile floor, flamboyant flower arrangements, shining brass plant tubs and bougainvillea vines fanning across the ceiling. And it seems immense, with arches opening to a huge outdoor terrace with a picture postcard view of Positano—the perfect place for a drink before dinner— and open on another side to an airy dining room with brickwork grilles, more bougainvillea vines and its own wrought-iron framed terrace. Here, over a tasty dish of grilled local fish or pasta fixed in umpteen different ways, you can count the twinkling lights of the hilltop town of Praiano. After dinner, sink into one of the big comfortable sofas in the lounge, have coffee or a drink from the bar tucked away in the corner and study your interesting-looking fellow guests. You may spy a writer celebrating the publication of his latest best-seller-to-be or a movie star taking a break between films.

In this uncommon place, no two rooms are alike, but all have hand-painted doors and minibars, cool tile floors, an antique or two and a wall of sliding glass doors opening to a balcony and a bird's eye view of sea. Try to

273

reserve a room with a number ending in three. Room 13 has that picturesque view of Positano from its balcony and a bathroom with a bougainvillea-framed glass wall. If the wall weren't there, you could jump straight out of the tub into the waves below. Room 33 has a cozy sleeping alcove and a large sitting area with its own miniature grotto, bougainvillea vines on the ceiling and a brave little lizard who will join you for breakfast if you offer him bread crumbs. An elevator from the lobby takes you straight into Suite 53: two large double bedrooms and bath, with white cotton-covered furniture, a handsome old fireplace and a glorious, bamboo-shaded wraparound terrace. The view is nothing less than spectacular.

Whether you have a sandwich by the beach, a four-course meal in your room or a drink by the pool, service is so smooth here it's almost invisible. Salvatore Attanasio, who happens to be Carlo Cinque's nephew, heads a happy staff, many of whom have been with the hotel since it opened.

There's a little cliff-top swimming pool if you prefer pools, and the view is pretty special, but that 80-meter elevator journey will take you down to some fine sea swimming, two tennis courts and a beach-side sunbathing terrace and bar built onto the rocks. Down here, Carlo Cinque didn't have it all his own way. He fights a running battle with the sea, which yearly carries off most of the small, pebbly beach, and the one jarring note during your stay may be a bulldozer brought in (by boat) to shore it up.

There's plenty to see in the area: the ruins of Pompeii and Sorrento up the coast, Amalfi down the coast and Capri, five miles out to sea. You'll soon understand why this neighborhood has had more than its fair share of songs written about it.

But don't feel guilty if you find it hard to budge from the San Pietro. After all, isn't this what you've been searching for all those years? (D.S.)

Name:	Hotel San Pietro
Manager:	Salvatore Attanasio
Address:	84017 Positano
Location:	On the Amalfi Coast, 1 kilometer south of Positano, about half-an-hour south of Naples
Telephone:	(089) 875455
Cables/Telex:	Sanpietrotel Positano/770072
Reps:	E & M Associates (Madison Avenue, New York) for U.S. and Canada, Blue Riband Travel, London for Europe
Credit Cards:	American Express, Visa, Diners Club
Rooms:	60, including 3 suites

Meals: Breakfast 7–11, lunch 1–3, dinner 8–10; dinner for two approx. $40–$45; tie and jacket; full room service 7 A.M.–10 P.M., drinks around the clock, but every room has a minibar

Entertainment: Piano bar in lounge

Sports: Tennis (2 courts, lighted), swimming pool (not heated), water-skiing, fishing

Sightseeing: The Amalfi Drive, Sorrento, Salerno, Paestum, Pompeii, Naples, Capri

P.S.   Closed November 1 through March 31; some small seminars in the off-season only

Hotel Punta Tragara
Capri

♨♨♨✕✕✕$$$

Everyone walks in the town of Capri. It's not just to catch a glimpse of handsome villas behind massive wrought-iron gates. It's not even for the mouth-watering window shopping in boutiques offering the kind of jewelry, clothes and leather accessories that will make you look like a full-fledged member of the jet set. Everyone walks in the town of Capri because cars are banned.

So when you step off the *aliscafo* from Naples, a porter from Punta Tragara will take your bags and give you some simple directions: up the *funicolare*, across the main piazza of town, down the Via Camerelle and along the Via Tragara as far as you can go. And there it is, its sun-baked terra-cotta colored walls rising on the point of a cliff that drops 500 hundred feet to the sea and the Faraglioni, Capri's landmark pair of needle rocks.

Punta Tragara was originally a villa designed by Le Corbusier for an Italian duke. The lobby with its marble floors, oriental rugs, baronial fireplace and chunky old oak tables was the duke's living room and, while it's grand, it's also cozy. And that just about sums up Punta Tragara's special charm. This is a haven for those who prefer their luxury on a small intimate scale, who want to be *near* the action of a lively resort but not in it.

Curving cream-painted corridors are dark and cool, but brightened with a brilliant coral carpet and enriched by huge tapestries and ancient clay water jugs.

Watched over by the alert eyes of Manager Roberto Ferraro, service is highly efficient but highly personal. Your breakfast order arrives almost instantaneously and is placed on your terrace with a cheerful "*buon giorno.*" Dishes on the dinner menu are proudly explained and presented at a leisurely pace so you can enjoy a fine view from Punta Tragara's thatch-roofed, open-sided dining terrace—and a meal that will boost Capri's reputation for good eating. Try the *fritto misto mare*, as light and fresh as you'll ever find, and *torta di mandorle*, a chocolate almond cake which is a specialty of the island. At the front desk, Heidi, Antoinetta and Claudio will cheerfully book you a Riva speedboat or a tennis court, reconfirm flights, arrange a tour of the island and tell you the locals' favorite restaurants and shops.

When the old duke died, his next-door neighbor Count Manfredi bought the property and converted the rooms into suites, intending to sell them as year-round condominium apartments. That no doubt accounts for their untypical and slightly overdone style of decoration: wall-to-wall raised-pile carpeting, patterned wallpaper and solid upholstered furniture, of which Le Corbusier would definitely not have approved. But it also accounts for their spaciousness and for the generous size of the balconies, all of which look out to sea.

The pièce-de-résistance at Punta Tragara is its unique pool: a miniamphitheater with mattressed tiers for sunbathing, rimmed with huge agaves, palm, pine and cypress trees, cactus, geraniums, marigolds and giant oil jars. At an upper level there are a few loungers, and, a few steps up, a very private little terrace where you can sunbathe and lunch completely on your own. If the sun gets too hot in this perfect sun trap, a couple of steps down from the pool is a breeze-cooled balcony with wacky hula-skirt sunbrellas, reclining chairs and a knobbly, tree-branch railing—another nice spot to have lunch. If you're fit and able, a foot path leads from the hotel to the rocks beside the towering *faraglioni.* It's a long, hot climb back up, but the sea swimming and a delicious lunch at Luigi's are worth the effort.

After a day in the sun you'll have plenty of time for a siesta—you'll need one after that climb up the *faraglioni*—as most people don't eat in Capri till 10:00. Stroll down to town, do some serious shopping in those glittering little shops, then have dinner on Punta Tragara's lovely terrace or pick from a dozen different interesting places in town. As you amble back to the hotel, you're accompanied by the scent of jasmine and the heady satisfaction that comes of having spent a perfect day. (D.S.)

Name: Hotel Punta Tragara

276   **Manager:**   Roberto Ferraro

Address: Via Tragara 57, 80073 Capri

Location: In town, so you must leave your car at the harbor after you leave the ferry, or *aliscafo*

Telephone: (081) 8370844

Cables/Telex: Punta Tragara Capri/710261

Reps: HRI in U.S., Canada and Europe

Credit Cards: American Express, Diners Club, Bankamericard

Rooms: 35 suites (with a/c)

Meals: Breakfast 7:30–10:30, lunch 12:30–3, dinner 7:30–10; dinner for two approx. $40–$45; informal; full room service anytime, minibar in every room

Entertainment: Disco, TV room

Sports: Heated seawater pool, thermal bath, massage (on request); tennis at Capri Sports Club (hotel makes reservations); water sports nearby

Sightseeing: A castle or two, a church or two, Tiberius' villa, various grottos—Blue, Green, Yellow, and so on

P.S. Closed October 1 to April; no children under 10; some very small seminars in spring; guests signing the register are expected to be over 18

La Scalinatella
Capri

WWWSSS

This sparkling little blue-and-white hotel sits enticingly just off the picturesque Via Tragara, partially screened by fir trees.

Owner-manager Mario Morgano comes from one of the oldest hotel families in Capri. His grandparents owned the Cafe Morgana, praised in a book by French author and critic Roger Peyrefitte, who wasn't always kind about Capri. As a boy, Mr. Morgano was put to work by his parents in the kitchen of their hotel and eventually did every job there was. Then, having learned the rules of running a hotel, he threw them out the window. Mr. Morgano changes your dollars at the *bank's* rate for the day. He's installed direct dialing in every room so you don't have to go through a switchboard.

If you've run out of money—which isn't hard to do with so many tempting shops nearby—he'll take your personal cheque for the bill. Since a third of his guests are regular clients and the rest have heard of La Scalinatella from friends who've been there—this hotel has no reps and no brochures—he's never had a bad debt. He'll book you a court at the tennis club five minutes away or a speedboat to take you on an outing around the island without including a cut for the house in the bill. And be sure to ask him about his canny safe arrangements to insure that no one but you knows what you're putting in and taking out.

Clearly, Mr. Morgano has an old-fashioned notion that his clients are his guests, and his hotel seems more like a private home—a private home, one should add, that looks like a modern villa belonging to a very rich Roman. There's no restaurant, so meals are simple—*prosciutto* and melon, mozzarella and tomato salad or *salade niçoise* and some of Capri's famously good ice cream—but, as there's no restaurant, there are no set hours to feel hungry. Have breakfast at midnight or lunch at sunrise, there's always someone in the kitchen to whip something up for you. and with so many good restaurants just down the road, you'll probably prefer to eat out anyway.

The antique writing desk in your room and the marble bust of the noble-looking gentleman outside your door may be Mr. Morgano's latest acquisitions from a local villa. Rooms are spare but not spartan. Pristine white walls, a shining tile floor, a firm six-foot bed, a couple of comfortable chairs, an antique chest of drawers, a painting or two on the wall, and that's about it. There's air-conditioning if you need it, but you probably won't. A wall of sliding glass doors opens to an airy balcony overlooking a jumble of rooftops and the Gulf of Salerno. Bathrooms are spacious, too, with brightly patterned tiles and a pair of basins set into a marble counter top.

There's plenty to do by the pool all day: settle down with a good book from a hefty bookshelf in the hall; study your fellow guests and play spot-the-celebrity; count the boats passing in the sea below; have a swim; lunch in the shade of a stately pine tree by a huge, hundred-year-old Ali Baba jar.

Once you get used to the cosseted life at La Scalinatella, it's hard to leave it for the hard world outside. If only there were more Mario Morganos! (D.S.)

Name: Hotel Scalinatella

Owner/Manager: Dr. Mario Morgano

Address: Via Tragara, Capri

Location: (See Punta Tragara)

Telephone: (081) 8370633

Cables:	Scalinatella Capri
Reps:	(None)
Credit Cards:	(None)
Rooms:	13 rooms, 2 suites and 15 junior suites

Meals: Breakfast anytime, lunchtime snacks by pool, no evening meal; round-the-clock room service, minibar in every room

Entertainment: TV in lounge

Sports: Pool

Sightseeing: (See Punta Tragara)

P.S. Closed November 10 to March 15; no children under 12; guests signing the register are expected to be 18 or over

Grand Hotel Quisisana
Capri

WWXXXSSS

For years, the Quisisana was *the* hotel on Capri and, by the strict standards of the Italian government, is still the only deluxe hotel on the island. But, like Capri itself, it's had its ups and downs, and some years back, the beautiful people deserted this idyllic island for newer haunts. Being one of the oldest resorts in the world—Tiberius ruled the Roman Empire from here for ten years—perhaps Capri needed the rest. While it waited for the pendulum to swing, the Quisisana changed hands and was rejuvenated. Now Capri and the Quisisana are back on top.

This is definitely the place to wear your smartest frocks and summer diamonds. Not that you wouldn't feel comfortable in a simple shirt and trousers—as long, of course, as they're by Yves St. Laurent or Armani—but the Quisisana attracts those who know what's good and believe, if you've got it, you should flaunt it.

Don't be fooled by the simple exterior. Behind that cream-colored Palladian facade, set back a terrace-width from the Via Camerelle, is the kind of luxury that takes years in the making.

The lofty-ceilinged lobby replete with marble floors, Murano glass wall lights, crystal chandeliers and murals in the manner of Fragonard may seem

279

a bit grand and the rooms on the floor above a bit bland, but elsewhere the Quisisana belies her age.

The outdoor restaurant with its butter-yellow awning and garden view is as pleasant a place to have dinner as you could wish for. And, thanks to the new chef, as good a place to eat. A typical room in the newer pool wing has a bougainvillea-edged balcony, pale blue tiles on the floor, golden-yellow-velvet sofa and chairs and a sparkling tiled bathroom. Duplexes in the other new wing have a sitting room with more blue floor tiles, an antique or two and a marble staircase leading to a balconied bedroom and his and her bathrooms. With its own high-walled courtyard entered from the gardens through an oaken door, it's like having your own little villa. And, as you're only ten steps from the pool, you can have a swim and a look at the sea before breakfast. Or a stroll through the rambling, tenderly tended gardens.

Lunch by the pool or on the terrace. Dine in your room or the indoor restaurant. Play bridge in the card room. Watch TV in the TV room. But whatever you do, don't miss having an evening drink on the Quisisana's street-front terrace at about 9:30. While you sip one of Marcello's perfect kirs and nibble on peanuts, you can watch Capri's famous nightly *passeggiata*. As the Quisisana is smack in the middle of town, just about everyone in Capri passes by, some of the sleekest, chicest people you'll ever see.

The Quisisana started life as a health clinic in the last century, and *qui si sana* means "here one gets well." Guests today are usually just suffering from a little stress and strain, but the Quisisana's promise still holds true. *Qui si sana.* (D.S.)

Name: Grand Hotel Quisisana

Manager: Dante Cattaruzza

Address: Via Camerelle 2, Capri

Location: In town. Again, leave your car at the harbor.

Telephone: (081) 8370788

Telex: 710520

Reps: Robert F. Warner in U.S. and Canada

Credit Cards: American Express

Rooms: 140, including 18 suites

Meals: Breakfast 7–11:30, lunch 12:30–3:30, dinner 7:30–11:30; dinner for two approx. $35–$40; informal; full room service 7 A.M.–midnight (some rooms have minibars)

| Entertainment: | Pianist in lobby evenings to 1 A.M., TV room |

Sports: Tennis (3 lighted courts), heated pool, sauna, massage, walking trails; water sports nearby

Sightseeing: (See Punta Tragara)

P.S. Closed November 1 through March 31; some small groups, even in the high season

Hotel Cervo
Sardinia

WWX$$$$

Crossing the wooden bridge from the old marina to the center of Porto Cervo at night, you might think you've wandered onto a film set: so many beautiful people strolling by, so many elegant little shops, a picture-book piazza overlooking the water, the obligatory candlelit restaurants and hardly a speck of dirt anywhere. Well, it's not a film set, but it was just as carefully planned twenty years ago as the center of activity for the 35 miles of Sardinian coast known as the Costa Smeralda. And right in the center of this center is the Hotel Cervo.

This is the youngest and bustliest of the Aga Khan's family of hotels, but it has the same kind of cool, comfortable chic that comes of using the best traditional materials and local crafts. Thick, white stucco walls are scooped out here and there to make little pockets for lights, floors are covered in uneven quarry tiles the color of well-polished cowhide, huge rough-hewn wooden beams stretch across ceilings and doorways, chunky antique coffers and chairs dot passageways to rooms.

Off the lobby is a courtyard where you can help yourself to olives from a fine old olive tree, and off the courtyard are walkways to rooms and a vine-covered pergola leading to the pool area. Once you get there, you don't have to stir all day. Have breakfast in the shade of the bamboo-covered restaurant, swim in the free-form pool, and sunbathe on well-padded white loungers while the chef and his helpers prepare a barbecue and buffet for lunch. If you must be by the sea, a hotel boat runs once an hour to the beach twenty minutes away, and, should you feel the need for more strenuous exercise, there are seven courts and a fully equipped gymnasium at the Cervo Tennis Club just down the road.

A few rooms off an upper gallery in the courtyard look out onto the 281 harbor, but you might find them a bit noisy if you like to go to bed early—people here tend to party until the small hours. Best bet, probably, is one of the rooms forming a courtyard around the pool. Though your balcony overlooks the courtyard, masses of flowering shrubs and bushes keep the view from seeming claustrophobic. Rooms are simply furnished but differ in details—like the color of the tile floor, or the design of the handwoven bedspread and curtains. But all have minibars, huge closets and a balcony or terrace.

People who stay at the Cervo aren't the type to spend much time in their rooms. After a day in the sun, there's only just time for a siesta and shower before the busy night life of Porto Cervo gets underway. Start with a glass of the local Vermentine in the Cervo's cosy little blue-and-white piano bar, or, better still, on the outdoor terrace just a few steps up from the piazza, a perfect vantage point for studying those beautiful strollers. Do a bit of shopping, then tuck into a meal at one of those candlelit restaurants or the Cervo's own inviting dining room, with a view through sliding glass doors of sleek yachts moored in the old marina.

When you stay at the Cervo, you're right in the midst of the action, and if that's what you like, you probably won't mind that service here tends to be more efficient than charming. (D.S.)

Name: Hotel Cervo

Manager: Carlo Ferraris

Address: 07020 Port Cervo, Costa Smeralda, Sardinia

Location: By the sea, about 20 miles from Olbia Airport, which is linked to several points in Italy by the DC9's of the island's own airline, Alisarda

Telephone: (0789) 92003

Cables/Telex: Cervotel/790037 Cosme

Reps: HRI in U.S., Canada and Europe

Credit Cards: American Express, Diners Club

Rooms: 90 rooms, 2 suites (all air-conditioned)

Meals: Breakfast 7:30–11, lunch 1–2:30, dinner 8–11; dinner for two approx. $46–$50; informal dress; room service 7:30 A.M.–11 P.M., drinks and snacks only (all rooms have minibars)

Entertainment: Piano bar in lounge, some folklore shows, taped music, TV room

282 **Sports:** Tennis (7 courts, 3 lighted), swimming pool (heated in winter),

golf (18 holes at Pevero Golf Club), walking trails, gymnasium, beach (20 minutes away, boat ride free of charge), water sports at Marinasarda

Sightseeing: Coastline and interior of Sardinia, *nuraghi* (the so-called giants' tombs); offshore islands like Maddalena and Caprera (but don't rush to get there); various folklore shows and festivals

P.S.   Closed December 17 through January 31; some groups during the low season (that is, everything except June to the first week of September); there *may* be some construction under way (extra rooms, convention center)

Hotel Cala di Volpe
Sardinia

♛♛♛✗✗ $$$$

It's hard to believe that the Cala di Volpe Hotel, like everything else in the Aga Khan's Costa Smeralda wonderland, didn't exist twenty years ago. Rambling round the curve of an aquamarine bay, changing levels as it goes, the hotel looks almost as old as the mysterious stone structures called *nuraghi*, which rise like watch towers over the landscape of Sardinia.

When the Aga Khan planned his now famous resort project, he picked this spot for his first hotel, and he chose an extraordinary architect to design it. Jacques Couelle never bothered with architectural school; he learned how to build by studying *nature*. But maybe only a man with no formal training could have mixed Moorish Village with Medieval Town, thrown in a dash of Sardinian Farmhouse and touches of Twentieth Century Glamour and gotten away with it. Walls are curved, windows are arched, arches are all askew. Chunky pillars and thick wooden beams support a bamboo-lined ceiling in the main lounge and dining room, and rough white stucco exteriors are set with jewellike chips of colored glass. Niches and doors are painted with bright figures or pale little bouquets of flowers like time-faded miniature frescoes. Crude, country-style furniture is carved or painted with traditional motifs, bed heads are hand-forged wrought iron, bedspreads and curtains are crunchy cotton woven locally by hand, just as it has been for centuries.

The rooms in the old wing, to the left of the main lounge, are the nicest. They come in all different shapes and sizes. Some have little upstairs sun terraces, several look out on a secret interior garden, a few have patios just a few feet from the water's edge. But the rooms in the new wing are bigger, and their fat-walled little balconies all have a view of the bay. Every room has a minibar, an up-to-the-minute tiled bathroom and a set of huge enveloping pale-blue terry-cloth robes for you to snuggle into. If all this doesn't sound comfortable enough, there's always the Presidential Suite: three bedrooms and a huge sitting area and terrace on the top floor with its own swimming pool.

Decisions, decisions. To play tennis on one of two all-weather courts or hire a speedboat or cabin cruiser and driver for some fishing or beach-hopping? To play golf on a nearby course designed by Robert Trent Jones (he considers it one of his best), or take the boat that leaves every half hour for the beach in the next bay? To sunbathe by the Olympic-sized pool or work up an appetite for lunch with a spot of waterskiing or wind surfing?

The buffet lunch in the poolside pavilion is a daily *event*: help yourself to twenty-five different salads; beef, fish, chicken or pork grilled on an open fire; cheese, fruit and several highly fattening desserts. Then start all over again. No wonder so many racy speedboats turn up at the hotel's minimarina at eight bells.

Without ever leaving the Cala di Volpe, you can also buy suntan oil and smart clothes, Sardinian pottery and fabrics and, if the headiness of it all gets to you, a gold trinket or silver tea service at Buccellati. You can have your hair done after a day by the sea. In the evening, test the mettle of a world champion bartender at the bar in the main lounge, then gorge yourself in the lofty dining room at another groaning table of antipasto. If you have a special request like lobster or a birthday cake, just give Signor Stacchine, the headwaiter, a bit of notice. He'll take care of it. After dinner, cross a covered wooden bridge to the terrace of the Pontile Bar overlooking the bay and enjoy the view over a long, cool *Tuttosi* (brandy, Canadian whiskey, Martini Rosso, a dash of Galliano and tangerine liqueur). And, if you're still feeling energetic, the discotheque stays open till the last reveler goes to bed.

Thanks to Jacques Couelle and a top-notch staff, the Cala di Volpe, even with all its facilities, manages to seem like a tiny village: idyllic, romantic, glamorous, but coolly efficient behind the scenes. The perfect place to unwind for the world's jettiest jet setters. (D.S.)

Name: Hotel Cala di Volpe

Manager: Giorgio Daina

Address: 07020 Port Cervo, Sardinia

Location: (See Hotel Cervo)

Telephone: (0789) 96083

Telex:	790274 Cavop
Reps:	HRI in U.S., Canada and Europe
Credit Cards:	American Express, Diners Club
Rooms:	125 rooms, 9 suites and 1 presidential suite (all air-conditioned)

Meals: Breakfast 7:30–10:30, lunch 1–5, dinner 8–10:30; dinner for two approx. $50–$55; informal dress; full room service 7 A.M.–10:30 P.M.

Entertainment: Piano in lounge, taped music, discotheque, folklore shows and fashion shows

Sports: Tennis (3 courts), seawater pool, beach, golf (18 holes at Pevero Golf Club), waterskiing, motorboat rentals

Sightseeing: (See Hotel Cervo)

P.S. Closed October 1 through April 30; some very small groups in off-season

Hotel Pitrizza
Sardinia

WWWWXX$$$$

When Princess Margaret came to stay at the Pitrizza a few years ago, it hardly caused a ripple. After all, scions of royal families and barons of big business have been coming to this perfect hideaway since it opened in 1964, the second built of the trio of hotels owned by the Aga Khan's consortium.

On four and half acres of a little point of land by the Bay of Liscia di Vacca, the Pitrizza is so much a part of the landscape that it's almost invisible to the outside world.

Six little villas with a central sitting room and four to six rooms each are tucked away like luxurious bunkers among clumps of trees and flowering shrubs. Rooms are almost monastically simple: rough stucco walls; ancient-looking tile floors; a few pieces of furniture hand-painted in faded blues and greens or carved from a dark, rich local wood called niboru. But they have wordly comforts too: fresh flowers, fresh fruit and mineral water; air-conditioning; sparkling tiled bathrooms; beautiful pastel sheets (if blue's not your favorite color, ask for pink or yellow). If you like to sunbathe while you breakfast, ask for a room with a terrace; if you prefer

285

your orange juice in the shade, ask for a garden room. By an ingenious arrangement of passageways and doors, most rooms can be made into suites. Or, if total privacy is what you're after, and never mind how much it costs, you can take over the self-contained half of Villa 2, as Princess Margaret did: a pergola-covered courtyard leads to a living room, single and double bedrooms, bathroom and very private garden.

When it comes time to venture out, you won't exactly feel crowded with only 48 fellow guests. And with 55 staff to look after you, you won't feel neglected. Excellent service is a fact of life at the Pitrizza, as you'll understand when you find that there's no service charge added to your bill. (But be warned: the cost of living here is very high.) The policy is, if you want to tip, you may. If you don't want to, you're not expected to. Heading the staff is Commendatore Ettore Bonomo, a jolly man with a twinkle in his eye, who admits proudly that he has an old-fashioned concept of management, and likes to meet all his guests. Signor Bonomo looks as if he enjoys his food and boasts that you can stay at the Pitrizza for two weeks and have a different meal every night (though with so many interesting restaurants nearby, you might be tempted to leave the fold from time to time). If you admire the flowers on your table, it's thanks to Mrs. Bonomo. Besides overseeing the housekeeping, she does all the floral arrangements at the hotel, and such is her talent that she was asked to do the same for *The Spy Who Loved Me*, which was made here.

If the Pitrizza begins to sound like a very exclusive private club, you have the right idea. The main building—reception area, lounge, dining room, bar and outdoor terrace—is actually called the clubhouse. Entering between two rough stone pillars topped by a methuselah of a wooden beam, you step into a long white space, broken only by arches and walled on one side with glass overlooking the brick-paved terrace and the startlingly blue sea. To the left, past a monumental double-sided fireplace, is a sitting area with plenty of plump, creamy linen sofas and, wherever they might be needed, chunky little dark wood tables. To the right is the bar and more sofas and, through an arch, the dining room with tables covered in cerulean blue cloths.

But if you think the clubhouse is nice, wait till you see the swimming pool. It looks as if it's been scooped out of a natural formation of pink rock, then smoothed over on the bottom with cement that's been painted to match the amazing blues and greens of the crystal-clear sea below. This is the place for your Esther Williams number if ever there was one. The beach isn't bad either: an apron of golden sand among the rocks dotted with coolie-hat sunbrellas and comfortable loungers.

Should such splendid isolation get too much for you, you're only a five-minute drive from town. But don't be surprised if, after the first trip, it just seems like too much trouble, and you decide to stay close to your luxurious bunker by the Bay of Liscia di Vacca. (D.S.)

286

Name: Hotel Pitrizza

Manager: Comm. Ettore Bonomo

Address: Via Lascia di Vacca, 07020 Porto Cervo, Sardinia

Location: On the Costa Smeralda, about 20 miles north of Olbia Airport (see Hotel Cervo)

Telephone: (0789) 92000

Cables/Telex: Hotel Pitrizza/790037 Cosme (attn. Pitrizza)

Reps: Relais-Châteaux in U.S., Canada and Europe

Credit Cards: American Express, Diners Club, Carte Blanche

Rooms: 28 rooms, 1 suite in 6 villas (all with private terraces and air-conditioning)

Meals: Breakfast 7–11, lunch 1–2:30, dinner 8–10; dinner for two approx. $70; informal dress; full room service during dining room hours

Entertainment: Pianist in lounge and dining room

Sports: Beach, seawater pool; tennis, golf, water sports nearby

Sightseeing: (See Hotel Cervo)

P.S. Closed October to April; no groups ever

Villa Igiea Grand Hotel
Sicily

WW X $$

The Villa Igiea is one of those places you dream about—a turn-of-the-century maze of gardens and corridors and stairways and overstuffed chairs to cosset you as you come in dusty and weary from seeing the great ruins.

Unfortunately some of the reality is just as dusty and weary, but it's nothing that a paint job, a little redecorating and a new chef couldn't fix because it's basically a delight. The bedrooms are large, some, in a sort-of-turret, quite enchanting; the grounds are well-kept; the pool overlooks the hotel's own little ruined temple (origin a little shady, but no matter) and the sweep of coastline. The broad terrace on which you drink or dine in the soft Sicilian air is luxury enough.

Villa Igiea Grand Hotel

The hotel is one of those golden-stone leftovers, originally the fairytale villa of an important wine dynasty; when they lost their money, it became home to visiting royalty whose deliciously stilted photographs line the public rooms and are stuffed into nooks as they would be at your great-aunt's. A different sort of royalty is found there now: vacationing, sleek Europeans moneyed Americans and the first families of Palermo, who come to spend the evening and lend a certain mystery. And blessedly, it remains turn-of-the-century in feeling—it's as if people are stopping here on the grand tour and use it as a base to make trips to the majestic Greek ruins at Agrigento, or to explore the city and the hills that are filled with the romantically decaying villas of another era. (I.S.)

Name: Villa Igiea Grand Hotel

Manager: Francesco Marcone

Address: Via Belmonte 43, Palermo, Sicily 90142

Location: In town (right on the edge of the city), about 20 miles from Punta Ráisi Airport

Telephone: (091) 543 744

Cables/Telex: Igieahotel / 91092 Villigea

Reps: Utell International

Credit Cards: American Express, Visa, Master Charge / Eurocard, Diners Club

288

Rooms: 92, all with private bath (some overlook the sea, some rear) and air-conditioning

Meals: Breakfast 8–10, lunch (on a terrace overlooking the water) 12–2, dinner (on the terrace) 8–10; 4-course dinner for two with a good Sicilian wine, approx. $30; dress casual; room service

Entertainment: TV can be found

Sports: One tennis court with a view, table tennis, swimming in a lovely pool, swimming from a small beach (or the rocks)

Sightseeing: The town of Palermo itself, which is surprisingly elegant— filled with palaces and grand squares; and up in the hills, Monreale with a cathedralful of world-renowned and unforgettable medieval mosaics

P.S.   The food is indifferent, but the setting on the broad terrace almost compensates for it

San Domenico Palace Hotel
Sicily

WW X $$

A dazzling example of the sacred with a generous overlay of the luxuriantly profane, the San Domenico is a sun-struck hotel grafted, seamlessly, onto the ruins of a 14th-century monastery towering above the Ionian Sea. And although it's run with exactly the proper degree of stuffiness, there is about its antique furniture, its cliff-top pool surrounded by oiled and cared-for bodies, its almost tropically dense gardens and hiding places, the moonlit terrace on which you dine, enough to make it a hedonist's mecca. And the town of Taormina, whose main street is also a mixture—of the chic and forgivably vulgar—adds to the headiness.

The hotel runs efficiently, but fortunately you never notice the whir. What you do notice is the unflurried way you are taken care of, almost maternally, and the maternal way in which the staff seems to have just polished the receding corridors of burnished furniture; the way the rooms (and beautifully tiled baths) are made up even if you are gone for three minutes; the way waiters suddenly appear when you want a drink in the great vaulted bar with its miles of upholstery or in the astonishingly lovely glassed-in cloister; in the way they offer you food as if it were a collection of jewels (it is definitely not); in the way they tend to the hallway shrine (doesn't every hotel have one?)

The rooms themselves are wonderful. The bedrooms in the newer wing are spacious, as are their balconies overlooking the sea. But even so, I prefer the ones in the original building—smaller but beautifully furnished and looking down, out of bougainvillea-framed windows, to the gardens and the water far below; they were once monk's cells, but much larger than that term might lead you to expect—they were, after all, *Italian* members of the church.

There is something ineffable about closing the curtains on the afternoon sun and the smell of jasmine to settle into linen sheets—I had the distinct impression that somewhere the monks were smiling. (I.S.)

Name: San Domenico Palace Hotel

Managers: Francesco Ferlano, Harold Glogner

Address: Piazza San Domenico 5, Taormina, Sicily 98039

Location: Right in town, right at the top of Taormina's climbing streets, which are at the top of a mountain

Telephone: (0942) 23701-2-3

Cables/Telex: Sandomenico/98013 Domhotel

Reps: Utell International

Credit Cards: American Express, Visa, Master Charge/Eurocard, Diners Club

Rooms: 100, all air-conditioned with private baths, all overlooking the gardens and sea

Meals: Breakfast 8–10, lunch 12–2, dinner (on terrace with a view of the sea); 4-course dinner for two, with wine, is about $30; room service. Dress at dinner is expensive Italian informal—glossy and artfully careless.

Entertainment: You can probably find a TV in one of the huge, vaulted public rooms.

Sports: Tennis, swimming in the pool (overlooking the cliffside and the water) or at the beach reached by hotel shuttle bus (the pool is preferable)

Sightseeing: The town of Taormina itself, down the stone steps of a few back streets, full of shops and bars and restaurants (wonderful pastry and phantasmagoric marzipan), squares and panoramas of the jagged shoreline; the Greek Theatre, second in size to that at Syracuse

---

For brief reports on other hotels in Italy turn to the chapter on Added Attractions at the end of this guide.

GREECE

GREECE

Lemnos

Delphi ②

Athens

③

1. Akti Myrina Hotel
2. Amalia Hotel
3. Xenia Palace Bungalows

Akti Myrina Hotel
Lemnos

♛♛♛✕✕✕$$

Put a Swiss architect and a Greek architect together on a Mediterranean island and what do you have? A luxury resort village of 125 charming bungalows designed in the fashion of the island's traditional sheepherders' stone-walled, red-tiled cottages, and set among 37 acres of vines and flowering shrubs reaching down to the sandy shore. Add a touch of history in the form of a hulking Venetian fortress on the hillside across the bay and—eureka!—Akti Myrina, a rare blend of Swiss luxury and efficiency with Greek charm and tranquillity.

Lemnos was not always so peaceful. Cretes, Persians, Venetians, Russians, Turks and assorted pirates have invaded Lemnos throughout a checkered history dating from Minoan times. But since 1912, when Greek ships finally freed the island, Lemnos has remained unspoiled by further invasions—including massed tourists, although it's within easy striking distance of Athens (just 45 minutes by air). Here, silence *is* golden. Your serenity is broken only by the "pong" of a well-hit tennis ball or the bray of mules carrying wheat from the fields.

"Lemnos" means "white" or "shiny" in the ancient Phoenician language, and like the island itself, Akti Myrina shines among resorts, attracting celebrities such as New York's former mayor John Lindsay and Maestro Carlo Maria Giulini. And, we might add, more than half of its clients are lured back to Lemnos again and again, often twice in the same year.

Service probably has something to do with this. The hotel personnel are attentive, friendly and efficient. And no one could ever say he or she went thirsty or hungry at Akti Myrina. To begin with, every bungalow has a well-stocked minibar; elsewhere in this pampering resort you have a choice of three bars and three restaurants, to say nothing of the open-air buffet by the beach where Chef Julio offers diners a choice of Greek and continental dishes.

Nor could any guest get bored at Akti Myrina. For the active, there are tennis courts, miniature golf, Ping-Pong, swimming in the sea or in a heated seawater pool, boating of all kinds—including sailing excursions to nearby islands on the resort's 45-ton caique, Evangelistria. When the sun goes down, guests can dance in the disco until their knees give out, although manager George Papadam readily admits that most guests prefer to listen to the quiet of the Mediterranean night on a moonlight cruise aboard the Evangelistria. Many guests, in fact, retire early (very early by Greek standards) and rise early to take advantage of whatever leisurely Lemnos

Akti Myrina Hotel

days have to offer. Although Akti Myrina has kept up with the Joneses of the resort world, it has still managed to retain its alluring island tempo.

The simple pleasures, then, are what make this resort so special. A half-hour stroll to the little river to feed the turtles. A donkey ride past almond orchards and vineyards to the pretty village of Kaspakas. A walk to Myrina village with its fishing fleet, waterfront *tavernas* and small shops, stopping en route to visit the tiny museum and its neolithic artifacts from ancient Droskopos on the island's east coast.

As the daylight fades, climb the hill to the Venetian fort to watch the fishing fleet leave and the sun set over Mount Athos. Ponder Lemnos' past. Think of the legendary princess, Hypsipyle, who stood on such a hill pining for the man who stole her heart and then went searching for the Golden Fleece—Jason, leader of the Argonauts. Or settle down for a refreshing sundown refresher on the lounger in your private garden. Fold down the window shutter that cleverly converts into a lounger-side table. Fetch a bottle from your minibar. Pluck a lemon from your private lemon tree.   293

Drink a silent toast to the architects who created this remarkable resort and to the owners who cared more for a dream-come-true than turning a profit. (S.H.)

Name: Akti Myrina Hotel

Owners/Managers: George Papadam, manager

Address: Lemnos *or* 4, Nikis Street, Athens, 126 (out of season)

Location: Next to the town of Myrina on the western coast of Lemnos Island in the Aegean Sea, between the islands of Imroz, (Turkey), the Sporades and Lesbos, a 45-minute flight (Olympic Airways) from Athens

Telephone: (in season) 22681-4, 22310, (area code 0276); (out-of-season) 3230249, 3230962 (area code 01)

Cables/Telex: Aktimyr Lemnos: 0294173 MYRI GR.; Aktimyr Athens: 216324 AKTI GR.

Reps: Robert F. Warner, Inc. (U.S.A. and Canada)

Credit Cards: American Express, Diners Club

Rooms: 125 bungalows

Meals: Breakfast 7–10 (in bungalow), lunch 1–2:30, dinner 8–10; dinner for two approx. $27; informal attire, although tie and jacket and dresses for dinner appreciated; room service 7 A.M.–11 P.M. (drinks and snacks only and minibars in all rooms)

Entertainment: No TV, no radio in rooms—just one TV in a private room off lounge; piped music in open-air restaurant and open-air bar—Greek and unobtrusive

Sports: Dimco (shuffleboard), *petanque* (French boccie), beach rackets, volley ball, minigolf, table tennis, tennis (2 courts), heated seawater pool (plus baby pool), sandy beach, wind surfing, snorkeling, pedaloes (paddle boats), waterskiing, boating (sailing, rowing, canoeing, motoring), fishing excursions, caique excursions to neighboring islands, donkeyback riding

Sightseeing: Caique excursions around the coast of Lemnos, as well as to the islands of Samothráki, Thásos, Ayios Evstratios and Mount Athos; walks to Venetian fortress, fishing village of Myrina, and Myrina Museum (archaeological); donkey ride to village of Kaspakas; archaeological sites of the Early Bronze and Neolithic Ages, dating back to the 4th millennium B.C., on the East Coast

P.S. Closed October 11 to May 9

Amalia Hotel
Delphi

Quite apart from its historic interest as the home of the ancient oracle, Delphi is one of the most romantic settings in Europe—ruined temples tucked away in the mountains, with Mount Parnassos on one side, rugged gorges on the other, the Gulf of Corinth off in the distance beyond the olive groves on Itea on the plain 2,000 feet below. It's a place that must be high on everyone's list of priorities in Greece. In the world. But to see Delphi at its romantic best—the calm as well as the magnificent, the haunting mystery as well as the grandeur—you must somehow contrive to be there before the tour groups have arrived and after they have gone for the day. This means staying over for the night, which means, in turn, staying at the best hotel in town.

The Amalia is not a beautiful hideaway in the context of this guide (its contemporary, terraced facade is almost "motelly") but it sits on a hill above the town, and the big-windowed dining room, verandas, garden and room balconies all offer unrivaled views across the surrounding countryside. There's sculpture in the garden, and the interiors have been decorated with sympathy for the surroundings of ruins and rocks—with textures of rough-hewn granite and marble, wood and leather and rush webbing. The 185 guest rooms are finished with less flair, but they are adequate for a night or two, and they do have those large windows and balconies when you escape to your room to avoid the crowds. The advantage of staying over is that you wake up in Delphi, in the hush of morning, and when you sit on your balcony and watch the mist swirling up from the plain, you half expect to see Apollo himself emerge. (S.H.)

Name: Amalia Hotel

Owner/Manager: Christ Coulouvatos, owner; Emmanuel Papilaris, manager

Address: Hotel Amalia, Delphi

Telephone: Delphi: 0265-82101

Cables/Telex: 21 51 61 Amalia Athens

Reps: Traveline (New York)

Credit Cards: American Express, Diners Club, Master Charge/Euro-card, Visa

295

Rooms: 185

Meals: Breakfast 7–10 (dining room or room service), lunch 12–3, dinner 8–10; dinner for two approx. $13–$15; informal attire; room service 7 A.M.–12 midnight, for drinks and snacks only. Café, 12–4, 6–12

Entertainment: Television in the cafeteria, taped music in the lounge and bar

Sports: Skiing nearby on Mount Parnassos

Sightseeing: Ancient ruins of Delphi, Marmaria, and Castalian Springs on the main road, Delphi Museum, shopping in town for handmade shawls and sweaters

P.S.   Children, conventions, and tour groups are, alas, welcomed with open arms

Xenia Palace Bungalows
Nafplion

WWX$

Even the Greek government, it seems, has a soft spot for Nafplion, a tiny fishing village said to have been founded by Nauplios, son of Poseidon. Here you find not one, not even two, but three government-owned, government-run Xenia hotels, built into the ramparts of a rambling Frankish fortress (actually, seven forts in one), 600 feet above the town. All three hotels command imposing views of the sloping tiled roofs below, the harbor and the bobbing boats, and the squat fortress of Bourdzi sitting forlornly on its tiny island out in the bay. But one of these Xenias is more special than the others, designed with the romantic qualities of Nafplion in mind. It's the deluxe complex of Xenia Palace Bungalows, nestled between the older first-class Xenia Hotel and the newer, cavernous Xenia Palace.

The three hotels get, of course, their fair share of tour groups throughout the year, the Bungalows less so than the others, but if you want to visit Nafplion (and you should) you really have no choice but to stay here. You simply plan your day to avoid the crowds—by spending much of the time enjoying your bungalow. The 54 bungalows are designed to mollycoddle you in privacy. The decor, to be sure, is Greek Modern—which means comfort and simplicity rather than frills and decoration. Stucco griffins and Greek-pattern plates embedded in concrete walls add the decorators' touch. But the view is the thing, and every room has a large balcony with table and chairs, and planters filled with flowers. Here you have your breakfast as you watch the sun brighten Bourdzi. Here, too, you can have your evening ouzo, since each room comes equipped with a well-stocked minibar. Since demipension, or Modified American Plan, is "obligatory," have your lunch on your balcony: simply call room service and have them send over platters of taramosalata and skara barbounia. In the evening, skip the dining room (an attractive salon when there are no groups) and follow the 899 steps down to Nafplion for dinner in a lantern-lit *taverna* beside the harbor and the boats of the latter-day sons of Poseidon.

Between meals, catch an hour or two by the pool when the groups have bussed off. Or take an afternoon drive. To Epidaurus, perhaps. Or Mycenae and the Palace of Agamemnon. When you return you'll discover one of the mollycoddliest features of your bungalow—a vibrating bed that massages limbs wearied from hours of trampling over rocks and cobbles. Too bad the bed is not on the balcony, too. (S.H.)

Name: Xenia Palace Bungalows

Manager: Nik. Smyrniotakis

Address: Nafplion

Location: On the Peloponessus, about 90 miles west of Athens

Telephone: (0752) 28981/5

Telex: 298154

Reps: (None)

Credit Cards: Master Charge/Eurocard, Diners Club, Visa

Rooms: 54 (a/c at extra charge)

Meals: Breakfast 7–10, lunch 12–2, dinner 8–10; dinner for two $12–$15; informal dress; full room service 7 A.M.–11 P.M. (and minibars in all rooms)

Entertainment: TV in rooms

Sports: Pool; beach and sailing nearby

Sightseeing: The village of Nafplion (or Nauplia)—citadel and fortress; Argolian Epidaurus (Epidhavros) (20 miles away)—sanctuary of Aesculapius (God of Healing), Roman baths, stadium, theater built by Polycleitus the Younger in 4 B.C., setting of drama festival every June and July; Mycenae; Tiryns

P.S. Group tours most of the year; if you want to stay here during the Epidaurus Festival, you must reserve a long time in advance; only a few of the staff speak English

For brief reports on other hotels in Greece turn to the chapter on Added Attractions at the end of this guide.

PORTUGAL and SPAIN

PORTUGAL AND SPAIN

1. Pousada do Castelo
2. Estalagem Albatroz
   Lennox Country Club Hotel
   Hotel do Guincho
3. Hotel Palacio dos Seteais
   York House
   Hotel Principe Real
   Pousada de Palmela
4. Hotel do Mar
   Quinta das Torres
   Pousada de São Filipe
   Pousada dos Lioios
5. Pousada do Infante
   Casa de São Gonçalo da Lagos
6. Estalagem do Cerro
   Pousada de São Bras
7. Hostal de la Gavina
8. Parador Marqués de Villena
9. Hotel Doña Maria
10. Parador Nacional Condestable Davalos
11. Parador Nacional San Francisco
12. Parador Nacional Gibralfaro

Portugal

Pousada do Castelo
Obidos

♛ ♛ ♛ ✕ ✕ $

The ancient city of Obidos, its 12th-century walls still encircling the city like a crown, was considered such a gem that Portuguese kings established a tradition of presenting it as a gift to their new queens.

The town is still a gem—and so is the *pousada* that has been installed in the castle that surveys it. Follow the uphill cobbled village lanes to the archway at the very top, pass through, climb the steep stairs, and you'll find not only a picture-postcard panorama of tile roofs, towers and battlements, but a tiny inn full of the flavor of the past.

The dim living room, with its tile floors, beams, tapestries, armor and antiques, is right in keeping with its atmospheric locale. Tiles line the walls of the bar and the stairway that leads to the upstairs lounge and dining room, both with half-tiled walls. The TV room is mostly modern, but with antique accents; the dining room is simple, and with its handsome stone fireplace, dark paintings and pieces of old porcelain, pewter and copper along the walls, makes a suitable setting for sampling the traditional foods of the region.

For starters, on the table you'll find coarse white fresh-baked bread, firm fresh goat's cheese and quail's eggs. *Sopa de pescada* is a rich and savory tomato chowder full of chunks of tender white fish, potatoes and carrots. For lunch, a good bet is the *omeleta*, prepared Portuguese style—a heaping platter of scrambled eggs cooked with chopped onions, highlights of pimiento and chunks of shellfish. The dessert cart, along with an assortment of custards, cakes and fresh fruit, features an unusual lemon pudding, a tasty concoction with a spongy soufflelike texture.

A trip to Portugal really ought to include a visit to Obidos and its *pousada*, but unless you act early, a meal may be all you can enjoy here. There are only six guests rooms and they are usually booked at least a month ahead.

The rooms aren't huge, but they are large on atmosphere—white walls and beams, long drapes, high carved headboards, excellent copies of antique lamps, wardrobe chests and writing tables. It's worth planning ahead for. (E.B.)

Name: Pousada do Castelo

Manager: José Manuel Nobae Pereia

Address: Obidos, 59 miles north of Lisbon, located in the castle overlooking the town

Telephone: 95105

Telex: P-2510

Reps: (None)

Credit Cards: Master Charge/Eurocard

Rooms: 6 rooms

Meals: Breakfast 7:30–10, lunch 12:30–2:30, dinner 7:30–9:30; dinner for two approx. $13; informal; room service for breakfast only

Entertainment: TV lounge

Sports: (None)

Sightseeing: The fascinating churches, cobbled streets and old walls of Obidos; many shops featuring local crafts and rugs

P.S. Reservations recommended at least a month in advance

Pousada do Castelo

Estalagem Albatroz

Cascais

Alas, we can't claim to have discovered the Albatroz—Princess Grace, Cary Grant, even the Queen of Bulgaria have beaten us to it. Still, it's a pleasant surprise to find this gem of a cliffside *estalagem* (or inn) tucked behind a terraced garden right next door to the Cascais beach and looking out on the most colorful part of the famous fishermens' harbor.

Everything here has been built around that harbor view. The original Portuguese-style tile-roofed mansion has been expanded with a glassed-in nautical decor gallery and the dining room has been remodeled with huge windows from one end to the other. That dining room, incidentally, is generally acknowledged as the best in town, so that many of the guests elect to take all their meals right here. Not surprisingly, the specialty is the fish fresh from the harbor, and watching the next fleet's catch coming in while you eat adds to the pleasure of your dinner.

Some of the gracious original structure of the old home remains, like the tiled walls and the latticework stairway that dominates the entry. The rooms upstairs are big, simply furnished and looking out to sea, or down at the garden, sometimes through half-round windows reminiscent of a porthole. The bar offers a change of mood; it's an interior room furnished with inviting brown-and-gold sofas, accented by leopard-skin pillows and hassocks.

Outside, there is a waterside garden with chaises for private sunbathing, in case you don't want to mingle with the masses on the beach. And all the shopping you can afford is just a stroll away.

Even if you're not the first, there's every good reason to add your name to the guest book at the Albatroz. (E.B)

Name:	Estalagem Albatroz
Manager:	Francisco Antunes
Address:	Rua Frederico Arouca 100, Cascais
Location:	Next door to Praia da Rainha, behind the railroad station
Telephone:	282821/22/23
Cables/Telex:	(None)
Reps:	(None)
Credit Cards:	(None)

Rooms:	16 rooms

Meals: Breakfast 8–10, lunch 12:30–3:30, dinner 7:30–10:30; dinner for two approx. $17; informal; room service for breakfast; outdoor terrace for drinks

Entertainment: (None)

Sports: Beach next door; golf, tennis, riding nearby

Sightseeing: Estoril (see Lennox Country Club); Sintra; Lisbon 18 miles

Lennox Country Club Hotel
Estoril

You don't have to be a golfer to love the Lennox Country Club, but it won't hurt. The Reids, the English couple who own this one-time villa, are obviously crazy about the game. They've put a practice green out front, named their pool-side bar The 19th Hole, lined the walls of the indoor bar-lounge with pictures of the pros—even named the rooms after the world's great golf courses, like St. Andrews or Porthcawl.

Still, even if you don't know a mashie from a niblick, you will appreciate the serenity here, just a block from the casino yet set apart on a quiet hilltop terraced with gardens. The nicely landscaped heated pool is peacefully placed next to a trickling waterfall, and the shaded terrace and lawns are strategically situated to look out at it all.

And while this is not a "country club" at all, it *is* a homey place where the help-yourself bars operate on the honor system and the forty guests, who are all on demipension plans, soon get to know one another. The lounges, furnished in loungeable leather, do have something of a clublike atmosphere; the rooms, while not elaborate, are also comfortable and all but one has a private balcony looking out on the town of Estoril.

Prices here vary according to the size of your room, but even the most expensive is a bargain in posh Estoril, including a big English breakfast, a five-course dinner, morning and afternoon coffee or tea and unlimited wine with your meals. The hotel also provides transportation to and from golf and horseback riding.

It's an unusually hospitable little hotel—a good place to stay, with or without your golf clubs. (E.B.)

Name:	Lennox Country Club Hotel
Owner/Manager:	Andrew Reid
Address:	Rua Eng. Alvaro Pedro de Sousa 5, Estoril
Location:	One block left of the casino off Rua Melo Sousa
Telephone:	2680424
Telex:	16470
Reps:	(None)
Credit Cards:	(None)
Rooms:	18 rooms

Meals: Breakfast 8–9:30, lunch 1:15–2, dinner 8:15–9; dinner for two approx. $20; informal; room service anytime

Entertainment: TV in lounge, occasional films, weekly outdoor barbecue in summer; casino in town

Sports: Pool on premises; beach, tennis, golf, riding available nearby (free transportation to golf and riding)

Sightseeing: Cascais, fishing harbor and bullfights; Sintra, national Palace, Pena Palace, Moorish Castle, Monserrate; Lisbon, 15 miles away, easily reached via electric train

P.S. Closed November through January

Hotel do Guincho
Cascais

♛♛ ✗✗ $

It looms on the horizon like a mirage—a stark white "Foreign Legion" fort standing alone on a wave-pounded cliff facing the Atlantic.

The entrance is in keeping with the stark surroundings—an old courtyard, bare except for potted cacti around the sides and an old well in the center.

Through the arched doorway, however, the mood changes. Six million dollars reputedly were spent transforming this 17th-century *fortaleza* into a luxury hotel, and while the thick walls, vaulted brick ceilings, columns and outer ramparts remain, the building has lost most of its ancient look. The old stone steps have been carpeted in red and are guarded now by a pair of ornate gilded statues. The two sitting rooms beyond have been completely modernized, furnished in comfortable traditional style with warm red, mustard and olive upholstered pieces picking up the colors in the floral sofas and the terra-cotta of the tiled floors. Roughhewn ceiling beams have been replaced with sleek polished wood and wall-to-wall windows have been installed to pick up the view, both in the sitting rooms and in the large and very formal dining room next door.

Upstairs, you'll sleep under those intriguing brick ceilings, perhaps in a hand-painted bed, with stone slabs as night tables, perhaps in a more formal room with upholstered headboards to match the bedspreads. Up or down, a decorator's touch is evident everywhere. All rooms come equipped with telephone, television, radio and air-conditioning.

Guincho is usually cited as a showplace, and its location is nothing short of spectacular, but as a seaside resort it has shortcomings. There's a crescent beach below on either side of the hotel, reached by steep steps down the hill, but the undertow is treacherous so few of the sunbathers

Hotel do Guincho

venture into the water. The hotel itself has no outdoor terrace on its windswept site, so unless you've snagged one of the rooms with a private balcony, you'll have to settle for a silent ocean scene through the picture windows. You won't even get that much in the bar, a dim, leathery place behind the reception desk.

You'll not find fault with the food here, or with the fine service. The seafood menu features everything from the traditional lowly Portuguese *bacalhau* (codfish) to king-sized shellfish, and the pork and veal dishes arrive tender and tasty.

If you are looking for dramatic seascapes and a place convenient to the action yet away from the crowds in Cascais and Estoril, Guincho is the place. It's no a beach resort in the usual sense, but it is a wonderful, windswept lighthouse sort of place where you jog on the beach before breakfast or walk off dinner as the moonlight shimmers on the Atlantic surf. (E.B.)

Name: Hotel do Guincho

Manager: Dr. Caldira Pais

Address: Guincho, Cascais

Location: Four miles north of Cascais on the coast road, route 247; 22 miles west of Lisbon

Telephone: 2850594, 2850491

Cables/Telex: Soltel P/12624

Reps: (None)

Credit Cards: American Express, Diners Club, Visa, Master Charge/ Eurocard

Rooms: 36 rooms

Meals: Breakfast 8–11, lunch 12:30–3, tea 4–7, dinner 7:30–10; dinner for two approx. $20; informal; room service all day and evening

Entertainment: TV in rooms and in lounge; taped music at dinner; casino at Estoril (under same ownership as the hotel)

Sports: Beach next door; free vouchers for golf and use of pool at Hotel Estoril Sol in Cascais

Sightseeing: Cascais, Estoril, Sintra are minutes away (see also Lennox Country Club for sights in Lisbon)

P.S. Some small meetings and dinners held in conference room

Hotel Palacio dos Seteais
Sintra

WWWXX $$

For centuries, the kings and aristocrats of Portugal chose to build their palaces in Sintra, the lush hilltop town Lord Byron once called a "glorious Eden." So it seems appropriate that the country's most palatial hotel should be located here, built into a wing of a magnificent 1787 estate.

Seteais is impressive inside and out. The stately stone building, set amidst formal gardens, looks to the mountains from the front, and the rear view downhill stretches all the way to the sea, miles away. In the lofty salons and corridors, you'll find marble floors, long velvet drapes, chandeliers, tapestry rugs, murals, hand-painted frescoes on the walls, carved ceilings and elaborate period furniture, antiques as well as fine reproductions.

The hallways, the rooms, even the bathrooms are enormous here. The ceilings seem a story and a half high and the windows are almost that full height. The furnishings are ornate, typically with tall wooden headboards with upholstered panels and individualized motifs, and with nice touches such as the delicate reproduction antique writing tables.

Down the wide stairs, the dining room is also grand, done in elegant soft shades of beige and green. The four-course menu features continental as well as local specialties, and here is a perfect place to sample the best of Portuguese wines. The *acepipes variados* (assorted hors d'oeuvres) are positively memorable—two large double-decker rolling carts filled with hot and cold dishes. And as if that weren't enough, the waiter appears with more—fish and meat tidbits wrapped in a delectable pastry crust served hot from the kitchen.

The bar is the smallest room in the house—just five tables—but right outside is a spacious terrace looking out to the distant sea.

The Palacio was actually built by a Dutchman, then later acquired and restored by the Marquis le Marialva. Byron supposedly worked on *Childe Harold* in the garden. In 1955 the government took over and turned one wing into a hotel with 18 rooms. It was leased to the owners of Lisbon's well-known Tivoli Hotel, who installed gracious manager Alberto de Vasconcelos at Seteais to look after things. He had done so in grand style for more than 20 years, taking personal pride in keeping things just so, and entertaining everyone from Melina Mercouri and Brigitte Bardot to Adlai Stevenson, Agatha Christie and Queen Juliana. The Dutch ambassador was in residence during our visit.

Senhor de Vasconcelos says he has just one current problem. Seteais has always been a prime choice for elegant weddings, the formal garden making a perfect background for nuptial portraits. Lately, he says, bridal couples have been driving up in full dress just to have their pictures taken in the garden, sometimes causing a wait for the bride in residence.

It's hard to blame the local couples. Settings like this one are hard to find. (E.B.)

Name: Hotel Palacio dos Seteais

Manager: Alberto de Vasconcelos

Address: Rua Barbosa du Bocage 8–12, Sintra

Location: Follow signs clearly marking uphill route from the center of town; 18 miles from Lisbon

Telephone: 2933200/25/50

Cables: SETEAIS-Sintra

Reps: (None)

Credit Cards: American Express, Diners, Master Charge/Eurocard, Visa

Rooms: 18 rooms, 1 suite

Meals: Breakfast 8–11, lunch 12:30–2:30, dinner 7:30–9:30; dinner for two approx. $20; informal; room service for breakfast; outdoor terrace

Entertainment: (None)

Sports: (None)

Sightseeing: The town of Sintra—National Palace, Pena Palace, Moorish Castle, Monserrate, Convento de Santa Cruz dos Capuchos

P.S. Some groups for lunch, occasional private parties or weddings

---

York House
Lisbon

WWXX$

Never underestimate the power of a woman—much less two of them.

Here was this wonderful 16th-century convent fading and crumbling away as it passed from owner to owner after its occupants were expelled by Prime Minister Marques de Pombal in the 1750s. For a while it was a hospital, then it was abandoned entirely until an Irish Evangelical association moved in, doing the minimum about fixing up the place.

The first pair of ladies on the scene were English and they turned a small wing of the complex into a modest six-room pension for international guests. Then in 1930 two Frenchwomen took over, and with a combination of Gallic charm, grit and good taste, set about transforming the place. They polished up the terra-cotta tiles, patched and painted the white walls and vaulted ceilings, added blue-and-white Oriental rugs, paintings, antiques and fine furnishings, and before they were done, they had created Lisbon's most interesting hotel.

In their enthusiasm, they even dug years of accumulated dirt out of an old cellar to discover a plaque in the wall commemorating a visit from "Pope Pio VI" way back in the 18th century—and to create an atmospheric downstairs dining room with a stone ceiling and thick old columns.

Nor are the improvements finished. Present owner Ginette Moreno, whose mother started it all, is still at work adding and renovating. She plans new living and dining rooms, a new reception area and, she declares firmly, a facelift for the stone steps to the street.

You'd never expect what awaits you when you ascend those worn steps. The entrance to York House is an unmarked gateway in an aging wall on a street near the waterfront—safe, of course but hardly fashionable.

It's a pleasant shock to find yourself suddenly in a tranquil courtyard shaded by ancient twisted trees and blooming bougainvillea. In the building to the right is the reception desk, on the left a handsome bar, modern in furnishings but with antique accents. One wall is a gallery of paintings, affectionate gifts to the hotel from former guests.

The main dining room, arched and beamed and lined with blue-and-white tiles, has elaborate brass chandeliers, a handsome old grandfather's clock against the wall, precious porcelains and other collectibles displayed in tile-bordered recesses in the wall. An upstairs sitting room has a TV set—but it is hidden hehind the doors of a tall antique chest.

The corridors wander, and the rooms off them range anywhere from small but adequate to apartment size—large enough to reside in. Some people *do* live in them, in fact—people like students, writers and members of the French diplomatic corps who are in Lisbon on long-term assignments. The decorating isn't elaborate, but it does have a pleasant old-fashioned air, lots of tiles and floral prints.

The bathrooms, though, are not old-fashioned. Senhora Moreno can tell you horror stories about what her mother went through installing plumbing in those thick walls so that most of the rooms could have private baths.

York House is away from central Lisbon, but a bus or trolley outside the door will have you in the heart of things in minutes; or you can take cabs, since Lisbon cab rates are less than buses in some U.S. cities. The reasonable room rates here allow for lots of taxis compared to what you might pay for comparable quarters elsewhere in the city. (E.B.)

Name: York House

Owner/Manager: Ginette Moreno

Address: Rua das Janelas Verdes 32, Lisbon

Location: West of the Rossio and the Bairro Alto almost on the waterfront, near the Museum of Ancient Art. (Better take a cab the first time—and write down the address before you start, since most cabdrivers don't speak English).

Telephone: 662435

Cables/Telex: (None)

Reps: (None)

Credit Cards: American Express, Master Charge/Eurocard, Visa

Rooms: 60 rooms

Meals: Breakfast served in your room 7:30–10, lunch 12:30–2, dinner 7:30–9; dinner for two approx. $12; ihformal; room service for breakfast only/

Entertainment: TV in lounge

Sports: (None)

Sightseeing: (See Principe Real)

P.S. The only group ever to be seen here was a gathering of 15 French professors one summer

Hotel Principe Real
Lisbon

Cabdrivers seem to have a hard time finding the Principe Real for though it is just a brief stroll from the stately Avenida da Liberdade, it is tucked away on a residential street up the hill and around the corner from the boulevard, next to the Botanical Garden.

Once found, however, this turns out to be an extremely convenient location for a rare kind of establishment—a four-star hotel in the heart of the city with just 24 rooms and lots of staff to look after them.

Most of the rooms are large, furnished in uninspiring Old World style with matching deep-colored red or gold floral bedspreads or drapes, lacy inner curtains, standing mirrors, old-fashioned secretary desks and gilt wall sconces. Each room has a minuscule balcony, just about large enough for testing out the day's weather before you set out to explore the city.

The sunny top-story breakfast room surely must be Lisbon's pleasantest, with a whole wall of windows that start your day with a view of St. George's Castle and all the hills of the city below, spread out in a tile-roofed, pastel-tinted panorama.

There's more of a living room than a lobby here—furniture comfortably grouped around a fireplace, the light filtered by a colorful stained-glass window, with plants and antiques all around the room. The tiny adjoining bar has a cozy feel, too.

You'll find no stacks of tour-group luggage in this lobby, or in the attractive tile-walled reception area at the door. And the friendly staff behind the desk is happy to help you with anything you might need, from reading a road map to making sightseeing suggestions. Everything is within easy walking distance, since you are just about midway between the Praça Marquês de Pombal and the Rossio, centers of the new and the old parts of the city.

There's a lot to be said for this very personal small hotel, but only with a word of caution. That seemingly quiet side street is deceptive. Trucks and motorcycles roar by far into the wee hours, and if your room fronts on the street, you'll need more than ambience to get you through the night.

If you want to avoid big, busy hotels, this is an ideal place. Just be sure to ask for—no, *insist* on—a room away from the street. (E.B.)

Name: Hotel Principe Real

Owner/Manager: Maria Cecilia Refende

Address: Rua da Alegria 53, Lisbon

Location: West of the Avenida da Liberdade, behind a little park called Praça da Alegria and near the Botanical Garden. (If you come by cab, write down the address clearly before you start—few cabdrivers speak English.)

Telephone: 360116/7/8

Cables: PRINREAL

Reps: (None)

Credit Cards: (None)

311

Rooms:	24 rooms
Meals:	Breakfast only, served 7:30–11:30; room service available
Entertainment:	(None)
Sports:	(None)
Sightseeing:	Midway between the chic area around the Praça Marquês de Pombal, and the shopping district at the Rossio; easy walking distance, too, from the atmospheric old quarter, the Alfama, and the Barrio Alto, where the *fado* clubs cluster

Pousada de Palmela
Palmela

WWXX$

Given a great old building to convert to a hotel, a designer can take one of two directions—try to re-create the past or attempt to blend past with present. At Palmela, the newest showplace of the government *pousadas*, the latter (and more perilous) route was taken, making the gray-stone architectural features of a vast old monastery the dominant elements of the decorating scheme, eschewing antiques in favor of stark modern furnishings and little more than plants and tapestries to soften the effect.

It works! Palmela is one of the most dramatic of the *pousadas*, both in its lofty site as part of the castle complex that dominates the city and in its austere decor. Everything here is on a grand scale, from the exquisite modern tapestry and the standing wrought-iron lanterns marking the entrance, to the ten-foot-wide hallways, double-height ceilings and enormous rooms, both public and private. The building is planned around a large stone courtyard, now brightened with wooden tables and chairs and umbrellas but still reflecting its monastic origins. All along the glassed-in arched arcade surrounding the court, identical sets of buttery-soft modern leather armchairs and sofas have been placed around marble-top tables, all in a gray-beige tone that picks up the gray stone outlining the archways. The only color comes from terra-cotta planters and the native patterned rugs at each sitting area.

The long narrow dining room is equally severe. One of the white walls is bare except for the stone supports around each shuttered window and the ferns in clay pots on each deep window ledge. On the inner wall three tremendous paintings hang, done in black and white like an artist's oversize pencil sketches of medieval scenes. The chairs are sleek walnut with black leather seats. Red carnations on the white tablecloths and red tile floors provide a bit of color, picked up by tall side arrangements of dried flowers.

The sitting rooms outside, a small lounge with television and a large one for before-dinner drinks, have used the same gray-beige furnishings as the arcade but with deep red rugs and religious paintings to relieve the severity—at least, a little.

As you would expect in these surroundings, the service is formal and so is the menu—a three- or four-course prix-fixe lunch or dinner with two choices in each category and a wine list that runs for pages. The fish soufflé here is a light and flaky "must."

Upstairs, the bedrooms are tremendous, with white stucco walls, handsome paneled doors with interesting hardware, tall windows with full-length shutters and fantastic views no matter which side of the building you face—hills and sea, the tile-roofed town or the great old castle ruins across the way, more romantic than ever bathed in soft floodlights at night.

The rooms are softer in feel, decorated with rough native materials— beige woven bedspreads with stripes of brown, rust and white, white woven drapes with a heavy fringed bottom. There are carpets on the tile floors and more of those soft leather chairs, set around a round marble table bearing an earthenware pitcher of cold water. Closets are built into an outer dressing room, white formica dressing tables are built into the walls and accented with leather hassocks.

Palmela's castle is historic. It was from here that Afonso Henriques, the first king of Portugal, drove out the Moors. Today, the grandeur of the *pousada* building speaks for itself, uncluttered by excess ornament. It makes an eloquent statement. (E.B.)

Name: Pousada de Palmela

Manager: Rene Gomes

Address: Palmela

Location: About 20 miles south of Lisbon; the *pousada* is within the castle complex above the town—follow blue and yellow "Pousada" signs from the village

Telephone: (235) 12 26/1395

Cables/Telex: (None)

Reps: (None)

Credit Cards: Master Charge/Eurocard, Visa

313

Rooms:	25 rooms, 2 suites

Meals: Breakfast 8–10, lunch 12:30–2:30, dinner 7:30–9:30; dinner for two approx. $14; informal; room service for breakfast

Entertainment: Taped music with dinner; TV in lounge

Sports: Beaches at Arrabida, Setúbal, Sesimbra

Sightseeing: Castle ruins and gardens in Palmela; castles in Setúbal and Sesimbra

Hotel do Mar
Sesimbra

♨ ✗✗ $$

Architect Conceicão Silva may have been ahead of his time. Back in 1965 when he built Hotel do Mar as a series of stair-steps from beach level to the tip of its hillside site, his concept was all but revolutionary. Even today the hotel is unique, with its white tiers stacked up like a cubist painting, softened by low rows of tropical greenery along each layer.

To find the hotel, you must follow the winding road as it tumbles down to the bustling fishing village of Sesimbra, then watch for signs pointing back up again to the hotel. The hilltop entrance is actually at the fifth level. Past the reception area with its tropical birds is an airy lounge with beamed ceilings, white globe hanging lamps and Danish modern furniture. There are long glass walls on two sides and an outside deck the width of both walls for taking in the view.

Up one flight, the long dining room has similar furnishings but a more formal feel, and once again, a view from end to end. There's an inside sitting room on a lower level with big leather armchairs and marble-top tables where you can write letters, play cards or catch the latest on Portuguese TV. Down at ground level you'll find a round snack bar and a tunnel leading underneath the road to the beach.

The heart of the hotel, however, is the living area, two sets of multitiers separated by a level green lawn and a big shimmering circular swimming pool. (Believe it or not, there's a disco underneath the pool, nicely muffled if you don't care to partake.)

The rooms are predictably sleek and modern, white walls with wood accents and lots of built-ins, including two cushioned stone seats on either side of the window. Out the louvered doors is a big terrace with red tile flooring and wicker furniture, high rounded side walls and a low garden in front—as well as an unobstructed vista of blue sea. Here's where you see that Silva's plan was for more than dramatic effect—it gave each room a maximum of terrace, view and privacy. From your terrace you can see Sesimbra's fisherman's beach and anticipate the pleasure of each day's catch in the dining room at night. Or you can have a try at catching your own tunny or swordfish in the hotel's private boat.

A modern 120-room resort hotel hardly qualifies as a lovers' hideaway, but Do Mar is extremely low key and it does offer the chance for an unusually varied vacation. Most of the guests here settle in for a full week, combining beach and boating with forays into the picturesque village and to explore the famous three castles in the vicinity. When they want city life, Lisbon is just 20 miles away. It's a good mix. (E.B.)

Name: Hotel do Mar

Manager: Mario Frede

Address: 2970 Sesimbra

Location: About 19 miles south of Lisbon off route 10; look for hotel signs off the road along the beach in town

Telephone: 2233 326/413/414

Cables/Telex: MARE/13883

Reps: (None)

Credit Cards: American Express, Diners, Master Charge/Eurocard, Visa

Rooms: 113 standard rooms, 6 deluxe rooms

Meals: Breakfast 7:30–10:30, lunch 12:30–3:30, dinner 7:30–10:30; dinner for two approx. $20; informal; room service available all day

Entertainment: Taped music with dinner, TV in lounge, disco

Sports: Swimming pool, beach, private boat for excursions

Sightseeing: Fisherman's beach in Sesimbra; castles in Sesimbra, Setúbal and Palmela

P.S. You'll definitely find both groups and children here, but the spread-out layout makes it possible to find your own private nook

Quinta das Torres
Azeitão

♛✗$

Quinta means "farm, country estate." Usually you see the word together with a family name on markers embedded in very high, very private walls along the roadside. But if you turn at the Quinta das Torres sign and proceed down the long tree-shaded drive to a grilled gate almost hidden in the vines, you'll be able to sample the way of life of Portugal's old landed gentry.

This 16th-century estate has been in the same family for generations. Like many estate owners before them, they found the old place becoming a burden, and in 1940 decided to earn a bit of upkeep by turning ten of their many rooms into lodgings for guests. Some of these rooms share the main building with the family quarters, but most are across a fountained courtyard, and each one is totally different. You may find yourself with a fireplace or an outdoor terrace, with a ruffled canopy bed or a bed with an old wrought-iron headboard, but you can be sure of finding a wealth of antiques and fine reproductions, patterned rugs on tile floors, high shuttered windows and religious artifacts as well as fresh flowers in your room.

The main reception hall, with a massive refectory table in the center, has two fireplaces as well as cabinets filled with antique guns. The dining room has a fireplace of its own, as well as a domed ceiling, Portuguese and Italian tiles on the walls and a window that looks out on a formal pool. A five-minute walk through the trees will bring you to a spring-fed pool for swimming.

The owners of Quinta das Torres are elderly now, and the house, too, is showing just a few signs of age, but its aristocratic past is unmistakable. It's a worthwhile stop for a rare look behind those time-mellowed walls. (E.B.)

Name: Quinta das Torres

Owner/Managers: Dr. Bento de Sousa, Maria Clementina Solza

Address: 5 Estrada Nacional, Azeitão

Location: On the main highway just across from the Jóse Maria de Fonseca winery (Lancers to U.S. wine lovers); between Palmela and Sesimbra; 15½ miles south of Lisbon, 9½ miles north of Setúbal

---

Telephone: 208 00 01

Cables/Telex: (None)

Reps: (None)

Credit Cards: (None)

Rooms: 10 rooms

Meals: Breakfast served in rooms until 10; lunch 12:30–2:30, dinner 7–9; dinner for two approx. $20; informal

Entertainment: (None)

Sports: Swimming pool; beaches nearby; hiking

Sightseeing: The three castles—Sesimbra, Setúbal, Palmela, drives into the Arrabida mountain range, fishing harbor at Setúbal

Pousada de São Filipe
Setúbal

WWXX$

Wind your way up the mountain road, walk through the old arched gate, along an echoing stone passage adorned with tiles, and you emerge at an outlook, the town and a startlingly blue sea below, a great crumbling yellow castle above.

The canopy of interconnected white umbrellas on an upper terrace are your clue that not all of this 15th-century fortress has been allowed to crumble. Climb the steps and you'll find that where soldiers once were quartered, you can now live in an atmospheric *pousada* with rooms and hallways filled with antiques.

The low-ceilinged living room is paneled with old blue and yellow tiles and furnished with native rugs, religious artifacts, old chests, engravings and red- and blue- and gold-painted wall sconces with the look of their heraldic past—but the TV set here is an eyesore. Through an arched stone doorway is a medieval-style bar with tiled tables.

Heading straight up from the entry hall, duck your head under another low arch and climb the time-worn stone stairs to the bedrooms and the second-floor dining room, a room with a wood-paneled ceiling, tile wall decorations and a panoramic view. There's excellent fresh fish here brought up from the bustling harbor, and there's no better place to try a Portuguese favorite, *sardinha assada* or charcoal-grilled sardines, from the town that is the center of the country's sardine industry.

317

There's a lot of variation in the rooms, which get larger as you go higher, the best being on the third floor. Room 16 is a winner, with its heavy carved headboard and paneled wardrobe chest. It's a pleasure to walk the halls here, where you may come upon all manner of antiques, including an interesting ancient door.

Don't leave São Filipe without asking to be shown the little chapel next door, built in 1581 by Isabel of Aragon in memory of her brother, Philip. It's a beauty with its blue-and-white tile murals and gold leaf altar.

Setúbal's fortress used to guard the city against attack from the sea. Today it is guarding something equally vulnerable—the heritage of the past. (E.B.)

Name: Pousada de São Filipe

Manager: Dr. Rui Gomes

Address: Setúbal

Location: On the right bank of the river, across the 25 de Abril bridge, 25 miles south of Lisbon. Signs from the center of town point the way uphill to the *pousada*.

Telephone: (065) 23844/24981

Cables/Telex: (None)

Reps: (None)

Credit Cards: Master Charge/Eurocard, Visa

Rooms: 15 rooms

Meals: Breakfast 8–10:30, lunch 12:45–2:30, dinner 7:45–9:30; dinner for two approx. $14; informal; room service breakfast only

Entertainment: TV in lounge

Sports: Beaches nearby

Sightseeing: Setúbal's fishing harbor, Manueline-style Church of Jesus, small town museum; castles at Palmela and Sesimbra

P.S. This is a popular *pousada*; reservations recommended two months ahead

Pousada dos Lioios
Evora

WWWXX$

Looks can be deceiving. Here's a small white building in the most historic square of Evora, seemingly distinguished mainly by its location facing the ruins of the Roman Temple of Diana.

But behind its plain facade, the Pousada dos Lioios, dedicated in the year 1491 as the simple home of a band of devout monks, has been embellished, enlarged and enriched with donations over the years to become a veritable mansion with pink and gray marble floors, spacious rooms and a memorable cloister, distinctive for its granite and marble fountain, pointed arches and twisted columns done in the ornate, Moorish-inspired style of architecture known as Manueline.

When the weather is mild, you'll dine in the colonnade around the cloister, seated on handsome chairs of hand-worked chestnut, looking out through the arches on a garden of flowers and fruit trees and serenaded by the peaceful plink of the fountain. The dining room is exceptional, rightfully noted for serving the very best of the specialties of Alentejo, the province whose menus have most strongly influenced the national cuisine. The *carne de porco a Alentejana*—tender roast pork morsels in a savory sauce with tiny baby clams—is a Portuguese classic. Here's your chance, too, to sample *gaspacho a regional*, a golden variation on the usual Spanish recipe, or one of the favored Portuguese sugared egg desserts—as well as the fine local wine known as Vidiguera.

In winter, meals are served in the old monks' refectory, now adorned with heavy wrought-iron chandeliers and brass-studded red-velvet straight-back chairs.

A magnificent tapestry reaches the entire length of the long marble stairway leading to the sleeping quarters. Each room is unique, though all are decorated in rich damasks, velvets and brocades. Room 2, a deluxe location, has a frescoed ceiling, crystal sconces, distinctive furnishings and a rare private terrace. Room 12, a smaller chamber, has an elaborately carved wooden headboard, with night tables, wardrobe, even a waste basket to match.

The public rooms are grand. A spacious entry holds an elaborately carved long table bearing plants and tall pewter candlesticks, as well as a four-door antique cupboard. Beyond is a sitting room in white and gold, and through an archway, a small bar. Walk down the corridor and through a back court and you'll come to a pleasant surprise—an open courtyard for sunning and an awninged terrace where tea is served in the afternoon.

Come evening, walk back into the town square to gaze at those ruins, doubly romantic by moonlight. For most visitors, Evora and its prize *pousada* rank among the most treasured memories of Portugal. (E.B)

Name: Pousada dos Lioios

Manager: Braga Lopes

Address: Evora

Location: Evora is about 96 miles from Lisbon, best reached via Setúbal. The *pousada* is up the hill from the shopping center of Evora, clearly marked by signs.

Telephone: 240-51

Cables: POUSADA

Reps: (None)

Credit Cards: Master Charge/Eurocard

Rooms: 29 rooms, 1 suite

Meals: Breakfast 7:30–10:30, lunch 12:30–2:30, dinner 7:30–9:30; dinner for two aprox. $14; informal; room service for breakfast only

Entertainment: TV in lounge

Sports: Pool, tennis, riding nearby

Sightseeing: Evora is said to have no fewer than 59 monuments; most important are the Temple of Diana, the Cathedral, Church of St. John the Evangelist, Royal Church of St. Francis, Church of Our Lady of Grace, the town museum, and the ancient university

---

Pousada do Infante
Sagres

The Atlantic and Mediterranean meet here, waves crashing against the rugged, rocky cliffs. It's a solitary spot, a place to contemplate the forces of nature—and it's a fitting site for a cliff-top *pousada* dedicated to the brave explorers and navigators who once battled the elements at sea for Portugal.

Pousada do Infante was built in 1960 in the timeless, traditional style

of the region, a long low white building with a red tile roof and lots of tall thin lacy carved chimneys. Across the back, an arched colonnade runs the length of the building, fronted by a wide terrace and an even wider lawn, all offering quiet space where you can settle in for hours to watch the sea. If you prefer doing your ocean-gazing in private, each bedroom has a balcony that shares the dramatic view. The rooms are spacious, traditional in feel and well-furnished, with formal draperies, floral bedspreads and comfortable upholstered armchairs. There are only fifteen of them, and getting one requires reserving about two months in advance.

The large olive and light-blue living room manages to be impressive and inviting at the same time. Your eye goes immediately to the two modernistic tapestry murals at either end, depicting the exploits of Henry the Navigator. On top of a sleek marble fireplace, an old gilded religious figure stands, between tall candlesticks and floral bouquets. The furniture is soft crushed velvet, the rugs are hand woven, the floors are polished tile.

The same polished tiles are on the dining-room floor, and there are traditional patterned tiles on the walls as well. One wall is dominated by a rounded fireplace and carved model of the kind of clipper ships that once plied the seas outside. Lots of Algarve visitors drive to Sagres just to eat here; the specialties of the house are as safe as fresh-caught sole or as adventurous as octopus in tomato sauce, and the fig and almond sweets and Lagos wine please almost everyone.

You can see the Sagres beach from the terrace and there's everything to do here or in the neighboring Algarve towns—fish, ride, play golf or tennis, gamble at the casino—you name it. But this *pousada* holds a fascination all its own. Just try sitting back on your terrace and watching the waves come crashing in. It may be all the entertainment you need. (E.B.)

Name: Pousada do Infante

Manager :   Alfredo de Azevedo

Address: Sagres, Algarve

Location: At the westernmost tip of the southern Algarve coast; signs in town clearly point the way to the *pousada*

Telephone: 64222/3

Cables/Telex: (None)

Reps: (None)

Credit Cards: Diners Club, Master Charge/Eurocard, Visa

Rooms: 15 rooms, 1 suite

Meals: Breakfast 8:30–11, lunch 12:30–2:30, dinner 7:30–9:30; dinner for two approx. $12; informal; room service for breakfast only

Entertainment: TV in lounge, casino nearby

Sports: Beaches, fishing, tennis, riding, golf all nearby

Sightseeing: Algarve towns—most scenic are Lagos and Albufeira; follow the *"Praia"* signs off the main highway to explore beaches

P.S. Lots of tour groups for lunch—busloads every Tuesday and Friday, good days for taking off to explore the area

Casa de São Gonçalo da Lagos
Lagos

You ring the bell and, in a moment, a pleasant young man appears to bid you welcome, take your bags to your room, hand you the key to the front door and discreetly disappear. You're on your own, cozily ensconced in your own private pink casa.

At least that's the way it feels here in this one-time villa, unmarked outside except for a small round porcelain plaque at the door. You're only a few steps from the busy heart of town, but you'd never know it, since everything is turned away from the traffic toward a peaceful patio draped in bougainvillea.

The casa rambles. Up the tiled stairway, the living room is homey, with big sofas and chairs in front of the fireplace and facing the TV, well-stocked bookshelves, antiques on the mantel. Just beyond is a vine-shaded terrace, bright with blue-and-white tiles and red geraniums, wicker tables and chairs turned toward the flower-draped patio and its trickling fountain in a lilypond.

Breakfast is served on the terrace—unless you prefer the dignified indoor dining room with painted ceilings and big old buffets and cupboards. There's a more formal sitting room, as well, lots of gilt and velvet in shades of rose, with old mirrors and paintings and an antique clavichord in the center.

All of it is much the same as it was when this was an aristocratic home dating back to the 18th century—which it remained until just a few years ago when the family decided to take advantage of their central location to take in a small number of paying guests. Present owner, Tereza da Cunha, who took over in 1978, has kept things as personal as ever. The bedrooms

322

have names rather than numbers—Lilas or Azul for the color scheme or perhaps Imperio for the furniture style. You'll find scalloped hand-embroidered linens and a snow-white embossed coverlet on the bed, lots of antique pieces in the room and varying period decor from rustic to rococo, depending on your location. The biggest rooms are on the second floor, but you'll have to contend with street noises if you choose one. The best accommodations are up the winding stairs to the third floor, especially those facing the patio. Don Jose has beautiful high carved wooden beds, Rustico has the choicest of the views.

There are no lobbies here; the bar off the living room looks as if it belongs in a home; the terrace has just three small tables. If a private pink villa appeals to you, it's easy to make yourself at home at the casa. (E.B.)

Name: Casa de São Gonçalo da Lagos

Owner/Manager: Tereza da Cunha

Address: Rua Candida dos Reis 73, Lagos, Algarve

Location: On the southern Algarve coast, about 50 miles west of Faro, 27 miles west of Sagres. To find the hotel, drive into the main square of town, drive around the traffic circle to continue straight on to a second square, then turn left onto Rua Candida dos Reis.

Telephone: 62171

Cables/Telex: (None)

Reps: (None)

Credit Cards: (None)

Rooms: 13 rooms

Meals: Breakfast only, 8:30–10:30; no room service

Entertainment: TV in the lounge

Sports: Beaches, tennis, golf, fishing, riding available nearby

Sightseeing: Igreja de Santo Antonio (Church of St. Anthony), regional museum, old customs house; flea markets and crafts shops; drives to visit other Algarve towns and beaches; casinos at Alvor, Monte Gordo and Vilamoura

P.S.   Parking can be a problem here

Estalagem do Cerro
Albufeira

It's one part Portuguese, one part North African—and unmistakably Algarve. From the white-washed curves and chimneys outside to the wicker and wood within, the Estalagem do Cerro has achieved what so many hotels here lack—the look and feel of its locale.

The inn is actually two buildings, an older native structure and a modern addition, connected by a two-story open court topped with trailing vines. The corridors wander up and down in all directions and terraces, alcoves and little gardens have a way of cropping up just where you least expect them.

Walk one way and you'll come upon a modernistic duplex lounge with cowhide chairs around a fireplace, tall plants to soften the bare walls and a TV for entertainment. There's a tiny terrace outside, just enough room for two tables.

Try another tack and you'll come to the bar, this time a room with a wooden slatted ceiling, tiles on the wall and chairs upholstered in black leather.

In still another direction is the dining room, simply furnished with wicker chairs and lamps, its major decoration the view that comes in through the big arched windows that fill the wall. That view is the best in town, for Do Cerro has a choice location at the top of the hill that twists and turns its steep way down to Albufeira and the sea. It's a mosaic of red roofs, white walls and blue ocean by day, a sea of twinkling lights at night.

All the rooms have access to some terrace, veranda or garden where you can take in the sun and the scenery. The rooms are varied in size and layout, some have private terraces, a few have fireplaces, some are made up as studio sitting rooms. But all are Algarve simple in their decor—tile floors, rattan chairs, woven straw headboards in simple wooden frames, mirrors, chests, benches and shelves built right into the walls, hanging baskets and tin lanterns for light, radios to supply soft music. Someone with a sense of humor has dubbed Room 10 the honeymoon suite—it's a small room almost entirely taken up with a large bed and with a terrace as big as the room itself.

The Algarve is gaining a growing number of hotels that could just as well be in Miami or Malibu or almost anywhere. Here's one, at least, that belongs right here. (E.B.)

Name: Estalagem do Cerro

Manager: Antonio Negrao Neto

Address: Albufeira, Algarve

Location: Albufeira is about 24 miles west of Faro; hotel is at the top of the hill above the town; there are no street names, but there are signs pointing the way if you look carefully

Telephone: 52191/2

Cables/Telex: (None)

Reps: (None)

Credit Cards: (None)

Rooms: 50 rooms

Meals: Breakfast 8–9:30, lunch 1–4:30, dinner 8–11:30; dinner for two approx. $10; informal; room service until 9:30 P.M.

Entertainment: Taped music at dinner, TV in lounge

Sports: Beaches, tennis, riding, fishing, golf all available nearby

Sightseeing: Algarve towns and beaches; casinos at Alvor, Monte Gordo and Vilamoura; fisherman's beach and cliff-top walks in town

Pousada de São Bras
São Bras de Alportel

"They like to drive to the beach during the day—we make them a map to the best ones—then come back to the cool and the quiet at night. Some don't even leave in the daytime—they come to paint the scenery."

Manager Gil Carvalho had answered neatly the question of why anyone would want to come to the Algarve and stay in the surrounding hills rather than on the beach. One of the first of the *pousadas* when it was built 37 years ago, São Bras fulfills the aim of these government-owned inns in drawing visitors to an oft-neglected but scenic area. Many of the guests here are repeats who feel they have a "find," returning year after year for the rustic informality and the tranquil feel of this hilltop villa.

325

The white, tile-roofed building is handsome, but there's no mistaking the fact that this is meant to be a simple country inn. The living room is furnished with leather chairs gathered around a fireplace and a TV, the bar is really part of the same comfortable room and the dining room is decorated with wagon-wheel chandeliers, wooden tavern chairs, native rugs and a big fireplace to keep things cozy in the winter. The bedrooms are simple, too, with plain wooden bedsteads, rustic mirrors and regional pieces. Each one has a private balcony for viewing the beautiful surrounding hills, and there's a terrace the whole length of the building for the same purpose.

The food is hearty here, the welcome warm, the rates reasonable. It's a pleasant change of pace, a surprisingly short drive from the beaches of the Algarve. (E.B.)

Name: Pousada de São Bras

Manager: Gil Carvalho

Address: 8150 São Bras de Alportel

Location: About 15 miles north of Faro; *pousada* is just north of the town—signs point the way.

Telephone: 42305

Cables/Telex: (None)

Reps: (None)

Credit Cards: Master Charge/Eurocard, Visa

Rooms: 16 rooms; five more presently being remodeled to include private baths

Meals: Breakfast 8–10, lunch 12:30–2:30, dinner 7:30–9:30; dinner for two approx. $13; informal; room service for breakfast only

Entertainment: (None)

Sports: Beaches nearby, lots of woods for hiking

Sightseeing: Algarve towns and beaches

For brief details of other hotels in Portugal turn to the chapter on Added Attractions at the end of the guide.

Spain

Hostal de la Gavina
S'Agaró

♛♛♛✕✕✕$$$

Hostal rather than *hotel* because the owner, Don José Ensesa, wants his guest to feel they are in a friend's home. Which presumably they do, if they're accustomed to walls of padded silk or hand-embroidered satin, floors inlaid with eight types of marble, ceilings of cross-beamed oak and paneled walls of glowing walnut hung with Flemish tapestries and portraits in gilded frames. The *hostal*'s bedchambers are fit for a grandee (four-poster bed, perhaps, chandeliers and furniture with gilt trim) so no one can raise an eyebrow if you elect to spend a lot of time *acostado*. La Gavina, the Seagull, a white-stucco *casa grande* with gray-green window blinds and red clay tiles on the roofs and turrets, is set among gardens of mimosa and bougainvillea, on a granite-cropped peninsula with sandy coves, in a parklike setting of pines and cedars and cypress trees. It's a place that encourages relaxation of the most languid kind. A morning by the pool (seawater in summer, heated fresh water in winter, poolside dining, fully equipped cabanas). An hour or two on the beach. A *paseo* along the pathway carved from the rocky foreshore. Lunch beneath a shady pergola. Siesta. Tennis. Leisurely sips of sherry on the breeze-cooled terrace before dinner. Sumptuous dining by candlelight, in what is generally acknowledged to be one of the finest restaurants in all of Spain.

This is the kind of ambience that attracts well-heeled jet-setters of the princess-and-president variety, but people are judged here less by title than by inclination—Hostal de la Gavina is strictly for vacationers who prefer low-key, almost sedate luxury. No piped music here to intrude on your contentment. No radio or TV in the rooms. The creator of this remarkable hotel, the aforementioned José Ensesa, is the scion of a prosperous Catalan family (chemicals and flour). He it was who filled his *casa grande* with antiques from his private collection, and staffed it with 75 family retainers who serve you punctiliously and graciously. He is something of a perfectionist, this Don José (the marble lobby was reconstructed three times before he was totally satisfied), and presumably something of an artist to have spotted the possibilities of this Mediterranean promontory. The sea

327

𝒽Hostal de la Gavina

plops against the rocks or trickles across the sand. Winds whisper. Mimosa scents the air. It's a lovely spot, this neck of land, this Gavina. To paraphrase Winston Churchill: some Seagull, some neck.

Name: Hostal de la Gavina

Manager: Alfonso Jordan Garcia

Address: S'Agaró, Gerona

Location: On the Costa Brava, 60 miles south of the French border, 68 miles north of Barcelona, 20 miles from the Gerona-Costa Brava Airport

Telephone: (972) 321100

Telex: 57132

Credit Cards: American Express

Rooms: 58 rooms, 16 suites

Meals: Breakfast 8–11, lunch 12–3, dinner 8–11, served on the terrace or in a trio of indoor dining rooms; dinner for two approx. $36–$40; informal dress; room service during dining room hours

Entertainment: Piano in the dining room

Sports: Tennis (2 courts), sauna, massage, exercise room, swimming pool, two beaches (not private), waterskiing, boating, American-style bowling alley, 3 miles of paths along the shore; golf and horseback riding nearby

Sightseeing: The Costa Brava coastline

P.S. Expect some groups, some special events—an International Bridge Tournament, music festivals, tennis tournaments, etc.

Parador Marqués de Villena
Alarcón

WW X $

The setting is dramatic, almost showy. Where the Rio Júcar flows in a wide loop to form a natural moat, the bluff soars steeply from its banks, and there, high up there, is the *al-arcon* or Moorish watchtower.

Its bouldery battlements seem to rise naturally out of the rock, its crenellations clawing at the sky. Here's the castle of romantic legend, a real live knights-on-white-chargers-damsels-in-distress fastness, crowning a crag above the plain of La Mancha. You reach it, by white charger or Ford Fiesta, up a winding roadway, precipices on either side, ending in a paved courtyard with an old well and a spreading fig tree, surrounded by walls of crushed boulders, oak-beamed galleries and a massive stone tower 75 feet high. This is the Marqués de Villena, a national *parador* within the old *al-arcon*. The original great hall is now the dining room, its exposed stonework set off by medieval paintings; waitresses in traditional costume (embroidered blouses with white lace stockings) serve you the regional dishes of La Mancha—*ensalada Manchega* (salad sprinkled with dried and salted cod flakes), *tortilla guisada* (potato omelet) or *cordero en saldereta* (ragout of lamb in a liver sauce).

329

Several of the guest rooms are located in that massive tower. Peek from your window. Down. There's a 500-foot drop, straight down to the Júcar. You begin to feel like you're in one of those cliff-hanging houses, or *casas colgadas*, you may have spotted at Cuenca on your way to Alarcón. Furnishings are regional rustic, functional rather than plush. But that doesn't mean no one wants to spend a storied night in one of the *parador*'s eleven rooms. On the contrary, if you want one of these cliff-hangers you'd better have a very swift white charger.

Name:	Parador Nacional Marqués de Villena
Manager:	Secundino Fuertes Alvarez
Address:	Alarcón, Cuenca
Location:	About halfway to the coast, just off highway N111 which links Madrid and Valencia
Telephone:	331350
Cables:	Paral Alarcon
Reps:	Hamsa, Madrid
Rooms:	11
Meals:	Breakfast 8–11, lunch 1–4, dinner 9–11; dinner for two approx. $18–$22; informal dress; room service during dining room hours
Entertainment:	Reading Cervantes
Sports:	(None)
Sightseeing:	Alarcón, Cuenca Province and the *casas colgadas* of the city of Cuenca

Hotel Doña Maria
Seville

If there is a tourism destination where the reality is a carbon-copy of a travel poster, it surely is Seville. It's operetta or *zarzuela* come alive. And that's before you have a sip of sherry or sangria.

The city's cathedral is the largest in Spain; indeed, the largest Gothic building in the world. But just an orange-blossom breath away is a small townhouse which we think is the most romantic hideaway in this most enchanting of towns. The four-star, antique-filled, Hotel Dona Maria seems to have been created just for lovers.

Take a guest room...any guest room. It will be discreetly illuminated, probably by low-watt lanterns or a crystal chandelier. The focus will be where it belongs—on the bed. If you insist, you can have twins, positioned side-by-side, like shy newlyweds, but unabashed romantics will insist on a double-size four-poster of antique brass, its canopy the most delicate of white lace, its coverlet a matching spread that could be the gauzy fabric of a bridal gown.

The hotel has 61 rooms, each decorated in regional style with authentic antiques and (if needed) reproductions. Each has a radio (to play at its very lowest volume, naturally) and a telephone (to take off the hook). You'll breakfast-in-bed at any time until 11, of course. Breakfast is the only "real" meal served at the Doña Maria. This hotel isn't for those who want (heavens!) to dress up and dine in a proper room. Rather, envision the two of you, bodies glistening from a postbath oil-massage, feeding each other snacks and sharing icy drinks, unobtrusively delivered by room service.

After your postbreakfast, postluncheon or postwhatever nap, take the tiny hotel elevator (note its brass door handle) to the roof. There, by the minuscule swimming pool, you can sun, order drinks from the poolside bar, then retreat to canvas-topped loungers where you're shielded from the sun while you admire each other and/or the panorama of the Seville skyline, dominated by the nearby Giralda Tower, formerly a Moorish minaret.

Should you have any questions about sightseeing, restaurants, where to engage a horse and carriage or such, ask for Manager Pedro (Peter) Oppawsky. Peter, born in East Germany, speaks English fluently, which he learned first in London, before polishing it with phrases picked up from the many English travelers who gravitate to the island of Ibiza, where he was long a hotelier. A romantic himself, Peter is married to a Sevillana who slowly lured him back to live in the fairytale city of her birth. (J.A.)

Name: Hotel Doña Maria

Manager: Pedro Oppawsky

Address: Don Remondo 19, Sevilla 4

Location: In the very heart of Sevilla

Telephone: (954) 224990

Cables: Maryhotel Sevilla

331

Reps: (None)

Credit Cards: American Express, Visa

Rooms: 61 rooms, 2 suites (all with air-conditioning)

Meals: Breakfast 7:30–11; room service for drinks and snacks 7:30 A.M.–11 P.M.

Entertainment: Taped music in lobby and lounge, TV in rooms; cafés and flamenco in town

Sports: Small cooling-off pool on roof; tennis, golf, horseback riding nearby.

Sightseeing: Seville—the Cathedral (with its art by Murillo, Morales and Zurbarañ) and Giralda Tower, the Alcázar and its gardens; Fine Arts Museum, Tower of Gold, the Santa Cruz Quarter; Holy Week processions, the Seville Fair (after Easter)

P.S. Some tour groups ("but very small ones")

Parador del Condestable Davalos
Ubeda

Time stopped in Ubeda somewhere around 1500. Black-clad matrons still scrub their narrow doorways here, the clip-clop of donkey hooves still echoes through the cobbled streets.

Actually, two cultures have survived in this tiny town—Moorish and Castilian. The twisting lanes of white-washed Andalusian houses open unexpectedly into hushed squares of plantings, or lead to Renaissance palaces whose stony honey-gold grandeur reflects the heritage of Castile. The mix is so unusual that the whole town has been declared a National Monument to preserve its unique atmosphere.

In the finest of Ubeda's squares, the Plaza de Vazquez de Molina, you'll find the town hall, two dazzling churches and a bed for the night in the Palacio del Condestable Davalos, built as a palace for Dean Ortega in the 1500s, now a *parador* offering palatial lodgings.

The entry leads to a tiled, plant-filled courtyard surrounded by an arcade of marble columns. At the top of a great arched staircase with heavy carved wooden bannisters, a glassed-in walkway overlooks the court and leads to the beamed bedrooms. Each is a story and a half high, with windows almost to the ceiling. From the carved headboards to the pottery inkwells on the massive wooden writing tables, the furnishings—both antiques and excellent copies—have obviously been chosen with great care to reflect the history of the house. Even the original window glass has been preserved wherever possible.

In a handsome dining room downstairs, costumed waitresses serve the typical foods of the region. Here in the heart of olive-growing country, you might want to try the *tajo redondo con aceitunas*—(roast veal with olives). A spicy concoction called *callos a la andalusia* (tripe with chick peas in tomato sauce) is another regional favorite, and a specialty of the house is *bezcocho barracho* or tipsy cake, laced with sherry.

The *parador* is small and it is easy to meet people when you want to. On the main floor, besides the dining room, you'll find a comfortable traditional sitting room, a cozier small lounge, and, across, the patio, a quiet library. Downstairs the old wine cellar has been turned into a tavern offering a rustic setting for a before-dinner drink.

Beyond the door, a dozen notable churches and palaces are waiting to be explored—as well as those old Andalusian lanes. Time may have stopped in Ubeda, but the memories will linger on for years. (E.B.)

Name: Parador Nacional Condestable Davalos

Manager: Juan A. Fernández

Address: Plaza Vasquez de Molina, Ubeda

Location: In the center of town, Ubeda is less than a hundred miles north of Granada, fifteen miles east of Linares.

Telephone: 750345, 750341 and 750347

Cables: Paral Ubeda

Reps: Hamsa

Credit Cards: American Express, Diners Club, Visa, Master Charge/ Eurocard

---

Rooms: 25

Meals: Breakfast 8-11, lunch 1-4, dinner 9-11; dinner for two approx. $14-$16; informal dress; room service during dining room hours

---

Entertainment: (None—but seven (*seven!*) discos in Ubeda)

Sports: (None)

Sightseeing: Ubeda, Jaén, Baeza, Granada and the Sierra Nevadas

333

Parador de San Francisco
Granada

WW✕$

Strolling among the fountains and gardens and delicately carved Moorish halls of the 13th century Alhambra is like stepping into a real-life *Arabian Nights*. And you can actually stay right within this fairytale complex, enjoying your Arabian or whatever nights—if you plan ahead.

The Parador de Francisco, at the southern end of the Jardines del Partal, was a convent built on the site of an old mosque by Queen Isabella, in thanks for the defeat of the Muslims in Granada in 1492. It held a national place of honor while the bodies of Ferdinand and Isabella were interred there, but when the royal couple were moved to Granada's main cathedral, the convent was first neglected, then commandeered as a barracks, a storehouse and finally an art school before it was rescued and transformed into a *parador* in 1944.

Some of the arches and towers, fretted plasterwork, cloister and gardens remain, as do some of the original rooms, notably one of the large square public rooms with an arabesque ceiling. The tile-ceilinged, massive-doored rooms on the second floor offer fine antiques and the colorfully figured native rugs and Andujarra fabrics of the region.

Gleaming copper and pottery accessories reflect the heavy hewn beams of the ceiling and the great stone fireplace that fills one wall of the dining room. From the wide windows you can feast on an unforgettable scene—the minaret towers of the Alhambra in all their majesty. From your table, you can feast on Serrano ham, sugar cured in the surrounding Sierra Nevada mountains, one of the superbly prepared provincial specialties here. Try, too, the unusual garlic soup, made with ground almonds, or the moorish *hojaldres* pastries.

Parador de San Francisco would be an atmospheric inn no matter where it was located, but its exceptional site is an experience not to be missed. It has been enlarged in recent years, but it is still booked many months in advance. Make your plans early. At the least, mark this down as a stop for lunch or dinner. If you can't have an Arabian Night's Dream, make sure you enjoy an Arabian Day's Dream here. (E.B.)

Name: Parador Nacional San Francisco

Manager: Enrique Martinez Ferrándiz

Address: Bosques de la Alhambra, Granada

---

334   **Location:**   In the ancient Alhambra, in town, which is about 90 miles

from the airport at Málaga, or more than 200 miles from Madrid

Telephone: 221493 or 221462

Cables: Paral Granada

Reps: Hamsa

Credit Cards: American Express, Diners Club, Visa, Master Charge/ Eurocard

Rooms: 59 (with air-conditioning)

Meals: Breakfast 8–11, lunch 1–4, dinner 9–11; dinner for two approx. $18–$22, informal dress; room service during dining room hours

Entertainment: Cafés, clubs and so on in town

Sports: Nearby only

Sightseeing: Granada, the Sierra Nevadas; various folk events and festivals

P.S. Because the Alhambra is one of *the* major tourist attractions, you can expect to rub shoulders now and then with groups

Parador Gibralfaro
Málaga

Perched on high cliffs just a breath away from the ruins of the ancient fortress from which it borrows its name, Málaga's Parador Gibralfaro appears as if it has been overlooking the magnificent port for as long as the fort. Not so. Gibralfaro, the fort, was founded by the Phoenicians and reconstructed by the Arabs in the 8th century, but this government-run *parador* wasn't built until 1948. Situated on a minimountain at the end of a winding, narrow road, the rough-stone structure functioned initially as a restaurant. Then, in 1966, guest rooms were added. The enchanting result is a three-star gem which has a dozen rooms and can accommodate 24 fortunate guests. Advance reservations are strongly suggested but sometimes (aren't lovers said to be always lucky?) you can drive right up and find a room.

The *parador*'s interior is quintessentially Hispanic: textured, white-washed walls, arched windows, marble or tile floors, rustic walnut

335

furniture. Thoughtful touches provide an individual imprint: poinsettias in hand-painted pottery cachepots for a flick of color, blue-and-white dishes embedded as integral parts of a wall, pierced tin lanterns to filter the light and flicker intriguing designs.

There are several diversions to keep you from dashing to your room: a walnut bar from which you can order your favorite libation, leather and black wrought-iron chairs in which to lounge, a long balcony from which to gaze at Andalusian stars while you savor the perfume from the exotic flowers which are Málagan delights.

Our favorite guest room is 6, entered by turning the big black metal knob in the center of its walnut door. It's a spacious retreat in which a pair of twin beds cozy close so that you can hold hands while resting on pristine linen (the maid has thoughtfully laid back the spreads). Each bed has not one but two down-filled pillows which extend its entire width, with a single leather headboard against a white wall. The restrained decoration is limited to a single Santos carving.

A pair of hand-woven area rugs add a dash of color but the red tile floor begs for bare feet. You'll probably want to snatch a minute or two on your large, private balcony, seated on a pair of tapestry-upholstered bergères, and you'll bathe (or shower) in a room almost as large as the bedroom.

Even Eden must have had its flaws, and here the discordant note is a minibar—convenient, perhaps, for a sudden thirst, but modern and jarring nonetheless. And the pretty dining room on the second floor is marred somewhat by the aromas (and loud conversation) coming from its adjacent kitchen. Although there is supposed to be an English-speaking head waiter, he was absent during the dinner hour and the three gray-uniformed waitresses with black aprons were, as often happens in these parts, a bit dour. An ample menu (and wine list), in Spanish throughout, features a three-course dinner that includes Spanish tortilla (*omelette,* Spanish style, with potato) or swordfish (a local specialty) and flan with sinfully rich chocolate sauce. Take your time over lunch and dinner, because there's not much else to do up here. No tennis, no golf, not even a swimming pool. Gibralfaro is for those who want a retreat, an opportunity to concentrate on each other. (J.A.)

Name:	Parador Nacional Gibralfaro
Manager:	José Antonio Goni Stroetgen
Address:	Málaga, Spain
Location:	In the hills above Málaga

Telephone: (952) 22-1902/3/4

Cables:	Paral Malaga
Reps:	Hamsa

Credit Cards: American Express, Diners Club, Visa, Master Charge/ Eurocard

Rooms: 12 (not air-conditioned)

Meals: Breakfast 8–11, lunch 1–4, dinner 9–11 (on the terrace in summer); dinner for two approx. $18–$20; informal dress; full room service during dining room hours

Entertainment: The lights of Málaga

Sports: None at the hotel; beaches, tennis, golf, horseback riding nearby

Sightseeing: In Málaga, several museums, Gibralfaro Castle, Alcazaba, Roman theater, Puerta Oscura gardens; bull fights (in a 100-year-old arena which can be visited even when no corridas are scheduled); various folk and religious festivals throughout the year; day trips to Granada in the north, Marbella and Gibraltar in the south

Paradores Nacional

The four *paradores* described above are part of a chain of similar hostelries set up by the Spanish government. They are usually in former monasteries, convents or castles, but a few are modern structures without much personality. Among those we have heard good reports about (that is, in relation to this guide) but have not yet had a chance to visit, include the following *paradores: Casa del Corregidor* in Arcos de la Frontera, *Conde de Orgaz* in Toledo, *Reyes Catolicos* in Mojácar and *El Emperador* in Fuenterrabia. Rates are similar to those mentioned above, and together they will allow you to visit a substantial cross section of Spain.

In the following pages, you will find a selection of inns, hotels and resorts that did not make the guide proper. In some cases, this was due to tight deadlines or budgets, in others to the fact that the establishments were visited as possibilities but didn't quite measure up. However, since most of them may help fill in a few gaps in your itinerary and since several of them are relatively inexpensive, I have included them for your consideration. They are arranged alphabetically by country and by location within the country; as with other entries in this guide, the $ evaluations are based on double occupancy, room only, peak season.

Austria

Gasthof Post, Lech

$$

Try to recall a postcard of a typical Alpine village and you'll come up with something very close to the way Lech looks today. Mountains all around. An impatient stream charging through the middle of the village, its banks lined by chalets with steep roofs and window boxes. The Gasthof Post is a traditional staging inn right in the center of the village (but relatively quiet because of triple-glazed windows), owned by the Moosbrugger family, who have run it since World War II, and renovated in 1972. What you have now is a gleaming, fresh staging inn filled with beautiful hand-painted furniture, wood paneling, matching *duvets* and pillows. There are now 42 spacious rooms and suites, some with working fireplaces, some with ceramic stoves or *Kachelofens*, some with TV, some with minibars. Corridors and halls are decorated with antique mirrors, chests, firearms, staghorns—and pictures of the Dutch royal family who vacation here most winters. The dining rooms are warm and welcoming, and there's a full-size pool with adjoining sauna. Lech is high on the mountains, off the main road between Zurich and Innsbruck. *Gasthof Post, A-6764 Lech am Arlberg. Telephone: (05583) 2060*

Hotel Fondachhof, Salzburg

$$$

This 200-year old mustard-colored villa sits in a large garden on the fringes of Salzburg. It's only 15 minutes from the center of town, but it could be far out in the Salzkammergut, judging from the peace and quiet. Musicians love it (I spotted conductor Christoph von Dohnányi there last time around, and I recall interviewing Zubin Mehta on the terrace several years ago). The lobby is tiny but tidy; a winding stairway leads you up to the 8 guest rooms (the remaining 7 are in a one-year-old annex in the garden). Decor is traditionally elegant, with many antiques; service is efficient and attentive. There's a swimming pool tucked away in a quiet corner of the garden, and just across the lawn from the main entrance, there's a gazebo where you can have afternoon tea and/or drinks. *Hotel Fondachhof, Gaisbergstrasse 46-48, A-5020 Salzburg. Telephone: (06222) 20906/7*

Hotel Österreichischerhof, Salzburg

It's right in the center of town, hardly a hideaway, but half of its 130 rooms face the River Salzach, with views across the old city's spires and domes to the hilltop fortress—surely one of the most romantic cityscapes in Europe. The hundred-year-old ÖH, the favored stop of legendary figures at the Salzburg Festival (Richard Strauss and Arturo Toscanini among them), is old fashioned in the nicest sort of way, with a huge stairwell rising to a glass roof and brightened by ferns and palms on each landing. Every room is different, some with traditional decor, some with modern touches; rooms on the 1st, 2nd and 3rd floors overlooking the Salzach have balconies—but have to be booked months in advance (years in advance during the period of the festival). Some of the rooms have minibars, they're all air-conditioned and double-glazed. The Österreichischerhof has an unusually interesting choice of restaurants—elegant salon, grill room, cellar *Stube*, coffee shop and riverside terrace. *Hotel Österreichischerhof, Schwarzstrasse 5-7, A-5024 Salzburg. Telephone: (06222) 72541*

Belgium

Duc de Bourgogne, Bruges

Bruges itself, with its narrow canals and bridges and spires, is such a charmer you'd almost be willing to stay in a motel just to visit the place. You don't have to, because here's a small (10 room) hotel in a historic building, right on one of the most picturesque corners of the city. Parts of it date from the 14th century, and parts of it still look that way today. The dining rooms are particularly grand, with decorative ceilings, statues, old master paintings, and welcoming place settings on the tables (dinners from $30 for 3 courses to $50 for 5 courses). The dining rooms accommodate over a hundred guests at a sitting, so don't expect to have the place all to yourselves. *Hotel-Restaurant Duc de Bourgogne, Huidenvettersplaats 12, 8000 Brugge. Telephone: (050) 332038*

Hotel Erasmus, Bruges

An alternative to the Duc de Bourgogne, just across the canal, the Erasmus has a fairly large *taveerne* on street level, with contemporary light wood decor, and 8 guest rooms upstairs. They're tastefully decorated (by the owners, a young couple called Allewaert) with tinted glass, snazzy bedside lamps and soft neutral colors. Each room has a minibar and radio, and a toilet kit with tube of bath oil, toilet soap, shower cap and shoe cleaner. The rooms are fairly snug (likewise the corridors) and only three of them face the canal, but it's a comfortable, pleasant inn, a shade overpriced, perhaps. You can dine inexpensively in the *taveerne* to compensate for the room rates. *Hotel Erasmus, Wollestraat 35, 8000 Brugge. Telephone: (050) 335781*

La Commanderie, Villers-le-Temple

This venerable building dates from the 13th century, when it became the Commandery of the Knights Templar. Old gray stones with climbing vine, cobbled courtyards, venerable trees, beamed ceilings, comfortable rustic furnishings—it has just about everything you look for in a secluded hideaway with personality. Unfortunately, the people who run it seem to think they're custodians of the Holy Grail rather than innkeepers, so we can't promise an enthusiastic reception. However, if you can't get a room in the three Ardennes hideaways listed elsewhere in this guide, La Commanderie could be considered an alternative possibility. It's a short drive southwest of Liège, a few backroads off highway N 36. *La Commanderie, Villers-le-Temple. Telephone: (085) 511701*

Denmark

The Plaza Hotel, Copenhagen

$$$

  If you want to be as close to Tivoli as possible, you can't do better than the Plaza. It's very well run, steeped in tradition and expectedly expensive. The Flora Danica restaurant at the Plaza is one of the city's best—and the library bar is a knockout. Brush off the autograph hounds who'll be sizing you up at the front door. Visiting celebs all seem to stay at the Plaza—Mick Jagger, Birgit Nilsson, Liza Minelli, Kris Kristofferson. 120 rooms, 10 suites. *The Plaza Hotel, 4 Bernstorffsgade, 1577 Copenhagen V. Telephone: (01) 14 92 62*

Schackenborg Slotskro, Møgeltønder

$

You wouldn't want to go out of your way to find this little pocket of antiquity in South Jutland, but if you happen to be tootling around in the general area, you'll find it a very pleasant stopover. Møgeltønder is a tiny town of 730 inhabitants. You may find it vaguely reminiscent of Williamsburg. Rows and rows of bay-windowed brick houses lined up on a cobblestone road. Keep those cobbles in mind when you're reserving a room. Ask for a room in back—it's quieter. Rooms are simple but quite appealing. The modern tiled bathrooms have adjustable thermostats—you can dial the temperature you want to step out into after your morning bath. The Slotskro's food is something special. Be sure you try the salmon soufflé in pastry crust. It's outstanding. And very rich. For dessert try the blackberry sorbet with cassis, so tart it may leave your mouth permanently puckered. *Schackenborg Slotskro, Møgeltønder, 72, 6270 Tonder. Telephone: (04) 74 83 83*

England

The Manor House, Castle Combe

If you saw the Rex Harrison movie *Dr. Doolittle*, you saw Castle Combe, as pretty a hamlet as you will find anywhere. Just on the edge of the marketplace, a curving driveway leads you through a 26-acre park with brooks and lawns, statues and arbors to this lovely, honey-colored 18-century mansion (parts of it are much older). The setting, then, is splendid, and the lobby and lounges try to preserve much of the charm of a gracious country home, but somehow the Manor House falls between two stools—just too big to be a cozy personable inn, too small to afford the comforts of a first-class hotel. One bedroom at least (the one in the brochure, of course) has a four-poster bed, the others available for inspection were routine, and the dining room at the rear looks as though it has been tacked on to cater to coach parties. The Manor House is one of the most famous country-house hotels in England, but you'll probably be happier at nearby places like Huntstrete House near Bath or Whatley Manor in Easton Grey. 34 rooms, some share bathrooms. *The Manor House, Castle Combe, Wiltshire SN147HR. Telephone: (0249) 782206*

The Crown Inn, Chiddingfold

A village green, a half-timbered inn with a vine-framed door that has welcomed guests for something like 700 years—what could be more "Olde England"? It was built originally as a rest home for Cistercian monks making the pilgrimage from Winchester to Canterbury; Edward VI, the Boy King, stayed here when his troops bivouacked on the green. In the 1950s, The Crown was completely restored. There are only five guest rooms, small to begin with, smaller still to accommodate private bathrooms. None of them would justify a detour just to stay here (the prize is the Four Poster Room) but if you collect old inns, this is an adequate overnight stop. But *mid*week. At weekends the place overflows with day trippers come to sample the fare in one of the inn's four dining spots—the Bistro (the oldest part of the inn, with an inglenook fireplace and linenfold paneling), the main restaurant (tapestries, fireplaces, Chiddingfold stained-glass windows), the pub (complete with dart board) and the courtyard barbecue ("We supply the food, you do the cooking"). The inn is about an hour's drive from London, in a lovely part of England, just off Highway A283. *The Crown Inn, Chiddingfold, Surrey. Telephone: (WO42879) 2255*

Petty France, Dunkirk

Petite France, alias Petty France, gets its name from an early settlement of Huguenot refugees, but the present country house dates from Georgian days. In recent years, new owners have spruced it up with decorator colors (apricot, melon, ecru, cafe au lait, mocha—that sort of thing), comfy sofas and log fires. All 17 bedrooms have private bath or shower, color TV and telephones, including the 8 rooms across the courtyard in the former stables (smaller rooms, with bathrooms upstairs). The dining room is particularly attractive. Ditto the rates, around $50 for two, including English breakfast. It sits on 4½ acres of gardens, on a back road (A46) just north of Bath. *Petty France Hotel, Dunkirk, nr. Badminton, Avon. Telephone: (045) 423361*

Lythe Hill Hotel, Haslemere

The concept is typical English/14th-century farmhouse converted into an atmospheric restaurant serving French cooking. It's in one of the loveliest (and most historic) corners of the English countryside, about an hour's drive southwest of London, and the restaurant is worth the drive. Across the courtyard, a group of 16th-century farm buildings have been renovated into additional guest rooms and drinking-and-dining spots, with decor that blends old and new very deftly. The most comfortable rooms are in the new wing, the most interesting in the 14th-century house; but alas, *the* most interesting room, the Tudor Room with its rafter ceiling and canopy bed, also has a sign on the door saying "Fire Exit." For energetic types there are walking trails, croquet, tennis and sauna. Lythe Hill is a pleasant spot for

345

an overnight stop, with lots of sights to see in the neighborhood, but expect to encounter a few business groups scuttling around. 27 rooms, 8 suites. *Lythe Hill Hotel, Petworth Road, Haslemere, Surrey GU372BQ. Telephone: (0428) 51251*

Wales

The Hand Hotel, Llanarmon

This village is well off the beaten track, 9 miles west of a town called Oswestry, and let's hope you find it without having to ask directions, in which case you might have to identify it by its full name—Llanarmon Dyffryn-Ceiriog. (There are two other Llanarmon.) It's up in the hills, along a winding country road, and over an old stone bridge that spans a mountain stream. The Hand is a typical Welsh country inn, with whitewashed stone walls and black trim on doors and gabled windows. A big open fire welcomes you into the cozy pub that doubles as reception; the raftered dining room is at the rear, facing the garden. The inn was bought several years ago by industrialist Sir Alfred McAlpine as a hunting lodge for his friends, but when they're not in residence, the 8 guest rooms upstairs (simply furnished, but each with private bathroom) are available for paying guests. *The Hand Hotel, Llanarmon D.C. Telephone:Llanarmon D.C. 666*

Ynyshir Hall, Machynlleth

To answer your question, it's pronounced (very approximately) *ma-hunk-lith*, and it's 12-miles inland from a place called Aberystwyth, halfway up the coast of Wales. Ynyshir, the "House on the Island," is just that—a house on an island that also happens to be a bird sanctuary. "Hall" is maybe too grand a title, although it was once the country estate of Mr. Mappin of Mappin & Webb, the famous silversmiths of Bond Street in London. Its peach-colored facade rises above gardens filled with magnolias and eaves-high rhododendrons. Rustic chairs and ta-bles dot the lawn, sheep graze in the pasture beyond the fence. A friendly English family, the Hugheses, recently took the place over, and although they're adding a few touches of their own, this is basically a pleasant guest house with homey country-cousin decor. Some of the decor in the dining room may suggest slightly eccentric country cousins, but the food is well-prepared, and served, as one would hope in the former home of a silversmith, on tables with silver candlesticks and cruets. Very peaceful. 10 rooms. *Ynyshir Hall, Eglwysfach, Machynlleth, Powys, SY208TA. Telephone: (065-474) 209*

France

Le Mas d'Aigret, Les Baux-de-Provence

Located on the opposite side of this village/fortress from its illustrious competitor, Oustau de Baumanière, Mas d'Aigret gives you a chance to explore this fascinating region at more moderate prices. It's relatively new, incorporating a Provençal farmhouse at the base of the cliff, with some attractive rustic design motifs using the cliffs and native stone and big open fires in the bar, lounge and restaurant. The bedrooms, however, play safe—pleasant, comfortable but undistinguised decor.15 rooms, small pool and garden. *Le Mas d'Aigret, 13520 Les Baux-de-Provence. Telephone: (90) 973354*

Auberge De La Benvengudo, Les Baux-de-Provence

Another inexpensive alternative to Baumanière, this time on the Route d'Arles. It's only about ten years old, although the bastide itself dates back to the 18th century, with a year-old annex. Only 16 rooms, pleasantly decorated, some with antiques; rustic dining room, where M. and Mme. Beaupied serve dinners for only 100 francs, or thereabouts, for two. The terrace and garden are pretty spots to relax and plan trips to Arles, Nimes, St.-Remy and all the interesting places nearby. *Hotel La Benvengudo, 13520 Les Baux-de-Provence. Telephone: (90) 973250*

Mas La Cascade, La Celle

D554 is not exactly a speedway, but even so you could easily pass the La Cascade before noticing it—a small ochre wall topped with ochre tiles, right by the edge of the road. It looks plain, maybe even dull, from the roadway, but once inside the driveway it's a different story—a rushing stream, birds singing, rustic tables set up beneath the trees. Indoors, the Mas has something of the atmosphere of the American Southwest—roughhewn beams overhead, tile floors underfoot, sturdy rustic furniture, and two big open fires, one in the lounge, one in the dining room. The kitchen is right there at the entrance, open to view, the chef cooking over a wood fire— steaks, brochettes, chops which fill the lobby with appetizing odors. The dining room seats at most three dozen diners, and most of them have some sort of view through the big windows beside the cascade. Mas La Cascade is really a *relais gastronomique*, that is, a place to stop off and have a meal, about $25–$30 for two, but the dozen rooms upstairs are average-sized, attractive (rustic again, with low beamed ceilings, period furnishings, comfy beds, tiled bathrooms) and you may want to spend the night here and wake up to the birds singing and the stream trickling over *la cascade*. It's located about 2½ kms. from Briguole, on the road to Toulon. *Hotel Mas La Cascade, La Celle (Var). Telephone: (1694) 690785*

Hotel Marc-Hely, La Colle-sur-Loup

Palms, olives and one very old fig tree shade the garden, and the view from your balcony (every room has one) covers a classic vista (give or take a telephone pole or two) of St.-Paul-de-Vence perched on its hilltop. La Colle-sur-Loup itself is also a popular spot with artists, but otherwise it makes an ideal center for touring this region (it's only 7 minutes from Nice Airport on a new highway). The Marc-Hely's 12 guest rooms are decorated in simple, country-inn style, but with modern bathrooms. It has a guest-house atmosphere, with a small lobby and a few shelves of paperbacks for rainy days; it's friendly, quiet, unpretentious and with its low rates it's a welcome haven in these parts. There's no restaurant, but there are several good eating spots in the neighborhood, including the inexpensive La Vieille Ferme a few yards down the road. *Hotel Marc-Hely, 06480 La Colle-sur-Loup. Telephone: 32.81.48*

La Mayanelle, Gordes

Gordes is one of those intriguing medieval hilltop towns that seem to grow out of the rocks, and La Mayanelle sits right on the edge of the rocky precipice. Of its 10 rooms, half a dozen face "the view," across the plain to the Luberon hills. All the rooms are comfortable; they all have toilets, and all but three of them have baths. The bar and the dining room are the two most interesting parts of the hotel, medieval in spirit, preserving the atmosphere of the narrow cobbled streets and squares, and the towering castle with its new Vasarely Museum. Dinner here is about $40–$50 for two. Closed January to mid-February. *La Mayanelle, 84220 Gordes (Vaucluse). Telephone: (90)720028*

Hotel Le Kilal, Grimaud-Village

$$$

Grimaud-Village is in the hills, and not to be confused with the Port-Grimaud you pass on the road into St.-Tropez. This is an authentic old hillside village with a ruined tower at its highest peak, but the hotel is only a few years old, an architectural sore thumb to many people, no doubt, but a very comfortable deluxe hotel nonetheless. Its fifty guest rooms have fluffy wall-to-wall carpets, artisan decor and contemporary art prints; many of them also have balconies overlooking the hillside and the sea at Port-Grimaud, where, as the Kilal brochure explains, "your boat will be quite safe." A few of the rooms on garden level are particularly attractive, with private, flower-decked terraces or patios, and really rather good value (around $50 for two with breakfast in the off season). Other attractions up here are the restaurant, Le Cabasson, and a hillside pool with sun terrace. This is a place to consider if you want deluxe comforts but don't want to pay St.-Tropez rates. Closed November through March. *Hotel Le Kilal, 83360 Grimaud-Village. Telephone: (94) 432002*

Château du Domaine de Beauvois, Luynes

$$$

What better way to get into the spirit of visiting France's great old châtcaux than to stay in one yourself? There are at least half a dozen in the Loire to choose from—all comfortably plugged into the 20th century without having lost any of their Sun King charm. At Beauvois, for instance, you can spend the night in a room (Room 1) inside a 15th-century stone tower complete with fireplace, stained-glass window, and ancient beams—and then spend the next morning on the tennis court or in the heated swimming pool. The food is quite good here, but the management could use a warmer, more attentive eye, and most of the furnishings would be more at home at a garage sale than in a grand château. *Domaine de Beauvois, 37230 Luynes. Telephone: (47) 555011*

Hôtellerie La Fuste, near Manosque

$$

It's highly regarded by French gourmets for its regional cusine, a lovely 350-year-old *relais de porte* in a leafy garden, filled with the French equivalent of Victoriana—hand-carved chairs, antimacassars, elaborate breakfasts and high decorative ceilings. Bouquets of flowers brighten the tables. The guest rooms are fluffy and French country-innish, mostly quite small but with adequate bathrooms, some with windows opening on to the garden, a few with television. You come here mainly for the food, and you enjoy your meal so much you don't feel like driving elsewhere after you've disposed of the *civet de caneton aux essences de cannelle et d'oranges* or *tranche de gigot de broutard à la crème d'ail*. The dining room personnel show the customary French concern with presentation and correct service, and the dishes certainly live up to expectation. In summer, you dine in the garden, beneath a 300-year-old plane tree. La Fuste is a former staging post on the road between Provence and the Alps, about 3½ miles from the nearest town, by the name of Manosque, which is about all you need to know about it. But it's an interesting drive up from Aix-en-Provence (about 40 miles), on the Route de Barême. Your hosts are La Famille Jourdan—papa in the kitchen, mama as hostess, daughter in the dining room. *Hôtellerie La Fuste, 04210 Valensole. Telephone: (80) 64.05.67*

Added Attractions

Le Baou, Ramatuelle

Ramatuelle is another of those Cote d'Azur hill towns, a circular huddle of cobbled streets and honey-colored stone, in this case, in the hills above St.-Tropez. Le Baou sits on the edge of town with handsome views across the St.-Tropez hinterlands. It's built in traditional style with stone and tile, but the 16 guest rooms have modern decor, a cut above a good motel, with comfortable furnishings and fine bathrooms. Rooms on the lower level have bigger terraces, each separated from its neighbors by hedges. The bar-lounge has TV and taped jazz, and the roomy restaurant has big windows with views of the old town (the restaurant is highly regarded, and you can expect a meal there to set you back $20–$25 a head), and the whole setting is wonderfully restful and unhurried. Closed mid-October to mid-March. *Hôtellerie le Baou, 83350 Ramatuelle. Telephone: (94) 792048 or 729049*

L'Aubergo dou Souleu, St.-Paul-de-Vence

The hillside setting is similar to the Marc-Hely (above) and the view of St.-Paul-de-Vence is, if anything, even more beautiful from the tree-shaded terrace. The Aubergo is primarily a restaurant (a lovely blue-and-white rustic salon), serving relatively inexpensive meals, but with eight rooms upstairs. They're not as stylish as the dining room, but pleasant, comfortably equipped (they all have private bathrooms) and they cost around $30 double, with breakfast and service charge included. There's a small swimming pool into the bargain. *Aubergo dou Souleu, Route de la Colle, 06570, St.-Paul-de-Vence. Telephone: (93) 32.80.60*

La Colombe d'Or, St.-Paul-de-Vence

$$$

This 3-story hotel on the edge of town is very famous on several counts: it's the place where the walls of the dining room are lined with paintings by some of the artists who congregated on the Riviera; where you dine in the leafy courtyard beside a Légèr mural, swim in the patio pool beside a Calder mobile. It's famous, too, because so many movie stars and celebrities have stayed here. Presumably to have an audience, because the problem is that the Golden Dove is *so* famous it's usually mobbed by sightseers; and since there's a steady, virtually captive clientele, the staff can rarely rustle up more than Gallic-shrug service. Unless, of course, you're one of the celebrities. All of which is a pity, because many of the 24 guest rooms are *very* romantic, and highly original in the way they've matched Contemporary Chic to the eccentric contours of a centuries-old house. All the rooms have private bath, TV, radio, some have open fires, and Room 11 has a bed so large that once you get into it you'll never notice the crowds downstairs. If you decide to try the Colombe d'Or, go in the off-season, when you'll probably have a better chance of restfulness and acceptable service. Closed mid-November to mid-December. *La Colombe d'Or, 06570 St.-Paul-de-Vence (Alpes-Maritime). Telephone: (93) 328002*

Mas de Chastelas, St.-Tropez

$$

This is a typical Provençal bastide, built a couple of hundred years ago, surrounded by vineyards and orchards, about ten minutes outside of town. It was restored and converted into a 19-room inn in 1978 by a Parisian architect and a Parisian businessman. It's a deft combination of city chic and country simplicity, its flagstone floors contrasting with banquettes in contemporary stripes, decorator colors offset by the rustic effect of straw mats and wicker chairs. Rooms have private bathrooms, each floor has a small library; there's a separate lounge for TV viewers, and there are four tennis courts (2 lighted) a few yards away. This *mas* is a pleasant alternative to a St.-Trop hotel—close enough to the action, detached enough for peace and quiet and fresh air, with a young, sophisticated clientele. Closed mid-October through March. *Le Mas de Chastelas, 83990 St.-Tropez. Telephone: (94) 560911*

Hotel La Ponche, St.-Tropez

$$

This is the sort of small, unassuming charmer favored by people like Françoise Sagan, Raymond Loewy and Juliette Greco. It's right in the middle of town, on an atmospheric street a short walk from the waterfront, a typical St.-Trop house converted into a small hotel—but with rare taste and style. The owner's son-in-law, Jacques Cordier, is a painter of some note in these parts and his works grace the walls of hallways and guest rooms. Decor is chic, each room is different, so here is a rundown of some of the more distinctive among the 22 rooms available: 5 is small, above the Ponche's restaurant, with a view of the sea a hundred yards away; 10 has a huge bed and a balcony with views of sea, rooftops, TV aerials and the citadel; 22 is an attractive attic, white-on-white with contemporary furnishings and a large terrace (but with its low ceilings, probably not for tall people—at least not in an upright position). All rooms have bath or shower, phone, 7 have TV, 4 have refrigerators. Very French, very special. Open all year. *Hotel-Restaurant La Ponche, 83 St.-Tropez. Telephone: (94) 970253 or 971327*

Le Ya Ca, St.-Tropez

Walk a few narrow streets up the hill from the Port des Pêcheurs and you come to this vine-covered hotel (guest house, really) behind a stone wall. In a courtyard at the rear, guests sit at tables in the shade of pepper and palm trees, or dunk themselves in the pool. High walls screen out the neighbors. It's a friendly, simple atmosphere. The lobby isn't too promising, but the 23 guest rooms (all with private bathroom and air-conditioning) are attractive. Especially Rooms 9 and 10, with views across the St.-Tropez rooftops and the harbor, and 26 and 27 which have roof-high terraces. Facilities include bar/lounge, restaurant and a sauna. Open all year. *Hotel Le Ya Ca, Boulevard d'Aumale, 83990 St.-Tropez. Telephone: (94) 971179 or 971299*

Hotel de l'Abbaye, Talloires

$$

A few yards down the shore of Lake Annecy from the renowned Auberge du Père Bise, this sober-sided four-story hotel was once the abbey of the Benedictines. It dates from the 11th century, but was largely restored in the 17th century, then restored once more before being converted to a hotel. Within its great stone walls you'll find ancient cobbled courtyards with weathered fountains, a dining terrace beneath the trees, hallways lined with sober antiques. The guest rooms are comfortable, without being exceptional, most of them with period furnishings; some have small balconies overlooking the courtyard and gardens, but the prime chambers are those overlooking the garden and the lake. Unfortunately, the staff on a recent visit was about as enthusiastic and welcoming as a Benedictine with *la gueule du bois*. 40 rooms. *Hotel de l'Abbaye, 74290 Talloires (Haute-Savoie). Telephone: (50) 447081 and 447202*

Germany

Romantik Hotel Post, Aschaffenburg

$$

If you're arriving at Frankfurt Airport and heading south, avoid the city traffic and spend the night in nearby Aschaffenburg. Though there's not much left to the original Royal Bavarian Post Station here, the cozy Hotel Post boasts kings, prime ministers and even the Dalai Lama in its guest book—and one good reason why is its dining room, known far and wide. The rooms are basic but comfortable, and with a well stocked minibar at hand. There's a nice indoor pool, sauna and solarium to ease your jet lag. But the high spot of your stay will be the menu, strongly influenced by the French *nouvelle cuisine* and changing with the seasons to feature the freshest of game and fish, the sweetest strawberries, the tenderest mushrooms and white asparagus, all freshly prepared to your order. And while you're waiting, the paneled dining room is chock full of interesting things to look at—illuminated paintings, an old stagecoach, copper tools, swords, rifles, hunters' horns and a big display of local Franken wines which you'll probably want to sample with your meal. 75 rooms. *Romantik Hotel Post, 8750 Aschaffenburg. Telephone: 06021/21333*

Hotel Weisses Rossle, Hinterzarten, Black Forest

$$

Here's another 600-year-old historic Black Forest inn in the beautiful town of Hinterzarten, but once you get past the traditional facade of the Weisses Rossle, you're likely to think it's brand new. Tasteful, too. The rooms, public and private, are large and well furnished. In the newer "sun wing," connected by an underground walkway to the main complex, every room is almost a suite and has a private balcony. Facilities galore: you can ski and skate, hike, play tennis, tone up in the sauna and solarium, swim in an indoor pool. There are two dining rooms, a low-ceilinged *Stube* and a pleasant airy room with big windows, as well as a wide outdoor terrace with a view and convivial bars indoors and out. The food is just fine, especially the local specialty, smoked trout. The Weisses Rossle is a place for all ages

355

(lots of families here) with a long list of planned activities, dancing every night, a place for a busy outdoorsy holiday. But it is a shame that they didn't keep just a bit more of that traditional atmosphere. *Hotel Weisses Rossle, Hochschwartzwald, Hinterzarten. Telephone: 07652/1411-13*

Hotel-Gaststätte zur Post, Unterwossen

Could the German tourist office have planted those perfect little Bavarian villages? Wait until you see them, lined with tiny wooden two-story chalets, balconies overrun with flowers, colorful paintings on many of the facades, those magnificent Alps hovering in the background. You mustn't miss them—in fact, you really should try to stop in one, at least for one night, and the Zur Post, located between Munich and Salzburg, is a good choice at a good price. It's not an elaborate place, just one that's typical of the region in one of the picturesque villages. Rooms are simple and comfortable, with tiny balconies with a view, and there's a great big outdoor terrace where you can contemplate the mountains while you drink or dine. If there's a chill in the air, come in and warm up around the old-fashioned stove in the lobby, and choose from three or four indoor dining rooms, all done up in rustic Bavarian style in varying color schemes, and most of them also with a view. There's skiing here in winter, lakes and places to walk in warm weather, and most of all, year-around, a taste of everyday country life in one of Germany's most delightful areas. 60 beds. *Hotel Gaststätte zur Post, 8211 Unterwossen. Telephone: 08641/8305/8117*

Greece

Athenian Inn, Athens

Inside, you could be on a Greek island (white stucco walls, dark beams, tiled floors) but in fact you're in one of the fashionable districts of Athens, known as Kolonaki. The streets here are lined with high-rent apartments and expensive (by Athens' standards) restaurants; the American Embassy is a few blocks in one direction, Kolonaki Square, with all its terrace cafés, in the other. The inn is owned by a Greek-American couple, who've decorated its 28 rooms with rustic beds and fabrics, but added wall-to-wall carpeting, bath or shower, radio and telephone. Most of the rooms have balconies of sorts, a few with views of Lycabettus Hill. At less than $30 double, including breakfast in the rustic lounge, this is one of the best values in Athens. (Parking would be a disaster—make sure you don't have a car.) *Athenian Inn, 22 Haritos Street, Athens. Telephone: 738097*

Xenia Hotel, Tsangarádha

The attraction here is the setting rather than the hotel—a rather mundane structure (albeit of natural stone), with balconies, small rooms, cot beds and a dull dining room. But it sits on the side of a precipitous hill, on the far side of Mount Pelion and Volos, high above the Aegean Sea. The village teeters on the side of the hill, its mule-wide, cobbled streets running from a square dominated by a large church and a massive plane tree said to be 800 years old. A flower-lined path leads up to a typical *taverna* with a vine-covered terrace, and a maze of mule paths crisscross the hillside. You can follow these paths all the way down the hill to the beach, but before you do anything so foolhardy, think about how you're going to get back up. There are beaches nearby, accessible by car, with beachside *tavernas* and refreshments; otherwise, there's nothing to do here but commune with each other and the shades of ancient Greeks. Tsangarádha is a wonderfully isolated corner of Greece, yet interesting simply because it's so different from the usual image of Athens or the Greek islands. *Xenia Hotel, Tsangarádha. Telephone: 29205, 29351*

Naxos Beach Hotel, Naxos

This is another get-away-from-it-all, back-to-basics spot. To begin with, you can't fly there, you have to take a ferry— a trip of at least 6 hours from Piraeus. Naxos is, if you recall, the island where Ariadne was abandoned by Theseus, the largest of the Cyclades but still virtually unspoiled. There are a few Byzantine things to see—towers, castles, churches and so on—but mostly you come here to loaf and lounge and laze. The Naxos Beach is the place to do just that. It's modern, small (20 rooms plus 5 suites for families), but decorated and furnished with more flair than you normally find on these islands, using styles and fabrics in keeping with its island heritage. It's located at the quiet end of the beach, but accessible to the best stretches of sand, and you can, if you feel so inclined (and show some respect for the sun) walk into town to drink or dine in a waterfront *taverna*. *Naxos Beach Hotel and Bungalows, Naxos. Telephone: (0285)22928*

Holland

Hotel Canal House, Amsterdam

For people who want to stay on one of those lovely canals, but can't afford the rates at the Pulitzer Hotel, this 17th-century patrician mansion on the Emperor's Canal is a short walk from the Royal Palace, the Westerkerk (where Rembrandt is buried) and the Anne Frank House. Breakfast is served in what was once a gracious dining salon with lofty ceilings, chandeliers and tall windows overlooking a garden shaded by walnut trees. The lobby and reception room are not quite so grand (not yet, the owners are slowly upgrading the entire house), but the guest rooms are pleasantly bright with beamed ceilings, exposed brick walls and colorful bedspreads and drapes. Some rooms overlook the canal (a few of them without private bath), while the newly renovated rooms at the rear, overlooking the walnut trees, have handsomely tiled modern bathrooms. *Hotel Canal House, 148 Keizersgracht, Amsterdam. Telephone: (020) 225182*

Hotel Oranjeoord, Hoog Soeren

$$

This is a country inn, pure and simple. what it lacks in comeliness and sophistication is more than made up in its general conviviality. Where else can you hear fascinating sea stories from a man who has sailed around the world alone? Not that owner/manager Eelco Kasemier is at all garrulous. He isn't, but when coaxed he can spin a tale or two about going around Cape Horn the hard way, against the wind, in a 40-foot ketch. He can also discuss macrobiotic food at length. But you must ask. The Oranjeoord is a very plain place but homey and comfortable. And it is beautifully situated, just skirting the magnificent grounds which surround the royal family's Het Loo Palace (now a museum). You're also quite close to one of the best restaurants in Holland, De Echoput—don't miss it. *Hotel Oranjeoord, Hoog Soeren. Telephone: (05769) 227*

Hotel-Restaurant Wolfheze, Wolfheze

$$

From the outside it looks like one big mansard roof nestling over an unseen building. From the inside, it is something else again. The lobby is dotted with fern-filled atriums which introduce daylight where you least expect it. Everywhere you look you see ingenious workings of beautiful birch woodwork amid punctuation points of jet-age Italian leather chairs. The imagination ends abruptly when you take the elevator upstairs, however. Rooms are pure assembly line, in the manner of any American motel chain you care to recall. But they are clean and comfortable, and quiet as the night. All rooms have small patios overlooking a lovely woodland. All have color TV. There's also an enormous indoor pool where you can swim away some of your travel fatigue. The dining room is all candlelight and old tradition. Try the *entrecôte Lady Chatterly* or the *sautéed filet of sole George Sand* about $17–$18 for either. Delicious. Though it somehow lacks the snap and singularity of hotels chosen for a full writeup in this guide, the Wolfheze is worth noting. *Hotel Wolfheze, Wolfhezerweg 17, Wolfheze. Telephone: (085) 337852*

Italy

Villa Serbelloni, Bellagio

This is a classic setting—terraces by the lake, palm trees and flowers ringing the lakeside pool, stone steps down to the water, and behind it all a grand yellow-stucco palazzo. The sumptuous interior of marble, chandeliers and frescoes may be fading, but the guest rooms are spacious, decorated in Louis XV or Venetian styles, half of them overlooking the lake, the others the park. (Ask for a room on the north side.) The ornate dining room with its blue-and-silk decorative ceiling is elegant, but you'll probably prefer to dine on the terrace beneath the big awnings so that you can enjoy that soul-stirring view across Lake Como to Monte Grona. 98 rooms (some with minibars, some without private bathrooms). Boating, tennis, ferry trips across the lake. *Grand Hotel Villa Serbelloni, 22021 Bellagio. Telephone: (031) 950261*

Il Pellicano, Port' Ercole

$$$

It sits where you would expect a pelican to sit—on the rocks, beside the shiny sea, in this case beside a cove on the Argentario peninsula. Steep hills that plunge like pelicans into the sea also serve to shut out the mainland and keep this lovely spot unspoiled, despite the fact that it's only a hundred miles from Rome. Il Pellicano is a stylish, open-to-the-breezes villa, with dark beams on white ceilings, colorful decor and tiled floors. Just over half the 31 rooms have sea views and these are the rooms you definitely want— but you must reserve far in advance. There are also a few deluxe apartments in private cottages. Sports facilities include a picturesque saltwater heated pool, water skiing and boat trips to offshore islands; on land, there's a tennis court, and some attractive sightseeing possibilities—to Orvieto, Siena, the Etruscan museum at Tarquinia, the Roman baths at Saturnia. Il Pellicano is pleasantly informal (although shirts or wraps must be worn indoors and on the terrace), quiet and restful ("...on behalf of the many guests who come here for a rest, no radios or other musical instruments are permitted at the pool and beach areas…"). Friday evenings in July and August are given over to buffet dining and dancing by candlelight on the terrace above the cove. *Hotel Il Pellicano, 58018 Port' Ercole. Telephone: (0564) 833801*

Hotel Cardinal, Rome

$$

Via Giulia is one of those narrow, quaint streets in the Trastevere section of Rome, full of atmosphere and character. The Tiber is half a block away, the Piazza Navona and Farnese Palace are within walking distance, St. Peter's is just across the river. This former palace and courthouse was designed by Donato Bramante, one of the great architects of the Renaissance, and the handsome, weathered exterior has been preserved. Much of the interior, too, for that matter, but adapted niftily to contemporary ideas. All rooms have television, minibars and air-conditioning; a few on the fifth floor have balconies overlooking Via Giulia, but the quietest rooms are on the inner courtyard. Guests are expected to wear jacket and tie in the dining room, but there are many delightful, informal *trattorie* in the neighborhood. The problem is: cardinals dress in a not-too-modest red, and so does this hotel—walls of red felt, carpets of red and black. But the lighting is muted, so the overall effect is quiet, formal, elegant. *Hotel Cardinal, Via Giulia 62, Rome. Telephone: (06) 6542787*

Hotel Forum, Rome

$$$

It's not by any means one of the more glamouous hotels in Rome, but you might rub shoulders in the lobby or rooftop restaurant with Robert Redford or Ingmar Bergman. On the other hand, in the rooftop restaurant you might not even notice them, so spectacular is the panorama all around you—the Forum, Colosseum, Forum of Augustus, Capitoline Hill and Trajan's Forum. You can do your sightseeing over a bottle of Frascati. The

361

Forum, as a hotel, is only 20 years old, but for centuries before that it was a monastery. Now all 80 rooms have air-conditioning and radios (TV is available at extra charge). The most private rooms (and most attractively furnished) are on the corners; those on the ground floor tend to pick up some noise from the traffic swirling around the Colosseum (but by day, you can always escape to the roof terrace). Other Forum features include around-the-clock room service and a garage. *Hotel Forum, Via Tor de'Conti 25-30, 00184 Rome. Telephone: (06) 6792446*

Hotel Internazionale, Rome

There are three hotels at the top of the Spanish Steps, on the Via Sistina—one of them, the Hassler, is very expensive and very chic; the other two, the De la Ville (below) and the Internazionale are only moderately expensive. The building itself is 300 or 400 years old, and when it became a hotel in the twenties, many of the grand architectural flourishes were preserved—like the hand-carved wooden stairway in the lobby and the coffered wood ceiling in the dining room. All 41 rooms are different, all have a few antiques, air-conditioning and minibars; 10 have balconies, 6 overlook the Via Sistina, 4 overlook the Villa Martine and its gardens. Rooms 59, 58 and 53 have private terraces—currently in the process of renovation—and they should ultimately be the prize accommodations in the house (but also the most expensive). The staff is very friendly. Parking facilities are available nearby. *Hotel Internazionale, Via Sistina, 00187 Rome. Telephone: 6793047*

Hotel Sitea, Rome

If you're traveling around Europe on a Eurailpass, this is a convenient spot—a hundred yards from the main railroad and airport terminal, directly across the street from the prestigious Grand Hotel. Rooms vary in decor and quality, but most of them have attractive antiques. Your best bets

362

are Rooms 204, 404, 207 and 206, which have balconies—particularly the first two, which overlook a quiet street with a circular church, San Bernardo. The largest rooms are also the noisiest, facing the Grand Hotel. Up on the roof, there's a bar/lounge with a grand piano—lovely place to have a drink in the cool of the evening. The Sitea is air-conditioned throughout. 40 rooms. No credit cards. *Hotel Sitea, Via Vittorio Emanuele Orlando 90, Rome. Telephone: (06) 4751560*

Grand Hotel de la Ville, Rome

$$$

This is one of the favorites of American movie stars, even those who could afford to stay in the more glamorous Hassler next door. It's larger than most hideaways in this guide (189 rooms), but manages to preserve the air of a smaller, more personal hotel. Rooms on the 7th and 8th floors have the grandest views across the rooftops of Rome; otherwise you want a room on the courtyard side, away from the traffic on the Via Sistina. All rooms here have air-conditioning and minibar (TV on request, extra charge). There's also around-the-clock room service; the terrace restaurant serves Italian and international cuisine; the parking garage holds 45 cars. This is a reliable, well-run hotel, watched over for the past quarter century by its elegant *direttore*, Tommaso Melotti. *Grand Hotel de la Ville, Via Sistina 69, 00187 Rome. Telephone: (06) 6798941*

Villa Cortine, Sirmione

$$$

Sirmione is a lovely old walled town at the tip of a peninsula jutting into Lake Garda. No cars clutter its narrow, café-lined streets except for those belonging to local businesses or tourists bound for hotels like the Villa Cortine Palace, which sits in a private estate right at the very tip of the peninsula. The park is filled with fountains and statuary, cypress and cedars (what the brochure calls "secular" trees), leading to the porticoed entrance of a magnificent mansion built at the turn of the century by a German

363
Added Attractions

aristocrat. Fine, up to this point. Unfortunately, the present owner has tacked on a dreary three-story modern wing with balconies, and the dining room is too vast and boring. The guest rooms are adequate, and a few of those in the original mansion are quite grand. Overpriced, perhaps, for what it is, but it certainly is quiet, and it does attract a lot of well-to-do elderly clients who come back year after year. 54 rooms, tennis, pool, private beach. *Villa Cortine Palace Hotel, 25019 Sirmione. Telephone: (081) 910621/2*

Grand Hotel, Stresa

$$$

The full name is Grand Hotel et Iles Borromées, since the hotel is on the shores of Lake Maggiore and almost (but not quite) opposite the three picturesque Borromean islets. Alas, between the terrace and the lake there's a roadway that seems to carry lots of trucks rumbling up to the Simplon Pass; and since Lake Maggiore is no longer one of the essential stops on the European Grand Tour, the Grand Hotel seems to be gearing up for a seminar/convention type of clientele. Nevertheless, Maggiore is a beautiful lake, the Grand is one of those splendid *palazzi* with spacious rooms and high ceilings, chandeliers and marble and grand stairways, so jot it down as a possible overnight stop if you happen to be heading, like the trucks, for the Simplon Pass—or visiting the isles. Of the 151 rooms and suites, almost half have balconies or terraces, some have minibars; the higher you are, the more you see of Lake Maggiore. There are two heated swimming pools in the garden among the cypress and pine trees; and quarter of a mile down the road in Stresa village you can board a boat for the trip over to the Iles Borromées. A CIGA hotel. Closed November through March. *Grand Hotel et Iles Borromées, Corso Umberto 1, 67, 28049 Stresa. Telephone: 30431*

Portugal

Hotel Boa Vista, Albufeira

Just in case the nearby Estalagem do Cerro is filled—or in case you prefer a pool or a more formal hotel setting—here's a pleasant small slab-modern hotel with the same choice location high in the hills above Albufeira. The entry is appealing—marble floors, tiles, comfortable blonde modern furniture with blue-and-beige cushions, jaunty blue sailcloth shades in case the sun gets out of hand. The bedrooms are modern, nothing out of the ordinary, but well furnished with bright red bedspreads and leather banquettes. The marble-decorated baths are a nice touch, as are the spacious balconies overlooking the sea. The dining room shares the lovely view, but it's an attraction in its own right with its parquet floors and patterned draperies. There are two bars—and, best of all, a big round pool perched right on the cliffside looking out at the Albufeira. It's a recommended alternate in one of the Algarve's most picturesque towns. 20 rooms. *Hotel Boa Vista, Albufeira. Telephone: 52175/6/7*

Hotel da Baleeira, Sagres

It's a fairly standard resort hotel (maybe a bit more interesting than most with its native mural out front and the super-modern lounges inside) but the Baleeira deserves special mention because of its extraordinary location, all by itself on a cliff looking down to the colorful fishing harbor at Sagres, out to the rugged coastline and magnificent bay. You can take it all in while sunning at the hexagonal pool, beautifully situated on a ledge at the edge of the cliff—or seated in a plush white modern chair enjoying fresh-caught fish or game in the picture-window dining room cantilevered over the sea. The bedrooms, furnished in spare modern style, have their own private terraces for further sea gazing. (Just be sure to insist on a newer room, since the older ones are smaller and not so well furnished.) If you want to get closer to the ocean, it's just a stroll down the hill to an inviting sandy private beach. 144 rooms. *Hotel da Baleeira, Sagres, Algarve. Telephone: 64212/3* 365

Scotland

Banchory Lodge Hotel, Banchory

The rivers Dee and Feugh come together here in a tumble of rocks and spume, lawns shaded by fir and beech reach down to the river banks, and the world could be miles away. The truth is a hundred yards will put you in the village's main street (passing a campsite along the way), and half-an-hour's drive will deposit you in oil-booming Aberdeen. Banchory Lodge has been an inn for a couple of decades (although the somber-looking house is much older); guest rooms are modest but comfortable (9 is the pick of the bunch, with bay windows overlooking the river, and quite romantic if you can persuade Manager Dugald Jeffreys to remove the extra bed). The restaurant is the big attraction here, with antique clocks and elaborate floral displays, silverware and period furnishings setting off the wholesome country fare—roast lamb, roast beef, heaps of garden-fresh vegetables. Budget about $30 for two, lunch or dinner. Margaret Jeffreys somehow manages to cope with both the cooking and the floral displays, the young staff is attentive and polite. 21 rooms (16 with private baths). *Banchory Lodge Hotel, Banchory, Kincardineshire. Telephone: Banchory 2625 (area code 03302)*

Seafield Arms Hotel, Cullen

The eponymous earls and countesses have owned the land for miles around, as their ancestors have done for some 500 years. An earlier earl built this inn over a hundred years ago, and one of his heirs had it deftly renovated a few years ago, retaining the heavy-beamed lopsided charm of the old while adding the customary comforts of contemporary hotels. Warm colors, splashes of tartan and a well-kept air give it a welcoming atmosphere; each room has coffeemakers and radios. There's even a summer courtyard, between the inn and the old stables, set up with white cast-iron tables and chairs, shaded, when and if the need arises, by sun umbrellas. Cullen is a granite-gray fishing village and summer resort (Scottish-style) in the northeast of Scotland, a relaxing overnight stopover and center for touring the Banffshire countryside between Aberdeen and Inverness. 25 rooms (17 with private bath). *The Seafield Arms Hotel, Cullen, Banffshire. Telephone: Cullen 40791 (area code 0542)*

Open Arms, Dirleton

Not many villages in Scotland have a village green, but Dirleton has; with the walls of a ruined castle at one end and a trim park within the old walls, with old stone cottages behind flower-decked gardens, it's also one of the loveliest villages in the country. Taking full advantage of all this picturesque charm, the Open Arms has fitted its restaurant with a wall of windows facing the old castle; it also happens to be one of the finest restaurants in these parts, so it's always busy with Edinburgh folk, only too willing to drive for an hour to savor the village and the food (about $6 a head for lunch, $12 to $14 for dinner). Since it's primarily a restaurant, the Open Arms has only eight rooms, each with private bathroom, windows opening onto either the village or the garden at the rear; decor in rooms and lounges is countrified and comfortable, and Brigitte Bardot, of all people, spent several nights here. *Open Arms Hotel, Dirleton, East Lothian. Telephone: 241 (area code 062085)*

Donmaree Hotel, Edinburgh

On the outside, it's a solid gray house like hundreds of other stone houses in Edinburgh, but inside it's all freshly aspidistraed and ferned to match its Victorian pedigree. Tall windows are framed with tasseled mocha drapes, walls and furniture are covered in gilt and velvet, the lounge is hung with portraits of eminent or would-be eminent Victorians. The 8 double rooms (most with private bath) are compact but comfortable; you'll probably prefer one facing the garden at the rear, with views across Queen's Park to Arthur's Seat. The new owners, the Kirkwood Whites, spent several years in top restaurants in California and New York (where mine host worked in Charley O's), so pride of place here goes to their intime, frilly dining room, already considered to be one of the better restaurants in town (dinner about $15–$20 for two). The Donmaree is located 15 minutes from the center of town, in a residential district, on one of the main routes into the city. Limited parking in the garden. *Donmaree Hotel, 21 Mayfield Gardens, Edinburgh EH92BX. Telephone: (031) 667 3641*

Prestonfield House, Edinburgh

They've all stayed here—Benjamin Franklin, Samuel Johnson, Robert Burns, assorted dukes and princes, and in one of its earlier incarnations it was actually burned down by a mob of protesting students. It's within the boundaries of Edinburgh, within sight of Arthur's Seat, yet it sits on its own 23 acres and partridges still feed on the lawn. The public rooms are bedecked with antiques, and after-dinner Drambuies are sipped in the patrician Tapestry Room. In the oval dining rooms continental and Scottish fare are offered, but if you feel the setting is too elegant for cullen skink soup, nuttie tattie or Highland casserole, order instead salmon Chambertin or guinea fowl *forestiere.* The wine list is impressive—except for a Cypriot wine named Othello (Desdemona would be more appropriate). There are 5 guest chambers upstairs, creaky with character, with enough comforts (including makeshift toilets and showers) for an overnight stop. The emphasis, then, is on dining—no, on *catering,* what with the pair of dining rooms and the conference tent in the garden—but for anyone searching for something out of the ordinary, Prestonfield House is the most unusual hotel in Edinburgh. *Prestonfield House Hotel, Edinburgh EH165UT. Telephone: 667-8055 (area code 031)*

Culag Hotel, Lochinver

This "sheltered corner," or *culag* in the Highlanders' tongue, is tucked away in the northwestern corner of Scotland, in a rocky bay beside a fishing village with white walled houses. Built in the early 19th century by the Macleods of Skye, it later became a summer lodge for the Dukes of Sutherland, and is now owned by Lord Vestey of the Blue Star shipping line. The hotel shares the village pier with a large ice-making plant and, at times, the heavy trucks that cart the cod catch to London and the continent, so ask for a quiet room away from the activity. Guest rooms are comfortable if undistinguished, but the main attraction is the sheltered corner and the surrounding Highlands—fishing on eight lochs, pathways across the moors to Suilven and through the woods to White Shore Lock, excursions to Glencarp Forest, Inverpolly Nature Reserve, Ben More Assynt and the ruins of Ardvrech Castle. That and the rates: 49 rooms, for less than $50, including full Scottish breakfast. Closed mid-October to mid-April. *Culag Hotel, Lochinver, Sutherland. Telephone: Lochinver 209 (area code 05714)*

Rothes Glen Hotel, Rothes

Here's another Balmoral look-alike, except in this case it was in fact designed by the architect of the royal castle. It sits in 40 acres of greenery, looking across the valley of the River Spey, a soothing, pastoral setting, but just beyond the hedges and the trees, you can tackle half a dozen golf courses and twice that number of whisky distilleries (many of which offer guided tours). The hotel's interior is stately and elegant, with oak paneling everywhere, antique chests and clocks, collections of swords and claymores, and an impressive nine-panel stained glass ceiling above the great stairway. The guest rooms are something of a letdown (coin-operated minibars on the walls don't help), but comfortably fitted out with heated towel rails and electric blankets. 19 rooms (8 with private baths). Closed mid-November to mid-March. *Rothes Glen Hotel, Rothes, Morayshire IV337AH. Telephone: Rothes 254*

Switzerland

Hotel Löwen, Appenzell

Better hurry if you want to get to Appenzell before the tour buses do the place in. Right now it's still an extraordinary little town, filled with brightly painted houses and surrounded by steep rolling farmland that has inspired a uniqe brand of folk art, a bit heavy on cows, but with a decided naive charm. The tourists are beginning to clog the streets, however, and the old hotels are modernizing to take care of their new influx of visitors. The Hotel Löwen, which has been done over from top to bottom, is worth mentioning because it is an example of how this can be accomplished without losing the spirit of the old town. The red tile floors, stucco walls and wooden ceiling, the rural motif of the art work in the lobby are all right at home and right in Appenzell. The rooms, still rustic with their brown and yellow print motif, have been made unusually comfortable for such a small place, each with color TV, radio and minibar, some with handsome skylights to let in the out-of-doors. A modern sauna and solarium have been added downstairs, but the second floor lace-curtained dining room remains old-fashioned, with cowbells, a handsome old wall clock and antique pieces all around. Owner Suther Guido is rightfully proud of his new old hotel. You'll find it a fine home base for exploring an interesting area. 30 rooms. *Hotel Lowen, 9050 Appenzell. Telephone: (071) 871402*

Hotel Garni Allalin, Zermatt

It's in the middle of town, and brand new, but it's built in the Alpine style with a long sloping roofline and an interior of the kind you didn't think people could do anymore—carved wood, with intricate ceilings and paneling, all crafted, like the rustic wooden furniture, specially for the Allalin. It's very tastefully designed and executed—by local contractors and artisans. All rooms have triple glazing and balcony (some with stunning views of the Matterhorn), and a few have kitchenettes and minibars. There's also a sauna somewhere in the basement; and a pleasant, cozy bar, but no restaurant. 30 rooms. Open all year. *Hotel Garni Allalin, CH-3920 Zermatt.*

Telephone: (028) 671631

Hotel Walliserhof, Zermatt

Another pleasant, small hotel right on the main street, but with most of the rooms facing the rear, so relatively quiet. Guest rooms are functional and comfortable, with just the right touches of Alpine decor. The breakfast room at the rear serves a buffet with great fresh-baked breads; for dinner, my preference would be the *Stube* rather than the more formal dining room. Friendly staff, 30 rooms. *Hotel Walliserhof, CH-3920 Zermatt. Telephone: (028) 671174*

The Rates—and how to figure them out

BEFORE WE GO ANY FURTHER: ALL ROOM RATES QUOTED IN THIS GUIDEBOOK ARE FOR TWO PEOPLE.

Every country in Europe and every hotel in every country seems to have its own way of calculating and presenting room rates. The variations would baffle an IBM computer. The best we can hope to do here, as we mentioned earlier, is to give you as accurately as possible the range of rates effective in 1979. This is not ideal, but we could spend the next six months compiling and revising rates as they arrive; some would be on-season, some off-season, some 1979, some 1980. Better that they should all be for the same year (1979) and for the same season (peak). *This way you can use them for comparison purposes, to weigh up Hotel A against Hotel B.* The rates you finally pay will be 10% to 15% higher—but presumably this will be true for both Hotel A and Hotel B.

The rates quoted here are for the peak season. This means that you may be pleasantly surprised if you follow our advice and go in the off-season, thereby saving anywhere from 10% to 50% on room rates. Hotels which offer special off-season rates are identified with an asterisk(*). In most cases, peak season in Europe (at least for the hotels in this guidebook) is the summer months—anywhere from June to and through September, with July and August being peak of the peak and insufferable. Unfortunately, each hotel sets its own limits on the season, and it would be impractical here to spell out the precise period when each rate is in effect; you can get this information from a travel agent, the appropriate hotel representative or the tourist offices for each country you are interested in visiting.

Four Types of Rates

EP	European Plan	You pay for the room only. No meals.
CP	Continental Plan	You get bed and breakfast. Usually "continental" breakfast of rolls or croissants and tea or coffee; in some cases it will include orange juice; in a few it may bring you a "full English/Scottish/Irish breakfast" complete with eggs, bacon, kippers or whatnot; in still others it may be a help-yourself buffet breakfast.

MAP	Modified American Plan	In Europe, this rate is known as "demipension." You get room and breakfast plus one full meal—usually dinner, but in some cases you can opt for lunch *or* dinner. In some hotels MAP gives you full run of the regular menu, in others you will have to settle for a special menu, with supplements for any dishes ordered from the a la carte menu.
FAP	Full American Plan	In Europe, "full pension." You get everything—room, breakfast, lunch, dinner, perhaps also morning coffee and afternoon tea.

Which rate should you choose? Each has its advantages. MAP and FAP sometimes work out to be less expensive than the combined EP rate plus the cost of meals. In many cases, too, you may be staying in a hotel mainly because of the reputation of its dining room and you will be intending to dine there anyway. In some cases the hotel may be the only or the best restaurant for miles around. And in some cases, you have no choice—the hotel may insist on MAP or FAP rates, particularly during peak seasons. However, since there will be many times when you will be surrounded by attractive *brasseries, trattorie, tavernas,* waterfront cafés or whatever, often with more local flavor than the hotel dining room, you will want to have the *option* of dining where and when you please; in which case you should ask for a CP or EP rate.

A few hotels will, incidentally, allow you a rebate on your MAP or FAP rate if you skip a meal; but probably not a full rebate and *only* if you let them know of your intentions the night before or, at least, at breakfast.

Taxes and Service Charges

In Europe, most hotels incorporate local taxes into their rates. All taxes and service charges are included in the rates unless otherwise specified. All member countries of the European Common Market have a Value Added Tax, which varies in name and amount from country to country. Normally you don't have to give it a second thought, since it's part of the rate. A few hotels in Italy do *not* include it; likewise in Scotland and England, where the tax was recently hoisted from 8% to 15%, so some hotels which included the lower figure in their rates may now add a supplement to pay for the additional tax—or they have simply raised their rates.

The service charge (usually 10%, 12½%, 15% or 20%) is also included in the rate in most European hotels. In theory, this sum should be distributed among the staff, according to magic formulas devised by the individual managers; in reality, many travelers still tip, and many porters and waiters still expect to be tipped. Occasionally, too, managers themselves will mumble that of course—*harumph*—there's a service charge included in the rate but—*harumph*—people are expected to tip nevertheless. It's up to you.

Some guidebooks recommend that, regardless of service charge, you should still tip porters, maids, waiters, room-service waiters and so on. We work on the assumption that if someone like a concierge or maid offers some *special* service, they should be tipped separately. Otherwise, since the service charge is supposed to be there to take care of all tipping, we never tip beyond that figure. Sometimes we get the impression the staff is happy to see us leave. Sometimes we're happy to leave.

Wherever possible (and you'd be surprised how difficult it is to get straight answers on this topic), we have indicated in the rate tables where the service charge is included, where you will be expected to add tips to the room rate and how much you will be expected to tip—or, more likely, the hotel will automatically add to the bill.

Note: All the rates are quoted in the local currency, but at the beginning of each country's listing you'll find the rate of exchange in effect in December 1979, the last possible date for fiddling with type before the guide went to press.

Beware

We've checked and double-checked all the rates in this guide, and at the time of turning in the manuscript to the publisher (October 1979), they are as accurate as we can make them without going (a) blind, (b) bankrupt. In the best of times it's difficult for an innkeeper to forecast his rates for two seasons hence; in these inflationary, oil-ransomed days it's virtually impossible. Therefore, we suggest you always double-check the rates of the hotels you're interested in visiting, preferably before you set off, certainly before you sign in. Please, *never* insist on a figure because you saw it printed in this guidebook. Even the hotels' official rate sheets, which are brought up to date every few months, include the words "subject to change without notice." We have to go along with that: ALL RATES PUBLISHED IN THIS GUIDE ARE SUBJECT TO CHANGE WITHOUT NOTICE.

Austria

Currency: Austrian schilling $1=S12.56

Hotel	Peak Season Rate	Type of Rate
Goldener Adler	600–800	CP[A]
Goldener Hirsch	900–1800*	CP
Grünwalderhof	520–720	CP
Schloss Füschl	1860–3460*	MAP
Schloss Igls	1700–2300[B]*	MAP
Schloss Mönchstein	1100–1400*	CP

[A]Includes buffet breakfast.
[B]Peak season is in winter.

Belgium

Currency: Belgian franc $1=BFR28.45

Hotel	Peak Season Rate	Type of Rate
Moulin Hideux	1900–2100	EP
Pieuré de Conques	1800–1950	CP
Trôs Marets	1200–2200	EP
	(plus an additional 50% if you don't have lunch or dinner in the hotel)	

Denmark

Currency: Danish krone $1=KR5.17

Hotel	Peak Season Rate	Type of Rate
Falsled Kro	335–365	CP
Hesselet	360–620	EP
Nyhavn	249–636	CP
Steensgaard	300[A] –425	CP
Store Kro	610	FAP

[A]Without bath or toilet.

Hotel	Peak Season Rate	Type of Rate

England

Currency: Pound sterling $1=£0.46

Hotel	Peak Season Rate	Type of Rate
The Bear	33–40	CP
Blakes Hotel	40–115	EP
Browns Hotel	55–78	EP
Chewton Glen	43.50–77*	CP
The Close	37	CP[A]
Grosvenor Hotel	40.50*	EP
Huntstrete House *(service charge–10%)*	32–40	CP[A]
Lygon Arms	43	EP
Maison Talbooth *(service charge–10%)*	37.50–45	CP
Miller Howe *(service charge–12½%)*	48–80	MAP[AB]
Number 16 *(service charge optional, plus tax)*	22–32	CP
Sharrow Bay Hotel *(plus tax)*	48–64	MAP[AB]
Whatley Manor *(service charge–12½%)*	30–40	CP[AB]
White Moss House	18[A]–20	MAP[A]
Ye Olde Bell *(service charge–12½%)*	24–35	EP

[A]Serves full English breakfast.
[B]Includes early morning tea and afternoon tea.

France

Currency: French franc $1=FR4.10

Hotel	Peak Season Rate	Type of Rate
Artigny (Ch. d') *(service charge–15%)*	360–840	MAP

Hotel	Peak Season Rate	Type of Rate
Artigny (Mas d')	200–685*	EP
Audrieu (Ch. d')	197–450*	EP
Bas-Bréau (Hôt. du) *(service charge–15%)*	350–800*	EP
Baumanière (Oustau de)	300–430	EP
Byblos (Hotel) *(service charge–15%)*	410–670*	CP
Cagnard (Le)	150–350	CP
Cap (Hotel du) *(service charge–15%)*	590–1800*	EP
Cap Estel (Hotel Le)	800–900*	MAP
Chèvre d'Or (Ch. du) *(service charge–15%)*	260–440	EP
Domaine des Hauts de Loire *(service charge–15%)*	200–450	EP
Domaine St.-Martin (Ch. du) *(service charge–15%)*	400–950*	CP
Entremont (Mas d')	135–190	EP
Hameau (Aub. Le)	97–170	EP
Herbes Blanches (Mas des)	210	EP
Hôtel (L')	300–1100	EP
Lutèce (Hotel)	185–220	EP
Mercues (Ch. de)	350–600	EP
Mère Blanc (Chez La)	200	EP
Métairie (La)	143–300	EP
Moulin des Ruats (Hôt. du)	150^A–160	EP
Moulin du Roc	150–200	EP
Noves (Aub. de)	250–360	EP
Oustau de Baumanière *(see* Baumanière*)*		
378 **Père Bise (Aub. du)**	300–600	CP

Hotel	Peak Season Rate	Type of Rate
Poste (Hôt. de la) *(service charge–15%)*	200–350	EP
Prés Fleuris (Hôtel Les)	220–380	EP
Priéure (Hôt. le)	180–380	EP
Residence du Bois	300–430	CP
Ritz (Hotel) *(service charge–15%)*	585–670	EP
Rochegude (Ch. de)	204–410	MAP
Templiers (Aub. des)	180–290	EP
Tortinière (La)	345–755*	MAP
Université (Hôtel de l')	175–250	EP
Vaumadeuc (Manoir du)	335–353*	MAP
Verniaz (Hôtel de la)	350–400*	EP
Vieux Logis (Les)	143–325	EP
Vieux Puits (Aub. du)	212–262	MAP
Vistaero (Hôtel Le)	400–550*	EP
Voile d'Or (Hotel La) *(service charge–15%)*	550–1020*	MAP

[A]Without private bathroom.

Germany

Currency: Deutsche mark $1=DM1.74

Hotel	Peak Season Rate	Type of Rate
Parkhotel Adler *(plus tax of 3.60 DM per day)*	90–125[A] 130–240	CP
Alte Thorschenke	59–83[A] 82–110	CP
Romantikhotel Alte Post	75–85	CP
Burghotel auf Schönberg	90–110	CP
Posthotel Clausings *(plus tax of 3.60 DM per day)*	51–72[A] 95–104	CP
Hotel Eisenhut	115–150*	CP

Hotel	Peak Season Rate	Type of Rate
Schlosshotel Friedrichsruhe	125–160	CP
Parkhotel Fürstenhof	105–240	CP
Hotel Schloss Heinsheim	75–120	CP
Kommende Lage	90–100	CP
Schlosshotel Lembeck	70	EP
Hotel Markusturm	60–95	CP
Jagdschloss Niederwald	96–104	CP
Hotel Schwan	100–150	CP
Parkhotel Wässerburg Anholt	99	CP
Schloss Zell	80–140	CP
Zum Ritter	65–70[A] 90–150	CP

[A]Without private bath.

Greece

Currency: Drachma $1=DR37.45

Akti Myrina	2,660–3,310*	MAP
Amalia	1,274	CP
Xenia Palace Bungalows	2,350	MAP

Holland

Currency: Guilder $1=G1.95

De l' Europe	190–230	EP
Auberge De Kieviet	150	CP
Lauswolt	150–165	CP
Kasteel Neubourg	85–110	CP
Pulitzer	155–175	EP
Waterland	170	CP
De Wiemsel	150	EP
Kasteel Wittem	95	CP

Hotel	Peak Season Rate	Type of Rate

Ireland

Currency: Irish pound $1=£0.47

Ashford Castle *(service charge-12½%plus tax)*	41.10*	CP
Dromoland Castle *(plus tax)*	40*	EP
Fitzpatrick Castle *(service charge-12½%* *plus tax)*	29.50*	EP
Newport House *(plus tax)*	23*	CP

Italy

Currency: Lira $1=L821.75

Cala di Volpe *(plus Value Added Tax)*	170,000*	MAP
Cenobio del Dogi	53,000*	EP
Cervo *(plus 14% VAT)*	140,000–170,000*	MAP
Cipriani *(plus 14% VAT, 1,200 L* *per day)*	98,000–300,000*	CP
Due Torri	57,000–84,000*	EP
Gabrieli Sandwirth	38,000[A]–74,000	EP
Gritti Palace *(plus 14% VAT, 1,200 L* *per day)*	110,000–270,000	CP
Inghilterra *(plus 720 L tax per day)*	69,000–120,000	EP
Lord Byron	85,000–110,000	CP
Miramare	78,000*	EP
Pittrizza *(plus VAT)*	220,000*	MAP

Hotel	Peak Season Rate	Type of Rate
Pomerio (Castello di)	43,000–53,000	CP
Punta Tragara	120,000–160,000*	MAP
Quisisana	53,000–164,000*	EP
San Domenico	79,500	EP
San Pietro	90,000–120,000*	EP
Scalinatella	65,000–95,000	EP
Splendido (Albergo)	85,000–150,000*	EP
Victoria	39,900	EP
Villa Cipriani (7,200 L per day)	54,000–76,000*	EP
Villa d' Este	103,000–138,000	CP
Villa Igeia	50,750–55,000	EP

[A]Without private bathroom.

Portugal

Currency: Portuguese escudo $1=ESC$50.15

Estalagem Albatroz	1,545	CP
Pousada do Castelo	1,100	CP
Estalagem do Cerro	1,250*	CP
Hotel do Guincho	1,500–2,400*	CP
Pousada do Infante	900	CP
Lennox Country Club	1,250–1,425*	MAP
Pousada dos Lioios	1,250	CP
Hotel do Mar	2,200–3,650*	CP
Hotel Palacio do Seteais	2,250–2,550	CP
Pousada do Palmela	1,250	CP
Hotel Príncipe Real	1,750	CP
Pousada de São Bras	950	CP
Pousada de São Felipe	1,250	CP

Hotel	Peak Season Rate	Type of Rate
Casa de São Goncalo da Lagos	1,250*	CP
Quinta das Torres	1,200	CP
York House	1,200	CP

Scotland

Currency: Pound sterling $1=£0.46

Hotel	Peak Season Rate	Type of Rate
Ballathie House	24*	CP[A]
Creggans Inn	25	CP
Culloden House *(service charge–15% plus 15% VAT)*	35–50	CP[A]
Dunkeld House	22–38.50	CP
Greywalls	30–40	CP
Inverlochy Castle *(service charge–12% plus 15% VAT)*	50–70	CP[A]
Isle of Eriska *(plus 15% VAT)*	52–64*	MAP[A]
Meldrum House	17.32–29.70	CP[A]
Newton Hotel	33.50	CP
Taychreggan Hotel *(plus 15% VAT)*	29–35*	CP[A]
Tullich Lodge	33	MAP
Turnberry	38.50*	CP[A]

[A]Serves full Scottish breakfast.

Spain

Currency: Peseta $1=PTS66.08

Hotel	Peak Season Rate	Type of Rate
Parador Condestable Davalos	1,615	EP
Hotel Doña Maria	2,880	EP
Hostal de la Gavina	6,800–7,500*	EP

Hotel	Peak Season Rate	Type of Rate
Parador Gibralfaro	1,405–1,615	EP
Parador Marques de Villena	1,615	EP
Parador San Francisco	2,775	EP

Switzerland

Currency: Swiss franc $1=FR1.65

Hotel	Peak Season Rate	Type of Rate
Alex	200–240[A]*	MAP
Drachenburg	54–58[B] 64–120	CP
Grand	150–250	CP
Ch. Gutsch	112–130*	CP
Hirschen	42[A]–60	CP
Monte Rosa	230–246[A]*	MAP
Tenne	170–200[A]*	CP
Le Vieux Manoir	120–150*	CP

[A] Peak season is in winter; 25%–50% less in spring and fall.
[B] Without private bath.

The Reps

Hotel representatives are primarily booking agents. They keep tabs on the availability of rooms in the hotels they represent, and they'll handle your reservations and confirmations at no extra charge to you (unless you wait until the last minute, in which case they may have to make an additional handling charge). The reps who have appeared most frequently in these pages are listed below; in the interests of simplicity, only the main North American and European office is listed for each one.

The list is in alphabetical order in the sense that it follows the "format" of the name as it appears in the guidebook—that is, Scott Calder is listed under S rather than under C.

AIHR (American-International Hotel Representatives)
500 Fifth Avenue, New York, NY 10036
Tel.: (212) 730-8105

BTH Hotels Inc.
P.O. Box 48, Rego Park, NY 11374
Tel.: 800-221-1354 (except in N.Y. State and Canada: 212-335-3200)
Telex: 236509

CIGA (Compagnia Italiana Grandi Alberghi)
745 Fifth Avenue, New York, NY 10022
Tel.: (212) 935-9540
or San Marco, Ramo dei Fuseri 1812, 30124 Venice
Tel.: (041) 26275/30310 Telex: 41004
or 67 Jermyn Street, London SW1
Tel.: (01) 930-4147 Telex: 261859

E&M Associates
667 Madison Avenue, New York, NY 10021
Tel.: (212) 755-7220 or 800-223-9832

Gast im Schloss
3526 Trendelburg, Postfach, W. Germany
Tel.: (05675) 331 Telex: 994812

Golden Tulip Hotels Worldwide
437 Madison Avenue, New York, NY 10022
Tel.: (212) 247-7950 Telex: 0125503
or Stationstraat 2, 1211EX Hilversum, Holland
Tel.: (035) 49079 or 43180 Telex: 43651NL
(or any office of KLM Royal Dutch Airlines, worldwide)

HAMSA (for the Spanish National Paradores)
Calle de Jacometrezo 4, planta 9, Madrid 13
Tel.: 2226357 Telex: 42195

HRI (Hotel Representative Inc.)
770 Lexington Avenue, New York, NY 10021
Tel.: 800-223-6800 (from N.Y. State and Canada call collect 212-838-3110)
Telex: 237158
(Offices also in Canada, Denmark, England, France, Holland, Italy, Sweden, Switzerland, W. Germany and throughout the world)

Prestige Hotels
Strand House, Great West Road, Brentford, Middlesex TW89EX England
Tel.: (01) 568-6841 Telex: 8811951
(For U.S.A. and Canada, see Scott Calder Int.)

Relais de Campagne-Châteaux Hotels
Hotel de Crillon, 10 Place de la Concorde, 75008 Paris, France
Tel.: 742-0020 Telex: 220319
(Represented in U.S.A. and Canada by Two World Tours, below)

Robert F. Warner Inc.
711 Third Avenue, New York, NY 10017
Tel.: (212) 687-5750 in N.Y., or 800-223-6625
(In Canada, call collect—212-986-2471)

Romantik Hotels
Freigerichtstrasse 5, D-8757 Karlstein a. Main, W. Germany
Tel.: (06188) 5020 Telex: 4184214

Scott Calder International
295 Madison Avenue, New York, NY 10017
Tel.: (212) 535-9530, or toll-free 800-223-5581
Telex: 425331

Trust Houses Forte Hotels
71/75 Uxbridge Road, London W55SL England
Tel.: (01) 567-3444 Telex: 934946
or 810 Seventh Avenue, New York, NY 10019
Tel.: (212) 541-4400

Two World Tours
(see also Relais-Châteaux)
245 Park Avenue, New York, NY 10017
Tel.: (212) 687-3418 or 800-221-4547

Utell International
119 West 57th Street, New York, NY 10019
Tel.: (212) 757-0434
(In Canada, toll-free 800-261-9328)

Wolfe International
500 Fifth Avenue, New York, NY 10036
Tel.: (212) 730-8100

Tourist Information

The national tourist offices of the countries you plan to visit are glad to provide literature and will do their best to answer your travel questions. Please write to the office nearest you.

Austrian National Tourist Office
545 Fifth Avenue, New York, NY 10017
200 E. Randolph, Chicago, IL 60601
3440 Wilshire Blvd., Los Angeles, CA 90010

Belgian National Tourist Office
720 Fifth Avenue, New York, NY 10019

British Tourist Authority
680 Fifth Avenue, New York, NY 10019
875 N. Michigan Avenue, John Hancock Center, Chicago, IL 60611
1712 Commerce Street, Empire Life Bldg., Dallas, TX 75201
612 S. Flower Street, Los Angeles, CA 90017

Danish National Tourist Office
75 Rockefeller Plaza, New York, NY 10020
3600 Wilshire Blvd., Los Angeles, CA 90010

French Government Tourist Office
610 Fifth Avenue, New York, NY 10020
9401 Wilshire Blvd., Beverly Hills, CA 90212
645 N. Michigan Avenue, Chicago, IL 60611
323 Geary Street, San Francisco, CA 94102

German National Tourist Office
630 Fifth Avenue, New York, NY 10020
104 S. Michigan Avenue, Chicago, IL 60603
700 S. Flower Street, Broadway Plaza, Los Angeles, CA 90017

Greek National Tourist Organization
645 Fifth Avenue, New York, NY 10022
168 N. Michigan Avenue, Chicago, IL 60601
627 W. Sixth Street, Los Angeles, CA 90017

Irish Tourist Board
590 Fifth Avenue, New York, NY 10036
224 N. Michigan Avenue, Chicago, IL 60601
510 W. Sixth Street, Los Angeles, CA 90014
681 Market Street, San Francisco, CA 94105

Italian Government Travel Office
630 Fifth Avenue, New York, NY 10020
500 N. Michigan Avenue, Chicago, IL 60611
360 Post Street, San Francisco, CA 94108

Netherlands National Tourist Office
576 Fifth Avenue, New York, NY 10036
681 Market Street, San Francisco, CA 94105

Portuguese National Tourist Office
548 Fifth Avenue, New York, NY 10036
17 E. Monroe Street, Chicago, IL 60603
3250 Wilshire Blvd., Los Angeles, CA 90010

Spanish National Tourist Office
665 Fifth Avenue, New York, NY 10022
664 N. Michigan Avenue, Chicago, IL 60611
338 Biscayne Blvd., Miami, FL 33132
209 Post Street, San Francisco, CA 94108
Casa del Hidalgo, St. Augustine, FL 32084

Swiss National Tourist Office
608 Fifth Avenue, New York, NY 10020
104 S. Michigan Avenue, Chicago, IL 60603
661 Market Street, San Francisco, CA 94105